THE NEW CAMBRIDGE SHAKESPEARE

GENERAL EDITOR
Brian Gibbons

ASSOCIATE GENERAL EDITOR
A. R. Braunmuller, *University of California, Los Angeles*

From the publication of the first volumes in 1984 the General Editor of the New Cambridge Shakespeare was Philip Brockbank and the Associate General Editors were Brian Gibbons and Robin Hood. From 1990 to 1994 the General Editor was Brian Gibbons and the Associate General Editors were A. R. Braunmuller and Robin Hood.

THE FIRST PART OF KING HENRY IV

This updated edition offers a strongly theatrical perspective on the origins of Shakespeare's *The First Part of King Henry IV* and the history of its interpretation. The introduction clarifies the play's surprising, de-centred dramatic structure, questioning the dominant assumption that the drama focuses on the education of Prince Hal. It calls attention to the effects of civil war upon a broad range of relationships. Falstaff's unpredictable vitality is explored, together with important contemporary values of honour, friendship, festivity and reformation.

Extensive lexical glosses of obscure, ambiguous or archaic meanings make the rich word-play accessible. The notes also provide a thorough commentary on Shakespeare's transformation of his sources (particularly Holinshed's *Chronicles*) and suggest alternative stagings. This updated edition contains a new introductory section by Katharine A. Craik, which describes recent stage, film and critical interpretations, and an updated reading list.

THE NEW CAMBRIDGE SHAKESPEARE

All's Well That Ends Well, edited by Russell Fraser
Antony and Cleopatra, edited by David Bevington
As You Like It, edited by Michael Hattaway
The Comedy of Errors, edited by T. S. Dorsch
Coriolanus, edited by Lee Bliss
Cymbeline, edited by Martin Butler
Hamlet, edited by Philip Edwards
Julius Caesar, edited by Marvin Spevack
King Edward III, edited by Giorgio Melchiori
The First Part of King Henry IV, edited by Herbert Weil and Judith Weil
The Second Part of King Henry IV, edited by Giorgio Melchiori
King Henry V, edited by Andrew Gurr
The First Part of King Henry VI, edited by Michael Hattaway
The Second Part of King Henry VI, edited by Michael Hattaway
The Third Part of King Henry VI, edited by Michael Hattaway
King Henry VIII, edited by John Margeson
King John, edited by L. A. Beaurline
The Tragedy of King Lear, edited by Jay L. Halio
King Richard II, edited by Andrew Gurr
King Richard III, edited by Janis Lull
Love's Labour's Lost, edited by William C. Carroll
Macbeth, edited by A. R. Braunmuller
Measure for Measure, edited by Brian Gibbons
The Merchant of Venice, edited by M. M. Mahood
The Merry Wives of Windsor, edited by David Crane
A Midsummer Night's Dream, edited by R. A. Foakes
Much Ado About Nothing, edited by F. H. Mares
Othello, edited by Norman Sanders
Pericles, edited by Doreen DelVecchio and Antony Hammond
The Poems, edited by John Roe
Romeo and Juliet, edited by G. Blakemore Evans
The Sonnets, edited by G. Blakemore Evans
The Taming of the Shrew, edited by Ann Thompson
The Tempest, edited by David Lindley
Timon of Athens, edited by Karl Klein
Titus Andronicus, edited by Alan Hughes
Troilus and Cressida, edited by Anthony B. Dawson
Twelfth Night, edited by Elizabeth Story Donno
The Two Gentlemen of Verona, edited by Kurt Schlueter
The Two Noble Kinsmen, edited by Robert Kean Turner and Patricia Tatspaugh
The Winter's Tale, edited by Susan Snyder and Deborah T. Curren-Aquino

THE EARLY QUARTOS

The First Quarto of Hamlet, edited by Kathleen O. Irace
The First Quarto of King Henry V, edited by Andrew Gurr
The First Quarto of King Lear, edited by Jay L. Halio
The First Quarto of King Richard III, edited by Peter Davison
The First Quarto of Othello, edited by Scott McMillin
The First Quarto of Romeo and Juliet, edited by Lukas Erne
The Taming of a Shrew: The 1594 Quarto, edited by Stephen Roy Miller

THE FIRST PART OF KING HENRY IV

Updated edition

Edited by
HERBERT WEIL
Emeritus Professor of English, University of Manitoba

JUDITH WEIL
Emeritus Professor of English, University of Manitoba

CAMBRIDGE
UNIVERSITY PRESS

CAMBRIDGE
UNIVERSITY PRESS

University Printing House, Cambridge CB2 8BS, United Kingdom

One Liberty Plaza, 20th Floor, New York, NY 10006, USA

477 Williamstown Road, Port Melbourne, VIC 3207, Australia

314-321, 3rd Floor, Plot 3, Splendor Forum, Jasola District Centre, New Delhi - 110025, India

79 Anson Road, #06-04/06, Singapore 079906

Cambridge University Press is part of the University of Cambridge.

It furthers the University's mission by disseminating knowledge in the pursuit of education, learning and research at the highest international levels of excellence.

www.cambridge.org
Information on this title: www.cambridge.org/9780521687430

© Cambridge University Press 1997, 2007

First published 1997
Updated edition 2007
11th printing 2018

A catalogue record for this publication is available from the British Library

ISBN 978-0-521-86801-3 Hardback
ISBN 978-0-521-68743-0 Paperback

CONTENTS

ILLUSTRATIONS

Illustrations 1, 3*a*, and 7*b* are reproduced by permission of Laurence Burns; illustrations 4 and 9 by permission of the Shakespeare Centre Library, Stratford-upon-Avon; illustration 5 by permission of the Angus McBean estate; illustration 6 by permission of Chris Davies; illustrations 7*a* and 8 by permission of the Shakespeare Centre Library: Joe Cocks Studio Collection and illustration 10 by permission of Catherine Ashmore.

PREFACE

This edition owes a special debt to a pair of scholars no longer here to read it: Philip Brockbank who followed his initial invitation with continuing encouragement and Richard David who criticised an earlier draft in the kindest possible light. Giorgio Melchiori shared many questions and concerns while he was editing *2 Henry IV*. With his learning and patience, Brian Gibbons has been responsible for improvements on almost every page. At Cambridge University Press, Sarah Stanton has astutely smoothed many ways over many years; Paul Chipchase and Margaret Berrill have provided expert advice. C. Walter Hodges at a very early stage vividly illustrated our inchoate suggestions. A. R. Humphreys and David Bevington, editors of the Arden and Oxford editions of *1 Henry IV*, helpfully answered our queries.

Among the many friends and colleagues who have listened, argued, criticised drafts, or sent us their own work in progress, we wish especially to thank Scott McMillin, Miriam Gilbert, Edward Pechter, Ernst Honigmann, Patrick Boyde, George Hunter, Barbara Hodgdon, Victor Cowie, Kenneth Muir, George Toles, Tom Roberts, Patricia Tatspaugh, and Inga-Stina Ewbank. At the Shakespeare Centre in Stratford-upon-Avon, Marian Pringle, Sylvia Morris, and Mary White gave invaluable help with illustrations and production records; the staff of the Cambridge English Faculty Library, too, has been exceptionally generous. We are also grateful to the staffs of the University of Manitoba Library, the Cambridge University Library, the Folger Library, and the Huntington Library. Lucia Flynn has often saved us with her skills at the computer. For financial support and research leaves, we are indebted to the University of Manitoba Faculty of Arts, the University of Manitoba Institute for the Humanities, and the Social Sciences and Humanities Research Council of Canada. Clare Hall and Robinson College, Cambridge, helped us work in a stimulating environment.

We would also like to express our gratitude to the larger communities of critics, scholars, and directors who keep testing the value of Shakespeare's plays. Many of them have, in effect, questioned a widespread assumption that *1 Henry IV* presents an inclusive picture of society. But relative absences – particularly those of women, or of middle- and lower-class characters – may figure as important presences. By identifying such presences in small roles or in the transforming energies of language and action, we have tried to indicate some of the newer ways in which *1 Henry IV* continues to challenge its audience. Finally, we acknowledge that any errors or misguided opinions which remain here are our own.

We dedicate this edition to our son and daughter, Fred and Leslie Weil, who have grown up in the company of Shakespeare and Shakespeareans, bearing our arguments and adventures with lively humour and grace.

ABBREVIATIONS AND CONVENTIONS

Shakespeare's plays, when cited in this edition, are abbreviated in a style modified slightly from that used in the *Harvard Concordance to Shakespeare*. Other editions of Shakespeare are abbreviated under the editor's surname (Theobald, Duthie) unless they are the work of more than one editor. In such cases, an abbreviated series title is used (Cam.). When more than one edition by the same editor is cited, later editions are discriminated with a raised figure (Rowe [3]). All quotations from Shakespeare, except those from *1 Henry IV*, use the text and lineation of *The Riverside Shakespeare*, under the general editorship of G. Blakemore Evans.

1. Shakespeare's plays

Ado	*Much Ado About Nothing*
Ant.	*Antony and Cleopatra*
AWW	*All's Well That Ends Well*
AYLI	*As You Like It*
Cor.	*Coriolanus*
Cym.	*Cymbeline*
Err.	*The Comedy of Errors*
Ham.	*Hamlet*
1H4	*The First Part of King Henry the Fourth*
2H4	*The Second Part of King Henry the Fourth*
H5	*King Henry the Fifth*
1H6	*The First Part of King Henry the Sixth*
2H6	*The Second Part of King Henry the Sixth*
3H6	*The Third Part of King Henry the Sixth*
H8	*King Henry the Eighth*
JC	*Julius Caesar*
John	*King John*
Lear	*King Lear*
LLL	*Love's Labour's Lost*
Mac.	*Macbeth*
MM	*Measure for Measure*
MND	*A Midsummer Night's Dream*
MV	*The Merchant of Venice*
Oth.	*Othello*
Per.	*Pericles*
R2	*King Richard the Second*
R3	*King Richard the Third*
Rom.	*Romeo and Juliet*
Shr.	*The Taming of the Shrew*
STM	*Sir Thomas More*
Temp.	*The Tempest*
TGV	*The Two Gentlemen of Verona*
Tim.	*Timon of Athens*

Tit.	*Titus Andronicus*
TN	*Twelfth Night*
TNK	*The Two Noble Kinsmen*
Tro.	*Troilus and Cressida*
Wiv.	*The Merry Wives of Windsor*
WT	*The Winter's Tale*

2. Other works cited and general references

Abbott	E. A. Abbott, *A Shakespearian Grammar*, 1894 (references are to numbered paragraphs)
AEB	*Analytical and Enumerative Bibliography*
Auden	W. H. Auden, *The Dyer's Hand and Other Essays*, 1962
Bailey	Nathaniel Bailey, *Dictionary of Cant Words*, added to *The New English Dictionary*, 4th edn, 1759
Barber	C. L. Barber, *Shakespeare's Festive Comedy*, 1959
Beaumont and Fletcher	*Dramatic Works in the Beaumont and Fletcher Canon*, ed. Fredson Bowers, 1966
Bevington	*Henry IV, Part I*, ed. David Bevington, 1987 (Oxford Shakespeare)
Bullough	*Narrative and Dramatic Sources of Shakespeare*, ed. Geoffrey Bullough, IV, 1962
Cam.	*The Works of William Shakespeare*, ed. W. G. Clark, J. Glover, and W. A. Wright, 9 vols., 1863–6 (Cambridge Shakespeare)
Capell	*Mr. William Shakespeare his Comedies, Histories, and Tragedies*, ed. Edward Capell, 10 vols., 1767–8
Cercignani	Fausto Cercignani, *Shakespeare's Works and Elizabethan Pronunciation*, 1981
Chambers, *Shakespeare*	E. K. Chambers, *William Shakespeare: A Study of Facts and Problems*, 2 vols., 1930
Chambers, *Stage*	E. K. Chambers, *The Elizabethan Stage*, 4 vols., 1923
Child	Harold Child, 'The stage history of *King Henry IV*', in Wilson, pp. xxix–xlvi
Collier	*The Works of William Shakespeare*, ed. John Payne Collier, 8 vols., 1842–4
Collier [3]	*Shakespeare's Comedies, Histories, Tragedies, and Poems*, 6 vols., 1858
Colman	E. A. M. Colman, *The Dramatic Use of Bawdy in Shakespeare*, 1974
conj.	conjecture
corr.	corrected
Cowl and Morgan	*The First Part of King Henry the Fourth*, ed. R. P. Cowl and A. E. Morgan, 1930 (Arden Shakespeare)
CQ	*Critical Quarterly*
Daniel	Samuel Daniel, *The First Fowre Bookes of the Civile Wars Between the Two Houses of Lancaster and Yorke*, 1595. Excerpts from Book III reprinted in Bullough, pp. 208–15
Davison	*The First Part of King Henry the Fourth*, ed. P. H. Davison, 1968 (New Penguin)

Dekker	*The Non-Dramatic Works of Thomas Dekker*, ed. A. B. Grosart, 5 vols., 1884–6
Dent	R. W. Dent, *Shakespeare's Proverbial Language: An Index*, 1981 (references are to numbered proverbs)
Dering MS.	*The History of King Henry the Fourth as revised by Sir Edward Dering, Bart.* (1623), a facsimile edition, ed. G. Walton Williams and G. Blakemore Evans, 1974
DNB	*Dictionary of National Biography*, 1953
Drake	Nathan Drake, *Shakespeare and his Times*, 1817
Dyce	*The Works of William Shakespeare*, ed. Alexander Dyce, 6 vols., 1857
Dyce ²	*The Works of William Shakespeare*, ed. Alexander Dyce, 9 vols., 1864–7
Empson	William Empson, *Essays on Shakespeare*, 1986
ESC	English Shakespeare Company
Evans	*The Riverside Shakespeare*, ed. G. Blakemore Evans *et al.*, 1974
F	*Mr William Shakespeares Comedies, Histories, and Tragedies*, 1623 (First Folio)
F2	*Mr William Shakespeares Comedies, Histories, and Tragedies*, 1632 (Second Folio)
F3	*Mr William Shakespear's Comedies, Histories and Tragedies*, 1664 (Third Folio)
F4	*Mr William Shakespear's Comedies, Histories and Tragedies*, 1685 (Fourth Folio)
FV	*The Famous Victories of Henry the fifth*, 1598, reprinted in Bullough, pp. 299–343
Geneva	Geneva translation of the Bible, 1560
Gibbons	*Measure for Measure*, ed. Brian Gibbons, 1991 (New Cambridge Shakespeare)
Gurr	*King Richard II*, ed. Andrew Gurr, 1984 (New Cambridge Shakespeare)
Gurr, *Stage*	Andrew Gurr, *The Shakespearean Stage 1574–1642*, 3rd edn, 1991
Hall	Edward Hall, *The Union of the two noble and illustre famelies of Lancastre and Yorke*, 1548 and 1550; 1809 edn, reprinted 1965
Hanmer	*The Works of Shakespear*, ed. Thomas Hanmer, 6 vols., 1743–4
Hazlitt	*Characters of Shakespear's Plays*, ed. P. P. Howe, 1930
Hemingway	*Henry The Fourth, Part I*, ed. Samuel Burdett Hemingway, 1936 (New Variorum)
Hinman	*Henry the Fourth, Part I*, Shakespeare Quarto Facsimiles no. 14, ed. Charlton Hinman, 1966
Holinshed	*Holinshed's Chronicles of England, Scotland, and Ireland*, 6 vols., 1587, 1808 edn, reprinted 1965
Humphreys	*The First Part of King Henry IV*, ed. A. R. Humphreys, 1960 (Arden Shakespeare)

Johnson	*The Plays of William Shakespeare*, ed. Samuel Johnson, 8 vols., 1765
T. Johnson	*The Works of Mr William Shakespear*, pub. T. Johnson, 1710
Jonson	*Ben Jonson*, ed. C. H. Herford and Percy Simpson, 11 vols., 1925–52
KR	*Kenyon Review*
Kittredge	*Sixteen Plays of Shakespeare*, ed. George Lyman Kittredge, 1946
Lyly	*The Complete Works of John Lyly*, ed. R. Warwick Bond, 3 vols., 1902
Mahood, *Bit Parts*	M. M. Mahood, *Bit Parts in Shakespeare's Plays*, 1992
Mahood, *Wordplay*	M. M. Mahood, *Shakespeare's Wordplay*, 1957
Malone	*The Plays and Poems of William Shakespeare*, ed. Edmond Malone, 10 vols., 1790
Marlowe	*The Complete Works of Christopher Marlowe*, ed. Fredson Bowers, 2 vols., 1973
McMillin	Scott McMillin, *Shakespeare in Performance: Henry IV, Part One*, 1991
Melchiori	*The Second Part of King Henry IV*, ed. Giorgio Melchiori, 1989 (New Cambridge Shakespeare)
MLN	*Modern Language Notes*
MLQ	*Modern Language Quarterly*
MLR	*Modern Language Review*
Morgann	Maurice Morgann, *Shakespearean Criticism*, ed. Daniel A. Fineman, 1972
Nashe	*The Works of Thomas Nashe*, ed. R. B. McKerrow, 5 vols., 1904–10; rev. edn F. P. Wilson, 1958
N&Q	*Notes and Queries*
Odell	George C. D. Odell, *Shakespeare from Betterton to Irving*, 2 vols., 1966
OED	*The Oxford English Dictionary*, 20 vols., 1989
Onions	C. T. Onions, *A Shakespeare Glossary*, revised by Robert D. Eagleson, 1986
Oxford	*William Shakespeare: The Complete Works*, ed. Stanley Wells and Gary Taylor, 1986
Oxford OS	*William Shakespeare: The Complete Works*, Original Spelling Edition, ed. Stanley Wells and Gary Taylor, 1987
Partridge	Eric Partridge, *Shakespeare's Bawdy*, 3rd edn, 1969
Patterson	Annabel Patterson, *Reading Holinshed's Chronicles*, 1994
Pope	*The Works of Shakespear*, ed. Alexander Pope, 6 vols., 1723–5
Pope[2]	*The Works of Shakespear*, ed. Alexander Pope, 10 vols., 1728
PBA	*Proceedings of the British Academy*
PMLA	*Publications of the Modern Language Association*
Q0	sig. C1–C4 [v] (fragment), 1598
Q1	*The History of Henrie the Fourth*, 1598 (first quarto)
Q2	*The History of Henrie the Fourth*, 1599 (second quarto)
Q3	*The History of Henrie the Fourth*, 1604 (third quarto)
Q4	*The History of Henry the Fourth*, 1608 (fourth quarto)
Q5	*The History of Henrie the Fourth*, 1613 (fifth quarto)
Q6	*The Historie of Henry the Fourth*, 1622 (sixth quarto)

Q7	*The Historie of Henry the Fourth*, 1632 (seventh quarto)
Qq	quartos
RES	*Review of English Studies*
Rowe	*The Works of Mr William Shakespear*, ed. Nicholas Rowe, 7 vols., 1709
Rowe[3]	*The Works of Mr William Shakespeare*, ed. Nicholas Rowe, 3rd edn, 8 vols., 1714
RSC	Royal Shakespeare Company
Salgādo	Gāmini Salgādo, *Eyewitnesses of Shakespeare: First Hand Accounts of Performances 1590–1890*, 1975
SB	*Studies in Bibliography*
Schäfer	Jürgen Schäfer, *Documentation in the OED: Shakespeare and Nashe as Test Cases*, 1980
SD	stage direction
SH	speech heading
Spenser	*The Works of Edmund Spenser*, ed. Edwin Greenlaw *et al.*, 8 vols., 1932–49 (Variorum)
Sprague, *Histories*	Arthur Colby Sprague, *Shakespeare's Histories*, 1975
Sprague and Trewin	Arthur Colby Sprague and J. C. Trewin, *Shakespeare's Plays Today*, 1970
SQ	*Shakespeare Quarterly*
S.St.	*Shakespeare Studies*
S.Sur.	*Shakespeare Survey*
Staunton	*The Plays of Shakespeare*, ed. Howard Staunton, 3 vols., 1858–60
Steevens	*The Plays of William Shakespeare*, notes by Samuel Johnson and George Steevens, 3rd edn, 10 vols., 1785
Stow, *Chronicles*	John Stow, *The Chronicles of England*, 1580. Excerpts reprinted in Bullough, pp. 215–19
Stow, *Survey*	John Stow, *A Survey of London*, ed. Charles L. Kingsford, 2 vols., 1908
subst.	substantively
Sugden	E. H. Sugden, *A Topographical Dictionary to the Works of Shakespeare and his Fellow Dramatists*, 1925
Textual Companion	Stanley Wells and Gary Taylor, with John Jowett and William Montgomery, *William Shakespeare: A Textual Companion*, 1987
Theobald	*The Works of Shakespeare*, ed. Lewis Theobald, 7 vols., 1733
Tilley	M. P. Tilley, *A Dictionary of the Proverbs in England in the Sixteenth and Seventeenth Centuries*, 1950 (references are to numbered proverbs)
Trewin	J. C. Trewin, *Shakespeare on the English Stage*, 1964
TSLL	*Texas Studies in Literature and Language*
uncorr.	uncorrected
Van Lennep	William Van Lennep, ed., *The London Stage: 1660–1800, Part I 1660–1700*, 1965
Var. 1773	*The Plays of William Shakespeare*, ed. Samuel Johnson and George Steevens, 10 vols., 1773
Var. 1778	*The Plays of William Shakespeare*, ed. Samuel Johnson and George Steevens, 10 vols., 1778

Walker	William S. Walker, *A Critical Examination of the Text of Shakespeare*, 3 vols., 1860
Warburton	*The Works of Shakespeare*, ed. William Warburton, 8 vols., 1747
West	Gilian West, '"Titan", "onyers", and other difficulties in the text of *1 Henry IV*', *SQ* 34 (1983), 330–33
Wilson	*The First Part of the History of Henry IV*, ed. John Dover Wilson, 1946 (New Shakespeare)
Wilson, *Fortunes*	John Dover Wilson, *The Fortunes of Falstaff*, 1943
Wright	*The First Part of King Henry IV*, ed. W. A. Wright, 1897 (Clarendon Press Series)
G. Wright	George T. Wright, *Shakespeare's Metrical Art*, 1991

Biblical quotations are from the Geneva edition, 1560, unless otherwise noted.

INTRODUCTION
The First Part of King Henry IV

Reputation

In the most highly regarded twentieth-century study of history plays from different periods and nationalities, Herbert Lindenberger argues: '*Henry IV* surely provides the supreme example of a complex and serious approach to history that diverts in the very act of instructing.'[1] G. R. Hibbard represents many leading critics and directors when he expands this evaluation beyond the confines of genre: 'In size, in significance, and above all, in the sheer wealth of invention that has gone into its making, *Henry IV* is among the major achievements.'[2]

For *1 Henry IV*, undisputed facts concerning the play's reception support these superlatives. From its first appearance, probably in 1597, *Part One* has enjoyed great popularity and has been performed with exceptional frequency. Between 1598 and 1622, before the First Folio of 1623, there were seven quarto editions – more than for any other play by Shakespeare. *Part One* continues to be among the plays most often published in general texts and anthologies of literature for students around the world.

Readers and audiences familiar with the reputation of *1 Henry IV* will often be surprised when they approach the play itself for the first time. If they anticipate stirring action or expect to laugh whole-heartedly with Falstaff, the first two scenes may seem relatively subdued. They contain a stimulating but unstable mixture of serious and comic qualities. During the third scene, political conflict does disrupt the King's Council, yet the next episodes, which focus on the robbery at Gad's Hill and on Hotspur's argument with his wife, Lady Percy, may even diffuse such political momentum as has built up during the Council scene. Only with the three great scenes of the central action – in the tavern with the Prince and Falstaff, in the household of Glendower, and in the court of Henry IV – does the dramatic intensity and richness for which the play has been celebrated burst upon us.

This delay between expectation and fulfilment provides evidence of the play's basic design: a restless, de-centred opening movement, followed by a mid-section filled with astonishing, highly theatrical surprises, and a concluding movement which powerfully intensifies the already discordant rhythms of uneasiness and elation. Shakespeare's willingness to postpone satisfactions reveals the confidence with which he reshaped historical and theatrical sources in composing his play. Early audiences, acquainted with some of these materials and aware of Shakespeare's prior history plays, were probably even more surprised by this first movement than are audiences today. For example, anyone who had recently watched *Richard II*

[1] *Historical Drama: The Relation of Literature and Reality*, 1975, p. 108.
[2] *The Making of Shakespeare's Dramatic Poetry*, 1981, p. 162.

(1595–6) would already know that, according to Shakespeare, Henry's reign had begun with a rebellion which the Percys helped put down, and with the assassination of Richard himself. The King's pointed reference to his 'unthrifty' son as a dissolute prodigal (*Richard II* 5.3.1) would prepare an audience to behold a ruffian Prince of Wales. So would the popular legends circulated through ballads and tales as well as in plays like *The Famous Victories of Henry the fifth* which celebrated the Prince's wild youth. But when the Prince suddenly confides to the audience his secret plans for self-reform – plans which necessarily 'falsify men's hopes' (1.2.171) – the audience realises that Shakespeare intends to give them something fresh and surprising.

The Prince's soliloquy offers the most emphatic among many examples of how, early in the play, Shakespeare unsettles preconceptions. If audiences believe the King in the opening scene, they may expect the Prince to be stained with 'riot and dishonour' (1.1.84). They may also surmise that Glendower, 'irregular and wild' (1.1.40) is a barbarian, that Hotspur is princely, and that the King, admiring Hotspur's virtues, will treat him with respect when they meet 'Wednesday next' (1.1.102) at Westminster. Expectations about all these matters will prove to be mistaken, at least in part.

Shakespeare fashions *1 Henry IV* as a sequence of three movements. Although his seventh play about English history, it is striking for its originality. Shakespeare forgoes the ceremonious, highly symbolic style of dramaturgy on which he had relied in *Richard II*. He leads the audience to a more gradual, detached understanding of complex characters who repeatedly foist their interpretations of the past upon one another. What is distinctive about Prince Henry is not that he so fervently remembers and predicts events, but that he ultimately succeeds in imposing his will on these events. With Henry IV, Shakespeare turned his attention to a king who had barely escaped the violent sacrificial death suffered by Henry VI, Richard III, and Richard II. He thereby freed himself to explore the volatile, disconcerting strategies of other would-be survivors.

Falstaff is probably the best-known survivor in western literature. Generations of spectators have watched to see if he can dodge the trap set for him by the Prince and Poins, and have been astonished by the way he escapes death at the battle of Shrewsbury. Falstaff's dramatic impact has become inseparable from his reputation. However widely critical responses to him may diverge, they are usually informed by some sense of his fame, of the debates he has inspired, and of the rejection he must ultimately experience. His reputation tends to enhance the vitality which shines through this extraordinary character, so that he may seem to enjoy a life almost independent of the play's design. Falstaff is an unpredictable presence throughout the three movements; his theatrical range extends from intimate banter to brilliant and uproarious scene-stealing. He is never more likely to surprise us than when he apparently adopts conventional roles or when he passes shrewd judgements upon the Prince – or on himself.

To elaborate a design which could register the energies of his characters in this history play, Shakespeare drew upon his own experiments with comedy; he also

1 'What trick, what device . . . canst thou now find out?' Act 2, Scene 4. Michael Pennington as the
Prince and John Woodvine as Falstaff in Michael Bogdanov's English Shakespeare Company touring
production, 1986

enriched *1 Henry IV* with imitations of popular festivity and entertainment. But
when he transferred his own grasp of exciting surprise and reversal to suspicious
rulers and ambitious courtiers, he moved far beyond the characterisation of such
earlier self-conscious tricksters as Richard of Gloucester in *Richard III* or the Bastard
in *King John*. Richard knows what he is doing and does it; the Bastard openly
experiments. But Henry IV, his son, and Falstaff deny us full confidence that they
can or will attempt to do what they say, for their success may at times depend on
obscuring their motives, both to others and to themselves.

As a consequence, this history play will divert and instruct different audiences in
remarkably different ways. Recorded critical reaction to the play begins with a nar-
rowly partisan response by the powerful Cobham family who apparently protested
against Shakespeare's treatment of their supposed ancestor Sir John Oldcastle,
thereby causing his name to be changed to Sir John Falstaff. The controversy that
seems to have arisen over Falstaff's name provides important information about
both the date and the early reception of *1 Henry IV*. These topics, to some extent
inseparable, will be distinguished for the sake of clarity. 'Date' focuses upon matters
of chronology – perhaps the last subjects we might expect to find closely associated

with Falstaff. The early reception of the play will be considered later, as a preface to selected contexts for interpretation.

Date

The few accepted facts about the date of *1 Henry IV* have enabled scholars to place its first performances tentatively in the early months of 1597. As we consider this limited evidence, it is helpful to remember that early performances of this play probably overlapped those of *The Merchant of Venice* (1596–7) and closely preceded those of *Much Ado About Nothing* (1598), *Julius Caesar* (1599), and *Hamlet* (1600–1). Furthermore, the text of Shakespeare's new play would have been especially flexible, subject to the pressure of contemporary political and theatrical circumstances.

On 25 February 1598, a play entitled *Henry IV* was entered in the Stationers' Register to Andrew Wyse:

1597 [1598, new style] xxv die ffebruariji. Andrew Wyse. Entred for his Copie, under t[he] handes of Master Dix: and master Warden man a booke intituled The historye of HENRY the IIIJth with his battaile of Shrewsburye against HENRY HOTTSPURRE of the Northe with The conceipted mirthe of Sr John Ffalstoff.

This entry makes no mention of 'Part One' or of 'The first Part', which may indicate that *Part Two* had not yet been written or performed, or that, if it had been, those who entered the copy saw no reason to identify this second play in any way.

Two separate quarto editions of *1 Henry IV* were printed in 1598, but only a fragment of the first (Q0) survives (see Textual Analysis, pp. 219–20). The second (Q1) was reprinted from the first by the same printing house, that of Peter Short. Its title modifies slightly the entry above:

THE / HISTORY OF / HENRIE THE / FOVRTH; / With the battell at Shrewsburie, / *betweene the King and Lord* / Henry Percy, surnamed / Henrie Hotspur of / the North. / *With the humorous conceits of Sir* / Iohn Fastalffe.

Only when, some months later, Francis Meres praised Shakespeare for his excellence in both comedy and tragedy in *Palladis Tamia* (entered in the Stationers' Register, 7 September 1598) do we have firmer evidence to support Shakespeare's authorship. As examples of 'tragedy', Meres submitted 'Richard the 2. Richard the 3. Henry the 4.' The titles of the quartos printed between 1599 and 1613 credit Shakespeare with having 'newly corrected' his play. None of the early quarto titles of the play show that it had an immediate sequel; our earliest specific reference to 'the firste part' comes from a Stationers' Register entry of 1603. In contrast, the sole quarto of *Part Two*, printed in 1600 as *THE Second part of Henrie the fourth . . . Written by William Shakespeare*, clearly indicates its relationship to *Part One*.

That the play was well received is beyond doubt. Following the two quarto editions of 1598, additional quartos were printed in 1599, 1604, 1608, 1613, and 1622, before the First Folio publication in 1623. New quartos in 1632 and 1639 strongly indicate the continuing appeal of the play. From the beginning, as the titles above suggest, Falstaff must have been counted upon to attract audiences. Indeed, Shakespeare's success in making Falstaff notorious seems to have displeased a small but influential group of courtiers.

In the earliest staged version of *1 Henry IV*, Falstaff was apparently called Old-castle, while Bardolph and Peto seem to have been named Rossill and Harvey. These names angered powerful aristocratic families, particularly the Cobhams who were descendants of Oldcastle's wife. The fifteenth-century Lollard, Sir John Oldcastle (d. 1417), would have been widely revered as a precursor of Protestant Reformation martyrs. Shakespeare changed these names, perhaps modifying the play in the process, but also leaving relics of his earlier intentions in his text. Two of the early names survive as speech headings, 'Ross.' in Q1 of *Part One* at 2.4.147, 149, and 153, and 'Old.' in Q of *Part Two* at 1.2.114. Poins names the four robbers-to-be as 'Falstaffe, Harvey, Rossill and Gadshill' in Q1 1.2.130–1, a line that endured through over twenty years of 'newly corrected' reprintings to appear in the Folio.[1]

The relationship of this controversy to the probable earliest performance of *1 Henry IV* is indirect but significant. Original performances are particularly elusive; the editors of *William Shakespeare: A Textual Companion* (1987) conclude, 'We can identify the first performances of only two plays: *All Is True* [usually called *Henry VIII*, 1613] and *1 Henry VI*.'[2] E. K. Chambers speculated that *1 Henry IV* may have been published 'unusually soon after its production. This can hardly have been earlier than 1597.'[3] He reasoned that the company would have wished 'to advertise the purging of the offence' which they had managed to give through the treatment of Oldcastle and others. An important consideration here is that William Brooke, Lord Cobham, served briefly as Queen Elizabeth's Lord Chamberlain between August 1596 and his death on 5 March 1597. Only then was he in a position to stop performances of a play which seemed to satirise his ancestor. Original performances before his death but fairly late in the season 1596–7 would also be consistent with the agreement among scholars that *Richard II*, entered in the Stationers' Register on 29 August 1597, had probably been first performed late in 1595. On the theory that Lord Cobham was responding to both parts of *Henry IV*, which 'increasingly misrepresent his ancestor', A. R. Humphreys conjectures that *Part One* might have been performed earlier in the season.[4]

Two other issues are closely bound up with the changing of names: the influence of censorship in reshaping the play and the form in which such a shape might be considered 'final'. We have no proof that Lord Cobham actively intervened, using his authority over the Revels Office or the licensing of plays. Why, one may wonder, would Shakespeare's normally cautious company have gone out of its way to

---

[1] On the premise that Lord Cobham required the name changes, they have been altered in the Oxford *Complete Works*, 1986; Falstaff becomes 'Sir John'; Bardolph becomes 'Russill'; and Peto becomes 'Harvey'.

[2] S. Wells and G. Taylor with J. Jowett and W. Montgomery, p. 89.

[3] Chambers, *Shakespeare*, I, 382–3.

[4] Humphreys, p. xiv. Gary Taylor argues that 'Oldcastle' was changed to 'Falstaff' before performance at court, Christmas 1596, in 'William Shakespeare, Richard James and the house of Cobham', *RES* 38 (1987), 347–9.

antagonise a Lord Chamberlain?[1] In the summer following the conjectured first performances of *Henry IV*, when the second Lord Hunsdon, the patron of Shakespeare's company, had become the new Lord Chamberlain, the Privy Council actually prohibited *all* performances from 28 July to about 10 October 1597. They were both reacting to an allegation from the City fathers that 'unruly apprentices' were gathering at plays, and terminating production of *The Isle of Dogs* by Jonson and Nashe, which they judged to be inflammatory.[2] In the light of such regulatory powers and attitudes, Gary Taylor argues credibly that official censors insisted that the name 'Oldcastle' be eliminated.[3] Yet no evidence has so far appeared which would suggest that Shakespeare resisted changing Oldcastle and the other names. Indeed, it is possible that having touched the nerves of honour and piety with 'Oldcastle', he would probe them more deeply with 'Falstaff', especially if, early in 1598, he were still developing his character for performance of *Part Two*.[4]

Whether 'Rossill' and 'Harvey', the original names of Bardolph and Peto, actually pleased or displeased powerful lords has been matter for careful but inconclusive speculation about Elizabethan patronage.[5] That these names survive in speech headings or in a list of thieves may give us evidence of another kind by contributing suggestions about playhouse practices. In the theatres, composition, rehearsal, revision, and performance may have overlapped extensively.[6] This could have been particularly true when the playwright, Shakespeare, as both a shareholder and an actor in the company, might well have exercised the powers of a modern director in preparing plays for the stage. From this theatrical perspective, survival of the names could reveal playhouse nonchalance where groups of attendants are concerned or reflect the irrelevance of precise identities where a deliberately confusing robbery, enlivened with improvisation, must have been enacted.[7] Because the naming of the thieves has contributed to the largest group of textual problems in *1 Henry IV*, further discussion is reserved for the Textual Analysis (pp. 220–1). In later productions, as well as in allusions to the play, Falstaff is occasionally called Oldcastle. Even if intended merely as neutral substitutions, such references might have stirred up the embers of ill will.

[1] See Bullough, p. 171; Robert J. Fehrenbach, 'When Lord Cobham and Edmund Tilney "were att odds": Oldcastle, Falstaff and the date of *1 Henry IV*', *S.St.* 18 (1986), 87–101. E. A. J. Honigmann believes that Shakespeare and his company deliberately provoked the Cobhams in order to please the Essex faction. See 'Sir John Oldcastle: Shakespeare's martyr', in *Fanned and Winnowed Opinions: Shakespearean Essays Presented to Harold Jenkins*, ed. John W. Mahon and Thomas A. Pendleton, 1987, pp. 118–32.

[2] See Chambers, *Stage*, 1, 298–9. He argues that the new Chamberlain may have persuaded the Council to permit performances to resume in October.

[3] 'The fortunes of Oldcastle', *S.Sur.* 38 (1985), 85–100. Janet Clare describes the 'Oldcastle' controversy in the context of developing regulation in *'Art Made Tongue-Tied by Authority': Elizabethan and Jacobean Dramatic Censorship*, 1990, pp. 76–9.

[4] Melchiori argues that *Part Two* was composed in 'late 1597/early 1598' and first performed 'after March 1598', p. 3.

[5] See John Jowett, 'The thieves in *1 Henry IV*', *RES* 38 (1987), 325–33.

[6] Scott McMillin, *The Elizabethan Theatre and 'The Book of Sir Thomas More'*, 1987, pp. 37–9.

[7] Mahood, *Bit Parts*, pp. 8–9, 15–16.

The design of the play

Who in Shakespeare's original audiences could have anticipated that he would take up the sober figure of a Lollard knight, regarded as a martyr by sixteenth-century religious reformers, and give him the theatrical genius of a great entertainer? *1 Henry IV* incorporates surprise within overall expectation as a principle of design. Shakespeare's skill at crafting an interplay of expectation and surprise, convention and experiment, becomes evident in the three-phase movement of his drama. The first movement of *1 Henry IV*, which includes six scenes, extends from the briefing session of Act 1, Scene 1, to the wrangling between Hotspur and Lady Percy in Act 2, Scene 3. The second movement begins with a long and vigorous scene set in the Eastcheap tavern (2.4) and ends two scenes later with the confrontation, so vividly anticipated in the tavern, between King and Prince at court (3.2). The third and final movement of ten scenes starts with another tavern gathering in Act 3, Scene 3 and ends after the victory by the King's party over Hotspur and his army at the long-awaited battle of Shrewsbury. Even so brief a survey can suggest some of the play's most important features: the economy with which Shakespeare links episodes; the combativeness of characters living in readiness for war; and the entanglement of public with private, political with domestic spheres of action. What such a survey of the play as a whole omits are the ways in which each movement differs from the other two. These are important differences; they may help to explain why, for many, the comic genre of *1 Henry IV* is a belated discovery rather than a foregone conclusion. Comedy arises surprisingly and with evident strain and stress from the grimly efficient dramaturgy of the third movement.

THE FIRST MOVEMENT: 'THEREFOR WE MEET NOT NOW'

In the opening speech King Henry describes his hopes for a crusade to the remote Holy Land which both he and his lords probably know will not take place: 'Therefor we meet not now' (1.1.30). They do meet to consider news from England's own borders: Mortimer's defeat and capture by the Welsh rebel, Glendower, and Henry Percy's (Hotspur's) victory at Holmedon, with his capture of several Scottish lords. Potential controversy over this 'honourable spoil' will become the occasion of the Council at the beginning of Scene 3. Shakespeare quickly plunges his audience into the political confusions for which the King is largely responsible. He has usurped power from his first cousin, King Richard II, and has caused Richard to be assassinated. Edward Hall, the Tudor chronicler, characterised as 'unquiet' the early years of Henry's reign. They were frequently disrupted when other rebels attempted to imitate the King's success and thereby replace him. By demonstrating that a king could be deposed, in spite of the divine sanctions which, all were taught, supported his rule, Henry had undermined a major prop of feudal monarchy. Feudal rulers were idealised as the first among equals in the legends of King Arthur supported by his Round Table; nevertheless such rulers were at the mercy of great landed noblemen, on whom they depended for arms and services. As *1 Henry IV* begins, the powerful Percy family who helped Henry become king is testing his authority.

In terms of staging, it is significant that this beginning has a business-like quality. Shakespeare may well have reserved for his third scene the striking visual props of royal power. There, a central throne and a spectacular display of crown and sceptre might serve as royal weapons with which to awe the unruly Percys.[1] Here, however, we appear to be in the royal equivalent of that workaday world which Shakespeare evokes throughout the first movement of his play, a world which includes household chambers and an innyard as well as the public highway where both the King's 'auditor' (2.1.46) and Falstaff will be robbed. A subdued conference in 1.1, followed by a surprising exhibition of regal might in 1.3, would not only deploy the resources of the Elizabethan stage; it would conform to the policy later explained by Henry to his son in Act 3, Scene 2. A ruler who avoids frequent and showy public appearances can have, he believes, the effect of a 'comet' when he does display his 'presence' (3.2.47, 54).

In terms of a developing structure, the opening scene introduces a series of episodes in which 'Therefor we meet not now' becomes almost a leitmotif. The King summons Hotspur to court, then drives him to rebel; the Prince agrees to participate in a robbery but robs the robbers; Hotspur talks of battle in his sleep yet refuses to confide his plans to his wife. Perhaps the King does more than any other character to establish a sense of uneasiness and mistrust during this first movement of the play. Although he is physically present in only two scenes, he epitomises, as cause and focus of rebellion, a range of political and familial disorders. He provides memorable and misleading accounts of Hotspur's honour and the Prince's 'dishonour' (1.1.84), initiating an opposition which he will accentuate when he has an opportunity. In Act 1, Scene 3, he imposes his own pessimistic interpretations upon the puzzling behaviour of Mortimer.

To set off the King from the characters who try to imitate or mimic him, Shakespeare creates a distinctive style.[2] In Henry's opening speech, images of body parts – 'lips' and 'blood' (6), 'hoofs' (8), and 'eyes' (9) – suggest dismemberment rather than identifiable wholes. By vaguely picturing uncontrollable forces – 'frighted peace' (2) or the 'edge of war' (17) – King Henry insinuates the divisions which trouble his kingdom and communicates a potential for violence.[3] Through a series of prophetic statements linked by the repetition of 'No more . . .', Henry promises peace but rhetorically stresses war. Such language is appropriate for a politician who, from his first appearance in *Richard II*, has been adept at activating the darker motives of others and at obscuring his own. The King's conduct raises questions to which

---

[1] On the theatrical dimensions of kingship, see Anne Righter [Barton], *Shakespeare and the Idea of the Play*, 1962, pp. 113–38; Stephen Orgel, *The Illusion of Power: Political Theatre in the English Renaissance*, 1975; David Scott Kastan, 'Proud majesty made a subject: Shakespeare and the spectacle of rule', *SQ* 37 (1986), 459–75.

[2] For the use of images which individualise characters, see Wolfgang Clemen, *The Development of Shakespeare's Imagery*, 1951, pp. 5 ff.; Katherine Eisaman Maus, 'Taking tropes seriously: language and violence in Shakespeare's *Rape of Lucrece*', *SQ* 37 (1986), 66–82.

[3] For a different view of allegorical language here, see Madeleine Doran, 'Imagery in *Richard II* and in *Henry IV*', *MLR* 37 (1942), 113–22.

there can be no reliable answers: would he really have gone crusading if not thwarted by rebellion? Is his rage at Hotspur calculated?

The opening episode of *1 Henry IV* demonstrates Shakespeare's skill in writing scenes which have the coherence of miniature plays, yet reflect and support his overall design. Scene 1 foreshadows the rhythm of subsequent scenes which move from irresolution to decisiveness. It also anticipates the shape of the overall dramatic narrative. King Henry controls the discourse of the conference through his questions.[1] By the end of the scene, the King has begun to recover the firmness which will be so conspicuous in Scene 3: 'I will from henceforth rather be myself, / Mighty and to be feared . . .' (5–6). When he emphatically concludes the third and final movement of the play, he has, at least for the time being, consolidated his authority.

The drama of moral choice

Showing how Shakespeare could achieve a 'continuous flow of action' on a bare thrust stage, Anthony Brennan observes: 'The progress of characters in time is embroidered in a pattern of contrasts and parallels, echoes and distortions.'[2] We may therefore notice again in Scene 2 several of the elements which both typify the first movement and echo Scene 1: informality; distinctive styles of speech; conscious anticipation of later events. Just as Scene 1 leads to a second and more complex court scene, Scene 2 points towards the first tavern scene, 2.4, which in turn pulls together and builds upon Hal's first appearance with Falstaff and the pair of robbery scenes, 2.1 and 2.2.

Yet such similarities bring out striking differences which repay very close attention. Falstaff's reiterated 'when thou art king' (1.2.12–13, 19, 47, 49) repeats King Henry's 'No more . . . no more', but in a far more hopeful key. The fluent prose style of the jests between Falstaff and the Prince introduces us to an unusual 'friendship' (see below, pp. 31–3). This style helps us begin to distinguish Falstaff's world from those of the King and of the Percy faction.[3] Falstaff exaggerates his freedom and social stature as a highwayman: 'Let us be Diana's foresters, gentlemen of the shade, minions of the moon' (1.2.20–2). His fantasies and his wonderful caricature of social order as 'the rusty curb of old Father Antic the law' (48) provoke the Prince's responses: imagining dire consequences for Falstaff's crimes and taunting him with the promise that he will be made official hangman.

The Prince and Falstaff are alone together onstage for the first eighty-five lines of Scene 2 and exchange thirty-three speeches. But the exact rapport between the two characters will vary from one production or reading to the next. A phrase like Falstaff's, 'Indeed, you come near me now, Hal' (10) can express a wide range of tones, from delighted approval and applause to ironic resentment. The productions described in 'Stage History' have shown that this relatively brief dialogue at the

---

[1] Joseph A. Porter, *The Drama of Speech Acts: Shakespeare's Lancastrian Tetralogy*, 1979, pp. 60–1.
[2] *Shakespeare's Dramatic Structures*, 1986, p. 5.
[3] See Jean E. Howard, *Shakespeare's Art of Orchestration: Stage Technique and Audience Response*, 1984, p. 27.

beginning of Scene 2 quickly suggests the nature of the bond between Falstaff and the Prince and is crucial for its later richer development.

Much more clear than the nature of their feelings for each other are the tacit rules which guide the relationship between them. As they plan the joke of the Gad's Hill robbery, the Prince and Poins count on Falstaff to amuse them in predictable ways. The repartee between Falstaff and the Prince is impersonal enough to accommodate other characters; Poins can enter into their non-stop bantering and baiting as if he had been present all along.

The Prince, having side-stepped questions about his future, suddenly reveals in his soliloquy that his behaviour has been intended to create a misleading impression. His speech probably surprises many readers and spectators, reversing their expectations about his character. The Prince's clear motives and plans contrast with his father's opaque calculations; his promises imply both a star performance as Henry V, and a unified dramatic narrative about his development. For Shakespeare, such a narrative model already existed in the form of popular Morality plays and Interludes which represented the testing of Christian youth beset by the temptations of the world, the flesh, and the Devil. Morality plays showed the influence of ingenious preaching techniques, as well as of folktales. They embodied, according to Robert Potter, archetypal narratives of innocence lost and salvation achieved through conversion and repentance.[1] Although this particular Morality pattern had flourished in the late fifteenth and earlier sixteenth centuries, it could probably still be recognised by Elizabethan audiences and reinforced through contemporary enthusiasm for the biblical theme of the prodigal son.[2]

Modern audiences and readers have often responded to the Prince's dramatic function by perceiving its similarity to more recent versions of the spiritual quest archetype: romantic and post-romantic stories of education and self-discovery, rebellion and initiation. Lindenberger points out that for a 'generation' of interpreters, the play explores the 'balance' which the Prince achieves or the ambivalence he learns to negotiate between values typified by Hotspur and Falstaff.[3] Yet this coming-of-age story provides only one of the conventions on which Shakespeare relied in designing *1 Henry IV*. Also important are chronicle histories, history plays, and poems which develop more sequentially as well as romance narratives like that of Edmund Spenser's *The Faerie Queene* (1590), composed of interlaced stories occurring simultaneously. Then too, we should reckon with traditions of celebration and entertainment which could have prepared Elizabethan audiences to find established conventions used in theatrically self-conscious and unconventional forms. Falstaff joyfully plays the Morality role of the Vice or 'Iniquity', but other functions of the Vice, tempting, mocking, and entertaining, seem to be shared out more equally between Falstaff and the Prince himself. Even the division of comic from serious scenes, often practised in Morality plays and stipulated by Renaissance theorists

[1] *The English Morality Play: Origin, History and Influence of a Dramatic Tradition*, 1975, pp. 8–10, 16–20.
[2] See Richard Helgerson, *The Elizabethan Prodigals*, 1976, pp. 2–3, 12–15. On similarities between Falstaff and the tempters in such plays, see Wilson, *Fortunes*, pp. 17–23, 31.
[3] Lindenberger, pp. 100, 180 n. 5.

mindful of classical decorum, breaks down when Hotspur provokes laughter or when the Prince promises to cast off his closest friend during the tavern revels of 2.4.

The Morality pattern of spiritual reform that underlies the Prince's soliloquy may be one method of inviting an audience into the play; it can engage concern with a whole series of moral choices rather than provide a sturdy framework for any one character's dilemma. Indeed, Shakespeare gave up a more conventional form of suspense by presenting a Prince who has already made his choice and feels armed against surprise: 'I know you all' (1.2.155). His soliloquy shows that he has the capacity later described by Hamlet, 'a large discourse, / Looking before and after' (4.4.36–7), but King Henry and the rebellious Percys will set the political agenda. Moreover, the Prince's speech operates 'before and after' in ways he cannot have intended. It furnishes one of several moments when the play appears to pivot on a fulcrum. In Walter Hodges' illustration for 'I know you all', the Prince looks back at least momentarily towards his departed friend, Poins, before facing forward towards the audience (see illustration 2). If we hear the speech while thinking back ourselves, we may remember the ambiguities in the King's overture. Within a few moments and a mere five lines into the next scene, we can recognise a strong likeness between the Prince, a hidden 'sun' who will eventually 'please again to be himself' (160) and the King who resolves, 'I will from henceforth rather be myself.' His 'all', which briefly stretches the world of the play, making a few characters stand for an entire society, will toll through the Prince's speeches even after, late in *Part Two*, he becomes King Henry V, suggesting his comprehensive sense of responsibility. He may prove successful, in part, because he youthfully underestimates the obstacles he faces.

Shakespeare complicates the pattern of moral choice in *Part One* by bringing Hotspur onstage right after the Prince's soliloquy. Perhaps he is reflecting here the designs of late sixteenth-century Morality plays which often present two antagonists rather than one central figure.[1] Through Hotspur's two long and brilliant speeches to the King in 1.3 – an alibi for ignoring the King's agent at Holmedon and an apology for Mortimer's honour – audiences discover why a king might want him for a son. In addition to his sincere passion for chivalry, he is humorous and imaginative – qualities markedly absent in his father, his uncle, and the King. That a naive Hotspur should regard the departed King as a 'vile politician' (238) and fail to notice how his own father and uncle 'train him on' (5.2.21) is one of the tragic ironies of the play.[2] Surfacing early, it encourages an audience to compare his relations to his elders with the Prince's and to look for more evidence of growth under pressure than one might otherwise expect from the Prince. Both young men are committed

---

[1] Alan C. Dessen, *Shakespeare and the Late Moral Plays*, 1986, pp. 55–90.
[2] See Robert Ornstein, *A Kingdom for a Stage: The Achievement of Shakespeare's History Plays*, 1972, p. 133. For an especially stimulating and influential argument on the complexity of 'two opposed value-judgements' that are necessary for any full experience of the plays, see A. P. Rossiter, 'Ambivalence: the dialectic of the Histories' in *Angel with Horns: Fifteen Lectures on Shakespeare*, 1961, p. 51.

2 'I know you all': a possible staging of Prince Hal's soliloquy, Act 1, Scene 2, as drawn by C. Walter Hodges. The position and stance of the Prince will determine whether he includes the audience in the theatre as part of 'you all'

to redeeming not only the times but also their fathers (see Commentary on 1.2.177 and 1.3.85).

Shakespeare juxtaposes the joke played by Poins and the Prince when they hide Falstaff's horse at Gad's Hill – 'Falstaff sweats to death, / And lards the lean earth as he walks along' (2.2.90–1) – with Hotspur's sharp satire on the 'frosty-spirited rogue' who runs away from the Percy plot (2.3.17). At the same time, he sets off a more subdued reverberation between two emotional bonds: Falstaff's friendship with the 'rogue' who has tricked him ('If the rascal have not given me medicines to make me love him, I'll be hanged' 2.2.15–16) and Lady Percy's compassionate dependence upon a husband almost wholly preoccupied with riding his horse into battle. Suggestions of good life, disrupted by robbers and rebels, run through the play from the flea-ridden inn of 2.1 to the later scenes set in Eastcheap and Wales. When Lady Percy asks, 'For what offence have I this fortnight been / A banished woman from my Harry's bed?' (2.3.32–3), Shakespeare brings the personal cost of such disorder home to his audiences.

THE SECOND MOVEMENT: '. . . BANISH ALL THE WORLD'
The second movement of *1 Henry IV* bursts forth with three exuberant scenes which have more lines than did the first six. All three are filled with mercurial changes of character, surprising images, and strikingly resonant clashes of personality. Although distinct in rhythm and mood, each of these scenes represents a fullness and richness of experience withheld during the first movement. That set in Eastcheap (2.4) and the latter part of the following scene, set in Wales (3.1), create a holiday humour. The duping of Falstaff, so easily brought off, hardly prepares us for his ability, within a frame of satisfied expectations, to surprise everyone, turning 2.4 into a feast of theatrical invention. And, after earlier references to Glendower as 'irregular and wild' (1.1.40) and as 'damned' (1.3.82), who would expect to find in Wales a haven of civility? C. L. Barber's observation that Shakespeare 'dramatizes not only holiday but also the need for holiday and the need to limit holiday' is especially pertinent to the second movement.[1] The festive energies of the tavern scene and the Welsh scene enhance the seriousness of the third (3.2) – an interview of great tension through which the Prince, here meeting his father for the first time in the play, earns his confidence. King Henry concludes the movement with grim and sharpened purpose: 'let's away, / Advantage feeds him fat while men delay'.

The first tavern scene, 2.4, easily the longest in the play with four hundred and sixty-one lines, has proved for many readers and spectators to be the most memorable. Like the play as a whole, this scene has three movements: an introduction during which the Prince, awaiting Falstaff, passes time by teasing Francis, the apprentice drawer; a mid-section devoted to the expected and the unexpected consequences of the joke played on Falstaff; and a climactic, more surprising pair of short plays improvised by the Prince and Falstaff (312–99), followed by a brief passage or coda in which the Prince hides Falstaff from the Sheriff, vows to make Falstaff 'answerable' for the money if he has 'robbed these men' (437–8), and, with Peto, picks Falstaff's pockets of their tavern reckonings. Although critics differ about the relative weighting of these components, most would probably agree that 'when examined, it is seen to be not at all a meandering effusion but a controlled structure, a skilfully threaded series of small firm units'.[2]

However carefully planned, this exuberance has led to great diversity of theatrical and critical interpretation.[3] As the plot thickens with the delayed entry of Falstaff and as the theatrical powers of the scene multiply, so too do possibilities

---

[1] Barber, p. 192.
[2] Emrys Jones, *Scenic Form in Shakespeare*, 1971, p. 30; he sees a two-part structure 'bridged' by the news of Northern and Western Rebellions. See also Mark Rose, *Shakespearean Design*, 1972, pp. 49–59.
[3] For extended discussion of 2.4 and of its relation to the rest of the play, see Gareth Lloyd Evans, 'The comical–tragical–historical method – *Henry IV*', *Stratford-upon-Avon Studies*, 3 (1961), 144–63; J. McLaverty, 'No abuse: the Prince and Falstaff in the tavern scenes of *Henry IV*', *S.Sur.* 34 (1981), 105–110; Edward Pechter, 'Falsifying men's hopes: the ending of *1 Henry IV*', *MLQ* 41 (1980), 211–30; John Shaw, 'The staging of parody and parallels in *1 Henry IV*', *S.Sur.* 20 (1967), 61–73.

for understanding Falstaff, the Prince, and the significance of their relationship. Falstaff incarnates humour 'unyoked' (1.2.156) – a tendency to claim too much and go too far – but a similar extravagance has been unleashed in the Prince: 'I am now of all humours that have showed themselves humours since the old days of goodman Adam to the pupil age of this present twelve o'clock at midnight' (2.4.81–3). Their imitations of Hotspur, Douglas, and the King are inspired. As T. S. Eliot said of Ben Jonson's satire, such parody is 'great in the end not by hitting off its object, but by creating it'.[1] Falstaff escalates his count of men said to have attacked him from two to eleven figures in buckram, then tosses in 'three misbegotten knaves in Kendal green' (186–7). The Prince expects to deflate Falstaff with his revelation that 'we two set on you four, and, with a word, out-faced you from your prize', but Falstaff in some productions and readings out-faces the Prince with his defence: 'By the Lord, I knew ye as well as he that made ye' (212–13, 221).

The climax of this unyoked humour comes when Falstaff, impersonating the Prince, pleads, 'Banish plump Jack, and banish all the world' (397–8). By replying 'I do. I will', the Prince (in some interpretations) brings the game, with its free spirits, to a close (see below pp. 50, 55, 75 and Commentary). Whether he momentarily reveals his long-range strategy and whether Falstaff grasps the nature of his game are indeed crucial problems. How they may be resolved depends upon these considerations: the wariness or warmth with which both the Prince and Falstaff play their roles; the degree to which their emotional dynamism is supported or ignored by the audience onstage; inclinations of readers or spectators either to trust or distrust acting and games; varying hypotheses about the 'history', social order, and royal power which interrupt and re-direct revelry when Falstaff returns to announce 'villainous news' (276) – that the King has summoned the Prince to court and that civil war has begun. Charged with hopes and desires which neither character can fully reveal, their improvised playing resonates far beyond its length. Energetic accusations and defences make their sport resemble a public trial. Yet despite the crowded stage, the Prince and Falstaff can seem to be acting out a two-handed drama essentially for one another. Their final exchange suggests both a common preoccupation with self and a gulf between their loyalties and commitments.

The tavern scene can function within the play much as does the Prince's soliloquy in 1.2 – as a fulcrum prompting revaluations of the past (did Falstaff see through the Prince's disguise at Gad's Hill?) and shaping expectations of the future (will the Prince be able to manage his father?). 'Depose me?', asks Falstaff when the Prince abruptly commands, 'Do thou stand for me, and I'll play my father' (2.4.357–8). But although this change of roles might symbolise King Henry's past usurpation and the Prince's future succession, it does not fulfil the immediate purpose proposed for their theatrical game, enabling the Prince to 'practise an answer' to the King (309). Both characters seize on another opportunity for competitive wit and caricature. Then, almost as if he had wished to distract audiences from focusing on English family politics, Shakespeare follows the first tavern scene with a Welsh episode,

---

[1] *Elizabethan Dramatists*, 1963, p. 80.

distinguished from the scenes surrounding it both by social climate, and by an independent time-scheme. Whereas 3.2 takes place later the same morning that began in 2.4, 3.1 shows the rebels still planning their rendezvous at Shrewsbury. Yet in the next scene, King Henry reports the rebel gathering there as an event already past.[1]

In Wales, the revels, if not the dialogue, are dominated by Glendower, a man who, historically, sought to be prince of an independent realm.[2] Whereas 2.4 seems to mirror aspects of the entire play, 3.1 (the third longest scene in *1 Henry IV*) dramatises qualities which would otherwise largely be absent. Just how strongly readers or spectators perceive these exceptional qualities may depend on how they are encouraged to view Glendower's response to Hotspur. If he becomes too angry, in the theatre or in our readings, Hotspur's spirited lines will make him seem a fool. If he graciously restrains himself, it may appear that at least one major character does not always assume a self either imposed by or addressed to others. Instead, he confidently proclaims his achievements, including three substantive defeats of the English King (here treated as a predatory troublemaker), as well as his skill in music, poetry, and occult science. Some stage Glendowers, while looking bizarre, have behaved tactfully, making it seem that Hotspur, with one of those delayed reactions for which he is noted, is exploiting an opportunity to bait the King who broke off their dialogue in 1.3.

During recent productions, Glendower's musicians and the Welsh singing of his daughter, almost invariably omitted for over two hundred years, have conveyed the enchantment which Mortimer finds in his wife's strange tongue; it seems 'as sweet', he says, 'as ditties highly penned, / Sung by a fair queen in a summer's bower / With ravishing division to her lute' (202–4). Within Glendower's court, love is not merely a distraction from politics. Interpretations of the play which ignore the exceptional qualities of 3.1 may erase a brief holiday from the attitudes and anxieties which emphatically return in 3.2.

Where Glendower is 'wondrous affable' (162), King Henry is often wondrous harsh. Peremptory with Hotspur for refusing to send him the Scottish prisoners, he gains the support of his own son by challenging his honour. In marked contrast to the 'play extempore' (2.4.231) with its balanced exchanges and more equal division of lines, the King has five of the scene's nine speeches, including the first and last, and utters one hundred and thirty lines to the Prince's forty-four. Shakespeare points for his hearers the repetitive nature of experience by giving father and son similar language. The Prince's vow, 'I shall hereafter, my thrice-gracious lord, / Be more myself (3.2.92–3) echoes his father's earlier threat to the Percys: 'I will from henceforth rather be myself' (1.3.5); the King's conviction that his 'being seldom seen' caused him to be 'wondered at' like a comet (3.2.46–7) parallels the Prince's plan in his soliloquy to 'imitate the sun', which 'Being wanted . . . may be more

[1] On the complex time-scheme employed in *1 Henry IV*, see Ricardo J. Quinones, *The Renaissance Discovery of Time*, 1972, pp. 340–1.
[2] Arthur Granville Bradley, *Owen Glyndwr and the Last Struggle for Welsh Independence, with a Brief Sketch of Welsh History*, 1901.

wondered at' (1.2.157, 161), and his opinion that people only wish for holidays when they 'seldom come' (166). Yet the scene can surprise an audience with the possibility that if anyone does teach the Prince how to answer his father, it may well be the mistrustful King himself.

THE THIRD MOVEMENT: '. . . IF A LIE MAY DO THEE GRACE'
Comparing Shakespeare's dramaturgy to that of medieval plays where a character may well have his own 'house' set up onstage, John Wilders comments that 'the action of *Henry IV* is distributed between different physical worlds or locations, each dominated by a unique and uniquely demanding character'.[1] In the third movement of the play, however, the Prince has a strong impact in spite of his relatively brief appearances onstage. Falstaff often becomes a more dominant theatrical presence, yet tends, at times, to lose some of his dramatic force. In contrast to their earlier scenes, Falstaff occupies the stage throughout 3.3 and 4.2, while the Prince arrives late and leaves before Falstaff. And beginning with 3.3, Falstaff not only gets the last, sometimes rude, word in five scenes (3.3, 4.2, 5.1, 5.3, and 5.4) but also speaks in soliloquy, as did the Prince at the end of 1.2.

Falstaff's questions which open 3.3, 'Bardolph, am I not fallen away vilely since this last action? Do I not bate? Do I not dwindle?' invert the King's call to action which closes 3.2: 'let's away, / Advantage feeds him fat while men delay'. They introduce a movement which 'bates' from its predecessor. Of the last ten scenes, only this second tavern scene lasts more than one hundred and seventy lines. Except for 3.3 and 5.4, these scenes replace complex interaction and vigorous repartee with political self-justification. The richness of language and character becomes less complex as the choreography of battle becomes increasingly important. Falstaff's new role of scavenging recruiter who leads his starving troops 'where they are peppered' (5.3.35) complements a new emphasis on the chivalric side of Prince Henry. The prospect of battle seems to simplify the life of this great play, although the fighting, when it does come, takes up only the first parts of two scenes in the text. Most of the scenes conclude in an anticlimactic vein.

Falstaff's lines about his own bating also parallel the lines with which the King opens the play, 'So shaken as we are, so wan with care.' In the third movement, Falstaff's resemblance to King Henry becomes more obvious. His anxieties about decline and death foreshadow a major motif associating the King and Falstaff in *Part Two*. Through this dwindling Falstaff, Shakespeare explores the ethical border between loyalty to others and self-preservation. In 3.3, Falstaff provokes the Hostess into a hilariously damning self-defence against his back-handed compliment to her as an 'otter': 'She's neither fish nor flesh, a man knows not where to have her.' 'Thou art an unjust man in saying so', protests the enraged Hostess, 'thou or any man knows where to have me, thou knave, thou' (102–7).

Responses to Falstaff's soliloquy on 'honour' may depend to an unusual extent not only on the values supported by particular interpretations or productions, but also on the views about war already held by readers and spectators. To confirm his

[1] *The Lost Garden: A View of Shakespeare's English and Roman History Plays*, 1978, p. 87.

own opinions, Falstaff employs the catechism, a device for indoctrinating students by teaching them correct answers to prescribed questions. While his technique helps him reduce military obligation to absurdity, his affirmation of life may be irresistible. Like the Prince's soliloquy, Falstaff's speech invites us to measure an emphatic viewpoint against other possibilities. After Falstaff attacks the vanity of dying to save face, the audience witnesses the King's strategy to protect his life by disguising loyal lords in his 'coats'. The Prince risks his life to save the King and then to kill Hotspur. In turn, Falstaff pretends that he is dead, then that Hotspur may revive, 'Why may not he rise as well as I?' (5.4.121–2), before claiming the honour he has mocked.

Shakespeare seems to limit diversity of experience and attitude during this third movement, then release them at its conclusion. But he does prepare for a comic ending, in part by transposing roles. Hotspur's similarity to the King as rebel and potential regicide grows, while the Prince takes up the role Hotspur played in earlier scenes: the forthright and generous young warrior. For the first time, in 5.4, the Prince meets Hotspur who has dismissed his challenge to single combat with rueful realism: 'O, would the quarrel lay upon our heads, / And that no man might draw short breath today / But I and Harry Monmouth!' (5.2.47–9). The dead Hotspur lies momentarily side-by-side with the supposedly dead Falstaff. Falstaff's ultimate resurgence when he takes credit, earned by the Prince, for killing Hotspur, will mirror the King's victory.

Belated comedy

King Henry's success is a strong probability based on well-known facts. The ending, however, could have been given a more tragic or a more heroic emphasis. Perhaps Shakespeare discovered, as he composed, how controlling was a comic vision for the action of *Part One;*[1] Shakespeare had learned to shape his dramatic presentation of history throughout groups of plays so that moments of humiliation, sacrifice, and festive joy would resonate with one another. By echoing earlier sequences in his own work, he produced effects often analogous to the typological repetitions which connected events of biblical history within the English mystery plays. (These popular cycles were still being staged in Shakespeare's youth, and he might well have seen one performed at Coventry, near Stratford-upon-Avon.)[2]

The primary type or model for the comic ending of *1 Henry IV* could well have been the first tavern scene. Act 5, Scene , the climactic episode in the final sequence, often recalls 2.4 because of its exceptional polish and tight-knit three-part design: (1) a 'breather' or pause in battle, emphasising the Prince's new solidarity with his brother and father, whose life he then saves from Douglas; (2) the verbal and physical combat between 'Harry' Monmouth and 'Harry' Hotspur, which ends with Hotspur's death and the Prince's epitaphs for Hotspur and Falstaff; and (3) the revival of Falstaff, leading to his virtual theft of the Prince's prize. Both scenes

---

[1] See Leonard F. Dean, 'From *Richard II* to *Henry IV*: a closer view', in *Studies in Honor of DeWitt T. Starnes*, ed. Thomas P. Harrison *et al.* (1967), pp. 37–52.
[2] Emrys Jones, *The Origins of Shakespeare*, 1977, pp. 35, 51.

a

3 Two battle scenes from Act 5, Scene 4:
   a The Prince saves the King from Douglas in the touring production of the English Shakespeare
       Company, directed by Michael Bogdanov, 1986
   b Hotspur fights the Prince while Douglas 'kills' Falstaff. A possible Elizabethan staging drawn
       by C. Walter Hodges

build on bustling entrances and exits. But the 'unyoked humour' of the first tavern
scene has become the unyoked violence of the battlefield, while the illusion of two-
handed performance by the Prince and Falstaff has turned into a series of deadly
duels. Before his mock death, Falstaff, an enormous target, wanders miraculously
unhurt through the thick of battle, like a spectre from the comic world of Eastcheap.
'Art thou alive? . . . I prithee speak' (5.4.129–31), says the Prince to his resurrected
companion. By gaining credit for defeating Hotspur, Falstaff enjoys a splendid fool's
revenge for the jokes practised upon him in the tavern. This vengeance proves truly
comic, because the Prince graciously agrees, 'if a lie may do thee grace, / I'll gild it
with the happiest terms I have' (5.4.148–9).

As in 2.4, the third episode serves as a fulcrum for reassessments and forecasts.
In a broader view of Shakespeare's design, this play may be approached as the first
of two plays about Henry IV, as the first play in the 'Henriad' of three plays, or as
the second play in a larger group of either four or eight. If we recall that Falstaff
will ultimately be rejected by the Prince or that Henry V will die young, after his
triumph at Agincourt, this will darken our sense of the ending with the shadows of
events that are '[p]ast and to come' (*2 Henry IV* 1.3.108). But for now the King's side

Hotspur

Prince

Douglas

Falstaff

b

has won. The final mood is improbably benign – comparable to those interludes of happiness in the mystery cycles, which are eventually swallowed up in a succession of harrowing episodes and violent sacrifices. Or to the elation shared by fans of a sports team after a rare season of success.

Transforming the sources

Among the sources for *1 Henry IV* are not only quite different narrative and dramatic histories, but also popular and widely accessible materials such as ballads, proverbs, and biblical passages. Following his own practice in *Richard II*, Shakespeare sifted historical accounts with care, at the same time treating them more independently. He frequently developed characters or situations from minimal suggestions, or recombined hints provided by his sources. Two of these are especially influential: one, Holinshed's *Chronicles* (1587) for the King's struggle with the Percys, leading to the battle of Shrewsbury; and the other, popular dramatic traditions for the behaviour of the prodigal Prince and his riotous companions. But as consideration of the play's design and of Falstaff's original name, Oldcastle, has already suggested, Shakespeare was able to cross the seriousness of civil disorder with the comic humours of popular entertainment, recalling his earlier experiments in the history play, but with significant differences.

HISTORY PLAYS

The genre of history play seems to have been largely created by Shakespeare himself. In his first historical tetralogy, the three parts of *Henry VI, and Richard III* (probably 1589–93) and subsequently in *King John* (probably 1595–6), Shakespeare began to develop a form of drama which could represent the ongoing nature of political conflicts and suggest their complicated, interactive causes. These early histories resemble contemporary tragedies and plays about conquerors which employ multiple story lines and portray sensational violence. Like these plays, they also emphasise the strategies and consequences of intrigue and revenge, especially in *Richard III*. But through a proliferation of agents and motives, such coherent patterns often lose their shaping force in the history plays and become more incidental. Conflict and crisis may occur at any time in the action, revealing how closely the dramatist depends on the apparent incoherence of history.

The possibility that such open and chaotic formal structures might be unified by concepts which contemporaries would have recognised has provided a focus for most twentieth-century studies of the Elizabethan history play. E. M. W. Tillyard maintained that both of Shakespeare's tetralogies express a divine plan: God punished the English people for the deposition and murder of Richard II, and redeemed them through the victory of Henry VII over Richard III at the battle of Bosworth in 1485. Tillyard's case for the authority of this 'Tudor myth' in Shakespeare's age rested on the arguments of Tudor historians and theologians, and on the preaching of homilies (sermons) against rebellion.[1] Irving Ribner contended that a structure derived from Morality plays helped to shape English historical drama by emphasising the struggle between good and evil forces.[2] Lily B. Campbell's investigation of how the plays are informed by Renaissance historiographic practices on one hand and addressed to current political concerns on the other, has been followed by numerous studies which stress historical thought and literature, the political themes of kingship, constitution, and popular resistance, and the social and political crises of the 1590s.[3] Those who approach the histories in secular terms have often agreed

---

[1] *Shakespeare's History Plays*, 1944.
[2] *The English History Play in the Age of Shakespeare*, 1957.
[3] *Shakespeare's 'Histories': Mirrors of Elizabethan Policy*, 1947.

with Tillyard and other exponents of ideological interpretation that Shakespeare wrote a national epic of fall and redemption, achieving Miltonic scope through an integrated sequence stretching through eighty-seven years and eight plays, from *Richard II* to *Richard III*.

While there can be no doubt that Shakespeare responded to such schemes of interpretation as the 'Tudor myth' – his characters expressed them and his spectators could have been quick to apply them – it is important to remember that Shakespeare's own plans were subject to the financial realities of theatrical production. Whether or not he conceived whole cycles of plays, his company seems never to have performed them as cycles; even two-part dramas like the *Henry IV* plays were not, as far as we know, staged on consecutive days. Shakespeare's company might have enjoyed more financial security, and have therefore planned more ambitious projects towards the end of the 1590s.[1] Yet, as the partisan responses of the Cobhams and the general theatre closing of 1597 (referred to above, pp. 5–6) make clear, theatrical fortunes remained precarious. It is safer to surmise that any design imposed by Shakespeare upon the endless disorders of fifteenth-century history would have been retrospective, emerging as he wrote, rather than as part of a consistent plan.

Although valuable not only for stimulating speculation about what history meant to Shakespeare and his audience, but also for the thematic continuities they have helped us to identify, theories of unity and order can also efface important differences between and within Shakespeare's tetralogies. *Richard II*, which begins the second tetralogy (1595), was composed perhaps three years after *Richard III* which concludes the first. The second group seems to be more deeply engaged with the role of private character in public life. It dramatises a far more problematic symbiosis between rulers and ruled. For extended passages in the *Henry IV* plays, overt political conflict like that which animates the first tetralogy or *King John* appears to recede. As we have seen, the style and movement of *1 Henry IV* distinguish it from *Richard II*. Moving from the comic design of *1 Henry IV*, Shakespeare presented in *Part Two* a more satiric anatomy of old King Henry's world, and approached tragedy with the turning away of Falstaff by the newly crowned King. Then, in *Henry V*, Shakespeare submitted the beliefs which sustain the social contract between king and people to rigorous testing. To understand the 'history' in any one play, therefore, is to understand distinctive combinations of characters and events, to recognise that important experiences and values may indeed occur only once, while others reverberate over long dramatic periods of time.

HISTORY IN THE PLAY

In addition to the 1587 edition of Holinshed's *Chronicles*, Shakespeare consulted and used less extensively Edward Hall's *The Union of the two noble and illustre families of Lancastre and Yorke* (1548), the *Chronicles* collected by John Stow (1580) and Stow's *Annals* (1592), as well as Thomas Phaer's verse portrait entitled 'Owen Glendower' from *A Mirror for Magistrates* (1559). Closely associated with these accounts, both

---

[1] Gurr, pp. 3–4.

as a source for *1 Henry IV* and as an analogue based on the same period of history, is Samuel Daniel's epic poem *The Civile Wars Between the Two Houses of Lancaster and Yorke* (1595).[1]

The group of middle-class writers, who together produced the volumes known as Holinshed's *Chronicles* (after their first editor, Raphael Holinshed, who died in 1586), nourished, and responded to, a growing fascination with historical writing of many kinds. The 1587 edition addresses those who are 'studious in antiquities, or take pleasure in the grounds of ancient histories'. Louis B. Wright believed that in Elizabethan eyes, history was 'the greatest of secular studies'. But earlier he stressed a more questionable 'middle-class' view: that history was 'safe, entertaining, instructive and useful'.[2] When Shakespeare had Richard of Gloucester boast in *3 Henry VI* of his ability to 'set the murtherous Machevil to school' (3.2.193), some spectators may have linked his villain to a stereotype for evil politicians. But members of the audience whose knowledge of historical writing included Machiavelli's political analyses might have brought to performances some of his attitudes towards causation.[3] These were famous or infamous, depending on one's viewpoint, because they stressed such secondary causes of events as character and accident, rather than the supposed primary cause, divine providence. That 'history' in its more restricted meaning, i.e. a narrative of government and political affairs, was not at all 'safe' became strikingly obvious when Sir John Hayward was imprisoned in the Tower of London in 1600.[4] Hayward had dedicated his *The First Part of the Life and Raigne of King Henrie IIII* to the Earl of Essex; he was suspected of having supported the Earl's ambitions by emphasising the deposition of Richard II. After the trial and execution of Essex in 1601, it became unwise for playwrights to scrutinise the postures and policies of English royalty. Shakespeare turned his attention to still more 'ancient' sources, the legends of early Britain, and the sophisticated biographies and histories by classical writers.

The fact that Shakespeare had anticipated and had helped to create strong interest in historical subjects does not mean that he relied on his audience to remember either *Richard II* or the chronicle descriptions of Henry's reign. Through the speeches of his characters, he quickly introduces necessary information: the play opens in 1400 (1.1.26), there is trouble on both borders (34–61), the royal Council will meet next Wednesday (102). If spectators *did* recall *Richard II*, they might well infer that the usurping King has ruled a year; he had concluded *Richard II* with a vow to expiate his guilt for the assassination of Richard by making a 'voyage to the Holy Land' (5.6.49), and he admits, during the speech which opens *1 Henry IV*, that 'our purpose now is twelve month old' (1.1.28).

---

[1] Bullough reprints excerpts from Holinshed, Stow's *Chronicles*, *A Mirror for Magistrates*, and Daniel, with several analogues including *The Famous Victories of Henry the fifth*.

[2] *Middle-Class Culture in Elizabethan England*, 1935, pp. 337, 301.

[3] Felix Raab devotes the second chapter of *The English Face of Machiavelli: A Changing Interpretation 1500–1700*, 1964, to 'Machiavelli's reception in Tudor England'.

[4] To write about politics rather than antiquarian matters, some historians believed, required personal experience in government. See D. R. Woolf, *The Idea of History in Early Stuart England: Erudition, Ideology and 'The Light of Truth' from the Accession of James I to the Civil War*, 1990, p. 22.

In comparing Shakespeare's versions of English history with chronicle accounts, there is always some risk that a focus upon source materials will over-emphasise details which Shakespeare has effectively submerged, co-ordinated or transformed. Another risk is that a broader sense of the chronicles and of their power to excite Shakespeare's imagination will be lost. Readers curious about the potential significance of Shakespeare's omissions or about his extraction of voices and opinions from Holinshed may consult the Appendix. Annabel Patterson has argued that one of the main purposes guiding the compilation of chronicles by Holinshed and others was the wish to represent conflicting viewpoints, which he terms 'indifference'.[1] Apparent inconsistencies, therefore, result from a wary and self-critical attempt to preserve the texture of controversy. If the writers identified as 'Holinshed' were as careful to achieve 'indifference' as they were to record rare documents, the inclusiveness for which they have been criticised was more discriminating than it appears. For our understanding of how Shakespeare used this archive, Patterson's revaluation of Holinshed has several implications: that Shakespeare's primary source was simultaneously a model of multiplicity and caution, that particular details or anecdotes may have resonated for Shakespeare because of far-flung connections in the chronicles themselves, and that serious students of the history in Shakespeare's plays can no longer limit their attention to 'Shakespeare's Holinshed' – those often cited passages on which he most heavily relied.

King Henry IV corresponds more closely than any other major character in this play to his prototype in Holinshed. Shakespeare seized upon his use of anticipatory violence ('policie often-times preventeth perill') and skill in fathoming the 'cloaked drift' of the Percy faction.[2] He attributed to Henry himself the fatalistic sense of retribution which in Holinshed, as earlier in Hall, becomes pervasive soon after Henry's coronation and recurs during the narrative of his reign. Bent upon staving off rebellions similar to his own, Shakespeare's King intends his rare public appearances to resemble the effects of a comet (3.2.47). Here Shakespeare probably picked up and transfigured Holinshed's belief that the comet or 'blasing starre' of 1402 was an omen for 'the great effusion of bloud that followed' (p. 19). Shakespeare apparently made his King more dependent on mental than on physical strength; Holinshed had credited him with killing thirty-six of his enemies at Shrewsbury, implying that his deeds inspired an unidentified 'other' to attack and kill Hotspur. Holinshed's Henry is partly victorious through the fighting of the 'lustie' Prince, but requires no life-saving intervention. Both kings are poisoned by guilt, but only Shakespeare's King claims, after one year of rule, that he might unify the English by leading them on a crusade to Jerusalem. In contrast, the year before he died (1412), according to Holinshed Henry did make preparations for a voyage to the Holy Land, 'there to recover the citie of Ierusalem from the Infidels' (p. 57). His motive, however, was more international than civil; he was disturbed by the 'malice' of Christian princes who fought one another rather than the enemies of their faith.

---

[1] Patterson, pp. vii–x, 15.
[2] Holinshed, III, 16, 23. References to this edition and volume will be placed in the text within parentheses.

Shakespeare developed both Hotspur and the Prince in a more original manner which meshes with his alteration of historical fact. He condensed the period between 1400 when his play begins and 1403, the date of the battle of Shrewsbury. At the same time, he greatly reduced the age of Hotspur, who was born in 1364, before the King (1367); this change is already apparent in *Richard II* when young Henry Percy makes his first appearance as a sober, loyal, and hard-working supporter of the rebellion against Richard II. The fiery and imaginative warrior so envied by the King in *1 Henry IV* is Shakespeare's invention, tinged perhaps with memories of stirring ballads about Northumbrian battles, *The Hunting of the Cheviot* and *The Battle of Otterburn*. By adding several years to the Prince's age, Shakespeare supported other parallels between 'Harry' Percy and 'Harry' Monmouth; one 'star' of England is made to extinguish the other in single combat at the end of the play. It is probable that Shakespeare derived his sense of rivalry between the two young men from Samuel Daniel's heroic lines in the *Civile Wars*:

> There shall young *Hotespur* with a fury lead
> Meete with thy forward sonne as fierce as he.   (III, st. 97)

Daniel credits the Prince with rescuing his father from Douglas, but not with killing Hotspur. Where Daniel blames Hotspur for being furious and violent as well as 'wrong counsail'd' (III, st. 109), Shakespeare makes possible a more rueful response to Hotspur's death. He turns the sickness of Northumberland, reported as occurring earlier by both Holinshed and Daniel, into a last-minute excuse and he follows Holinshed in stressing the role of Worcester, who betrayed Hotspur by misrepresenting the King's final terms for peace and then whetting him on to fight. Shakespeare surrounds the final encounter of the Prince and Hotspur with intimations of a brotherhood they might have shared in less tragic circumstances.

The characterisation of Prince Hal builds on specific sources, but branches off from the myths and popular dramatic traditions described in more detail below. Hall and Holinshed mention his military service on the Welsh marches, not his carousing in London taverns. According to Holinshed, towards the end of the reign King Henry feared that the Prince might be planning to 'usurpe the crowne' (p. 53). He had heard 'tales' from his servants, not only about the Prince's 'evill rule', but also about the large number of people who followed him. The Prince then publicly vowed his loyalty to the King. Otherwise Holinshed records no evidence that Henry seriously doubted his son's allegiance. In his *Chronicles* (1580), John Stow picks up several stories about the legendary wild Prince which Shakespeare may have noticed. For example, he describes how the Prince and his men would waylay the Prince's 'own receivers' in disguise, and 'distresse them of theyr money'. When they later complained to him, the Prince would pay them back and reward them for their trouble. This particular tale may be more historically accurate than others because it derives from the recollections of the Earl of Ormonde, a contemporary of the Prince, who later knighted him in France shortly before Agincourt.[1]

---

[1] Charles L. Kingford, ed., *The First English Life of King Henry the Fifth*, 1911, pp. xvii, xix, 17.

'O that Glendower were come!' (4.1.124), exclaims Hotspur before the battle.
Welsh fighters did assist the Percys at Shrewsbury according to Holinshed; in the
play, however, we learn from the Archbishop of York that Glendower 'comes not
in, o'erruled by prophecies' (4.4.18). The first rebel to be mentioned in Scene 1
and the reason why King Henry must march to Wales at the end (in Holinshed
he marches to York), Shakespeare's puzzling Glendower owes little to historical
accounts. His prototype studied law in England; Holinshed says that he served
Richard II, but records the chronicler Walsingham's contrary view that he served
Henry Bullingbrook. Holinshed refers obscurely to '[s]trange wonders' at Glendower's birth (p. 21), (perhaps confusing the birth of Glendower with that of Mortimer), and is emphatic about quoting Hall on the folly of Welsh prophets (p. 23).
Thomas Phaer, author of 'Owen Glendower' in *A Mirror for Magistrates*, zestfully
describes how this foolish rebel died of exposure in the Welsh mountains. Shakespeare borrows Phaer's sentiment, echoed by Holinshed, to fuel the King's rage at
Mortimer's defection: 'on the barren mountains let him starve' (1.3.88), but pro-
longs the dramatic life of Glendower himself, who is certainly the last rebel defeated
in *Part Two*.[1]

THE WILD PRINCE

Shakespeare probably knew earlier dramatic versions of the material which he presented in his three plays about Henry IV and Henry V. Thomas Nashe had referred
in *Pierce Penilesse his Supplication to the Divell* (1592) to '*Henrie* the fifth represented
on the stage', while Henslowe's *Diary* recorded that a 'harey the v' was performed as
'ne' (new) by his company the Admiral's Men in 1595–6.[2] Kenneth Muir concludes
his survey of sources for the *Henry IV* plays with a particularly tantalising allusion by Gabriel Harvey, who mentioned in *Foure Letters* (1592), '"clownes; gowty
Divels, and buckram Giants ... hypocritical hoat spurres" and "some old lads of the
Castell"'. 'Was there', asks Muir, 'a play as early as 1592 in which Oldcastle talked
of men in buckram?[3]

One of these popular plays has survived, but in a text that many scholars consider
corrupt. *The Famous Victories of Henry the fifth* may have been first acted in the late
1580s or early 1590s; its title page (1598) links it to 'the Queenes Majesties Players',
a prominent earlier troupe that had been disbanded. A play of the same title was
entered in the Stationers' Register for 1594. *The Famous Victories* appears to abridge
a longer play which covered the career of Henry V, from his youthful escapades
to his victory at Agincourt and his marriage to Katherine of France. It therefore
corresponds roughly to the plots of *1 Henry IV*, *2 Henry IV*, and *Henry V*.

That *The Famous Victories* can have been a direct source for much of *1 Henry IV*
seems unlikely. As an analogue, it throws light on two major aspects of Shakespeare's
play: the character of the Prince and the comic liveliness of Falstaff. The robbery

---

[1] For the supposition that the Welsh Captain of *Richard II* might be Glendower, see Peter Ure, ed., *King
Richard II*, 1956, note to 3.1.43.
[2] Nashe, I, 213; *Henslowe's Diary*, ed. R. A. Foakes and R. T. Rickert, 1961, p. 33.
[3] *The Sources of Shakespeare's Plays*, 1978, p. 103.

episode which constitutes the main link between *The Famous Victories* and *Part One* quickly demonstrates that the Prince is a prodigal son. The King's receivers who have been attacked (before the play begins) suspect what has happened. When they enter, they cannot help but see the stolen money, laid out in a 'brave shewe'; they recognise the horses and identify the 'bignesse' of the Prince himself. One of them claims that he has 'belambd' this figure 'about the shoulders'. The Prince bullies the receivers into re-telling their 'tale' of robbery by 'foure', debunks the beating he has been given ('Gog's wounds you lamd them faierly, / So that they have carried away your money' *FV* 70–1), and threatens to have them hanged 'and all your kin' if they report him.

No delight in 'incomprehensible' lies inflates this jest or redeems its perpetrators from vindictiveness; no money is given back. Sir John ('Jockey') Oldcastle, a cautious flatterer scarcely distinguishable from the other companions, Ned and Tom, tamely echoes the Prince's lawless, parricidal schemes: 'Nobly spoken *Harry*, we shall never have a mery world til the old king be dead' (*FV* 475–6). With good reason, 'the old king' calls himself 'thrice accursed' for getting a son who 'with greefe / Will end his fathers days' (*FV* 262–4). In *The Famous Victories*, the Prince's relationship with the King is never complicated by the Percy rebellion. Shakespeare seems to have invented the scene in which Henry uses his grievances to turn the Prince against the Percys in the third Act of *1 Henry IV*; it owes little to the historical reconciliation which occurred shortly before the King's death, a scene described at length by Holinshed and Stow and dramatised in both *The Famous Victories* and *2 Henry IV*.

Incidents comparable to the robbery portraying the wild youth of Henry V were introduced and passed down through Thomas Walsingham's *Historia Anglicana* (1418), Tito Livio's *Vita Henrici Quinti* (1437), the *Brut* chronicle (1479), Fabyan's *Chronicle* (1516), and the English manuscript translation of Livio (1513) which added new matter from de Monstrelet's *Chroniques* and from the reminiscences of the Earl of Ormonde. John Stow, as we have seen, picks up the story about the Prince robbing his own receivers. Playwrights surely noted the potential appeal of such stories, replete with drunken brawling and a radical conversion by the prodigal son; in *The Famous Victories*, he approaches his father with dagger in hand and the King weeps. Shakespeare could turn, therefore, to a popular dramatic tradition centred on the life of Henry V which combined serious and comic styles of presentation.

This popular tradition tended to juxtapose rather than mingle serious and comic elements, enhancing the autonomy of comedians and clowns. An anecdote in *Tarlton's Jests*, an informal collection of practical jokes, shows how a resourceful clown might exaggerate his independence by improvising. Richard Tarlton (d. 1588), seems to have played a role similar to that of the clown, Dericke, in *The Famous Victories*. Referring to his performance at the 'Bull' in 'a play of *Henry the fifth* wherein the judge was to take a box on the eare', the jest-book describes what happened when the actor playing the judge was apparently absent. Tarlton, therefore, 'ever forward to please, tooke upon him to play the same judge, besides his owne part of the clowne'.[1] After the corresponding scene in *The Famous Victories*, which focuses on the legend that the Prince struck the Lord Chief Justice, Dericke talks John Cobbler into impersonating a judge, then beats him for thinking he really is one.

By mingling comedy and history, Shakespeare made his play potentially more subversive. He altered the dramatic convention of juxtaposing history and comedy by fusing them within a more complex, provocative synthesis. Simultaneously, he upset social decorum by presenting the aristocratic Oldcastle as a notorious wit; the Cobhams were offended when Oldcastle, a colourless follower in *The Famous Victories*, merged with a figure 'ever forward to please' and entertain. Above all, by drawing the clown into his serious plot, Shakespeare transformed his role and heightened tensions between the truths of history and of drama.

HISTORY AND TRUTH

Two established attitudes would have influenced ways of perceiving the truth of history plays. On one hand, many people believed that staging could create a verisimilar effect so that history would appear to transpire before the eyes of the spectators. On the other hand, they thought that, after careful assessment and reconciliation of available evidence, historians could reach an understanding of the past which was largely accurate.[2] Just how powerful the first type of truth might have seemed in a dramatic history is suggested by Thomas Nashe's defence of drama in *Pierce Penilesse*:

How would it have joyed brave *Talbot* . . . to thinke that after he had lyne two hundred years in his Tomb, hee should triumphe againe on the Stage, and have his bones newe embalmed with the teares of ten thousand spectators . . . who, in the Tragedian that represents his person, imagine they behold him fresh bleeding.[3]

Attackers and defenders of the theatre recognised the force of such illusions. Titles of the period which repeatedly assert that history plays are 'true' may appeal both to the exciting effects of verisimilitude and to a faith in historical accuracy little mediated by fiction or art.[4]

Falstaff's resurrection at Shrewsbury activates these two senses of truth. As a clown who can suddenly improvise his death and rebirth, he seems to be filled with a dramatic life of his own. At the same time, Shakespeare partly created this rebirth by combining scattered facts and observations in Holinshed. From the first year of Henry V's reign came the information that Sir John Oldcastle, 'highlie in the kings favour' (p. 62) was accused of heresy but escaped from the Tower of London. He seems to have drawn, too, on rumours that had surfaced early in the reign of

---

[1] *Tarlton's Jests*, 1611, ed. J. O. Halliwell-Phillips, *Shakespeare Society* 20 (1844), 24–5.
[2] Woolf, p. 34.
[3] *Pierce Pennilesse his Supplication to the Divell* in Nashe 1, 212.
[4] G. K. Hunter, 'Truth and art in history plays', *S.Sur.* 42 (1990), 15–24, finds thirteen examples in titles between 1573 and 1616. See also Herschel Baker, *The Race of Time: Three Lectures in Renaissance Historiography*, 1967, chap. 1, 'The truth of history'.

Henry IV, that Richard II was alive after all. And one especially striking detail from Holinshed's account of Shrewsbury (1403) surely helped to sow another seed for Falstaff's resurgence. Following Douglas' response when he has killed Blunt and three others in king's clothing – 'I marvell to see so many kings thus suddenlie arise one in the necke of an other' – the chronicler comments, 'The king in deed was raised' (p. 26). By connecting some of this wonder and relief to Falstaff, Shakespeare fashioned a theatrical miracle.

Shakespeare, finally, gave an unforgettable twist to the narrative and to the whole question of historical truth. How can the Prince, who has killed Hotspur and seen Falstaff 'dead', contradict Falstaff's revision of the facts: 'we rose both at an instant, and fought a long hour by Shrewsbury clock' (5.4.139–40)? Through the Prince, spectators may experience the slipperiness of history, which within the play often means to the characters what they remember or choose to believe.[1]

A multitude of competing views within an open-ended play about civil war would not necessarily create scepticism or undermine a faith that history might attain truth. Shakespeare the dramatist seems to be more interested in the visible results of ideas and arguments than in their philosophical significance. It seems ironically appropriate that Falstaff can transform history by carrying away the corpse of Hotspur – the character who has naively assented to a partisan version of history. But the incongruous image of Falstaff with Hotspur on his back lodges in our memories whether or not we unravel the complex of truths which knots it together.

The appeal of Falstaff and the contexts of interpretation

The popularity of *1 Henry IV* has always depended upon the great appeal of Falstaff, who engages readers and audiences through his surprising wit. In his numerous roles – including companion, entertainer, father-figure, satirist, and thief – Falstaff brings us to the heart of the play's key relationships and draws our attention to its problematic themes. At the same time, his theatrical genius opens up the stricter boundaries of political and familial strife to a reflection of issues which have concerned different spectators, then and now. Decisions about which issues and which contexts of interpretation are appropriate have traditionally been inseparable from choices among Falstaff's many roles. He rarely leads us towards the whole truth, but he can never be ignored. We have therefore included many references to or opinions about Falstaff in the following discussion of contexts which can expand a view of the play. It begins with echoes and reverberations of the Oldcastle controversy (see Date, pp. 5–6). To conclude this survey, we look briefly at the most influential responses to Falstaff's character.

EARLY RECEPTION

In an Epilogue written for *Part Two* before *Henry V* was performed, Shakespeare promised the audience that in the following play 'Sir John' will 'make you merry'

---

[1] Robert C. Jones, *These Valiant Dead: Renewing the Past in Shakespeare's Histories*, 1991, pp. 100–7.

and perhaps 'die of a sweat, unless already 'a be killed with your hard opinions, for Oldcastle died [a] martyr, and this is not the man'. Public 'opinions' may have surprised the playwright, causing him to reshape his game of arousing an audience's curiosity. Falstaff makes no one 'merry' in expected ways in *Henry V*; he dies offstage, leaving the audience to decide whether to blame his 'sweat', or the young King who has 'kill'd his heart' (2.1.88), or the 'hard' and contentious responses he had provoked offstage. By 1599 the reception of Falstaff generated a competing dramatic interpretation of the 'martyr' by the Lord Admiral's Men, entitled *The first part of the true and honorable historie, of the life of Sir John Old-castle, the good Lord Cobham*. The authors, Michael Drayton, Richard Hathway, Antony Munday, and Robert Wilson, warn their audience, 'It is no pampered glutton we present, / Nor agèd counsellor to youthful sins; / But one whose virtues shone above the rest, / A valiant martyr, and a virtuous peer.'[1]

Topical references to Falstaff/Oldcastle confirm his powerful effect upon early viewers, and clarify in retrospect the displeasure of the Cobham family. The Earl of Essex seems to have been referring contemptuously to Henry Brooke, the son of Lord Cobham, when he wrote to Sir Robert Cecil in February 1598, encouraging him to tell their friend, Sir Alex Ratcliffe, that 'his sister is maryed to Sr Jo. Falstaff'.[2] Much later, in 1633, Richard James, the librarian to Sir Robert Cotton, attempted to explain in a dedicatory epistle why Shakespeare had replaced 'Oldcastle' with the name of another historical figure who in fact outlived both Oldcastle and Henry V:

in Shakespeare's first show of Harrie the Fifth, the person with which he undertook to play a buffoon was not Falstaffe, but Sir Jhon Oldcastle, and that offence being worthily taken by personages descended from his title, as peradventure by many others also who ought to have him in honourable memory, the poet was put to make an ignorant shift of abusing Sir Jhon Fastolphe, a man not inferior of virtue though not so famous in piety as the other . . .[3]

James' judgement on Shakespeare as an unscrupulous entertainer and on his Falstaff as a buffoon was repeated by George Daniel of Beswick in his poem *Trinarchordia* (1647) and by the influential Thomas Fuller, both in *The Church History of Britain* (1655) and in his *Worthies of England* (1662).

Such reactions sever many of the lines mooring Falstaff to the larger vessel of Shakespeare's play. Although informed by condescension towards popular theatre, they help initiate a tendency, also evident in the quarto titles, to give Falstaff independent stature as a source of humours and 'conceits'. On one hand, their bias might well have been encouraged by Falstaff's growing prominence within a dramatic design which Francis Meres (above, p. 4), perhaps thinking of both parts, had in 1598 regarded as tragic. By treating Falstaff as a buffoon, James and others testify to his kinship with such fools and clowns as Richard Tarlton and William Kemp

---

[1] Prologue 6–9 in *The Oldcastle controversy: Sir John Oldcastle, Part I and The Famous Victories of Henry V*, ed. Peter Corbin and Douglas Sedge, 1991.
[2] Leslie Hotson, *Shakespeare's Sonnets Dated and Other Essays*, 1949, p. 147.
[3] Samuel Schoenbaum, *William Shakespeare: A Compact Documentary Life*, 1978, pp. 195–6.

who were famous for pleasing crowds and stealing shows. On the other hand, the Oldcastle controversy exemplifies the kind of intensely topical interpretation from which the editors of the First Folio sought to free Shakespeare.[1] 'He was not of an age, but for all time', wrote Ben Jonson in his Folio poem celebrating Shakespeare's memory. The Oldcastle controversy reminds us that Shakespeare was also 'of an age', one in which Reformation passions ran high. It invites us to rethink the attitudes of spectators who needed either to censure Falstaff or to enjoy him mainly as a welcome distraction from their own concerns.

HONOUR

During the last decade of the sixteenth century, the rising fortunes of the Earl of Essex demonstrated the continuing power of 'honour' as a political value. Becoming the Queen's favourite, Essex also attracted a large group of dependent supporters. Chivalry had become largely ceremonial and recreational, an occasion for tournaments and jousts, while the English nobility had lost many of its feudal privileges to the centralised power of the crown. Yet the great prestige of mighty war lords lived on in an age which offered many opportunities for violent adventure. Mervyn James has shown that Essex defined himself and his objectives through a proud and militant code of honour which preserved medieval features.[2] Hotspur, 'the theme of honour's tongue' (1.1.80), might not have seemed anachronistic to Shakespeare's first audience.

A particularly interesting manifestation of 'honour' relevant to conflicts in *1 Henry IV* appears in the reason which Essex later gave to justify his treacherous behaviour: he sought only to circumvent 'flatterers' who surrounded the Queen, cutting off his channels of communication and keeping him from fulfilling his obligations.[3] A similar excuse was used by the leaders of the Northern Rebellion of 1569, and by the earlier representatives of the same Percy family, who in 1403 send out letters explaining that they cannot directly approach the King with their grievances because of 'the slanderous reports of their enimies' (Holinshed, p. 23). In the rebellion of 1405, which he leads with Northumberland, the Archbishop of York maintains that he is in arms for 'feare of the king, to whom he could have no free accesse, by reason of such a multitude of flatterers as were about him' (p. 37). In *Richard II*, Henry Bullingbrook removes and destroys the King's 'flatterers', claiming that his aim is reform, not revolution. And in *1 Henry IV*, Worcester explains to the King that the Percys, 'the first and dearest of your friends', have rebelled to protect themselves against 'unkind usage, dangerous countenance, / And violation of all faith and troth / Sworn to us in your younger enterprise' (5.1.69–71). Here, 'dangerous countenance' implies not only that the King's 'looks of love' (1.3.284) have vanished, but also that the Percys can no longer rely upon support from a

[1] Leah S. Marcus, *Puzzling Shakespeare: Local Reading and its Discontents*, 1988, p. 28.
[2] *Society, Politics and Culture: Studies in Early Modern England*, 1986, pp. 416–65.
[3] *Ibid.*, p. 445.

relationship characterised at best by what Marc Bloch has called 'reciprocity in unequal obligations'.[1]

The 'honour' at stake in these exchanges refers to the capacities which equip an individual for public trust or responsibility, to the opinions or 'credit' which make possible the performance of tasks or duties, and to the primary reward of such performance in a time when most public or governing roles were unsalaried.[2] Falstaff's allegation that 'honour' is merely a 'word' (5.1.132) aptly represents its fleeting quality. Sixteenth-century advice on noble behaviour or military conduct rarely emphasises the interactive fluidity of reputation, although this quality may help to explain why the honourable man had to be 'constant' and true to his word. What Falstaff himself misses by equating honour with a quick recipe for death ('I like not such grinning honour as Sir Walter hath' (5.3.56–7)) is that honour may have helped to reduce violence. Honour communities flourish where the means of control exerted by elite groups are precarious and personal. In Thomas Hobbes' opinion, honour provides the power to secure obedience.[3] It may also have functioned for Elizabethans as a method of turning envy into emulation, as a stimulus for hospitality, and as a means of policing the borders of gender and class.[4] At one extreme, honour brightened into the armour of reputation and public faith which made it possible for Queen Elizabeth to rule without a standing army. At the other, it shaded into confidence tricks and protection rackets, not to mention robberies in which thieves 'cannot be true one to another' (2.2.22–3).

A much darker depiction of 'honour' within both parts of *Henry IV* occurs when Falstaff abuses his authority as a captain; Shakespeare directly reflects current scandals by showing how Falstaff robs the wealthier citizens (who buy out of military service) and exploits the poorer ones who are helpless. When Falstaff leads his 'ragamuffins' where they are 'peppered' (5.3.34–5) and maimed for life, he abandons a responsibility 'which, in its paternalism, far exceeded the normal duty of an officer towards his troops'.[5] Falstaff applies this duty only in one direction; he has already asked the Prince to stand over him if he falls in battle: ' . . .'tis a point of friendship', he suggests (5.1.121–2). The Prince's answer offers an example of how 'detraction', as Falstaff soon remarks, does not 'suffer' honour to 'live with the living' (136). He reduces Falstaff's point of honour to grotesque absurdity: 'Nothing but a Colossus can do thee that friendship' (123).

[1] *Feudal Society*, vol. 1, *The Growth of Ties of Dependence*, 1961, p. 228. Bloch is referring to vassalage at an earlier period, but the description is pertinent here. Graham Holderness, *Shakespeare's History*, 1985, pp. 30–9, argues that Shakespeare understood and consciously reconstructed feudalism.

[2] See Anthony J. Fletcher, 'Honour, reputation, and local office-holding in Elizabethan and Stuart England', in Fletcher and John Stevenson, eds., *Order and Disorder in Early Modern England*, 1985, pp. 92–115.

[3] *Leviathan*, ed. Michael Oakeshott, 1946, p. 58.

[4] Felicity Heal, *Hospitality in Early Modern England*, 1990, p. 23; Michael Hattaway, 'Fleshing his will in the spoil of her honour: desire, misogyny and the perils of chivalry', *S.Sur.* 46 (1994), 121–35.

[5] Lindsay Boynton, *The Elizabethan Militia 1558–1638*, 1967, p. 104.

FRIENDSHIP

The examples above suggest that Elizabethan friendship would often have been entangled with political alliances, codes of conduct, and public opinions. As Essex knew, one method of acquiring honour was to attract a large following.[1] This practice continued well into the next century. Troops of such 'friends' are temporarily assembled by the hero of Thomas Middleton's *A Mad World My Masters* (1604–7) so that he will be mistaken for a lord. Five hundred followers, an extraordinarily large group, lost the security of 'good lordship' when Prince Henry suddenly died in 1611.[2] Hotspur deplores the contaminating effects of alliance upon the 'bright honour' of the Percy family, which he longs to redeem from 'half-faced fellowship' with the King, a 'vile politician' (1.3.206, 238). To the King, the Prince's choice of friends is inevitably a public, political issue which brings dishonour upon his son. Anxious in Holinshed, as we have seen, when he hears about a 'great resort of people' at the Prince's house, the King suffers in Shakespeare because the Prince has one follower who is evidently 'known as well as Paul's' (2.4.442).

Montaigne believed that princes must forgo friendship altogether, for 'no friendship can be knit where there is so little relation and correspondence'. Men follow not the prince but his fortune, hoping 'by countenance and custom' to increase their own.[3] Montaigne was convinced that a true friendship like his bond with Etienne de La Boétie must be 'free', that is, unencumbered by kinship, marriage, domestic ties, or questions of benefit and obligation. It would be impossible to sustain two such friendships because one's friends might require competing services. The complete mingling of souls and wills in genuine as opposed to 'common' friendships, which were short-lived, might occur but once in a lifetime, he thought.[4]

With his emphasis on disinterested virtue and suspicion of allies or flattering dependants, Montaigne echoes discussions of friendship by Cicero and Plutarch. His influential contribution to an important humanist theme and literary topic strongly implies that many friendships must have been fraught with social and political differences. In a society built upon patronage and hierarchy, true marriages of male minds would have been almost impossible. As if drawn to complicated attachments, Shakespeare represents friendships which are marked by conspicuous disparities of age, rank, and emotional need. Perhaps the most challenging and unlikely of all these friendships is the one between Falstaff and the Prince. Paradoxically, their relationship, by far the closest in the play, achieves the freedom which Montaigne prized, not in spite of, but because of obstacles and constraints.

By approaching Falstaff in the ambiguous terms of Renaissance friendship, we may be able to balance interpretations which treat him as a temptation to cast away, a problem to outgrow, or as the occasion for indulgences which can be wilder because

---

[1] On large contemporary households, see G. R. Batho, ed., *The Household Papers of Henry Percy Ninth Earl of Northumberland 1564–1632*, 1962, pp. xxii–iii.

[2] See Leonard Tennenhouse, 'Sir Walter Ralegh and the literature of clientage', in Guy Fitch Lytle and Stephen Orgel, eds., *Patronage in the Renaissance*, 1981, p. 253.

[3] 'Of the inequality that is between us', in *Complete Works*, trans. Donald M. Frame, 1958, p. 195.

[4] *Ibid.*, 'Of friendship', pp. 135–44.

they are also temporary.[1] Barbara Everett appeals from a recent critical tradition preoccupied with the Prince's growth to an earlier focus upon Falstaff, once 'widely agreed to be the dramatist's greatest character'.[2] Because the play so effectively fuses history and comedy, one may also appeal to a perspective which emphasises relations between characters: without their friendship, neither Falstaff nor the Prince would engage our attention so fully. Ronald A. Sharp explains the power of friends to transform each other by using an analogy with Edward Hyde's theory of the gift. Gifts, according to Hyde, accumulate value as they circulate; they create abundance by sharing it.[3] So conceived, friendship becomes a comic art, one that is richer and riskier for its inclusion of utilitarian selfishness, competition, and the occasional reckoning.

Through his patronage, the Prince extends hospitality to Falstaff by paying his bills. Through his imagination, Falstaff gives the Prince opportunities to play serious games. Together they turn patriarchal society upside down and inside out, when the young Prince becomes a nurturing and protective lord or the old man mentors him by playing the roles of prodigal youth and childlike dependant. As a father who can be mocked or manipulated, or as a 'plump' maternal figure who serves up food for the Prince's keen wit, Falstaff has frequently been approached in the context of psychoanalytic theories oriented, like many political readings, towards the future of the developing young man.[4] It is also possible, however, that Falstaff's familial traits reflect ways, especially in great households like Burleigh's, in which roles overlap among friends, followers, servants, wives, and children.[5]

Flourishing outside the court, which was often seen as inimical to friendship, these friends speak a social and physical language of burlesque, rather than the erotic language of compliment more typical of ideal and instrumental male friendships.[6] The Prince uses the words 'friend' or 'friends' nineteen times to Falstaff's one, but never about Falstaff. Except during the first part of Act 1, Scene 2 (a mere eighty–five lines) and on three brief occasions in Act 5, these friends are never alone together onstage. Falstaff complains, when his fellow thieves hide his horse and themselves, that

I have forsworn his company hourly any time this two-and-twenty years, and yet I am bewitched with the rogue's company. If the rascal have not given me medicines to make me love him, I'll be hanged. It could not be else. I have drunk medicines.   (2.2.13–16)

To speak of his love at all, Falstaff resorts to a superstitious explanation favoured by the fathers of rebellious daughters; he also speaks very loudly for an audience just

---

[1] For example, see D. J. Palmer, 'Casting off the old man: history and St Paul in *Henry IV*', *CQ* 12 (1970), 267–83.
[2] 'The fatness of Falstaff: Shakespeare and character', *PBA* 76 (1991), 109.
[3] *Friendship and Literature: Spirit and Form*, 1986, pp. 84–8, 93.
[4] Valerie Traub, *Desire and Anxiety: Circulations of Sexuality in Shakespearean Drama*, 1992, pp. 50–70.
[5] See Richard C. Barnett, *Place, Profit, and Power: A Study of the Servants of William Cecil, Elizabethan Statesman*, 1969, pp. 5, 9.
[6] Alan Bray, 'Homosexuality and the signs of male friendship in Elizabethan England', *History Workshop Journal* 29 (1990), 1–19.

offstage: the Prince, who has surely not known Falstaff for twenty-two years, and Poins, who just as surely bewitches no one during *1 Henry IV*. Another mention of love could be taken as an indirect confession, but it also signals to the Prince that their balancing act demands some restraint. When Falstaff first proposes 'a play extempore', Hal, hanging on to Falstaff's supposed cowardice, replies, 'Content, and the argument shall be thy running away.' In one of the most poignant lines of the play, Falstaff responds, 'Ah, no more of that Hal, an thou lovest me' (2.4.230–33).

Falstaff seems to understand that one friend can only win a battle of wits if both do, hard as each must try to top the other. And so he urges the Prince: 'Play out the play' (2.4.402). Trust in their bond makes possible such experiments with the self, just as it allows Falstaff to fall asleep confidently behind the arras. Perhaps the Prince forgets, in the heroic loneliness of his conquest over Hotspur, that his 'old acquaintance', apparently slain, has been more to him than a 'vanity' (5.4.105). Falstaff soon puts him out of this simple, honourable humour. With an independence typical of their friendship, he acts out a duplicity often typical of honour, and beats the Prince at his new chivalric game.

FESTIVITY

Holiday in *1 Henry IV* is both a basic principle of structure and a rich trove of dramatic experience. To early modern religious reformers who sharply regulated or even eliminated holidays, viewed as pagan disorders, plays themselves seemed dangerous.[1] In addition to exploiting the theatricality associated with unruly entertainment and revelry, Shakespeare draws upon archetypes familiar from sports and celebrations as one clear way to identify his characters and to associate them with the forces of time and change, ritualised through festivity.

Popular dramatic traditions had long been animated through physical proximity of performer to spectator in dining-halls, churchyards, streets, and market-places.[2] Elizabethan clowns like Richard Tarlton were notorious for adopting the actor's potential autonomy as their special privilege. David Wiles has argued that William Kemp, an enormously popular and talented clown, would have played Falstaff. Because Kemp left the company before *Henry V* was completed, Wiles believes, Shakespeare chose to make Falstaff die offstage.[3] Some sense of the clown's irrepressible vigour might have prepared early audiences at *Part One* for Falstaff's resurrection. Perhaps they might also have noticed how Shakespeare gives *his* clown an added challenge, that of provoking laughter in the midst of violence and death. By tempering sympathy for Falstaff, Shakespeare seems to play him against the grain of a convention which would otherwise have given him overwhelming dramatic advantages.

---

[1] See Jonas A. Barish, *The Antitheatrical Prejudice*, 1981; Jean E. Howard, *The Stage and Social Struggle in Early Modern England*, 1994.
[2] Robert Weimann, *Shakespeare and the Popular Traditon in the Theatre: Studies in the Social Dimension of Dramatic Form and Function*, 1978.
[3] *Shakespeare's Clown: Actor and Text in the Elizabethan Playhouse*, 1987, p. 128; see also Wilson, *Fortunes*, pp. 124–5.

When he jokingly impersonates the King, Falstaff resembles household jesters and fools, whose wisdom and careful observation taught them how and when to subvert authority.[1] When he wildly insults the Prince, or conjures up attackers in Kendal green, he embodies the excessive energies of carnival.[2] As with their Morality-play roles of Vice and Prodigal, both Falstaff and the Prince self-consciously portray the battle between Shrovetide (the English equivalent of carnival) and Lent, between an old fat man and a young lean one, a 'huge hill of flesh' and a 'starveling' (2.4.202–3).[3] They compete, as well, for control of their jokes and games, recalling the Lords of Misrule chosen to preside over amateur entertainments, especially during the Christmas season. The Prince, who as Henry V will found the feast of Crispin Crispianus to commemorate his victory at Agincourt, already shows an English monarch's sensitivity to the political powers of spectacle and holiday.[4] In effect, he censors Falstaff's performance as king, and tries to turn the 'play extempore' into an exhibition of royal displeasure. Whereas Falstaff prefers to fuse holiday and everyday, the Prince draws a line between them, culminating on the battlefield when he throws Falstaff's own bottle of sack at him, demanding whether it is 'a time to jest and dally now' (5.3.52). In a society where special clothing, dishes, foods, and pastimes were reserved for use on particular holidays, the Prince's attitude might have found a more sympathetic response at other times as well.

Whether festivals provided outlets for social tensions or methods of sustaining resistance to authority, they seem to have been deeply rooted in popular practices. Shakespeare's play suggests that such roots may be tapped for negative as well as positive purposes, and that festive liberties may even be used against the people. Prince Hal wins the hearts of his drinking companions, the tavern drawers, who, he claims, consider him 'no proud Jack like Falstaff' (2.4.9–10), then urges Francis to rebel against his master by breaking his indentures and running away (38–40). Even when his own festive humour runs away with him, the Prince may be trying to find out how popularity works to empower one king or to get rid of another.[5] Perhaps he is sometimes inclined to get back, through Falstaff, at the people of England, the very people, Holinshed said, who had been 'so readie to joine and clappe hands' with his usurping father (p. 58). Holinshed commended the Prince for 'recreations, exercises, and delights' which were not 'offensive or at least tending to the damage of anie bodie' (p. 54). But Shakespeare emphasised his determination to 'make offence a skill' (1.2.176). By taunting Falstaff for his fat body and repeatedly comparing him to slaughtered meat, the Prince may prefigure the end of carnival and the rejection of his friend.

---

[1] Walter J. Kaiser, *Praisers of Folly: Erasmus, Rabelais, Shakespeare*, 1964, pp. 267–75; Enid Welsford, *The Fool: His Social and Literary History*, 1961, pp. 163 ff.

[2] Michael D. Bristol, *Carnival and Theatre: Plebeian Culture and the Structure of Authority in Renaissance England*, 1985, pp. 204–7.

[3] For an illuminating discussion of Shrovetide customs, see François Laroque, *Shakespeare's Festive World: Elizabethan Seasonal Entertainment and the Professional Stage*, 1993, pp. 96–104.

[4] David Cressy, *Bonfires and Bells: National Memory and the Protestant Calendar in Elizabethan and Stuart England*, 1989, pp. xii, 67.

[5] Sheldon Zitner, 'Anon, anon: or a Mirror for a Magistrate', *SQ* 19 (1968), 63–70.

C. L. Barber argued, in his seminal treatment of Shakespearean festivity, that characters experience a ritual process which moves them 'through release to clarification'.[1] Barber's formula accords with the way in which the Prince and Falstaff can test and strengthen one another through their differences. It illuminates Falstaff's unparalleled candour about his own weaknesses and connects his resurrection, through folk plays and motifs, to fertility rituals which reconcile human with natural cycles. What Barber's harmonising concept does not address are the repeated hints within the play of rituals which are far more contradictory and sacrificial.

REFORMATION

How would Falstaff have appealed to those concerned with religious issues? When Ben Jonson anatomised English society in *Bartholomew Fair* (1614), he included references to the slaughter of the innocents ('childermass'), the martyrdom of St Bartholomew (patron saint of butchers), the massacre of Protestant Huguenots by Catholics in France on St Bartholomew's Day, 1572, and the burning of English Protestants in adjoining Smithfield during the reign of Queen Mary (1553–8). Through a travesty of epic heroes and Puritan zealots, Jonson encouraged his audience to laugh at the fears and hatreds which eventually helped propel England into a religious civil war. It is possible that passages from *1 Henry IV* could have been written in a similar spirit; Falstaff's biblical citations should have been amusing for the audience and safe for Shakespeare because Falstaff mocks his own pretensions, along with those of pious Puritans.[2] But Shakespeare was sailing much closer than Jonson to the high winds of Reformation controversy. Instead of merely alluding to a dark history of religious violence, he took it upon himself to burlesque Oldcastle the martyr, and to treat Falstaff's promises of 'amendment' as a running joke. Emphasising the Prince's plan for '[r]edeeming time' (see 1.2.177 and note), he initiated an exploration of this reformer's career.

Whereas 'honour' and 'festivity' tend to be associated with impulses which fix social patterns, 'friendship' and 'reformation' have more dynamic properties. Gerhart B. Ladner emphasises a definition of reform which is theologically Catholic but also consistent with the comic design of *1 Henry IV*. He distinguishes reform from revolution which claims total improvement, from the cyclical Machiavellian 'ricorso' which minimises human agency, and from the Protestant spiritual rebirth which occurs once. Reform is a process of *multiple* repetition which permits the most inventive elements in human history to survive.[3] So defined, reformation in *Part One* can point ahead, to *2 Henry IV*, with its numerous meditations on time, and to the secular apocalypse of Agincourt in *Henry V*. In his edition of *2 Henry IV*,

---

[1] Barber, pp. 6–10.
[2] Naseeb Shaheen points out that twenty-six of the fifty-four biblical allusions that he counts in *Part One* are spoken by Falstaff, 'probably suggested by Oldcastle's religious background', in *Biblical References in Shakespeare's History Plays*, 1989, p. 137.
[3] *The Idea of Reform: Its Impact on Christian Thought and Action in the Age of the Fathers*, 1959, pp. 25–35, 436.

Giorgio Melchiori explores the hypothesis that for Shakespeare, who was trying to put new shapes on old and familiar dramatic materials, the entire 'Henriad' is a 'remake'.[1]

Within *1 Henry IV*, the evidence of reformation in Ladner's sense is more limited but nonetheless vivid. When the King lectures his son on the lessons ot his own past, he employs a highly tendentious parallel between then and now, between King Richard and Henry Bullingbrook as they were, the Prince and Hotspur as they are. These equations slot Richard into the role of a 'skipping King' who

> ambled up and down,
> With shallow jesters, and rash bavin wits,
> Soon kindled and soon burnt, carded his state,
> Mingled his royalty with capering fools . . .   (3.2.60–3)

So described, Richard himself resembles a lively theatre clown; William Kemp, who perhaps played Falstaff, would later dance from London to Norwich in 1599. Long before he literally digs up King Richard and re-buries him (*Henry V*, 4. 1. 295–305), the Prince, by 'mingling' with Falstaff, may be redeeming both Richard's time and his own.

Whether Shakespeare lighted by accident or intention upon Oldcastle as a figure to couple with his princely reformer, there is wonderful propriety in his choice. For after the Reformation, Oldcastle the Lollard became 'one of those cultural icons in which are epitomized a society's conflicting and shifting values'.[2] There are also multiple ironies in the fact that the Cobham descendants of Oldcastle belonged not to a persecuted sectarian minority but to a ruling class which fervently supported the union of church and state. For all their disagreements over the regulation of religion, members of this consensus came together in attacking religious independents who questioned such a union.[3] Because Lollard views frequently coincided with those of the later radical independents and sectarians, Oldcastle's theology could have been as embarrassing to his heirs as was his alleged rebellion against Henry V – and not so easily explained away.[4] In an intellectual climate hostile to unorthodox attitudes, Shakespeare may have managed to approach religious radicalism by couching a 'damnable iteration' (1.2.72) of the Bible in the language of folly.

APOLOGIES FOR FALSTAFF

Falstaff may not be the central figure in his play, but during four hundred years he has become more familiar than almost every hero and heroine. Like Hamlet and Cleopatra, Falstaff enjoys a privileged existence in our cultural awareness; many feel they 'know' him, including some who have neither read nor seen any of the

---

[1] Melchiori, pp. 9–15.

[2] Patterson, p. 131.

[3] G. H. Williams, *The Radical Reformation*, 1962, pp. xxiii–xxxi. See also, for a 'third body of ideas' that was rejected by the court and the established church on one hand, and by orthodox Puritanism on the other, Christopher Hill, *Milton and the English Revolution*, 1979, p. 69.

[4] A. G. Dickens, *The English Reformation*, 1967, chap. 2, describes the survival of Lollardry into the sixteenth century.

three plays in which he appears. He has lent his name to an opera, a novel, and, most appropriately, a beer. As Shakespeare does for his greatest heroes and villains, he gives Falstaff weaknesses which are never completely effaced by the qualities which please audiences, qualities which are much easier to experience than to describe or recapture.

For over three hundred years after the play was first performed, allusions to and commentary about *1 Henry IV* overwhelmingly emphasised Falstaff. Most of these writers appear to assume that enthusiasm for Falstaff is general. At the same time, they try to explain why Falstaff should be so charismatic when his faults are so glaring. By far the most influential earlier commentaries are those by Samuel Johnson in the notes to his edition of 1765, and by Maurice Morgann in his monograph, *Essay on the Dramatic Character of Sir John Falstaff* (1777).

Johnson considered the two parts of *Henry IV* to be more widely read than Shakespeare's other works; no two plays had ever 'afforded so much delight'. He apostrophised Falstaff as 'unimitated, unimitable', then asked, '[H]ow shall I describe thee?' Answering his own question must have strained Johnson's professed admiration for Shakespeare's 'mingled drama'; it would be difficult to find, in the many critical references to Falstaff as a parasite or tempter, a stronger condemnation than Johnson's. 'Falstaff is a character loaded with faults, and with those faults which naturally produce contempt . . . At once obsequious and malignant, he satirises in their absence those whom he lives by flattering. He is familiar with the Prince only as an agent of vice . . .' But in explaining Falstaff's necessity to 'the prince that despises him', Johnson shifted quickly to an unsentimental appreciation of Falstaff's 'perpetual gaiety', which, he suggested, is in no way criminal or ambitious. We are left, then, to ponder Johnson's final harshness and to puzzle over his emotional withdrawal in declaring that 'neither wit nor honesty ought to think themselves safe with such a companion when they see Henry seduced by Falstaff'.[1]

Johnson revealed his disproportionate interest in Falstaff by spending in his concluding note more than twice as many words upon him as upon the Prince and Hotspur combined. Maurice Morgann, defending Falstaff against what he takes to be a universal verdict on his cowardice, wrote the longest and the most often cited early discussion of any Shakespeare character. 'There is no better piece of Shakespearian criticism in the world', said A. C. Bradley (1902). Certainly, as Jonathan Bate suggests, there can be few more 'generous' ones.[2]

Like Johnson, Morgann saw how repellent Falstaff's vices may become: 'here we shall behold him most villainously unprincipled and debauched; possessing indeed the same Courage and ability, yet stained with numerous vices'. These vices 'become still more intolerable by an excess of unfeeling insolence on one hand, and of base accommodation on the other'.[3] But by coupling these traits with the 'leading quality' of quick wit, by showing what happens when such an individual is 'grouped' with

[1] *Johnson on Shakespeare*, ed. Arthur Sherbo, *The Works of Samuel Johnson*, vol. VII, 1968, pp. 522–4.
[2] Ed., *The Romantics on Shakespeare*, 1992, p. 8. Bradley's praise is cited by Fineman in Morgann, p. 27.
[3] Morgann, p. 210.

or related to others, and by imposing upon him the limits of genre and artifice, Shakespeare produced a comic figure who 'passes thro' the Play as a lawless meteor, and we wish to know what course he is afterwards likely to take'.[1]

This paradox – a carefully wrought character who is simultaneously a 'lawless meteor' – seems designed to astound a 'jury' of moralistic readers and spectators. Distracted by the issue of Falstaff's cowardice, critics and theatre historians often neglect Morgann's implicit attack upon this audience. His defence of a constitutional or 'natural' courage, of a capacity for pragmatic behaviour which may even 'avail itself of flight', is a way of demonstrating that Shakespeare 'makes a character act and speak from those parts of the composition, which are *inferred* only, and not directly shown'.[2] In building his case, Morgann wrote as if Falstaff had a past: 'He found himself esteemed and beloved with all his faults, nay *for* his faults, which were all connected with humour, and for the most part, grew out of it.'[3] But Morgann also undertook, as the 'jury' he cajoled did not, a disciplined scrutiny of the evidence against his own argument. The guilty parties in this trial were those who responded to Falstaff superficially, missing the substance and the true pleasure of Shakespeare's art.

Morgann was followed by A. W. Schlegel (1808), William Hazlitt (1817), and A. C. Bradley, while James Gillray and Isaac Cruikshank, cartoonists active in the 1790s, and later Samuel Taylor Coleridge (1812–13), carried on Johnson's view of Falstaff as an immoral, destructive tempter. Coleridge associated Falstaff with the dynamic villains Richard III and Iago.[4] (Alexander Pushkin would later group him with Angelo and Shylock.) Falstaff's defenders emphasised instead his love of life, laughter, and society. For Hazlitt, he was 'the most substantial comic character that ever was invented'. The same keen mind which Coleridge thought corrupt, seemed for Hazlitt to be 'an emanation of a fine constitution; an exuberance of good-humour and good nature'. Hazlitt regarded his vices as 'characters' assumed by Falstaff:

He is represented as a liar, a braggart, a coward, a glutton, etc. and yet we are not offended but delighted with him; for he is all these as much to amuse others as to gratify himself . . . The unrestrained indulgence of his own ease, appetites, and convenience, has neither malice nor hypocrisy in it.[5]

Although the rejection of Falstaff was not treated as a major issue before Bradley, both Morgann and Hazlitt seem to have been disturbed by the ending of *Part Two*.[6] Morgann assumed that the Prince knew Falstaff's faults as well as he did, but unlike Hal, he wanted to rescue Falstaff from detractors anyway. Hazlitt conceded that Shakespeare himself knew best, but admitted, 'we never could forgive the Prince's

---

[1] *Ibid.*, pp. 214–15.
[2] *Ibid.*, pp. 154, 168.
[3] *Ibid.*, pp. 151–2.
[4] *Lectures 1808–1819 on Literature*, ed. R. A. Foakes, *The Collected Works of Samuel Taylor Coleridge*, vol. v, pt 1, 1987, pp. 575–6.
[5] Hazlitt, p. 279.
[6] See G. K. Hunter, 'Shakespeare's politics and the rejection of Falstaff', *CQ* 1 (1959), 232–3.

treatment of Falstaff'.[1] Bradley largely discounted Falstaff's vices while stressing his novelty, as had Morgann. Bradley celebrated Falstaff's 'freedom of soul' which was 'illusory only in part, and attainable only by a mind which had received from Shakespeare's own the inexplicable touch of infinity which he bestowed on Hamlet and MacBeth and Cleopatra, but denied to Henry the Fifth'.[2]

In reaction against a romantic tendency to take characters out of their contexts in plays, early twentieth-century critics often approached Falstaff as a dramatic role or function. They also subordinated his vitality to the unifying effects of more general themes and images. The most influential study, John Dover Wilson's *The Fortunes of Falstaff*, emphasised his similarities to the Vice, the conventional tempter–entertainer of the Morality plays.

Dissenting from this paradigm, W. H. Auden and William Empson took their own strong responses in surprising directions. Without the Falstaff scenes, Auden suggested, *Henry IV* would become the 'middle section of a political trilogy, which could be entitled *Looking for the Doctor*'.[3] He reflected that Falstaff's love for the Prince was 'tragic' because Falstaff himself, lacking any sense of time or consequences, cannot see it is hopeless. This ever youthful and creative figure (a fat man, wrote Auden, looks like 'a cross between a very young child and a pregnant mother') is both a 'Lord of Misrule' and 'a comic symbol for the supernatural order of Charity'.[4]

Empson's qualified defence of Falstaff ('It is hard to defend this strange figure without doing it too much') questioned the lack of ambivalence in Dover Wilson's view. To explain why Falstaff has a 'heart' that can be broken when the new King rejects him, Empson joined the conflicting insights of Johnson and Morgann in a new apology. As Morgann acknowledged, Falstaff had 'sordid' inner vices; and as Johnson suggested, Falstaff 'feels in himself the pain of deformity' even if he does 'make sport of it among those whom it is in his interest to please'. If Falstaff was Dover Wilson's medieval Vice, thought Empson, he would have no inner life, 'no interior at all'.[5]

Empson's tact, so unexpected, in accounting for the 'heart' of a Falstaff 'driven on by an obscure personal shame of an amoral sort' was remarkably similar to the tact he found in Shakespeare, who included what had to be made 'obvious' for his first audiences but, going beyond unambiguous meanings, 'rode remarkably near the edge'.[6] What seemed clear 'to Empson was Falstaff's Renaissance role as an aristocratic, Machiavellian tutor who initiated a future ruler into a flawed world. What seemed more perplexing was the 'power' of Falstaff, connected to his 'shame' and somehow realised in 'love': the love which attracted the 'young thieves' he

---

[1] Hazlitt, p. 285.
[2] 'The rejection of Falstaff' in *Oxford Lectures on Poetry*, 1909, p. 273.
[3] Auden, p. 186.
[4] *Ibid.*, pp. 195–8.
[5] Empson, p. 65. This chapter is a revision of 'Falstaff and Mr Dover Wilson', *KR* 15 (1953), 213–62. Johnson's comment on 'deformity' comes from his note on 'the Burning Lamp' (3.3.20); he suggested that Falstaff bitterly resents insults about his being fat.
[6] Empson, p. 39.

tutored, and the 'love' he himself expressed for them. Baffled, he admitted, by the potent compound of shame, charm, desire, and drink in Falstaff's 'heart', Empson stated unforgettably, 'Indeed, if you compare Hal to his brother and his father, whom the plays describe so very unflinchingly, it is surely obvious that to love Falstaff was a liberal education for him.'[1]

Stage history

PLAYHOUSE BEGINNINGS

When *1 Henry IV* was first performed in 1596–7, Shakespeare's company may have been in transition among several playhouses. Until the former Theatre was taken apart, moved from the northern edge of the City to the south bank of the Thames, and reconstructed as the Globe (1599), they probably used either the Curtain or the Swan.[2] *1 Henry IV* would have been well adapted to travel within London – or beyond, when the theatres were temporarily closed. From the text we can conjecture that the players must have required only a few portable properties: a crown, a throne, a joint stool, Falstaff's mug, cushion, and bottle, Hotspur's letter, and assorted weapons. Spectators entering the playhouse might well have seen a stage which would be bare except, perhaps, for a throne, some rushes on the floor, and hangings at the rear. An upper playing area, used to represent castle battlements in *Richard II*, would not be required.

The Curtain and the Swan were probably, like the Globe, capable of holding three thousand spectators who sat in tiers of galleries or stood in the yard or 'pit' which was lower than a platform stage thrust out from one side of the amphitheatre.[3] During daylight performances in the open air, spectators would have seen one another, and their faces would have been visible to the actors. Other distinctive features of Elizabethan staging were the rapid pace of performance and the symbolic quality of some techniques.[4] Within the 'two hours traffic of the stage' (Prologue, *Rom.*), the rhythm of scenes was enhanced by their continuity. Not only costumes or actions, but also different parts of the stage and its structure could quickly take on significant meanings. A flurry of entrances and exits, as in the tavern scene of *1 Henry IV*, might distinguish a public from a more private setting.

Of all the arts used to engage spectators in the Elizabethan theatre, the most important would have been the skills of the actors who could exploit their physical proximity to the audience.[5] Specific speeches would have created immediate and flexible relationships between actors and audiences, varying not only with cast

---

[1] *Ibid.*, p. 67.

[2] Gurr, *Stage*, pp. 45–8, 118–20.

[3] Gurr, *ibid.*, pp. 123–31, describes the excavations of the Rose Theatre site in 1989 which indicated differences in the designs of the Southwark playhouses.

[4] Glynne Wickham stresses the shift from an 'emblematic' towards a more naturalistic staging style during this period, in *Early English Stages 1300–1600*, 3 vols., 1959–81.

[5] John Russell Brown discusses the new naturalism of Elizabethan acting in *Shakespeare's Plays in Performance*, 1969, pp. 22–39. Cf. Gurr, *Stage*, pp. 100–3. For the influence of playhouse conditions on acting, see Bernard Beckerman, *Shakespeare at the Globe 1599–1609*, 1962, pp. 127–37.

changes but also from day to day. Because many plays encouraged actors to address the audience directly, even using 'asides' when other actors were onstage, it may be difficult to determine the inwardness or privacy of speeches in which a character seems to think aloud. The Prince's soliloquy in 1.2 plainly provides, in a non-realistic manner, necessary information about his secret plans. But by stepping forward to say 'I know you all', the actor can also implicate the audience, catching the attention of spectators who might have been waiting for the next appearance of Falstaff and ready to chime in whenever the comedy became more raucous.[1] The development of modern theatres which simulate the dimensions of Shakespeare's playhouses has not extended to the inclusion of noisy 'groundlings' like the ones referred to by Sir Thomas Palmer, in a commendatory poem prefaced to the Folio edition of Beaumont and Fletcher in 1647: 'I could praise Heywood now, or tell how long/Falstaff from cracking nuts hath kept the throng.'

Writing his plays for his own company of all male actors, Shakespeare must often have shaped the script to the performer. He would have anticipated the skills of his players, a group which included thirteen men (some of whom were shareholders in the company) and four boys. For example, he could only have written the part of Lady Mortimer, Glendower's daughter, if he could count upon the talents of a boy able to act and sing in Welsh (see 3.1.191 SD and note). Continuing experience with one another and specialisation in particular types of role equipped this company to develop and sustain a remarkably large repertoire. In performing *1 Henry IV*, which presents thirty-three characters and additional attendants, travellers, and soldiers, the majority of actors in Shakespeare's company must have played several roles. The question of which actors took major parts in *1 Henry IV* has caused much speculation: Richard Burbage has been proposed as the Prince; John Heminges, Thomas Pope, and Will Kemp (the clown) as Falstaff. Shakespeare perhaps conceived Falstaff's role as a clown part; then, when the role became more challenging, it might have been assumed by the actor who would eventually play the King to Burbage's Hamlet.[2]

THE GROWTH OF ACTING TRADITIONS

The allusions and references which substantiate the Oldcastle controversy show that Falstaff must have made a strong immediate impression. But evidence for actual early performances of *1 Henry IV* is minimal. After 1700, with much more frequent staging, evidence increases; spectators and actors add their memories and biographers add their lives of theatre personalities to the record supplied by acting editions, official documents, and cast lists. Later, surviving playbills and newspaper reviews become valuable historical sources, while editors, essayists, and critics begin to take notice of current stage practices. In the twentieth century, most aspects of

---

[1] See Herbert Weil, 'On expectation and surprise: Shakespeare's construction of character', *S.Sur.* 34 (1981), 39–50.

[2] Useful, but not authoritative, are T. W. Baldwin, *The Organization and Personnel of the Shakespearean Company*, 1927, p. 312 and Henry David Gray, 'The roles of William Kemp', *MLR* 25 (1930), 261–73.

production have become the objects of careful study by scholars and critics interested in performance and its traditions.

The first recorded production of *1 Henry IV* may be the play put on for the Lord Chamberlain's private entertainment of the Flemish ambassador in 1600; a letter from Rowland Whyte to Sir Robert Sidney referred to it as 'Sir John Old Castell', which could mean either *Part One* or *Part Two*.[1] In 1612–13, one or both parts were among twenty plays staged at court during celebrations for the marriage of Princess Elizabeth to the Elector Palatine.[2] *The First Part of Sir John Falstaff* was staged at Whitehall in 1625. Before all theatres were closed by Parliament in 1642, the only other performance recorded was of 'ould Castel', probably Shakespeare's play, at the 'Cocpit' at court in 1638.[3] In this early period, information about the popular, as opposed to the courtly, appeal of *1 Henry IV* comes primarily from the repeated publication of quarto editions, from Palmer's poem, cited above, and from an allusion by Leonard Digges in some lines prefaced to the 1640 edition of Shakespeare's poems. Digges declared that 'though the Fox and subtill Alchimist, / Long intermitted could not quite be mist . . . when let but Falstaffe come, / Hall, Poines, the rest you shall scarce have a roome, / All is so pester'd'.[4]

A manuscript discovered in 1844 preserves a conflation and adaptation of both parts for private performance in 1622–3. Named after Sir Edward Dering (1598–1644), this manuscript is of special interest because, of its 3,401 lines, roughly two-thirds come from *Part One*. The Dering MS. cut only 11 per cent of *Part One* – two complete scenes (2.1 and 4.4) and some two hundred additional lines. The second longest deletion was the seventy-four lines of Glendower's scene with Lady Mortimer. These changes eliminated eight characters, all of them minor except Westmoreland, whose lines in the first scene were spoken by Prince John and by Sir Walter Blunt. These deletions reveal close knowledge of the text and anticipate those in later acting editions and adaptations, especially John Barton's *When Thou Art King* in 1969 (see below, p. 54).

With the restoration of kingship and the re-opening of the theatres in 1660, *1 Henry IV* seems to have been revived almost immediately. It played three times before the year was out, at the Red Bull theatre, and later at the Vere.[5] In the division of the existing repertory between two companies, Davenant's and Killigrew's, the play went with a mere handful of Shakespeare's works to Killigrew's troupe. Samuel Pepys, who was to record his attendance at some three hundred and fifty London performances between 1660 and 1669, saw *1 Henry IV* in December 1660 and complained that reading the play beforehand reduced his pleasure in the production, 'my expectation being too great'.[6]

---

[1] Chambers, *Shakespeare*, II, 322.
[2] Chambers, *Stage*, II, 217; IV, 127, 180.
[3] Chambers, *Shakespeare*, II, 353.
[4] *The Shakespeare Allusion Book: A Collection of Allusions to Shakespeare from 1591 to 1700*, ed. John Munro, 1932, I, 457.
[5] Van Lennep, pp. 12, 19, 23.
[6] *Ibid.*, p. 23.

1 Henry IV seems to have been acted even when Shakespeare became temporarily unfashionable in the 1670s.[1] The publication of a 'droll' or skit entitled *The Bouncing Knight, or The Robbers Robbed*, in *The Wits, or, Sport upon Sport* (1662, 1672), which portrays Falstaff and the Hostess on its frontispiece, suggests that the tavern scenes, exploited in the skit, may have helped to keep the play itself upon the boards.

In 1682, the two London theatre companies merged, and *1 Henry IV* came under the control of Thomas Betterton. Colley Cibber, the actor, would later recall how Betterton played Hotspur (at the age of forty-seven) with 'wild impatient starts' and 'fierce and flashing fire'.[2] Betterton initiated two significant traditions when, eighteen years later in 1700, he acted Falstaff at Lincoln's Inn Fields in a performance billed as 'King Henry the Fourth: With the Humours of Sir John Falstaff'. Praised for hitting these humours, Betterton became the first in a succession of stage Falstaffs who, playing the role year after year, could be compared with one another. The cuts which he made in the text established patterns which John Bell and John Kemble later used in their editions of Shakespeare, 1773–5 and 1815.[3] Betterton trimmed the King's opening speech to ten lines and removed nearly thirty of his lines from Act 3, Scene 2. Also cut were a large segment of Lady Percy's speech to Hotspur in 2.3, a portion of the 'play extempore' in 2.4, 3.1 after line 140, all of 4.4, and the Prince's rescue of the King before Hotspur's entry (5.4.1–57).[4] This revival seems to have been planned as competition for Cibber's thoroughly altered *Richard III* at Drury Lane, and its capacity to draw 'all the town' proved to one observer that 'Shakespeare's wit will always last.'[5]

According to Harold Child, 'the vogue of *Henry IV* reached its zenith in the eighteenth century . . . [with] two hundred and twenty performances of *Part One* in London, 1704–50 [in contrast to] eighty of *Part Two* for . . . 1720–50'.[6] After Betterton, the most successful Falstaff was James Quin (1693–1766). He too began with Hotspur (1718), went on to King Henry two seasons later, and regularly played Falstaff from 1722 until his retirement in 1751. The bookseller Thomas Davies praised this intelligent Falstaff for his excellence at 'satire and sarcasm', while Francis Gentleman, editor of the Bell edition (1773–5), later recalled his 'glow of feature and expression' when exposed by the Prince and Poins.[7] Quin further reduced the acting script for *1 Henry IV* by curtailing Falstaff's role in the robbery and by eliminating the 'play extempore' altogether. Gentleman said that it 'rather choked and loaded the main business'.[8] Quin also created the gag of introducing

[1] Odell, I, 42.
[2] Child, p. xxxiii.
[3] Bell's edition was printed from the prompt-books of two Theatres Royal, Drury Lane and Covent Garden. See Odell, II, 15–19, 40–1.
[4] C. B. Hogan, *Shakespeare in the Theatre, 1701–1800*, vol. I, *London 1701–50*, 1952, p. 144. See also Odell, II, 84.
[5] Van Lennep, p. 523.
[6] Child, p. xxxv.
[7] Davies' *Dramatic Miscellanies*, 1785, reprinted in Salgādo, p. 176; Sprague, *Histories*, p. 61. Sprague emphasises the frequent mention of Falstaff's eyes.
[8] Child, p. xxxvii.

Falstaff's escape from 'open and apparent shame' with 'Ha, ha, ha! d'ye think I did not know ye?' This trick was still being used in Sir Herbert Beerbohm Tree's production in 1896.[1]

Compared with the many references to Falstaff, comments on other roles are extremely rare during these years. After Cibber described Edward Kynaston (1619–87) as Henry IV, noting the 'terrible menace' of a whispered 'Send us your prisoners' to Betterton's Hotspur and his 'affecting scene' with his son in 3.2, the King and the Prince received little attention.[2] David Garrick, perceived to be miscast as Hotspur, because of his flexible voice and small size (Quin could easily carry him off), quickly dropped the part. Of the many eighteenth-century Falstaffs besides Quin, the most popular seems to have been John Henderson (1747–85). Contrasting his 'frolicksome, gay, and humorous' qualities with Quin's 'impudent dignity', Davies remembered his description of his 'ragamuffin regiment' and his pleasure at misusing 'the king's press money'.[3]

INNOVATIONS: 1800–1945
The enthusiasm of earlier audiences apparently promoted tendencies to 'exalt the Falstaff scenes at the expense of the historical part of the play'.[4] Gentleman was reflecting one extreme contemporary attitude to *1 Henry IV*, when he declared that 'want of ladies, and matter to interest female auditors, lies so heavy on it' that only 'an excellent Falstaff' can give it 'occasional life'.[5] This trend continues into the nine-teenth century as actors build reputations by playing Falstaff, often sacrificing subtlety for new stage business and costumes. The common practice of dressing Falstaff in thick, high boots probably began as a means of disguising an actor's thin legs. Because his role at Shrewsbury could be strenuous, it became customary to send him into stage battle without armour.[6] By the late eighteenth century, Davies claimed, 'No joke ever raised such loud and repeated mirth, in the galleries, as Sir John's labour in getting the body of Hotspur on his back.'[7] Morgann strongly objected to seated Falstaffs so fat that they had to be picked up off the edge of the stage by the Prince and Poins disguised as robbers, or who resembled 'piteous' tortoises while the Prince fought Hotspur.[8] Some later Falstaffs seem to have been so badly beaten in the robbery scene that they crawled from the stage, and to have emphasised their cowardice upon rising from the dead.[9] When in 1816 Stephen Kemble needed no padding to play Falstaff, he provoked Hazlitt into a cascade of insults rivalling the Prince's; another spectator recalled that it had been 'painful' to watch the obese

---

[1] *Ibid.*, p. xxxvi.
[2] Citations in Salgādo, pp. 174–5.
[3] *Ibid.*, p. 177.
[4] Child, p. xxxiv.
[5] Odell, II, 41.
[6] Sprague and Trewin, pp. 80–1.
[7] Davies, cited by Child, p. xxxvii.
[8] Morgann, p. 154.
[9] Arthur Colby Sprague, *Shakespeare and the Actors: The Stage Business in His Plays, 1660–1905*, 1945, p. 85; Sprague, *Histories*, p. 71.

Kemble, who 'evidently suffered under the exertion'.[1] Kemble began the tradition of discovering Falstaff asleep in 1.2, continued by many later productions.[2] Sharp differences of opinion began to appear in recollections of specific stage Falstaffs, just as they have always attached themselves to the character. Samuel Phelps was both noted for 'unctuosity' and pronounced lacking in 'unction'.[3] In mid-century, Phelps carried on the tradition of specialising in Falstaff by acting him more than three hundred times.[4] In the United States, James Hackett portrayed Falstaff, starting in 1828, for over forty years.[5]

More innovative was the attempt to achieve authenticity in scenes and costumes. A 'bill' advertising Charles Kemble's 1824 production at Covent Garden listed, among other authorities for its period accuracy, effigies, portraits, stained glass, illuminated manuscripts, sumptuary laws, and chronicles.[6] This production closely followed and was influenced by a spectacular *2 Henry IV* staged for the coronation of George IV in 1821 and a highly successful, 'picturesque' *King John*. For the 1864 centenary production directed by Phelps (playing Falstaff), there appear to have been thirteen painted scenes, plus a sunset.[7] Between each of the fifteen scene changes in Beerbohm Tree's 1914 production, the curtain fell and the band played.[8] Such a production style, described by J. C. Trewin as 'the great canvas pavilions of spectacular Shakespeare', also depended upon crowds of supernumeraries.[9]

In the long run, the 1864 production may have been more important for its text than for its scenery. Phelps, who had restored the 'play extempore' in 1846 and taken it out again in 1856, decisively returned it in 1864, along with all of Act 3, Scene 1. Reviews of Beerbohm Tree's 1896 production disagreed about the merits of Tree's believable Falstaff, but recognised a new kind of acting which appeared less mannered or 'tragic'.[10] In the twentieth century, influenced by the boldly simplified stagings of Granville Barker and by William Poel's attempt to revive Elizabethan conventions, directors began to seek a more 'classical' style. Poel's impact seems to have been apparent in Robert Atkins' 1935 production, although the great vaudeville comedian and crowd-pleaser, George Robey, alleged to have 'hardly ever seen a Shakespearean performance', stole the show as Falstaff. Reviewing the first night, James Agate suggested that Robey only fell into his music-hall trick of raising his eyebrows when he needed time to recall his lines, but that the delighted crowd kept him going.[11] In a purer theatrical experiment designed to reproduce Elizabethan stage conditions in the Harrow School Speech Room, Ronald Watkins worked with

---

[1] J. R. Planché, *Recollections and Reflections*, 1901, reprinted in Salgādo, pp. 180–1.
[2] Sprague and Trewin, p. 28.
[3] Hemingway, 'Appendix on stage history', p. 490.
[4] *Ibid.*
[5] George C. D. Odell, *Annals of the New York Stage*, 1931, II, 493.
[6] Odell II, 173.
[7] *Ibid.*, p. 361.
[8] Sprague, *Histories*, p. 52.
[9] Trewin, p. 58; Odell, II, 174.
[10] Child, p. xlii.
[11] *Brief Chronicles: A Survey of the Plays of Shakespeare and the Elizabethans in Actual Performance*, 1943, p. 102.

'[n]o curtain here in front, no darkened hall, no scenery, no lights, nothing at all'.[1] Such developments were behind the simple timber framework set up on the stage of the Memorial Theatre at Stratford in 1951 for the performance of the entire second tetralogy.

One other significant development, originating in nineteenth-century Germany, was the production of *1 Henry IV* as part of a group or cycle. Franz Dingelstadt directed *1 Henry IV* in Munich in 1851 and began to work on a series of seven histories from the two 'tetralogies'. In 1864, to celebrate the tercentenary of Shakespeare's birth, Dingelstadt produced these histories in Weimar, taking a week to complete his cycle.[2] At Stratford-upon-Avon, between 1899 and 1916, F. R. Benson regularly directed productions of plays from the 'second tetralogy', emphasising *Richard II* and *Henry V*; he apparently presented all four plays on consecutive days in May 1905.[3] The two parts of *Henry IV* were finally staged together on Shakespeare's birthday by Sir Barry Jackson for the Birmingham Repertory Company in 1921, and again, for the opening of the new Memorial Theatre building at Stratford in 1932.

PERFORMANCES, CELEBRATIONS, AND NEW AUDIENCES: 1945-91
Because performances of *1 Henry IV* often reach a broad spectrum of the theatregoing public, modern English companies have produced the play for special occasions. During the Festival of Britain, 1951, and the centenary year of Shakespeare's birth, 1964, it was staged as part of a cycle of histories. The Royal Shakespeare Company selected *1 Henry IV* as the play to open its new London theatre, the Barbican, in 1982. Again, in 1991, beginning his term as artistic director for the RSC, Adrian Noble directed *1* and *2 Henry IV* as the featured plays on the main stage in Stratford-upon-Avon. While such productions have affirmed the vitality of the play for contemporary audiences, cycle stagings, developing much further the experiments of Dingelstadt, Benson, and Jackson (above), have radically changed its meanings. Audiences have been able to observe *1 Henry IV* as the first of two or of three, or as the second of four plays. In 1951 and in 1964, the Royal Shakespeare Company performed the entire second tetralogy; spectators in 1964 might have seen their three-play version of the first tetralogy in 1963. Then in 1988 the touring English Shakespeare Company presented both tetralogies within a single season. Eager addicts could see seven plays in less than sixty-two hours. New dimensions of *1 Henry IV* have also been revealed by one major film adaptation, a television production, and a video based directly upon a stage performance.

This account of stage history after the Second World War concentrates on the most influential productions. Whereas resources for the study of earlier stage history are often meagre – anecdotes or generalities abound, but only for Falstaff's role do we have much evidence – contemporary productions have been much more thoroughly

[1] Trewin, p. 207, n. 1.
[2] Simon Williams, *Shakespeare on the German Stage*, 1990, 1, 153–4.
[3] Michael Mullin, ed. *Theatre at Stratford-upon-Avon: A Catalogue Index to Productions of the Shakespeare Memorial/Royal Shakespeare Theatre, 1879–1978*, 1980, 1, 395, 139, 146, 153.

4   A non-theatrical version of the robbery, Act 2, Scene 2: Falstaff, a 'huge hill of flesh', nimbly runs away. Etching by George Cruikshank, 1858. In 1945, Ralph Richardson was praised for his agile footwork, surprising when combined with his heavily padded figure

documented. Because recent studies have described some of these productions extensively, we will focus upon their most innovative qualities and emphasise their dramatisation of four important sequences: the soliloquy of the Prince; the 'play extempore'; the reconciliation of the King and the Prince; and the combat between Hotspur and the Prince with its sequel.[1]

John Burrell's production for the Old Vic Company in 1945 was part of a classical repertory planned to show 'that the London Theatre had not only survived the years of devastating air raids but had survived with unmatchable ability'.[2] In at least one key respect, this extremely popular production followed stage tradition: the leading actors played Hotspur and Falstaff. They received by far the most comments from reviewers. Laurence Olivier, who had recently triumphed as the hero in his film of *Henry V*, chose to play Henry Percy rather than the future Henry V. His romantic, inscrutable Hotspur spoke quickly, even incomprehensibly, with a stammer which culminated in his last broken line, 'food for w – w –'. (The idea of having Hotspur stammer, probably based upon a misreading of 'speaking thick', i.e. 'fast', in *2 Henry IV* 2.3.24, dates at least from the Beerbohm Tree production of 1914.) Olivier concluded Hotspur's speech and life by pitching face forward in full

---

[1]   See especially McMillin; Barbara Hodgdon, *The End Crowns All: Closure and Contradiction in Shake-speare's History*, 1991; T. F. Wharton, *Text and Performance: Henry the Fourth, Parts 1 and 2*, 1983; and Sprague, *Histories*.
[2]   McMillin, p. 14.

armour down some steps.[1] The young and relatively inexperienced actor who played the Prince was overshadowed by Ralph Richardson's engaging Falstaff. Spectators saw 'little of the glutton or the sensualist' in a performance distinguished for great mental and physical agility. Although Richardson followed Robey and other stage Falstaffs who had exaggerated the expressiveness of their eyes, he dispensed with one traditional gag, a shield used to hide his face before he peeped out from behind it and exclaimed in his next line, 'By the Lord, I knew ye, as well as he that made ye.'[2] Richardson's mobile countenance told the story of his exposure and joyous recovery; caught out when his invention of men in buckram ran away with him, he was defenceless until his wit suggested an escape route. For Kenneth Tynan, recalling this production, Richardson's humane and vulnerable performance, with its 'charity', 'magnanimity', and 'grief', seemed to confirm W. H. Auden's hyperbolic suggestion that Falstaff was a comic symbol for Jesus Christ.[3]

It is striking that in a company of such overall strength as the Old Vic's in 1945, well-known actors in minor roles – Harcourt Williams as Glendower, Sybil Thorndike as Mistress Quickly, Margaret Leighton as Lady Percy – should have received more praise than did Nicholas Hannen as the King or Michael Warre as the Prince. Compared with later interpretations, these roles seem to have been presented in relatively straightforward fashion: a capable, conscientious ruler and father; a Prince who used his soliloquy more for information than for self-expression. Later though, after 'I do, I will', he playfully threw the royal cushion back to Falstaff.

In the next major production, directed by Anthony Quayle at Stratford-upon-Avon in 1951, Falstaff and Hotspur drew less attention, while, probably for the first time, the characters of the King and the Prince and the relationship between them became more prominent. This occurred both through staging the entire second tetralogy and through strong casting: Harry Andrews as the King, and Richard Burton as the Prince. Quayle himself acted Falstaff, not as a scene-stealing charmer but as a potentially vicious clown. The exceptionally large company of forty-six (the Old Vic had twenty-seven), including seventeen supernumeraries, presented all four plays within a frame structure, created by designer Tanya Moiseiwitsch to simulate a more Elizabethan theatrical environment.

In the eighteenth century, Edmond Malone believed that Nicholas Rowe's edition (1709) enhanced the stage popularity of *1 Henry IV*.[4] Scholarship seems to have had a large, if indirect, influence upon the 1951 production, visible not only in the more authentic staging but in the conception of Falstaff as a tempter. Above all, Tillyard's approach to Shakespeare's eight histories as a national epic seemed particularly attractive while the struggle to recover from the Second World War

---

[1] Trewin, p. 195.
[2] On persistent gags, see Sprague, *Histories*, p. 61.
[3] *Showpeople: Profiles in Entertainment*, 1970, p. 43. For Tynan's early review, stressing Richardson's dignity and youthful heart, see *He That Plays the King: A View of the Theatre*, 1950, pp. 49–50.
[4] Hemingway, p. 480.

5 A typical publicity photograph: Prince Hal (Richard Burton) and Poins taunt Falstaff (Anthony
Quayle) while Bardolph looks on in Act 2, Scene 4. Quayle directed this production at Stratford-upon-
Avon in 1951

continued. It may well have given confidence to directors and actors staging a cycle
of plays in the year of the Festival of Britain, celebrated throughout the country.[1]

When *1 Henry IV* opened a month after *Richard II*, audiences could see for
themselves that King Henry was declining from his role as energetic, ambitious
usurper in *Richard II*. They could experience the anxieties of kingship when they
recognised Michael Redgrave, the assassinated Richard II, returning in the role
of Hotspur. They would have seen in Richard Burton a far more complex Prince,
already somewhat alienated from his companions and so preoccupied with his future
that he developed minimally through the cycle. Richard David's description of the
Prince's soliloquy suggests Burton's 'sobriety and self-knowledge': 'Hal had turned
to watch [Poins] leave the stage; for a moment he stood looking after him; then
his head moved slowly to regard the audience over his shoulder.' His soliloquy
'followed, with a curious simplicity and tonelessness, and yet with a suggestion of
strong emotion held in check'.[2] In the first tavern scene, the Prince turned jovial
play to deadly earnest assault so that the laughter of the watchers became uneasy
and stopped with the momentous pause, preceding Prince Hal's 'I do, I will.' Never

[1] McMillin, p. 36.
[2] David, 'Shakespeare's history plays: epic or drama?', *S.Sur.* 6 (1953), 136.

until he thought Falstaff dead did Burton's Prince reveal any friendly feeling. In
the scene of reconciliation (3.2), father and son spoke at cross-purposes and with
mutual mistrust.

Playing Falstaff to this much less responsive Prince, Quayle, said the *Times*
reviewer, 'speaks the jests with metallic precision; and his smile when it appears
is a painted smile'.[1] After he was criticised for make-up which turned him into
'a cross between an aged circus clown and a Hallowe'en turnip', Quayle subdued
his appearance. Nevertheless, spectators found him too cold and unsympathetic.
By letting audiences glimpse the evil behind his jester's mask, Quayle prepared
them early for his ultimate rejection. Redgrave's Hotspur was a simpler and far
cruder figure, who spoke his own version of a dialect he had studied in the pubs
of Northumberland. Hotspur's wife, played by Barbara Jefford, shared his rough
manners, so that their boisterous physical argument received new emphasis; it has
since been copied frequently. Quayle included all of 2.1 (Gadshill had often been cut
because of his obscure language), 4.4, and 3.1. This last 'was given in full, with long
and passionate speeches in Welsh for Glendower's daughter . . . there was no sense
of flagging'. Hugh Griffith as Glendower captured the 'dangerous, enigmatical, and
compelling personality that alone can cast the spell the scene demands'.[2]

By the time that Peter Hall and the newly named Royal Shakespeare Company
returned to the four plays thirteen years later, in 1964, the heroic temper of 1951 had
diminished. Influenced by the Theatre of the Absurd, by the Theatre of Alienation,
and probably by excitement over Bertolt Brecht's Berliner Ensemble, which had
performed in England beginning in 1956, this production of *1 Henry IV* had little
in common with its most influential predecessors: Quayle's 1951 epic or the more
tempered mingling of comedy and history in Douglas Seale's production for the
Old Vic in 1954–5.[3] In 1963 the RSC had achieved great success with *The Wars of
the Roses*, John Barton's adaptation of the three parts of *Henry VI* and *Richard III*
as a trilogy. Therefore, when audiences came to see the second tetralogy, staged in
1964, many would have been familiar with the bleak, anti-military *Wars of the Roses*,
which begin just after Henry V has died, leaving an infant ruler, Henry VI, who
will prove temperamentally incapable of controlling factions at home or of holding
on to his father's French conquests. They watched Ian Holm, who had starred in
the role of the tyrant Richard III, now portray the Prince who becomes Henry V.
Reviewers found more similarities than contrasts between the Machiavellian villain
and the model ruler. All four plays used John Bury's set which consisted of large,
movable, oppressive armoured walls to present a world of corrupt power politics.

Audiences seem to have been enthusiastic about the vision and style of these
cycles. Harold Hobson wrote, 'I doubt if anything as valuable has ever been done for
Shakespeare in the whole previous history of the world's stage.'[4] When the company
revived their productions of the second tetralogy in 1966 some critics, looking back

---

[1] John Dover Wilson and T. C. Worsley, *Shakespeare's Histories at Stratford, 1951*, 1952, p. 67.
[2] David, 'Shakespeare's history plays', 135.
[3] For an account of Seale's production, see Tynan, *A View of the English Stage*, 1975, pp. 153–4.
[4] *Sunday Times*, 19 April 1964, cited by McMillin, pp. 60–1.

over Hall's reign, praised the unified direction given to the histories as his greatest achievement.[1]

Individual performances, as opposed to company style, however, evoked mixed reactions. King Henry, strongly acted first by Eric Porter and then in 1966 by Tony Church, was an unpredictable but also obviously sick and exhausted figure. Holm, playing the Prince as another unpredictable character, was criticised for his detachment. Gareth Lloyd Evans wrote, 'He tends . . . to act from the outside of a character, and to engage in tricksiness of speech and gesture.'[2] The small Holm physically dominated much larger actors playing Falstaff (Hugh Griffith) and Hotspur (Roy Dotrice). Merciless when promising to banish Falstaff, he killed Hotspur and then dumped him into a pig trough. The most disputed performance was that of Hugh Griffith. He came to *1 Henry IV* not, with the rest of the company, from the ironic *Wars of the Roses* but from the robust comedy of the *Tom Jones* film, in which he portrayed Squire Western. Perhaps because his performance seemed reminiscent of kinder Falstaffs like Richardson's, reviewers were disoriented. He would, McMillin concludes, 'have been more at home in another production of the play'.[3]

Audiences who watched the RSC tetralogy revived for London in 1966 could also have gone to see the extraordinary rearrangement of lines and episodes from this tetralogy in Orson Welles' film, *Chimes at Midnight*. By transposition and cutting (principally Glendower and Douglas), Welles crammed into one hundred and fifteen minutes much of *Part One*, a medley of materials from *Part Two*, and brief passages from both *Richard II* and *Henry V*. In this bravura adaptation, Welles played Falstaff, recalling the tradition of actor-managers like Betterton and Beerbohm Tree. At the same time, he explored the play in the film medium with a genius that most critics were slow to appreciate.[4]

The film begins by showing two figures in the distance slowly struggling through snow towards an ancient oak tree, before it cuts to a beamed room with an immense roaring fire. The first lines heard, taken from late in *Part Two*, are those of the frail Justice Shallow, who croaks, 'Jesus, Sir John, the days that we have seen.' The rest of the film creates the effect of a flash-back remembered by Falstaff shortly before he dies. After the film credits – displayed against a background of marching troops, with lively music and a voice-over based on Holinshed ('King Richard the Second was murdered, some say at the command of Henry Bolingbroke . . .'), the film moves to Westminster where King Henry, his lines superbly spoken by John Gielgud, coldly confronts the rebels (1.3). This scene was shot in the cathedral of

---

[1] In contrast, Ronald Bryden (*New Statesman*, 24 April 1964) astutely questioned this unifying conception, emphasising both distinctions among the plays and the inadequacy of the Prince's education as a coherent organising theme.

[2] 'Shakespeare, the twentieth century and behaviourism', *S.Sur.* 20 (1967), 137.

[3] McMillin, p. 62.

[4] This film has itself become legendary, the subject of many articles and several books; we do know that major financial difficulties led to filming in Spain, that very long delays (some lasting over a year) caused many in the international cast to leave, and – reportedly – that the financier believed he was paying for a movie of *Treasure Island*.

Cardona in Spain, using a low-angle perspective that makes emphatic the elevation, distance, and rigidity of the King. In a remarkably surreal effect, only the King's breath is visible as a rising vapour.

The camera then shifts to a close-up of a pot of ale (probably suggested here by Hotspur's threat to poison the Prince), moves back to reveal the Prince drinking, and searches through several rooms, up and down stairs, for the missing Falstaff. We are in the Boar's Head tavern instead of the Prince's chamber. When the camera and the Prince find the sleeping Falstaff, Poins has already picked his pocket (2.4), which, in this film, Falstaff quickly discovers. Three tavern scenes in quick succession incorporate lines from 1.2, 2.4, and 3.3, as well as passages from *Part Two*. In contrast to the technique for the Westminster scene, the camera tracks, cuts, and wheels about in the tavern sequence, suggesting both the intricacy and festivity of the tavern world, especially when we see Falstaff chase the Prince down a twisting staircase. The escaping Prince will become more and more eager, as the film continues, to get away from Falstaff once and for all.

Through a series of staged adaptations, beginning in 1938, Welles had evolved this version with his view of Falstaff as 'the most completely good man in all drama', an interpretation that no critic found in the finished film. Yet Welles wanted Falstaff to be no more important than the Prince in the film as a whole. A melancholy and transparent figure, he conveyed an affection for the Prince which more than balanced his vices and frivolity. Welles made it clear that Falstaff, anxious about the Prince's feelings, does not foresee his rejection.

For the soliloquy, 'I know you all', the Prince stood at the tavern gate, faced both the camera and the ramparts of his father's castle, and spoke with his back towards Falstaff, who, we see, is standing on the edge of the frame. The film viewer may observe that Falstaff strains but manages to hear few words, if any. Then, on 'offend', the Prince turns and winks at Falstaff, who smiles back. Soon, after the Prince's 'I do, I will', during a long silence before the rapping on the door, the camera catches the same bemused expression on Falstaff's face. Samuel Crowl comments that for all Falstaff's 'alertness to the sham hollowness of the political rhetoric . . . the one person he does not see through is his own pupil, Hal – the most powerfully shrewd character in the play'.[1]

To escape the Sheriff, Falstaff does not hide behind an arras, but is dropped through a trap-door. This foreshadows his rejection and burial in the last two sequences. Welles edits the battle of Shrewsbury so that it illustrates Falstaff's vision of honour. Falstaff and the camera bear witness to terrible violence which lasts for ten minutes before a word is spoken. Pauline Kael considered this sequence, 'the most brutally sombre battle ever filmed'.[2] Both the Prince and Hotspur seem worn out when they begin to fight. Later, as the Prince tells Falstaff's dead body,

[1] 'The long goodbye: Welles and Falstaff', *SQ* 31 (1980), 376. For the development of Welles' version, see Robert Hapgood, '*Chimes at Midnight* from stage to screen: the art of adaptation', *S.Sur.* 39 (1987), 39–52; and, for Welles' treatment of Shakespeare's text, Jack Jorgens, *Shakespeare on Film*, 1977, pp. 106–21.
[2] *Kiss Kiss Bang Bang*, 1968, p. 202.

'I could have better spared a better man', he sees vapour rising through Falstaff's visor. Changing tone in mid-speech, he angrily taunts the corpse, 'Embowelled will I see thee by and by.' Welles altered the conclusion of *Part One* even more drastically by having Falstaff drag Hotspur into the presence of the King. He thereby trapped and humiliated the Prince, who lost both his prize and his father's regard by failing to contradict Falstaff's lie. When Falstaff follows up this victory by delivering his speech in praise of sherris-sack from *Part Two*, the Prince throws down his tankard and follows his father towards the castle.

Of special interest for the light it cast upon Elizabethan stagings outside the London theatres was the history cycle entitled *When Thou Art King*. Adapted by John Barton from the second tetralogy, and directed by Barton and Gareth Morgan for the RSC's Theatregoround, this production toured schools and community centres in 1969 and 1970. *Part One*, called *The Battle of Shrewsbury*, lasted ninety-five minutes, while *Part Two*, called *The Rejection of Falstaff*, and *Henry V*, titled *The Battle of Agincourt*, each ran about eighty minutes. The Theatregoround company could present any one segment alone without an interval, two with a single break, and on special occasions, all three with one short interval and another long enough for a meal. This company of ten actors included eight men and two women; it mingled established leading actors, veteran players of secondary roles, and young apprentices, replicating the make-up (except for the women) of Shakespeare's own somewhat larger company. Only two actors never doubled: Charles Thomas, fresh from playing Mark Antony on the company's main stage, who acted the Prince of Wales and Henry V, and Brewster Mason who played Falstaff but no part in *Henry V*. Other actors played multiple roles, notably Jeffrey Dench as King Henry IV and Gadshill (and later, Pistol and King Charles of France), and Peter Geddes who was Poins and Sir Walter Blunt (and later, the Chorus and Gower). *The Battle of Shrewsbury* included twenty-three characters (six without individual or personal names) and deleted eight: Westmoreland (with some of his lines given to Prince John and some to Blunt), Worcester, Vernon, Glendower, Mortimer, Lady Mortimer, the Archbishop, and Sir Michael.

Sets for the Theatregoround production were simple, flexible, and portable, easily set up in a variety of acting spaces. Ideas from the directors' rehearsal notes that were reprinted in the programme suggest that Barton and Morgan tried to see the action through Elizabethan eyes. The Prince is said to experience a 'Morality school': 'After contact with all kinds of humanity, Hal returns to the palace better equipped to govern himself and his people.' Both Hotspur and Falstaff are figures of 'Vanity'. To prevent Falstaff from winning audience sympathy too quickly or too thoroughly, Barton borrowed from *The Famous Victories* the Prince's conflict with the Lord Chief Justice and used it to open *The Battle of Shrewsbury*.[1]

In 1975, Terry Hands transformed the original sequence of the plays by beginning with *Henry V*. *Part One* followed several weeks later, then *Part Two*, and finally,

---

[1] These explanations come from unpublished conversations between Barton and H. Weil, who was an observer at rehearsals for this production.

before the end of the season, *The Merry Wives of Windsor*. His productions exaggerated a theatrically self-conscious style which had been given stong impetus by Peter
Brook in his *A Midsummer Night's Dream* (1970). They also created a much more
informal mood, partly a response to a much tighter budget. Spectators who arrived
early for *Henry V* saw on the stage, apparently in rehearsal clothing, twenty-five
actors who gradually put on historical costumes and became a coherent group.

Because of the re-ordering by Hands, many in the audiences came to *Part One* having recently seen, not the assassination of Richard II, but the triumphs of Henry V.
Alan Howard presented this Henry as a consummate role-player; his voice and stage
presence seemed convincingly to inspire his army. Those who had seen *Henry V*
might therefore have been particularly surprised to discover, during the first tavern
scene of *1 Henry IV*, that Howard, as the young Prince, had been genuinely afraid
of 'that fiend Douglas, that spirit Percy, and that devil Glendower' (2.4.304–5). The
'play extempore' became a device which the Prince could use to control his terror. In
the process, Richard David pointed out, Howard showed such aversion to Falstaff
that he seemed 'to freeze the whole company at the inn'.[1]

Central to both parts of *Henry IV* in Hands' cycle, was a particularly vexed
relationship of the Prince with his two 'fathers', the King and Falstaff. Emrys
James, who acted Henry IV, had previously played the Chorus in *Henry V* as
a fervent supporter of that young King. But in the role of Henry IV he became a
guilt-racked autocrat; his behaviour under stress removed any basis for a convincing
reconciliation with his son. By contrast, Brewster Mason, returning to Falstaff after
The Merry Wives of Windsor (1968) and *When Thou Art King* (1969–70), seemed
gentlemanly and restrained, a counterbalance to the sometimes hysterical monarch.
Hands intensified the Prince's father-complex by treating the centre of the play,
from the first to the second tavern scene, as one unusually long act between the
two intervals. He also drew attention to overtly theatrical techniques throughout
this cycle: characters from one scene repeatedly would watch what happened in
another, while props as well as furniture could be used by characters separated in
time and space. After his soliloquy, the Prince remained onstage at the beginning
of 1.3 to observe the quarrel between his father and Hotspur, neither of whom he
would otherwise meet for many scenes. During the reconciliation scene (3.2), father
and son could at first observe the end of the scene in Wales (3.1), then later drink
out of the same cup of sack, left from the tavern scene (2.4).

The BBC, with major support from Time–Life publishers, created for television
another cycle of histories which aimed for a 'definitive' and 'neutral' style. *1* and
2 Henry IV and *Henry V*, all directed by David Giles, appeared in 1979, the second
year of the new series, when the original producer, Cedric Messina, asserted that
the plays should be allowed to 'speak for themselves'. Like *Chimes at Midnight* in at
least this one respect, these productions were filmed without the long rehearsal
periods and the two seasons of repertory playing which so often strengthened
RSC productions. Falstaff (Anthony Quayle) and Hotspur (Tim Piggott Smith)

---

[1] *Shakespeare in the Theatre*, 1978, p. 197.

overshadowed the rest of the characters, in a throwback to the days before the staging of cycles. Returning to a role he had performed nearly thirty years before in
1951, Quayle played to the cameras with a zest which qualified his brutal stabbing of
Hotspur's corpse. But this Falstaff also owed something to cycle-thinking in that his
essential corruption seemed to have worked backwards from Quayle's conception
of *Part Two*. Because this production lacked a strong directorial theme or strategy,
specific scenes like the Council episode (1.3) and the Welsh sequence proved more
memorable than most of the film.

To launch the long-heralded RSC theatre at the Barbican in London on 7 May
1982, Trevor Nunn chose to direct *1 Henry IV*. *Part Two* followed six nights later.
Nunn introduced as a prologue a hymn and a procession of monks bearing candles.
John Napier's set, three towering wooden structures moved by hydraulic trucks,
provided 'a magnificent folly of balconies, gangways, rotting beams and rusting
armour'.[1] Robert Smallwood observed, 'It is a big set, on a very big stage, and it is
one of the great successes of the production that one never feels that the company is
failing to fill it.'[2] More direct engagement of actors with audiences was created by the
architecture of the Barbican itself, which, despite its capacity of 1,160 seats, reduced
the usual distance between auditorium and stage, and eliminated a proscenium
arch. Another of the company's successes, reviewers agreed, was their depth and
strength as a group, called by Stephen Wall their 'flair for the communal and the
collective', which had been widely acclaimed in their recent adaptation of *Nicholas
Nickleby*.[3]

To the extent that this energetic, highly physical production had any specific
emphasis, it explored new versions of father–son relationships. Both Hotspur and
the Prince were boyish, immature. The Prince clearly preferred the animated,
friendly world of Eastcheap to a severe and lonely court; Patrick Stewart played
King Henry as a priest-like figure who stepped out of the monastic procession to
emerge as an individual. This King chose to repress his affection for his son. Joss
Ackland's tough and ambitious Falstaff, on the other hand, occasionally showed the
Prince genuine warmth. During their first scene, Gerard Murphy's Prince sat on
Falstaff's knee and embraced his friend while he insulted him; another embrace
followed 'I do, I will.' Wall commented that 'As modern criticism has often dourly
insisted, it is clear that Falstaff is impossible. Ackland reminds us that he is irresistible.' Whether Murphy's Prince had the intelligence to learn anything from
Falstaff seemed less certain. One reviewer saw as the key moment in the production
the encounter between the Prince's two fathers. Just before the battle (5.1), 'Hal
finds himself poised between his two fathers, but instinctively responds to Falstaff's
cry of "Hal" as the King regretfully departs.'[4]

In 1986–7, Michael Bogdanov directed his new English Shakespeare Company
in productions of *1* and *2 Henry IV* and *Henry V* which toured Britain, Europe,

---

[1] Michael Coveney, *Financial Times*, 14 May 1982.
[2] '*Henry IV, Parts 1 and 2* at the Barbican Theatre', *CQ* 25 (1983), 15.
[3] *TLS*, 25 June 1982.
[4] *Guardian*, 11 June 1982.

6   King Henry (Patrick Stewart) steps from a procession to speak the first lines in the Royal Shakespeare Company production which opened the Barbican Theatre, London in 1982. Trevor Nunn gave
Scene 1, often presented more intimately, a ceremonial style

and North America. Bogdanov's were probably the most praised and most disputed
theatrical interpretations of these history plays during the past twenty years. Each
play was presented in a nearly full text, with *Part One* lasting almost three hours.
Eager spectators could join in a single-day marathon: *Part One* in the late morning;
Part Two after a long break for lunch; and *Henry V* in the evening after a longer break
for dinner. Then the next year, the company expanded its repertory to perform all
the plays from both tetralogies, combining the three plays of *Henry VI* into two;
it travelled to Hong Kong, Tokyo, the United States, Australia, and Europe, and
toured Britain, before playing a London season in 1989.

   To reduce what he called 'repetition' in *Part Two*, Bogdanov sacrificed some of
the more affirmative qualities in *1 Henry IV*. When the Prince first met his father
onstage in 3.2, Michael Pennington delivered his lines in the bored, insolent manner
of a truant teenager. The Prince seemed to be telling the King what he wanted to
hear – almost as if he had memorised a text composed by his father – but suggested
that he did not mean a word of it. The effect of this interpretation was to emphasise
sincerity of feeling when father and son are really reconciled, shortly before the
King's death in *Part Two*. Interestingly, when the ESC revived its productions
the following year, but performed them after the first tetralogy and *Richard II*,
Pennington played 3.2 in *Part One* without irony. Another alteration apparently

7 Two versions of the 'play extempore' in Act 2, Scene 4:
   a Alan Howard, as the Prince, playing the King in the 1975 production directed by Terry Hands
   b John Woodvine as Falstaff plays the King to Michael Pennington's Prince Hal in Michael
       Bogdanov's touring production, 1986. Both Howard and Pennington played the young Prince
       only after starring at the Royal Shakespeare Company in larger roles for older men

drew upon and simplified Orson Welles' treatment of Falstaff's lie about killing Hotspur. In Bogdanov's revision of Shakespeare and Welles, the Prince receives praise from the King for his deed, only to be interrupted by the entry of Falstaff carrying the body of Hotspur. Both the King and Prince John, neither present in the text, clearly believe Falstaff's version. They stare at the Prince in disgust and depart without a word, suggesting that, for them, the Prince's account of his combat – and implicitly, his promises to reform – are worthless. This change gives *Part One* a forceful conclusion, but the Prince's generous offer to Falstaff, 'If a lie may do thee grace', turns into an unrooted, perhaps futile gesture.

Like the RSC, the new ESC was using *1 Henry IV* and the other histories to display its range. But unlike the cycles which had focused on the education of the good ruler, Machiavellian kingship, or family psychology, Bogdanov's productions were explicitly anti-Establishment and charged with class-consciousness. Both the social consensus and the inexpensive tickets which had helped the Burrell production become so popular in 1945 were things of the past. King, court, rebels, and Sir John Falstaff all embodied the corruption and selfishness of the aristocracy. In its *Henry V*, the company outrageously parodied the chauvinistic violence of the campaign against the French. *Part One* began upon a stage littered with grubby props. A group of actors, dressed in rehearsal clothes, was singing a 'Ballad of Harry le Roy'; the Prince, in blue jeans, stepped out of this ensemble and watched the other actors prepare for the beginning of Scene 1. Although the chilly detachment of Pennington's Prince could make his presence and behaviour arresting, it was given an obnoxious twist on the battlefield. When Hotspur disarmed the Prince and chivalrously returned his sword, the Prince promptly stabbed him in the back.

Such a 'hunter', as John Peter termed him, had little to learn from John Woodvine's Falstaff, also portrayed as selfish and watchful.[1] Woodvine's outstanding performance gained part of its vitality, McMillin has argued, from a bizarre contrast between his wearing the green velvet jacket and red-checked trousers of a seedy gentleman, and the chaotic jumble of clothing styles on the other actors. 'Through it all, Woodvine's Falstaff was, of all things, a centre of stability, a classical performance visible through those outlandish costumes, a figure one could almost count on in the midst of the image-breaking around him.'[2] Both the subtlety and the accuracy of his acting were exceptional. Indeed, Woodvine's appeal so overbalanced the flaws he made no effort to hide, that when he appeared as the Chorus at the beginning of *Henry V*, slimmed down and tossing out the cushions that had filled Falstaff's baggy costumes, he regularly received a standing ovation.

At the end of its second season (1989), Bogdanov's entire seven-play cycle was filmed in the Grand Theatre, Swansea. Distributed primarily on educational television, in schools and universities, the video of *Part One* provides a faithful record of its theatrical life. Some skilful camera work in the tavern scenes, incorporating close-ups of Bardolph and Mistress Quickly shouting and banging on tables, captures

[1] *Sunday Times*, 29 March 1987.
[2] McMillin, p. 111.

the contagious skills of Barry Stanton, who replaced Woodvine for the second season. One reviewer epitomised his technique and vision: 'He keeps buffoonery at a
minimum, and doesn't even strive for wit. Like all great comics he simply describes
the world as he sees it, and is appalled.'[1] Another strong new performance was that
of Andrew Jarvis, who followed the late John Price in the role of Hotspur. Jarvis
himself had been both a flute-playing Gadshill and a fanatic Douglas during the
first ESC season. Ingeniously he turned what might have been a broad caricature
of Percy – this bowlegged Northumbrian centaur clomped across the stage – into
an engaging sketch of trust barely tainted by prevailing decadence.

In 1991, Adrian Noble directed for the RSC a production which was remarkable
for its staging and its fresh conception of characters. As in the productions of Welles,
Nunn, and Bogdanov, a carnivalesque tavern was opposed to an austere court.
The elaborate tavern set, presenting a multi-level flourishing bordello, recalled the
Barbican set of 1982. But in staging the battle, Noble emphatically distinguished this
production from its predecessors. Trucking off the massive tavern structures at the
Barbican had exposed the empty space upstage used for the battlefield. At Stratford,
to the sound of drumming with a Japanese timbre, a tableau of the battlefield was
lifted hydraulically from under the stage. Robert Smallwood's description captures
the effect of this spectacle, with the King 'in the center, a heaving mass of armored
soldiers on either side, seething and writhing in slow-motion combat around him,
the clash and cacophony of the music and the falling bits of arms and armor seeming
to catch something of the futile destructiveness of war'.[2] The swift transition from
stylised tableau to intense realism when Prince Harry fought Harry Hotspur was
extraordinary. Vertical dynamics were emphasised by other staging devices: a small
replica of the Sepulchre Church of Jerusalem, which resembled a golden crown,
and hung high above the stage, where it was flown after the King prayed to it at
the beginning of Scene 1; a very high ladder which the Prince climbed part way, in
order to speak with Falstaff on the march through Warwickshire (4.2); traffic up and
down stairs in the tavern. Playing the second tavern scene (3.3) before a front cloth,
Falstaff arrived and left through a trap; after his stabbing of Hotspur, they sank
down together through this trap while Falstaff kissed the top of Hotspur's head.

Especially rich and resonant were the performances of Robert Stephens as Falstaff
and Julian Glover as King Henry. Stephens provided an exceptional example of
casting against type. In his first season with the company, after a long career of
leading parts both onstage and in films, his only other role was Julius Caesar. After
two years of playing Falstaff, he would assume the title role in *King Lear*. Stephens'
awkward bulk and his absurd leather doublet were at odds with his cunning face
or the delicate, expressive hands which he scrutinised for evidence of decay on
'Do I not dwindle?' He managed to suggest that he delighted in the Prince's youth
and wished to gaze upon or touch it because he himself might once have been a

[1] Thomas M. Disch, *The Nation*, 25 June 1988, cited by Barbara Hodgdon, *Shakespeare in Performance: Henry IV, Part Two*, 1993, p. 134.
[2] 'Shakespeare at Stratford-upon-Avon, 1991', SQ 43 (1992), 342.

8   The tavern scene in Act 2, Scene 4 was dominated by Robert Stephens as Falstaff in Adrian Noble's
production for the Royal Shakespeare Company, 1991

charismatic charmer; his melancholy lay in his perception that few fat old men,
however companionable, are likely to be loved. '*Part One*' wrote Peter Holland,
'seemed to hinge on the search for an embrace' that Hal could not give to this
childless Falstaff, an embrace like the one which the Prince so deeply wanted from
his father and could not receive.[1]

What sort of father could have moved his son's feelings in so surprising a way?
Julian Glover's King Henry superbly complemented Stephens' imposing Falstaff, as
if one performance had heightened the other. Glover was unquestionably majestic,
a wise and authoritative ruler who made few mistakes and no uncalculated moves.
He saw through young men like Hotspur and his son whom he had to control. If the
Prince himself had been presented as a Machiavellian street-fighter or proto-Henry
V, this characterisation of the King might have been ineffective. But Michael Mal-
oney's Prince, though nimble and wholesome, was also young, confused, unformed,
and small enough to be over-shadowed by tall old men and by the vertical dimensions
of his stage environment. Even when the battle tableau lifted into the air, the Prince
was tucked in behind his father, seemingly unready to emerge on his own.

In the stage history of the past fifty years, when *Part Two* has regularly followed
Part One, we cannot always treat either as an independent work. But throughout the
preceding three hundred and fifty years of performance, *Part One*, almost without

[1] 'Shakespeare performances in England 1990–91', *S.Sur.* 45 (1993), 143.

exception, stood alone. We have seen that its reputation among audiences, scholars, and the public has made it the most admired of all Shakespeare's histories. And not the least of reasons for this acclaim is its ending. *Part Two* ends with Henry V's near-definitive rejection of Falstaff after the death of Henry IV and long after the death of Henry Percy. In the last two hundred lines of *Part One*, each major character reaches an oddly affirmative conclusion. Hotspur, who would not want life without honour, dies heroically. Each of the other three – the Prince, the King, and Falstaff – fights his own battle by vastly different rules. Who could have predicted that all three would win the day?

Recent stage, film and critical interpretations, by Katharine A. Craik

I HENRY IV AND RECENT CRITICISM

The following discussion summarises critical interpretations of *I Henry IV* since the early 1990s, and provides an account of recent high profile productions on stage and screen. The play remains as popular among readers as it does on the stage, and scholars no less than directors have approached it from a wide variety of perspectives.

NATIONHOOD

I Henry IV deals with the shift from a medieval monarchy towards a modern nation. But what did 'England' mean to Shakespeare, besides a community ruled by a common government? Given that the definition and description of the emergent nation state were urgent tasks for Renaissance thinkers, what opportunities and dilemmas did Shakespeare face as a history-teller?[1] Many readers consider the 'Henriad' to offer an epic portrait of England, for, as David Read argues, the kings in these plays achieve 'an ideal consonance with the land of England, and thus an iconic status in history'.[2] But this commonplace has been challenged in recent years by critics who have concentrated on the play's 'edginess', or preoccupation with territories on the fringes of England. In what ways did Welshness, Scottishness and Irishness contribute to a sense of English nationhood? If cultural outsiders posed a threat to English civility, why are they nevertheless associated in *I Henry IV* with the pleasures and mysteries of the strange? And in what ways does Shakespeare's depiction of nationhood dramatise the problems his own government experienced as they challenged local feudalism by attempting to unify diffuse geographical areas, languages and cultures?

The action of *Henry IV* is divided between several different physical worlds, as the above introduction makes clear. The new critical interest in Tudor cartography

---

[1] For a discussion of history as 'a matter of urgent self-interest', see Derek Cohen, 'History and the nation in *Richard II* and *Henry IV*', *Studies in English Literature*, 42.2 (2002), 293–315 (294); and Phyllis Rackin, *Stages of History: Shakespeare's English Chronicles* (1990), pp. 4–8.

[2] David Read, 'Losing the map: topographical understanding in the *Henriad*' in *Modern Philology*, 94 (1996/7), 475–95 (494–5). Alvin Kernan used the phrase 'the Henriad' to suggest the 'remarkable coherence' between the four plays of the second tetralogy. See 'The Henriad: Shakespeare's major history plays', *Yale Review*, 59 (1969), 3–32 (p. 3).

has recently shed further light on the play's 'geographical heterogeneity'.[1] As Read points out, 'notions of physical orientation in the world are crucial' in *1 Henry IV*, and not only during the stage business with the map in 3.1. Shakespeare's audience watched the play in the Globe, a theatre whose name made explicit the connection between the circular theatrical space and the larger sphere of the world outside. The famous 1592 Ditchley portrait of Elizabeth I shows the Queen standing gigantically above her kingdom with her feet planted on Oxfordshire, suggesting that territoriality was inseparable from sovereignty.[2] Shakespeare stresses the importance of material and conceptual 'landedness' at moments of dramatic crisis in *Henry IV*. Before his duel with Hotspur, for example, Hal links himself with 'one England' which cannot 'brook a double reign / Of Harry Percy and the Prince of Wales' (5.4.65–6). And when Hal reinstates the chief justice in *2 Henry IV* he describes himself as a body of land - perhaps London itself - whose 'tide of blood' (5.3.129) turns and ebbs towards the sea.[3] James E. Berg writes that both plays are indeed 'informed by impossible dreams of immediate royal control over land'. King Henry's opening speech in *1 Henry IV* fantasises that the territories of the realm have all been brought under control, but the play's final line ('Let us not leave till all our own be won') suggest that a king's rights did not inevitably include proprietary entitlement over the landscape.[4]

Shakespeare explores Englishness in *1 Henry IV* partly by considering what it means *not* to be English. The song Glendower's daughter sings to Mortimer in 3.1 suggests to Terence Hawkes the capacity of the Welsh language 'to sap the claim of English to be the transparent, fully referential transmitter of a new-minted Britishness'. Wales and Welshness are both eroticised and demonised as a narcotic force capable of damaging the 'order-giving boundaries of an English-speaking world'.[5] Christopher Highley points out that the Irish and the Welsh were conceptually linked in the early modern imagination, and concentrates on the play's parallels with contemporary Irish affairs. The first performances of the play coincided with the imminent collapse of English rule in Ireland and the escalation of Irish resistance, and Highley argues that Falstaff's rabble army invites comparison with Elizabeth's wretched, malnourished band of conscripts.[6] Shakespeare may have based his portrait of Owen Glendower on Hugh O'Neill, Earl of Tyrone, who initially helped secure Irish co-operation with the English colonialists but later fostered resistance and was declared a traitor. If Shakespeare had in mind Tyrone's Irish insurrection

---

[1] See above, pp. 14–15. The quotation is from Jean E. Howard and Phyllis Rackin, *Engendering a Nation: A Feminist Account of Shakespeare's English Histories* (1997), p. 161

[2] Read, 'Losing the map', 475 and 493.

[3] Read, 'Losing the map', 481, 480, 483 and 482.

[4] James E. Berg, 'This dear, dear land: "dearth" and the fantasy of the land-grab in *Richard II* and *Henry IV*', *English Literary Renaissance*, 29.2 (1999), 225–45 (229).

[5] Terence Hawkes, 'Bryn Glas' in Ania Loomba and Martin Orkin, eds., *Post-Colonial Shakespeares* (1998), 117–40 (127 and 124). Michael Cronin relates this scene to contemporary Anglo-Irish politics in 'Rug-headed kerns speaking tongues: Shakespeare, translation and the Irish language' in Mark Thornton Burnett and Ramona Wray, *Shakespeare and Ireland: History, Politics, Culture* (1997), pp. 193–212 (201).

[6] Christopher Highley, 'Wales, Ireland, and *1 Henry IV*', *Renaissance Drama*, n.s. 21 (1990), 91–114 (93).

when he was dramatising Glendower's part in the Percy rebellion, then '*Henry IV Part One* constitutes an intervention in the discursive field of Anglo-Irish relations'.[1]

HISTORY

Although Shakespeare is undoubtedly the best-known Renaissance historiographer, recent criticism has contextualised his plays alongside the works of Tudor chroniclers such as Polydore Vergil, Edward Hall and Raphael Holinshed as well as contemporary historical dramatists such as Christopher Marlowe and George Chapman.[2] Shakespeare was one historian among many, then, but critics agree that he was uniquely self-conscious about the complex project of history-telling. According to Michael Hattaway, Shakespeare's plays can be described as 'historiographical metafictions' which reflect upon a variety of historical processes and contain characters who behave as though they know they are acting in a drama about the past.[3] Part of Shakespeare's self-consciousness about historiography is realised through his innovative use of the genre of the history play. Studying the past was a newly pressing imperative in the transitional moment of the play's composition, and the scenes set at court and on the battlefield, 'where historically based characters quarrel in blank verse and play out the scripts written by Tudor historiography', clearly demonstrate a debt to chronicle history.[4] But Paul Dean takes issue with the critically orthodox position (derived originally from E. M. W. Tillyard's work in the 1940s) that Shakespeare was influenced only by the chronicles, pointing out the popularity of two-part plays in the late Elizabethan and early Jacobean theatre. Whereas earlier critics emphasised the debt of the *Henry IV* plays to both chronicle and comedy, Dean argues that the two-part structure enabled Shakespeare 'to explore, through juxtaposition, the boundaries between chronicle and romance as modes of historical perception'.[5]

Phyllis Rackin has explored the play's historicity from a different perspective, suggesting that Eastcheap reveals a 'stagy atemporal world' which parallels the scenes set at court. Falstaff's very first question to the prince, 'Now Hal, what

[1] Highley, 'Wales, Ireland, and *1 Henry IV* ', 98. Andrew Hadfield also discusses the link between *1 Henry IV* and Tyrone in '"Hitherto she ne're could fancy him": Shakespeare's 'British' plays and the exclusion of Ireland' in Burnett and Wray, eds., *Shakespeare and Ireland*, pp. 47–67 (p. 60).

[2] For a survey of contemporary historical drama, and Tudor chronicle history, see A. J. Hoenselaars, 'Shakespeare and the early modern history play' and Dominique Goy-Blanquet, 'Elizabethan historiography and Shakespeare's sources', both in Michael Hattaway, ed., *The Cambridge Companion to Shakespeare's Histories* (2002), pp. 25–40 and 57–70. Gilian West has recently argued that John Hardyng's *Chronicle* was an important source for *1 Henry IV*. See 'Hardyng's *Chronicle* and Shakespeare's Hotspur', *Shakespeare Quarterly*, 41 (1990), 348–51.

[3] Michael Hattaway quotes from Linda Hutcheon's 'classic definition' of the postmodern novel in 'The Shakespearean history play' in Hattaway, ed., *The Cambridge Companion to Shakespeare's Histories*, pp. 3–24 (p. 19). Hutcheon's definition is found in *A Poetics of Postmodernism: History, Theory, Fiction* (1988), p. 5. On Shakespeare's awareness of history's 'fraught process', see also Derek Cohen, 'History and the nation', 295.

[4] Rackin, *Stages of History*, p. 138. On Shakespeare's debt to chronicle history, see also above, pp. 21–5, and p. 71, n.4 below.

[5] Paul Dean, 'Forms of time: some Elizabethan two-part history plays', *Renaissance Studies*, 4.4 (1990), 410–30 (410). On the debt of *1 Henry IV* to popular comedy, see above pp. 26–7.

time of day is it, lad?' (1.2.1), suggests that the scenes set in the tavern take place outside of time, an impression bolstered by their ubiquitous anachronisms. In placing these two temporal realms side by side, Rackin argues, Shakespeare highlights the theatrical process of history-making. 'The historical world never takes on the illusion of full presence. The double plot in the *Henry IV* plays, in fact, can be seen as a kind of allegory of mediation, representing in dramatic structure the split between the historical past that is represented and the theatrical mediation required to make it present'. It is a delicate illusion which the 'opportunistic, self-willed, and dangerously charming' Falstaff continually threatens to overturn.[1]

POLITICS AND KINGSHIP

According to another important early modern historian, Sir Walter Ralegh, history can reflect critically on the present 'and tax the vices of those that are yet living, in their persons that are long since dead'. Such is its power to expose error, vice and corruption, indeed, that Ralegh – perhaps remembering the example of Sir John Hayward – famously advised the historian not to follow truth too near the heels for fear of having his teeth struck out.[2] Much recent criticism explores Shakespeare's engagement, through history, with topical concerns of his day. Was Shakespeare writing about contemporary problems such as the role of the Tudor monarchy in a centralised government, and did he have in mind events such as the Northern Rising of 1569? If Hal has to earn legitimacy rather than being born into it, does his situation reflect that of the new gentry of Elizabethan England? Does the play's interest in 'material goods and economic practices' engage with concerns raised by the early modern marketplace?[3] If aggression is central to the play's exploration of honour, can the play be seen to offer insight into the 'culture of violence in which Shakespeare came to maturity'?[4]

The question of theatre's role in early modern society has preoccupied many critics, especially since the publication in 1988 of Stephen Greenblatt's essay 'Invisible Bullets'. Using *Henry IV* and *Henry V* as case-studies, Greenblatt argued that early modern society permitted various threats to the established order when it condoned the liberality and experimentation associated with theatrical representation. Such threats were however always carefully managed: 'theatricality then is not set over against power but is one of power's essential modes'.[5] More recently, Greenblatt's theory has been vigorously contested by Tom McAlindon, who objects to the 'cult

---

[1] Rackin, *Stages of History*, pp. 138, 139 and 238.

[2] Goy-Blanquet quotes here from Ralegh's *The History of the World* (1614) in 'Elizabethan historiography and Shakespeare's sources', p. 61. On the imprisonment of the historian Sir John Hayward, see above p. 22.

[3] The quotation is found in Nina Levine's essay on early modern economics, 'Extending credit in the *Henry IV* plays', *Shakespeare Quarterly*, 51 (2000), 403–31 (404). James C. Bulman compares Hal to Elizabethan new-made gentry in 'Henry IV Parts 1 and 2' in Hattaway, ed., *The Cambridge Companion to Shakespeare's Histories*, pp. 158–76 (p. 165).

[4] This is R. A. Foakes's phrase, from *Shakespeare and Violence* (2003), p. 9.

[5] Stephen Greenblatt, *Shakespearean Negotiations: The Circulation of Social Energy in Renaissance England* (1988), p. 46.

status' of 'Invisible Bullets' and the degree of influence it has exerted over subsequent responses to the plays - and, indeed, the interpretation of Elizabethan theatre more generally. McAlindon suggests that Greenblatt employs selective analogy and rhetoric (rather than logic) to make persuasive the idea that Shakespeare led his audience 'through subversive thoughts to a positive acceptance of the dominant order'.[1] Since *1 Henry IV* presents a 'fiercely negative' view of monarchical authority, it seems unlikely that Shakespeare's intent was 'to beguile the audience into enthusiastic acceptance' of the status quo. McAlindon criticises Greenblatt's selective use of Renaissance 'witnesses' to support his argument, especially his ascribing to Machiavelli the notion that the origins of religion lie in forms of social coercion which depend on deceit. Whereas Greenblatt regarded Hal as the perfect expression of Machiavellianism, McAlindon sees the prince inviting us 'to match his words against his deeds, actively repudiating the Machiavellian ethic'.[2]

In *Shakespeare After Theory*, David Scott Kastan begins with the familiar assumption that 'the production of power' is a central concern of *1 Henry IV*. Unlike Greenblatt, however, Kastan argues that the popular, subversive, Falstaffian elements of the play cannot be readily contained. The title page of the 1598 quarto highlights 'the humorous conceits of Sir John Falstaff' alongside 'the battell at Shrewsburie', and readers should not assume (as Hal does) 'that the tavern world exists only for the production of aristocratic pleasure and value'. The play indeed works by countering such 'totalizing fantasies of power', and by disrupting the hierarchies upon which they depend. Kastan links Shakespeare's achievement in this regard to the increasing inclusivity of the public theatres which now admitted all classes of the population together without discrimination.[3]

Whereas critics such as Kastan (and Rackin) argue that Shakespeare's vision of history was remarkable for its inclusivity, Richard Helgerson proposes on the contrary that 'Shakespeare's history plays are concerned above all with the consolidation and maintenance of royal power'. The theatres may have been patronised by every level of society, but it would be a mistake to neglect the efforts Shakespeare and his company took 'to exclude and to alienate the popular, the socially marginal, the subversive, and the folk'.[4] According to Helgerson, *1 Henry IV* finally insists on the subordination of 'subplot to main plot, commoners to aristocrats, comedy to history'. Shakespeare may be participating in popular culture by rehearsing popular festive customs, but by staging the impossibility of 'comical' (or popular) history through Hal's eventual rejection of Falstaff, he is staging 'the exclusion of the common people both from the English nation and from what would come to be recognised as the canonical literature of that nation'.[5] Hal's banishment of Falstaff in *2 Henry IV*

---

[1] Tom McAlindon, 'Testing the new historicism: "Invisible bullets" reconsidered', *Studies in Philology*, 92 (1995), 411–38 (411 and 412).

[2] McAlindon, 'Testing the new historicism', 424, 423 and 429.

[3] David Scott Kastan, *Shakespeare After Theory* (1999), pp. 129 and 133.

[4] Richard Helgerson, *Forms of Nationhood: The Elizabethan Writing of England* (1994), pp. 234 and 245.

[5] Helgerson, *Forms of Nationhood*, pp. 227 and 233.

is also central to Laurie Shannon's exploration of friendship and sovereign author-ity in both plays. Hal's association with Falstaff is an example of *mignonnerie*, or improper friendship between men of different social rank, which appears to threaten his becoming a proper king. But this threat (as Hal knows) is a false one, for friend-ship involves 'a special power of self-disposition and expression that only the private person can exercise.' Shakespeare was sketching an idea of authority free from 'affec-tive aberrations', Shannon argues, in which both sovereigns and subjects are defined through protocols of friendship.[1]

Several recent critics have understood *1 Henry IV* as a commentary on one par-ticular political concern of the 1590s: the succession crisis which emerged as it became clear that Elizabeth I was going to die without producing an heir, thus end-ing the line of Henry VIII. Who then was the legitimate successor to the throne? Howard Erskine-Hill attends to the question of sovereign legitimacy and explores the hypothesis that the rebels (Worcester, Northumberland, Hotspur) had a legit-imate cause. Querying the very idea that the play stages a rebellion, Erskine-Hill suggests the rebels are more accurately described as 'legitimists'.[2] The play may therefore be seen to offer a highly topical reflection on the problem of succession. Richard Dutton also regards the play as a commentary on royal legitimacy, explor-ing the historical significance of the duchy of Lancaster. He concludes that the duchy functioned as 'an inescapable reminder that the monarchy after Richard II was compromised . . . the duchy, with its constitutional separation from the crown, is a permanent expression of the expulsion from Eden, the careful expedient of a monarch with a less-than-perfect claim to the throne'.[3]

The business of politics extends beyond the monarchy, of course, but Shake-speare's sources, including Holinshed, had tended to marginalise the voices of com-moners in the telling of history. Critics have concentrated on whether Shakespeare tried to redress the balance in *Henry IV* by incorporating the voices of tapsters, vintners, carriers, travellers and servants. Does Hal have the 'common touch', and what is the relationship between the play's 'low' characters and its tendency to extend in generic terms towards comedy? *1 Henry IV* is indeed remarkable for 'the social heterogeneity of the characters' and for its 'mixing of the momentous and the mundane'.[4] When Falstaff remarks 'You may buy land now as cheap as stinking mackerel' (2.4.296–7), for example, his idiom reflects everyday life and offers a real-istic portrait of the city alongside the play's high politics.[5] Remembering Henry's remark about 'moody beggars starving for a time / Of pell-mell havoc and confusion' (5.1.81–2), Charles Whitney suggests that Shakespeare had in mind the crisis of 1596

---

[1] Laurie Shannon, *Sovereign Amity: Figures of Friendship in Shakespearean Contexts* (2002), pp. 159 and 184.

[2] Howard Erskine-Hill, *Poetry and the Realm of Politics: Shakespeare to Dryden* (1996), p. 80.

[3] Richard Dutton, 'Shakespeare and Lancaster', *Shakespeare Quarterly*, 49 (1998), 1–21 (10).

[4] These quotations are found in Howard and Rackin, *Engendering a Nation*, p. 160; and Michael Billing-ton's review essay on the National Theatre productions of *1 Henry IV* and *2 Henry IV*, 'Crown and country', the *Guardian*, Review, 30 April 2005, p. 19.

[5] Erskine-Hill discusses the play's juxtaposition of high political affairs alongside a 'relatively realistic portrayal of national life' in *Poetry and the Realm of Politics*, p. 79.

when vagrancy, famine, unrest and insurrection were sparked by a rapid increase in food prices. Like Highley, Whitney argues that Falstaff's rounding-up of recruits in 4.2 recalls the unprecedented levels of military recruitment the same year to satisfy the need for soldiers for the Irish, Netherlands, Calais and Cadiz campaigns. The destitute were often used to swell the ranks.[1] An important aspect of the play's politics therefore resides in Shakespeare's simultaneous exploration of 'high' and 'low' culture. This mixing of popular and aristocratic preoccupations has broader implications, too, for the play raises the problem - explored at great length in *Richard II* - that 'popularity may successfully overcome hereditary right'.[2]

FALSTAFF

Responses to *1 Henry IV* were dominated in the 1980s by 'new historicist' readings which sought to recover the political, constitutional and cultural contexts of both Shakespeare's England and the medieval landscapes he evoked. Falstaff's fortunes in contemporary criticism have been mixed, perhaps because the imperative to 'always historicise' sits uneasily with the notion, first formulated in the eighteenth century, that his character reveals the timeless 'principles of human nature itself'.[3] It is perhaps for this reason that 'we now tend not to believe in Character in general, or in Falstaff in particular'.[4] One of the objections levelled against new historicism, however, is its tendency to privilege 'all-encompassing systems of power' over the more intimate history of the subject.[5] Barbara Everett offered a challenge to historicist analysis when she quoted in her 1991 essay (mentioned above) from the autobiography of Shakespearean actor Simon Callow who argues that 'there is nothing in a play *but* the characters'.[6] The enduring fascination with Falstaff's 'unfettered subjectivity' indeed suggests that questions about Shakespearean character - and related questions about interiority, motive and morality - are still far from resolved. As Hugh Grady argues, Falstaff has 'become a classic successively of high bourgeois, Modernist, and postmodernist cultures', his 'libido-infused, pleasure-oriented' gregariousness now obliging us to re-examine our recent assumptions about early modern selfhood – especially the belief that Renaissance subjectivity always involved painful self-scrutiny.[7]

To those 'joyless scholars' whom Falstaff has failed to captivate, Harold Bloom offered the following dark warning in 1999: 'You define who you are by your reaction

[1] Charles Whitney, 'Festivity and topicality in the Coventry scene of *1 Henry IV*', *English Literary Renaissance*, 24 (1994), 410–48 (418–19).
[2] Erskine-Hill, *Poetry and the Realm of Politics*, p. 84.
[3] Maurice Morgann, 'An essay on the dramatic character of Sir John Falstaff' (1777), repr. in G. K. Hunter, ed., *King Henry IV Parts 1 & 2: A Casebook* (1970), pp. 25–55 (p. 55). Morgann's essay is discussed above, pp. 38–9.
[4] Barbara Everett, 'The fatness of Falstaff: Shakespeare and character', *Proceedings of the British Academy*, 76 (1991), 109–128 (110). See also above, p. 33.
[5] Hugh Grady, 'Falstaff: subjectivity between the carnival and the aesthetic', *Modern Language Review*, 96 (2001), 609–23 (609).
[6] Everett, 'The fatness of Falstaff', 124.
[7] Grady, 'Falstaff', 612 and 620.

to Falstaff.' Drawing from Hegel's assertion that Shakespeare made his best characters 'free artists of themselves', and from Hazlitt's celebratory account of Falstaff, Bloom sketches a close relationship between Shakespeare and his best-loved character in *Shakespeare: The Invention of the Human*.[1] Falstaff's linguistic resourcefulness suggests to Bloom his enduring (Shakespearean) faith in language: 'Falstaff *is* Shakespeare's wit at its very limits.' Much is at stake here, for the Falstaffian spirit has the power to sustain civilization and resist any attempt to impose conformity or stifle creativity. Bloom celebrates the freedom and 'authentic vitalism' offered by this most irreducible of Shakespeare's characters by renaming *1 Henry IV* and *2 Henry IV* 'the Falstaffiad'.[2] This impassioned return to character raised some equally passionate objections, however, from readers determined to resist the return of Shakespearean scholarship to 'outmoded Romantic bardolatry' which merely reproduces 'the very notions of Romantic transcendental subjectivity that have been so effectively dismantled in recent years'.[3]

Other critics have tackled the problem of Falstaff's character from different angles. As the introduction to the present volume makes clear, scholars have long recognised that Shakespeare originally called Falstaff 'Sir John Oldcastle' in a 1596 performance text of *1 Henry IV* which has not survived. The original Oldcastle was the Lollard leader Lord Cobham, martyred for his Protestant beliefs during reign of Henry V.[4] The decision of the 1986 Oxford editors of Shakespeare's *Works* to revert to 'Oldcastle' sparked renewed interest in this debate, and several critics have since suggested that Shakespeare's original use of the name may have been intended as a puritan satire.[5] Richard Helgerson argues in *Forms of Nationhood* (1991) that Falstaff's language is 'replete with the telltale phrases of Puritan spirituality' which suggest Shakespeare's intention to pillory the adulatory version of the Oldcastle story offered by Protestant historiographers such as John Foxe and John Bale.[6] David Scott Kastan concurs that Shakespeare was mocking the radical forms of Puritanism associated with Lollardy. Taking issue with Gary Taylor's argument in the Oxford *Works* that Shakespeare's satire confirms his leanings towards Catholicism, Kastan proposes on the contrary that lampooning a Lollard martyr

---

[1] Harold Bloom, *Shakespeare: The Invention of the Human* (1999), pp. 306, 288 and 271. On Hazlitt and the romantic tradition of scholarship, see above pp. 39–40.

[2] Bloom, *Shakespeare*, pp. 273, 314 and 276.

[3] Grady, 'Falstaff', p. 609. David Womersley also objects to the 'romantic' idea of Falstaff representing Shakespeare's creative genius in 'Why is Falstaff fat?', *Review of English Studies*, 47 (1996), 1–22 (p. 1).

[4] See above, pp. 5–6 and 29. For a summary of Cobham's life and martyrdom, see Kristen Poole's *Radical Religion: From Shakespeare to Milton. Figures of Nonconformity in Early Modern England* (2000), pp. 16–18.

[5] Gary Taylor's 1985 essay 'The fortunes of Oldcastle' in *Shakespeare* Survey, 38 (1985) argued for the importance of restoring the name 'Oldcastle' in editions of *1 Henry IV*. The essay is discussed by Jonathan Goldberg in 'The commodity of names: "Falstaff" and "Oldcastle" in *1 Henry IV*' in Jonathan Crewe, ed., *Reconfiguring the Renaissance: Essays in Critical Materialism* (1992), pp. 76–88 (p. 77). Goldberg argues that Taylor's banishment of 'plump Jack' echoed Hal's: 'What Taylor proposes is not restoration but censorship of the texts we have' (p. 82).

[6] Helgerson, *Forms of Nationhood*, p. 249. Tom McAlindon agrees that Shakespeare was writing a 'deliberate and audacious caricature of a Protestant hero'. See 'Perfect answers: religious inquisition, Falstaffian wit', *Sh.S. 54* (2001), 100–107 (100).

was an act of religious orthodoxy at a time when Protestant nonconformity was being vigorously suppressed. Rather than assuming that Shakespeare was reluctantly obliged by an act of censorship to remove Oldcastle's name, Kastan suggests instead that the name change was the result of 'complex social and theatrical activity in which authorship was only one determinant'.[1] Kristen Poole traces Oldcastle's appearances in works by Shakespeare's contemporaries including Michael Drayton, Anthony Munday and John Weever. Whereas these writers attempt to 'restore Falstaff's righteous Lollard origins', Shakespeare's Oldcastle appears as a Lord of Misrule. Falstaff 'in all of his sack-swilling glory both catalyzed and epitomized the early modern representation of the stage puritan' as a grotesque, carnal figure, and *1 Henry IV* therefore sheds light on the controversy raised in the late 1580s by the illicit, anti-episcopal tracts of the pseudonymous 'Martin Marprelate'. Although the play was staged for the first time six or seven years after the Marprelate tracts died out, Shakespeare followed the anti-Martinist pattern for voicing religious dissent through grotesque comic prose: 'Falstaff thus plays the role of satirist even as he is the object of satire.'[2]

The grotesque aspects of Falstaff's character have indeed attracted the attention of many scholars whose work builds on earlier studies by C. L. Barber and J. Dover Wilson.[3] François Laroque argues that whether or not Shakespeare was familiar with the work of François Rabelais, 'by creating a character like Falstaff, Shakespeare comes as close as he possibly could to Rabelais's particular style of comedy' which centres on the body – especially the belly – and celebrates life through carnival. If Hal's eventual banishment of the fat knight in *2 Henry IV* is a *carne vale*, or 'farewell to the flesh', Falstaff's bulk nevertheless ultimately stands for the triumph of life over death, fatness over leanness, and festivity over Lent.[4] David Ruiter suggests that Hal gains popular support by developing an idea of 'kinship-through-shared-festivity' in which Falstaff plays 'the role of the main course, the fatted calf, in the holiday feast'.[5] It is for this reason that Falstaff is described in Act 2 as a 'damned brawn' (2.4.95), (a fatted pig ready for roasting) and a 'roasted Manningtree ox with the pudding in its belly' (2.4.374–5) (a whole roasted ox stuffed with sausages, served on festival occasions). It is in Hal's interests to keep Falstaff uncorrected and unfettered, Ruiter argues, for the metaphorical feast he represents unites the community behind the crown. Falstaff's fatness was however not the invention of

[1] Kastan, *Shakespeare After Theory*, pp. 93–106 (p. 102).

[2] Poole, *Radical Religion*, pp. 20, 21 and 39.

[3] Previous studies of Falstaffian grotesque are found in J. Dover Wilson, *The Fortunes of Falstaff* (1944); C. L. Barber, *Shakespeare's Festive Comedy: A Study of Dramatic Form and its Relation to Social Custom* (1963); and Neil Rhodes, *Elizabethan Grotesque* (1980). See also above, pp. 34–6.

[4] François Laroque, 'Shakespeare's 'battle of carnival and lent': The Falstaff scenes reconsidered (*1 & 2 Henry IV*)' in Ronald Knowles, ed., *Shakespeare and Carnival: After Bakhtin* (1998), pp. 83–96 (pp. 83 and 94). Cathleen T. McLoughlin provides 'an intertextual reading of Shakespeare's *Henry IV Part One* and *Two* with François Rabelais's *Gargantua and Pantagruel*' in *Shakespeare, Rabelais, and the Comical-Historical* (2000), p. 1.

[5] David Ruiter, *Shakespeare's Festive History: Feasting, Festivity, Fasting and Lent in the Second Henriad* (2003), pp. 69 and 73.

Shakespeare. David Womersley has recently traced its origins to a bitter religious altercation in which Foxe defended Oldcastle against the accusation of Nicholas Harpsfield, a Catholic theologian, that he was 'some grandpanch Epicure of this world'.[1]

WOMEN AND MEN

Shakespeare's histories have traditionally been regarded as plays about men, and the relationship of feminist critics to them has until recently been one of 'not-so-benign neglect'.[2] There are no women at Henry's court; only the rebel leaders (Hotspur and Mortimer) have wives; and the play contains just two brief references to Henry's queen in the form of jokes in the tavern at Eastcheap. When women appear on the battlefield in 1.1, they do so as Welsh intruders who mutilate the corpses of the English fallen, an act that 'may not be / Without much shame retold or spoken of' (1.1.45–6).[3] The play's marginalisation of women is perhaps inevitable, for, as Rackin points out, 'the restrictions that excluded women from the profession of acting collaborated with the exclusions of patriarchal history to marginalize the roles of female characters in Shakespeare's representations of the English past'.[4] Recent work has however established the crucial roles played by women – and the absence of women – in *1 Henry IV*. Valerie Traub argues that women are not simply excluded from Shakespeare's retelling of history, but that their exclusion is explicitly staged. Shakespeare therefore highlights society's constant repression of women, and the necessity of this repression for maintaining the status quo. Considering *1 Henry IV* in psycho-dramatic terms, Traub concentrates on Hal's relationship with Falstaff. Unlike many critics who regard Falstaff as the father substitute whom Hal must reject in order to assume the crown, Traub argues that he functions in the play as 'a projected fantasy of the pre-Oedipal maternal' against whom Hal finally differentiates himself.[5] Like W. H. Auden, Traub argues that Falstaff's swollen, bulging, porous body, 'gross as a mountain, open, palpable' (2.4.189–90), resembles a grotesque maternal one, and when he is metaphorically killed in *2 Henry IV* his

[1] Womersley, 'Why is Falstaff fat?', 3.
[2] The phrase is Valerie Traub's in *Desire and Anxiety: Circulations of Sexuality in Shakespearean Drama* (1992), p. 52.
[3] These points are made in Howard and Rackin, *Engendering a Nation*, pp. 45 and 163; and Barbara Hodgdon, *The End Crowns All: Closure and Contradiction in Shakespeare's History* (1991), p. 155.
[4] Rackin, *Stages of History*, p. 205. Rackin's view of chronicle history as emphatically patriarchal has more recently been qualified by Annabel Patterson, who argues that the world displayed in the chronicles 'was by no means simply or unproblematically "patriarchal" to the chroniclers themselves, whatever the dominant ideology of male superiority or social and legal structures might dictate'. See *Reading Holinshed's Chronicles* (1994), pp. 215–33 (p. 215).
[5] Traub, *Desire and Anxiety*, p. 55; see also above, p. 33, n. 4. Traub also discusses Falstaff's lament in *2 Henry IV*: 'My womb, my womb, my womb undoes me' (4.3.22), p. 57. On the masculinity of Falstaff (or 'false-staff') more generally, see Hodgdon, *The End Crowns All*, p. 160. Jonathan Goldberg argues on the other hand that critics have called him a woman 'in order not to have to think about his sexual relations with men'. *Sodometries: Renaissance Texts, Modern Sexualities* (1992), p. 173.

'death' stands for the rejection of a threat to adult heterosexuality – a rejection which is necessary for Hal's eventual emergence as a military hero in *Henry V*.[1]

Women may be excluded from the English court in *1 Henry IV*, but they play prominent roles in the scenes set in Wales and in the tavern at Eastcheap. Rackin and Jean E. Howard argue that the Welsh scenes represent 'the dangerous allure of a world that is both feminine and effeminating' in which Glendower's daughter 'embodies a dangerous sexuality that disables the man who succumbs to its temptation'. The Boar's Head presents a parallel, feminised world peopled by women who are 'theatregoers, entrepreneurs, and purveyors of commercial sex'.[2] Rackin and Howard argue that both locations are seductive 'domains of idleness and play' which call to mind the Elizabethan playhouse. Antitheatrical polemics of the late sixteenth century warned that the liberty and experimentation associated with the theatre was liable to corrupt audiences by inciting dangerous feelings of lust and discontent. In Rackin's account, the feminine worlds of Eastcheap and Wales pose a threat not only to English masculinity, however, but also to 'the discourse of patriarchal history' itself. Their intense theatricality impedes, parodies and interrupts historical narrative, replacing it with digressive dramatic enactment.[3] Jonathan Goldberg has taken issue with Rackin's pitting of history against theatrical representation, and with the argument that women are excluded from the play's history-telling. He argues on the contrary that *1 Henry IV*, especially 3.1, 'depicts the invidious terms upon which women may be included in the production of the sovereign male subject' – as well as the difficulty of finding such women. He stops short of calling Shakespeare a protofeminist but argues that responses to the play should do more than simply 'tell one more time the story of women's exclusion from culture'.[4]

The play's interest in masculinity is realised partly through Shakespeare's treatment of the psychology of kingship. After the Second World War, critics tended to follow J. Dover Wilson's account of Hal's heroic masculinity in *The Fortunes of Falstaff* (1943), reading *1 Henry IV* as a morality play centring on Hal's embodiment of English virtue. Although some critics still propose that the play stages 'the development of Hal as an ideal proto-Protestant hero', Goldberg's psychoanalytical reading of the play points out the shortcomings of unthinking critical attachment to 'Hal as the nation, as the mature individual, as the dazzling fabricator, English essence'.[5] To Goldberg, 'Hal's sovereignty reflects a sovereign subject; between him and his admiring critic there is a trajectory of desired identification'. William Empson pointed out in *Some Versions of Pastoral* (1935) that Hal resembles the fair young man addressed in Shakespeare's *Sonnets*, not least in his desirability and in his habit of taking on 'low' friends in order to abandon them. Recent critics who celebrate

---

[1] Auden's remarks on Falstaff are summarised above on p. 40.
[2] Howard and Rackin, *Engendering a Nation*, pp. 172, 170 and 164.
[3] Howard and Rackin, *Engendering a Nation*, pp. 164 and 174.
[4] Goldberg, *Sodometries*, p. 164.
[5] Goldberg, *Sodometries*, p. 145. The earlier quotation appears in Michael Davies, 'Falstaff's lateness: Calvinism and the Protestant hero in *Henry IV*', *Review of English Studies*, n.s. 56 (2005), 351–78 (353).

Hal's maturity and heroism therefore demonstrate 'a misogynist heterosexuality', for an attachment to Hal 'goes hand in hand with the patriarchal effacement of women'.[1]

RECENT STAGE AND FILM PRODUCTIONS

Michael Attenborough's *1 Henry IV* opened at the Swan in Stratford-upon-Avon in April 2000, followed by *2 Henry IV* in June, and moved to London's Barbican Theatre in 2001. Attenborough's production was part of the RSC's millennium project, 'This England', which staged all the plays in the first and second Lancastrian tetralogies. For the first time in the history of British theatre all eight plays were performed together, making it possible to see the entire sequence in less than a week.[2] The project involved two companies (one for each of the tetralogies) and a total of around 100 actors, attracting vast sponsorship. Its success suggests the continuing importance of the history plays at moments of national self-definition, and the millennium indeed brought a resurgence of interest in history, sparking other initiatives such as Simon Schama's BBC television series *A History of Britain* (2000). 'This England' was completed shortly before Project Fleet, the 2001 reorganisation of the RSC, which increased the number of independent productions and introduced shorter contracts for actors. Since these changes made further projects on the scale of 'This England' unfeasible, audiences in the near future are less likely to encounter the *Henry IV* plays as part of a full history cycle.[3]

The second tetralogy opened at Stratford's The Other Place with Steven Pimlott's modern dress *Richard II* where the set resembled a 'brutal white antechamber' shining an unforgiving fluorescent lighting on both audience and actors.[4] By contrast Attenborough's *1 Henry IV* was regarded by many as 'unashamedly old-fashioned'.[5] Es Devlin's set design represented England as bare and smoking, as though the ground were covered in cinder and glowing ashes, 'civil war seeming to burn the very land itself'. The costumes were more or less medieval, 'in a range of hues that suggested the autumnal'.[6] David Troughton's Henry IV opened the production crouched in front of his throne 'in a monkish robe, on his knees and penitentially clutching a great wooden crucifix', receiving news of the fortunes of war with 'a mix of defiance, desperation for reassurance, bitterness at his son, yearning for

---

[1] Goldberg, *Sodometries*, pp. 147 and 148.
[2] Robert Smallwood, *Players of Shakespeare 6: Essays in the Performance of Shakespeare's History Plays* (2004), p. ix. In 1988 the English Shakespeare Company had performed all of the plays in the second tetralogy within a single season, but combined the three parts of *Henry VI* into two. See above, pp. 47 and 56–60.
[3] The Chicago Shakespeare Theatre's 1999 production of *1 Henry IV*, for example, which later formed part of the RSC's Complete Works festival (Stratford, 2005/6), was not performed alongside the other plays of the second tetralogy.
[4] This phrase is Michael Coveney's, from his review of *1 Henry IV* in *The Daily Mail*, 21 April 2000.
[5] See for example Charles Spencer's review, 'Delicate debauchery', in *The Daily Telegraph*, 21 April 2000.
[6] These two quotations are found in Smallwood, *Players of Shakespeare*, p. 7.

9 Henry IV (David Troughton) battles with crown and conscience in Michael Attenborough's 2000 Royal Shakespeare Company production of *1 Henry IV* at the Swan Theatre, Stratford-upon-Avon.

tranquillity, remorse, exhaustion and near-despair'.[1] After comparing the warlike Hotspur to his own riotous son, Troughton bent dejectedly over the throne: 'But let him from my thoughts' (1.1.90).

Attenborough's production made *1 Henry IV* above all the story of a father and a son – and the failed relationship between them. Troughton later pointed out that Henry never mentions Falstaff by name, and suggested that this 'inability to speak of Falstaff is part of his failure as a father'.[2] Attenborough pointedly left them together on stage for a few moments between the play's first two scenes.

---

[1] Smallwood, *Players of Shakespeare*, p. 7; and Benedict Nightingale's review, 'Henry IV Part I', *The Times*, 21 April 2000.
[2] David Troughton, 'Bolingbroke in *Richard II*, and King Henry IV' in Smallwood, ed., *Players of Shakespeare*, p. 110.

Here Falstaff (Desmond Barrit) made his first entrance, 'struggling, old-mole-like' out of the earth through a rubber flange in the floor, then keeling over and landing spread-eagled while Henry lingered above in the council chamber.[1] William Houston's Hal appeared a few moments later, crawling bleary-eyed from beneath his father's empty throne into a freshly lit space which contrasted starkly to the dimly lit environment of the court. The throne remained onstage throughout the second scene. It served as a perch for Falstaff during his banter with Hal, then the prince staged his own 'reformation' (1.2.173) by theatrically installing himself there during the scene's closing soliloquy. In the first tavern scene (2.4), Falstaff took to the throne again to assume the role of the king, but ended up kneeling before it as Hal delivered – with chilling precision – the prescient words 'I do. I will' (2.4.399).

In the courtroom of 1.3, the stage returned to semi-darkness with the floor divided by criss-cross shadows which suggested both formality and tension. Henry's dismissal of Worcester was designed to humiliate him, and his enraged response to Hotspur's account of 'noble Mortimer' (1.3.109) culminated with him pushing Northumberland's son violently to the ground. Henry's 'absolutely calculated' goading of Hal in 3.2, especially his unfavourable comparison of Hal's manhood to Hotspur's, indicated that the king was 'a brutal pragmatist' at home as well as in politics.[2] After Hal's regretful reply at 3.2.129–59 to his father's accusations, Henry stretched his arms out towards his son – but Hal failed to notice, obliging his father to content himself instead with 'a little push on his shoulder' with his fist. Their embrace was postponed until 5.4, in the heat of battle, when Henry at last tells Hal 'Thou hast redeemed thy lost opinion, / And showed thou mak'st some tender of my life' (5.4.47–8).

Barrit was a gentle, philosophical Falstaff, and critics commented on the elegiac quality of his performance.[3] Attenborough emphasised Falstaff's profound affection for Hal, setting 1.2 in the morning and so suggesting he has spent the night in Hal's quarters. Falstaff hugged his 'sweet wag' (1.2.12), tousling his hair and holding his cheeks. Despite their emotional closeness, Barrit insisted that he found nothing of the 'homosexual element that some commentators on the play have wanted to detect', arguing that Falstaff's affection for the prince resembles more closely 'that deep, elemental love of parent for child'.[4] Houston was indeed a boyish Hal, but his jests at Eastcheap had a cruel, swaggering edge. 'Thuggishly attractive with a lean, whippet-like body and a dangerous predatory smile', he was clearly his father's son.[5]

---

[1] Smallwood, *Players of Shakespeare*, p. 7. Terry Hands used a similar technique of 'overlapping' in his 1975 production. See above p. 55; and Scott McMillin, *Shakespeare in Performance, Henry IV Part One* (1991), p. 74.
[2] Troughton, 'Bolingbroke in *Richard II*, and King Henry IV', p. 111; Michael Billington, 'Penitence bound', the *Guardian*, 21 April 2000.
[3] Michael Coveney, 'At last night's first night', *The Daily Mail*, 20 April 2000.
[4] Desmond Barrit, 'Falstaff in Parts 1 and 2 of *Henry IV*' in Smallwood, ed., *Players of Shakespeare*, pp. 132 and 143.
[5] See John Peter's review, 'Too nice to bite', *The Sunday Telegraph*, 30 April 2000.

Nicholas Hytner's production of both parts of *Henry IV* opened at the National Theatre on 4 May 2005, on the eve of a general election. This was the first time that these two plays had been mounted together at the National, and, as Michael Billington remarked in *The Guardian*, the productions furthered 'Hytner's ongoing plan to use [the National's] three stages to explore England's national and cultural identity'.[1] Whereas Hytner's 2003 modern-dress *Henry V* re-imagined the play in the context of the early days of the Iraq conflict, the costumes in this production were mainly period with some modern touches. Mark Thompson's set was simple and direct, a muted landscape divided by a wooden planked walkway and flanked by stumps of dead trees. Hytner made extensive use of projection screens on a back-cloth above the stage, using photographic images of London's rooftops for the scenes set in Eastcheap, castle crenellations for the scenes at court – and billowing clouds to suggest the unpredictability of English weather.

Michael Gambon's much-anticipated Falstaff brought out the old knight's 'predatory cruelty'.[2] Morally bankrupt enough to pickpocket the purses of the corpses that littered the battlefield, and genuinely 'blasted with antiquity', Gambon's Falstaff was resolutely unsentimental. Dressed in velvet trousers, with a feather in his hat and 'gout-friendly slippers', he resembled a 'wily, drunken bohemian tramp' not above shovelling the leftovers of the full English breakfast he enjoyed in 1.2 straight into his knapsack to enjoy at his leisure.[3] His first appearance with Hal saw the pair urinating on the smoke-blackened tree stumps – Falstaff in a majestic arc, Hal more discreetly – suggesting their shared disregard for the vestiges of war.

A cadaverous and world-weary Henry IV, David Bradley delivered his opening speech not in the council chamber at Westminster but 'on a smoke-filled public highway' surrounded by the survivors of England's 'trenching war' (1.1.7) weeping for its victims.[4] The play ended in the same manner as it began, as the king and his retinue progressed slowly down the same walkway surrounded by women wailing over the bodies of the fallen – suggesting history's circularity and terrible inevitability. Even the exhausted, bag-laden Carriers in the intimate, night-time setting of 2.1 seemed touched by the deprivations of wartime. In the space of the court in 1.3, however, Henry's battle-fatigue translated into hard-headed political expediency. Sir Walter Blunt took his place next to the king at table while Hotspur, Northumberland and Worcester were seated awkwardly before them on bare chairs. A 'fiercely driven' king, Bradley's much-praised Henry captured a sense of both his righteousness and restlessness as a ruler.[5]

Among the rebels, the powerful physicality of David Harewood's energetic Hotspur contrasted in a clever piece of casting with the litheness and lassitude of Alistair Petrie's Mortimer. In 3.1, an irascible Owen Glendower (Robert Blythe) translated

---

[1] Billington, 'Crown and country', p. 19.
[2] See Billington's review in the *Guardian*, 5 May 2005.
[3] See Victoria Segal's review in *The Sunday Times*, 8 May 2005; and Paul Taylor's in *The Independent*, 6 May 2005.
[4] This quotation is taken from Billington's review in the *Guardian*, 5 May 2005.
[5] See Jane Edwardes's review in *Time Out London*, 11 May 2005.

10   Hal (Matthew Macfadyen) and Falstaff (Michael Gambon) in Act 1 Scene 2 of Nicholas Hytner's
2005 National Theatre production in London.

with an eye-roll the sweet nothings his daughter (Eve Myles) had been offering in
Welsh to her husband: 'She bids you on the wanton rushes lay you down, / And
rest your gentle head upon her lap' (3.1.207–8). Mortimer settled across the lap
of his wife as if in a swoon – calling poignantly to mind the fallen soldiers of the
opening scene and acting as a reminder of the bloodshed to come. In this production it was Glendower who put a stop to his daughter's song, as though her slow
lament presaged future sadness. Whereas Hotspur ended the scene by impatiently
hurrying along a girlish Kate (Naomi Frederick) to bed, Mortimer forbade his wife
to follow with a wave of his hand. The first half of the play therefore closed with
Lady Mortimer alone and weeping on the edge of the stage.

   Matthew Macfadyen's Hal was a brooding, 'cold playboy prince', already 'well-
practised in contempt' before he cast Falstaff aside.[1] His friendship with Falstaff seemed designed in this production as a method to gain the attention of his
disapproving father. Macfadyen's Hal displayed 'an intriguing mix of arrogance
and insecurity' especially in 3.2.[2] As the courtiers solemnly prepared themselves
for worship beneath a vast silver cross, Hal stumbled into the church before hur-
riedly taking his place kneeling to face the audience next to his pious, waiting
father. The depth of Henry's 'headmasterly' disapproval (and love) towards Hal was

[1] See Nicholas de Jongh's review in *The Evening Standard*, 6 May 2005; and Susannah Clapp's in *The
Observer*, 8 May 2005.
[2] See Kate Bassett's review in *The Independent on Sunday*, 8 May 2005.

suggested by his first tossing a prayer book in exasperation at his son's feet before clasping him by the throat in an embrace. Hal's reactions to his father's torrent of 'withering irony' switched from boredom, to cringing embarrassment, to shame, and finally to anger – encapsulating in miniature Hal's transition from prodigal son to hero-warrior which takes place over the course of three plays.[1]

Gus Van Sant's 1991 film *My Own Private Idaho* is a popular reworking of *Henry IV*. Its relationship to Shakespeare's plays, and to Orson Welles' 1966 film about the rejection of Falstaff, *Chimes at Midnight*, is however by no means straightforward. Van Sant worked from several different scripts, including a modernised version of Shakespeare's plays, and the film includes some verbatim quotations from *1 Henry IV*.[2] More often, however, Shakespeare's lines are loosely quoted like an 'imitative quirk' in a work densely freighted with cultural and literary allusion.[3] The film tells the story of Scott Favor (Keanu Reeves) and Mike Waters (River Phoenix) who work as prostitutes in the backstreets of Portland. Scott's father, Jack Favor, the wheelchair-bound mayor of Portland, attempts to reform his delinquent son. Echoing Hal's promised reformation in *1 Henry IV* 1.2.155–77, Scott promises that his wild lifestyle is temporary. The film's episodic structure follows the journeys of Scott and Mike between Idaho and Rome where Mike searches unsuccessfully for his missing mother. Scott finally abandons Mike, who is in love with him, and returns to America where he makes a calculated 'social ascendance' from indolence to industry, adolescence to adulthood, homosexuality to heterosexuality, and poverty to affluence.[4]

My Own Private Idaho makes explicit the homoerotic subtext some readers have found in *1 Henry IV*, and, in so doing, offers a more general portrait of American masculinity and sexuality in the late 1980s.[5] In this respect, as Paul Arthur has argued, Van Sant drew from two important American cinematic genres: the western and the road movie. The night-time scene in which Mike confesses his love for Scott alludes to campfire scenes in countless westerns. The largely urban environment of *Idaho* presents a 'modern equivalent of the wilderness', however, which allows Van Sant to rethink familiar cinematic codes of the frontier and the outcast. Mike is an example of that 'primal American figure', the drifter, whose nostalgia for home takes the form of an endless search for his mother.[6] *Idaho* explores questions of personal development and self-realisation, but, as Arthur makes clear, the rite of passage which is so central to the road movie genre finally eludes Mike. The film begins and ends on the same mercilessly straight road in Idaho which, Mike remarks, 'probably

---

[1] The quotations are from Billington's review in the *Guardian*, 5 May 2005.

[2] Curtis Breight discusses the origins of the script in 'Elizabethan world pictures' in John Joughin, ed., *Shakespeare and National Culture* (1997), pp. 295–325 (p. 301).

[3] This phrase is Paul Arthur's from 'Kings of the road', his audio-visual discussion of the film which accompanies the commercial DVD of *My Own Private Idaho*.

[4] Paul Arthur, 'Kings of the road'.

[5] For an extended discussion of Van Sant's use of Shakespeare, see Sue Wiseman, 'The family tree motel: subliming Shakespeare in *My Own Private Idaho*' in Lynda E. Boose and Richard Burt, eds., *Shakespeare the Movie: Popularizing the Plays on Film, TV, and Video* (1998), pp. 225–39 (p. 238).

[6] Paul Arthur, 'Kings of the road'.

goes all the way around the world'. When Mike suffers the last of many episodes of narcolepsy in the film's concluding frames, he seems somehow trapped in the landscape which has been testing him.

Van Sant replicates Shakespeare's interest in the social underclass by making central the lives of the poor and the vulnerable. His equivalent of the Boar's Head tavern is a derelict hotel which Portland's homeless street hustlers have made their home. Van Sant reverses Shakespeare's main and sub-plots, focusing primarily on 'the most carnivalesque, anti-authoritarian, potentially *politically* subversive moments of the Shakespeare texts' - especially the class conflict raised through Hal's relationship with Falstaff.[1] Scott first appears swigging from a bottle of 'Falstaff' beer, suggesting that Van Sant reconceptualised Hal's relationship to Falstaff as one of consumer to commodity.[2] The hierarchical, moneyed world of Scott's family is vastly different from the chaotic, impoverished environment of the hustlers. As Van Sant's villainous Falstaff figure Bob Pigeon (William Richert) tells Scott, his future inheritance is their 'only ticket out' of life on the street. But when Scott finally embraces high society (and a possible career in politics), Van Sant's own sympathies are hard to discern. The film ends with two funerals: the staid, formal interment of Jack Favor, and a riotous farewell to Bob Pigeon conducted by the street boys. The film is punctuated by repeats of 'America, the Beautiful', played in fragments, and many have seen it as a pointed satire on contemporary America focusing on the dispossessed. Whatever the contemporary allusions in *Idaho* to the economically and erotically marginalised, however, Van Sant himself claimed that the Shakespearean material was included in an attempt 'to transcend time, to show that those things have always happened, everywhere'.[3]

---

[1] Sue Wiseman, 'The family tree motel', p. 238.

[2] See Kathy M. Howlett's discussion of Van Sant's 'commodification of art' in 'Utopian revisioning of Falstaff's tavern world: Orson Welles's *Chimes at Midnight* and Gus van Sant's *My Own Private Idaho*' in Lisa S. Starks and Courtney Lehmann, eds., *The Reel Shakespeare: Alternative Cinema and Theory* (2002), pp. 165–88 (pp. 168–9).

[3] Gus van Sant, *Even Cowgirls Get the Blues and My Own Private Idaho* (London and Boston: Faber and Faber, 1993), pp. xlii–xliii, quoted in Howlett, 'Utopian Revisioning of Falstaff's Tavern World', p. 179.

NOTE ON THE TEXT

The text for this edition is based on the first quarto (Q1, 1598), with the exception of 1.3.199–2.2.93. This passage relies primarily upon the only surviving fragment of a slightly earlier quarto (Q0, also 1598), from which Q1 was faithfully reprinted. Q0 and Q1 are widely acknowledged to be among the most carefully printed quartos for any play by Shakespeare. They provide the only authoritative copy-text for *1 Henry IV*. Most spellings have been modernised in accordance with the conventions of the *New Cambridge Shakespeare*. In one case, an earlier form, 'Bullingbrook', indicates pronunciation ('Bullinbrook') and has been retained, as in the NCS *Richard II*, ed. Gurr. Speech headings have been regularised, including 'Prince' for 'Prin.' and 'Pr.' (rather than 'Prince of Wales' or 'Prince Hal').

'Falstaff,' the familiar version for the name of the most famous character in *1 Henry IV*, has been used throughout as a speech heading. Although Sir John 'Oldcastle' is known to have been the character's original name, we have no evidence that Shakespeare resisted changing it to Falstaff. To adopt 'Sir John' as the speech heading would unduly weight a class-inflected form used most often by the Hostess and Bardolph in a single scene (3.3), and thereby undervalue other contexts in which Falstaff vigorously participates. For a discussion of 'Oldcastle', 'Rossill', and 'Harvey', the names altered after the earliest performances of the play, see Introduction pp. 5–6 and 69–70, and Textual Analysis, pp. 220–23. This edition follows Melchiori, ed., *2 Henry IV*, in identifying 'Bardolph' as a name change for 'Rossill' (red nose), hence 'Peto' for 'Harvey'.

The light punctuation of Qq01 has been retained when it offers more flexible choices to the actor and the reader. Changes in punctuation which significantly alter the meaning of the copy-text have been collated. Several elisions have been introduced, in keeping with Qq01's general preference for these colloquial forms. A grave accent in verse (as in armèd, impressèd) shows that the vowel should be pronounced. Elision of 'ed' or 'd' may otherwise be assumed. The treatment of short or irregular verse lines is explained in the Textual Analysis pp. 228–30, where special attention is given to 'shared' or 'split' lines.

When stage directions are added, they (like other changes to the copy-text) are enclosed in square brackets and recorded in the Collation. Such directions either replace obvious omissions or make explicit specific actions which are clearly indicated by lines in the copy-text.

In the format used for the Collation, a lemma or citation from the text is followed, after a square bracket, by the authority for the reading given. When additional readings help to illustrate the history of interpretation, these follow in chronological order. The Collation includes: (1) all significant departures from Qq01; (2) plausible emendations from later editions that have not been adopted; and (3) several emendations, which have historical importance even though they no longer seem to be credible choices. Spelling variants are not normally considered to be significant departures from the copy-text.

The Commentary explains meanings of terms, phrases, and short passages. When meanings are numbered in a sequence, each is acceptable; the first is not necessarily preferred. Illustrative examples often include conjectures about original staging, supplemented by reference to recent productions. To ensure that the basic historical background for *1 Henry IV* is immediately accessible, pertinent information has been incorporated in head-notes and in numerous glosses.

The First Part of King Henry IV

LIST OF CHARACTERS
In order of appearance (for speaking characters only)

KING *Henry the Fourth*
Lord John of LANCASTER
Earl of WESTMORELAND
Sir Walter BLUNT

PRINCE *Henry*

Sir John FALSTAFF
POINS

Earl of NORTHUMBERLAND
Earl of WORCESTER
HOTSPUR, *Sir Henry Percy*

FIRST CARRIER
OSTLER
SECOND CARRIER
GADSHILL
CHAMBERLAIN
PETO
BARDOLPH
FIRST TRAVELLER
SECOND TRAVELLER

LADY PERCY
SERVANT *to Hotspur*

FRANCIS
VINTNER
HOSTESS
SHERIFF

Lord Edmund MORTIMER
Owen GLENDOWER
LADY MORTIMER
DOUGLAS
MESSENGER
Sir Richard VERNON
ARCHBISHOP *of York*
SIR MICHAEL
Soldiers, other travellers, and attendants

84

Notes

Q Q F of *Henry IV, Part One* do not have a list of characters. The first list was provided by Rowe. The following notes are selective; they contain information on biography and on the significance of some names.

KING *Henry the Fourth* (1367–1413) Son of John of Gaunt, the Duke of Lancaster, and first cousin of Richard II, whom he supplanted in 1399. Hotspur calls him 'Bullingbrook' (his place of birth in Lincolnshire); Glendower calls him 'Lancaster' (his inherited ducal title). Both men question his legitimacy as monarch. He dies in *Part Two* 5.2.

Lord John of LANCASTER (1389–1435) The third son of Henry IV. He was made Duke of Bedford by his brother, Henry V, and became Regent of France in the reign of Henry VI. He presided over the execution of Sir John Oldcastle, was responsible for burning Joan of Arc, and caused Douglas to fall in battle.

Earl of WESTMORELAND (1364–1425) Ralph Neville, a northern baron and a kinsman of the King through marriage ('my gentle cousin', 1.1.31). Although never mentioned in *R2*, he had been one of King Henry's earliest supporters.

Sir Walter BLUNT An older knight. Not mentioned in *R2*, he had been a loyal follower of John of Gaunt and of his son, King Henry.

PRINCE *Henry* (1387–1422) The Prince of Wales, eldest son and heir to Henry IV, later crowned Henry V (1413). He is called 'the Prince of Wales' and 'Harry' by the King, 'Hal' primarily by Falstaff, and 'Harry Monmouth' (for his birthplace in Wales) by Hotspur.

Sir John FALSTAFF The Prince's companion. In the earliest version of the play, he was called 'Sir John Oldcastle', the name of a character in *FV* and, historically, a Lollard knight burned as a heretic in 1417. 'Falstaff' may have been suggested by 'Fastolffe', a historical figure who appears in *1H6* (spelled 'Falstaffe' in F and subsequent editions). It is possible, however, that his name (perhaps an ironic analogy to 'Shake-spear') symbolises his disposition. See Robert F. Willson, 'Falstaff in *1 Henry IV*: what's in a name?', *SQ* 27 (1976), 199–200, and George Walton Williams, 'Some thoughts on Falstaff's name', *SQ* 30 (1979), 82–4.

POINS A companion of the Prince and of Falstaff, self-described in *2H4* as a 'second brother', 2.2.67, i.e. a wild 'gallant' or a gentleman with little money (see *Wiv.* 3.2.73). He is also called 'Ned' and 'Yedward'.

Earl of NORTHUMBERLAND Henry Percy (1342–1408), the greatest of the northern barons and the most powerful of King Henry's early supporters in *R2*. In *2H4*, he flees to Scotland; after he returns he is 'overthrown' by the shrieve of Yorkshire, 4.4.97–9.

Earl of WORCESTER Thomas Percy (1344–1403), the younger brother of Henry. In *R2*, he forsook his position as steward of the royal household to support Bullingbrook.

HOTSPUR Sir Henry Percy (1364–1403), the eldest son of the Earl of Northumberland, generally referred to by his 'adopted name of privilege', 5.2.18, or nickname, which his historical prototype earned in border warfare with the Scots. He inspires other titles and epithets, ranging from 'Harry Percy' to 'the Hotspur of the North' or 'this gun-powder Percy'.

GADSHILL The 'setter' who arranges the robbery. His name probably comes from *FV*, where it is the nickname of the thief Cutbert Cutter, said to be 'a taking fellow / upon Gad's Hill in Kent', 165–6. Confusion often arises because of the similar names of the character and the location.

PETO A follower of the Prince. He is given an 'honourable' position in the arrangements preceding the battle, 2.4.456–7. He appears briefly as a messenger in *2H4*. In the early version of *1H4*, he was apparently called 'Harvey'. No historical significance has been found for 'Peto', a Warwickshire family name.

BARDOLPH Falstaff's companion and attendant of many years. He reappears in *2H4* and *Wiv.*, and is executed in *H5* for having stolen a 'pax' from a church, 3.6. He probably was first named 'Rossill', perhaps to annoy the Russell family. See Q 1.2.131; Melchiori, ed. *2H4*, p. 5, suggests a play upon the Italian *'rosso'*, i.e. red, because of his nose. 'Bardolph', confusingly, is also the name of a rebel lord in *2H4*.

LADY PERCY Katherine (1371–1444?), Hotspur's wife and Edmund Mortimer's sister, called 'Elianor' in Holinshed (probably through confusion with her niece), but, in fact, named Elizabeth. Shakespeare may have made her a Katherine because he associated her with qualities represented by 'Kates' in *Shr.* and later in *H5*. See Laurie Maguire, '"Household Kates": *chez* Petruchio, Percy, and Plantagenet', in *Gloriana's Face: Women Public and Private in the English Renaissance*, ed. S. P. Cerasano and Marion Wynne-Davies, 1992, pp. 129–65.

FRANCIS An apprentice drawer or tapster. He will assist the Prince and Poins in *2H4* when they disguise themselves in 'two of our jerkins and aprons', 2.4.16–17.

HOSTESS The landlady of the tavern in Eastcheap. The Prince and his companions in *FV* 83–4 refer to 'our old hostess / At *Feversham*', and to 'a prettie wench / That can talke well' at the 'olde Taverne in Eastcheape', 87–9. Also called 'Mistress Quickly', in *2H4* she becomes 'Helen of thy noble thoughts' (5.5.33) and in *H5*, married to ancient Pistol, 'Nell'. In *Wiv.*, Mistress Quickly is servant to Dr Caius.

Lord Edmund MORTIMER (1376–1409) The son of the third Earl of March and the brother-in-law of Hotspur. Holinshed and Shakespeare incorrectly identify him as the legitimate heir of Richard II. Edmund's elder brother, Roger, fourth Earl of March, was proclaimed heir presumptive in 1385 (Holinshed, II, 768). When Roger was killed in Ireland in 1398, his title and royal claim descended to his son, another Edmund (b. 1391), nephew of Shakespeare's character. The latter continued to support Glendower and died in the siege of Harlech (Barkloughly) castle.

Owen GLENDOWER (1359?–1416?) In Welsh, Owain ab Gruffydd (*DNB*). He 'dwelled . . . in a place called Glindourwie', i.e. 'The vallie by the side of the water of Dee, by occasion whereof he was surnamed Glindour Dew' (Holinshed, III, 17). He led the Welsh rebellion, both a movement for independence and a protest against the deposition of Richard. He may well be the Welsh Captain in *R2* 2.4, and is reported dead in *2H4* 3.1.103. Historically he was offered a pardon on the accession of Henry V, but refused it. Some report that he died of starvation in the mountains, others that he reached a ripe old age.

DOUGLAS (1369–1424) Archibald, fourth Earl of Douglas, often referred to as 'the' Douglas to indicate that he is the head of a noble Scottish family. Known in history as a great warrior and a poor general, he was killed at the battle of Verneuil by the English forces under the Duke of Bedford (Prince John).

ARCHBISHOP *of York* Richard Scroop (1350?–1405), the leader of the ongoing rebellion in *2H4*, entrapped and executed at Gaultree Forest by Prince John and Westmoreland, 4.1. He was the cousin (not the brother, as in Holinshed and Shakespeare) of William Scroop, Earl of Wiltshire and Lord Treasurer under Richard II, who was beheaded by Bullingbrook in 1399.

THE FIRST PART OF KING HENRY IV

[1.1]   *Enter the* KING, LORD JOHN OF LANCASTER, EARL OF
WESTMORELAND, [SIR WALTER BLUNT,] *with others*

KING   So shaken as we are, so wan with care,
          Find we a time for frighted peace to pant,
          And breathe short-winded accents of new broils
          To be commenced in strands afar remote;
          No more the thirsty entrance of this soil   5

Title] F (The First Part of Henry the Fourth); THE / HISTORYOF / HENRIETHE / FOVRTH Q1;
KING *Hanmer*   1.1] *Actus Primus, Scœna Prima.* F; *not in* Qq   0 SD.1–2 EARL OF WESTMORELAND] QqF (Earle
of Westmerland) *throughout*   0 SD.2 SIR WALTER BLUNT] *Dering MS., Capell; not in* QqF   4 strands] QqF (stronds)

Act 1, Scene 1
[1.1] Q marks neither act nor scene divisions.
This edition uses the divisions in F except when
noted.

[1.1] Shakespeare compresses the first two years
of Henry's reign, beginning in 1399, into one; the
Welsh victory described by Westmoreland, 38ff.,
came in 1401. According to Holinshed (III, 16),
the new King was almost immediately threatened
by civil disturbances and border wars. In contrast
to the formal Council meeting in 1.3, Shakespeare
here presents an informal exchange of views, dominated by a general mood of uncertainty.

The stage could be bare or there might be a
throne. In the latter case, decision must be made
whether the King confidently takes this seat or
leaves the throne conspicuously vacant.

0 SD John, younger brother of the Prince,
appears only in this scene and in Act 5; he has
no lines to speak until 5.4. The copy-text, Q1,
provides no entry for Sir Walter Blunt, who is
referred to as 'here' at 62–3 below. If he is included
with the group as the scene opens, the King, who
will already know the good news he brings, may
speak more forcefully. If the King has already dis-
patched a messenger to Hotspur (99), he might
have learned from Blunt, just before the scene
begins, of Hotspur's victory at Holmedon. Alternatively, Blunt is 'here' in court, but remains offstage. Much like the 'post from Wales' of the preceding night (37), he could interrupt the scene
at 62 and change its mood by encouraging the
King. This might require more stage business: a

letter from which the King reads (67–73, 91–4)
and a silent gesture as he sends a messenger to
summon Hotspur. A sense of urgency created by
rapid reassessments may be more important than
the clarity of the King's motivation. On Shakespeare's imprecision about some entries and exits
for messengers and minor characters, see Textual
Analysis, pp. 221–2.

1 we The royal pronoun, and perhaps the
nation as well.

1 wan pale, also weary and melancholy.

2–3 Find ... breathe The grammar is ambiguous, either 'we' or 'peace' being the subject of
'pant'. Because 'we' governs line 3's 'breathe', a
pause after 'peace' could indicate that 'we' also
governs 'find', and 'pant'.

2 Find we (1) Let us try to find, (2) We happen
to find.

3 breathe This verb is transitive and here
means 'speak' (though in 1.3.101 'breathed' is
intransitive, meaning 'paused', rested for breath).

3 accents words, language.

3 broils fighting.

4 strands i.e. 'the shore of the Holy Land, to
which, in *Richard II* (5.6.49), King Henry vowed
a crusade' (Bevington).

5 thirsty entrance ... soil i.e. dry mouth.
The metaphor presents the earth as an unnatural mother devouring her own children. It has
strong biblical overtones. Compare Gen. 4.11: the
earth 'opened her mouth to receive thy brothers
blood from thine hand'. This initiates a sequence
of images which convey the horror of civil war.

Shall daub her lips with her own children's blood,
No more shall trenching war channel her fields
Nor bruise her flow'rets with the armèd hoofs
Of hostile paces. Those opposèd eyes
Which, like the meteors of a troubled heaven,   10
All of one nature, of one substance bred,
Did lately meet in the intestine shock
And furious close of civil butchery,
Shall now in mutual well-beseeming ranks
March all one way, and be no more opposed   15
Against acquaintance, kindred, and allies.
The edge of war, like an ill-sheathèd knife,
No more shall cut his master. Therefore, friends,
As far as to the sepulchre of Christ –
Whose soldier now, under whose blessèd cross   20
We are impressèd and engaged to fight –
Forthwith a power of English shall we levy,
Whose arms were moulded in their mother's womb

23 mother's] QqF (mothers)

6 daub (1) cover with plaster or clay, (2) soil (*OED* sv *v* 1 and 3).

7 trenching ploughing (*OED* sv *v* 3b) and in a military sense, the use of ditches as fortification (*OED* sv *v* 5). As does the suggestion of whitewashing in 'daub', 6, the agricultural metaphor obscures the responsibility of the participants, including King Henry, for their destructive actions. Blood, running down the channels like rain, fertilises the gashed earth.

8 flow'rets small flowers.

8 armèd hoofs i.e. horses' hoofs that have been shod. Henry's imagery resembles the use of vivid montage in Eisenstein's films.

9 paces the gait or swift motion of war-horses.

9 opposèd eyes hostile as well as physically opposite. This use of the rhetorical figure metonymy, representing armies through some of their parts, carries ironic undertones of the body politic being dismembered by civil war.

10 meteors of a troubled heaven Meteors are taken as ominous (see *1H6* 1.1.1–5). An anxious concern for portents, omens, and prophecies typifies many characters in this play.

12 intestine internal, domestic (with a suggestion of the physiological sense). A choice of grave yet showy words, which preserve latinate or archaic meanings, distinguishes the King's personal idiom. Compare 'impressèd' (21), 'expedience' (33), 'industrious' (62), 'adventure' (92), and 'utterèd' (106).

13 close grappling, hand-to-hand fighting.

13 civil civic or communal. Mahood (*Wordplay*, p. 26) suggests that the phrase 'civil butchery' gains vigour through a 'mainly unconscious' rejection of the meaning 'polite'.

14 mutual well-beseeming interdependent, well-ordered (Humphreys).

17–18 ill-sheathèd . . . master A common saying as in *WT* 1.2.156–7. That he adds this well-worn metaphor may hint at Henry's exhaustion, belying his more hopeful syntax, 'No more . . ., no more'.

18–27 Therefore . . . bitter cross The King concludes his speech with a momentum designed to emphasise the necessity for union and express his own impatience to seek absolution for his guilt.

19–22 As far . . . levy By advancing Henry's wish to go on a crusade from the end of his reign (Holinshed III, 57) to a time near its inception, Shakespeare links the opening of *1H4* more tightly to the concluding scene of *R2*.

21 impressèd and engaged conscripted and pledged by oath.

22 power army, force.

23 arms Punning on weapons/limbs (as 'chase' implies, 24).

23 mother England. The metaphor of soldiers born from the earth may echo the myths of Cadmus and of Medea.

To chase these pagans in those holy fields
Over whose acres walked those blessèd feet   25
Which fourteen hundred years ago were nailed
For our advantage on the bitter cross.
But this our purpose now is twelve month old,
And bootless 'tis to tell you we will go.
Therefor we meet not now. Then let me hear   30
Of you, my gentle cousin Westmoreland,
What yesternight our Council did decree
In forwarding this dear expedience.
WESTMORELAND My liege, this haste was hot in question,
And many limits of the charge set down   35
But yesternight, when all athwart there came
A post from Wales, loaden with heavy news,
Whose worst was that the noble Mortimer,
Leading the men of Herefordshire to fight
Against the irregular and wild Glendower,   40
Was by the rude hands of that Welshman taken,
A thousand of his people butcherèd,
Upon whose dead corpse there was such misuse,

26 fourteen hundred] Q (1400)   30 Therefor] *Davison;* Therefore QqF   31 Westmoreland] QqF (Westmerland)
throughout   39 Herefordshire] F; Herdforshire Qq1–3; Herdfordshire Qq4, 5   43 corpse] Q1, F (corpes); corps Qq2–5;
corses *Staunton conj.*

26–7 Which . . . cross The emphasis falls not on 'advantage' but on 'nailed' and 'bitter cross'. This is significant for the speaker and for the action to come. See Introduction, pp. 8–9.

29 bootless useless, without reward.

30 Therefor . . . now That is not the reason we now meet. The short sentence ending in mid-line signals a major shift in tone.

31 Of From.

31 gentle cousin noble kinsman. 'Cousin' can indicate any relationship of kin except direct descent.

33 dear expedience urgent and cherished enterprise; 'expedience' carries the sense (now obsolete) of an expedition that requires speed (*OED* 1a); compare *Ant.* 1.2.178.

34 liege liege lord, the 'superior to whom one owes feudal allegiance and service' (*OED* sv *sb* 1).

34 hot in question i.e. being planned with zeal. Compare 'hot incursions and great name in arms' (3.2.108).

35 limits of the charge specified orders and defined responsibilities for military and financial needs.

36 all athwart contradicting our purposes.

37 post messenger who rides hastily.

37 heavy grave, of great importance (*OED* sv *a*[1] 12, citing 2.3.57).

38 the noble Mortimer See List of Characters for a detailed explanation of Shakespeare's confusing Lord Edmund Mortimer, captured by Glendower, with his nephew Edmund, the fifth Earl of March. This same confused substitution follows at 1.3.83, 142–4.

40 irregular engaged in guerilla warfare, i.e. not observing the rules.

43 corpse corpses. The Elizabethan usage of 'corpse' in a plural sense is common.

43–6 Upon . . . spoken of Westmoreland's relatively tactful version rephrases Holinshed, 'The shamefull villanie used by the Welshwomen towards the dead carcasses, was such, as honest eares would be ashamed to heare, and continent toongs to speak thereof' III, 20. For a much more explicit account of the women's atrocities, see Holinshed III, 34.

Such beastly shameless transformation,
By those Welshwomen done, as may not be   45
Without much shame retold or spoken of.
KING   It seems then that the tidings of this broil
      Brake off our business for the Holy Land.
WESTMORELAND This, matched with other, did, my gracious lord,
      For more uneven and unwelcome news   50
      Came from the north, and thus it did import:
      On Holy-rood day, the gallant Hotspur there,
      Young Harry Percy, and brave Archibald,
      That ever valiant and approvèd Scot,
      At Holmedon met, where they did spend   55
      A sad and bloody hour;
      As by discharge of their artillery,
      And shape of likelihood, the news was told;
      For he that brought them, in the very heat
      And pride of their contention did take horse,   60
      Uncertain of the issue any way.
KING   Here is a dear and true industrious friend,
      Sir Walter Blunt, new lighted from his horse,
      Stained with the variation of each soil
      Betwixt that Holmedon and this seat of ours;   65
      And he hath brought us smooth and welcome news.
      The Earl of Douglas is discomfited.
      Ten thousand bold Scots, two-and-twenty knights,

55–6 At . . . spend / A . . . hour| QqF; At . . . met / Where . . . hour *Capell*   62 a dear and true| Q5, F; deere, a true Qq1–4

49–55 This . . . met Shakespeare brings the two events together to show how the King's authority is being challenged on the borders of his realm. The battle of Holmedon, according to Holinshed, took place three months after Mortimer's capture.

50 uneven (1) not uniform or 'smooth', as 66, (2) uncertain.

52 Holy-rood day 14 September, the day dedicated to the Holy Cross in the church calendar. This is an ironic coincidence in the light of the King's deferred crusade to the Holy Land.

53 Archibald The fourth Earl of Douglas. See List of Characters.

54 approvèd tested by experience.

55 Holmedon In Northumberland, near Wooler (there are many variant spellings, e.g. Humbleton), where in 1402 the Percys stopped one of the frequent invasions of northern England by the Scots.

57–8 As by discharge . . . told The severity

of the fighting is being estimated from the amount of shooting. Holinshed speaks of archery, but 'artillery' could refer to any missile, as well as to the engine used to fire it (*OED* 2). At 2.3.47 Hotspur dreams of basilisks, cannon, and culverin.

60 pride highest pitch, intensity.

62–3 Here . . . Blunt See 0 SD.

62 dear and true This F reading is more consistent with the King's style. He often couples words and phrases as in 'smooth and welcome', 66. The copy-text Q's 'Here is deere, a true' clearly requires some emendation.

62 industrious painstaking, attentive (*OED* 2).

64 Stained with the variation of each soil The King praises Blunt's diligence and may suggest his native integrity. His figures do not necessarily describe the way Blunt looks.

66 smooth pleasant.

67 discomfited overthrown, routed in battle.

Balked in their own blood, did Sir Walter see
On Holmedon's plains. Of prisoners Hotspur took   70
Mordake, Earl of Fife and eldest son
To beaten Douglas, and the Earl of Atholl,
Of Murray, Angus, and Menteith.
And is not this an honourable spoil?
A gallant prize? Ha, cousin, is it not?   75
WESTMORELAND In faith, it is a conquest for a prince to boast of.
KING Yea, there thou makest me sad, and makest me sin
In envy that my Lord Northumberland
Should be the father to so blest a son –
A son who is the theme of honour's tongue,   80
Amongst a grove the very straightest plant,
Who is sweet Fortune's minion and her pride –
Whilst I by looking on the praise of him
See riot and dishonour stain the brow
Of my young Harry. O that it could be proved   85
That some night-tripping fairy had exchanged
In cradle-clothes our children where they lay,
And called mine Percy, his Plantagenet!
Then would I have his Harry, and he mine.
But let him from my thoughts. What think you, coz,   90
Of this young Percy's pride? The prisoners

---

69 blood, did] Q5, F (blood did); bloud. Did QQ1–4   76 SH WESTMORELAND] QQF (Westmerland) (*throughout*)
76 WESTMORELAND In faith . . . boast of] *As Bevington;* [*King*] In faith . . . is. / *West.* A conquest . . . of QQF

69 Balked Heaped up, perhaps in rows. A 'balk' was a ridge between two furrows.

70 prisoners Henry seems to know that Hotspur has captured Douglas, but his name is not included in the list of prisoners. Compare 3.2.112–17.

71 Mordake Shakespeare may have wrongly identified him as Douglas' son because of a missing comma in Holinshed's list of prisoners (III, 21). Murdoch Stewart was the eldest son of Robert, Duke of Albany, Regent of Scotland.

73 Menteith One of 'Mordake's' titles, not a separate person historically (an apparent mistake by the dramatist).

74 honourable spoil Henry may be contrasting Hotspur's behaviour with that of the Welshwomen. He maintains his public commitment to chivalric standards.

82 minion Here, favourite; elsewhere, servant or lover, as at 1.2.21.

84 riot debauchery of the worst kind (*OED sv sb* 1a) or (more mildly), wanton revelling. The term, used only three times in *1* and *2 H 4*, always refers

to the Prince.

84 stain the brow From his first appearance in *R2* Henry conceptualises dishonour or shame in physical terms.

85–7 O that . . . lay Shakespeare probably follows Daniel in making Hal and Hotspur the same age. Historically Hotspur was twenty-one years older than Hal and two years older than the King himself. See Introduction, p. 24.

86 fairy had exchanged Alluding to the folk belief that fairies exchanged their own ugly offspring for beautiful human children. This shows an atypical side of Henry who is often hardheaded.

88 Plantagenet The dynastic surname of the royal family.

90 coz cousin, kinsman.

91–4 The prisoners . . . Fife According to the law of arms (referred to in *H5* 4.7.2), Hotspur could hold for ransom all prisoners except those of royal blood. He was therefore obliged to surrender only Mordake, grandson of Robert II of Scotland.

> Which he in this adventure hath surprised
> To his own use he keeps, and sends me word
> I shall have none but Mordake, Earl of Fife.

WESTMORELAND This is his uncle's teaching, this is Worcester,   95
> Malevolent to you in all aspects,
> Which makes him prune himself, and bristle up
> The crest of youth against your dignity.

KING   But I have sent for him to answer this;
> And for this cause a while we must neglect   100
> Our holy purpose to Jerusalem.
> Cousin, on Wednesday next our Council we
> Will hold at Windsor, so inform the lords.
> But come yourself with speed to us again,
> For more is to be said and to be done   105
> Than out of anger can be utter èd.

WESTMORELAND I will, my liege.

Exeunt

[1.2] *Enter* PRINCE OF WALES *and* SIR JOHN FALSTAFF

FALSTAFF Now Hal, what time of day is it, lad?

102–3 we / Will hold at| *T. Johnson, Pope;* wil hold / At QqF   Act 1, Scene 2   1.2| *Scæna Secunda.* F; *not in* Qq
0 SD| Qq; *Enter Henry Prince of Wales, Sir John Falstaffe, and Pointz* F

92 adventure a daring enterprise.
92 surprised captured (*OED* sv *v* 2b).
96 Malevolent . . . aspects Like a comet or meteor, 'malevolent' or unfavourable in all positions.
97 prune Worcester teaches Hotspur, as a hawk, to preen. The hawk trims his feathers for action; he *prunes* them with his beak.
97–8 bristle up . . . youth Carrying on the image of the bird of prey which demonstrates its readiness for attack. The bird's aggression is especially clear when it raises the feathers on its head. 'Crest' may also suggest a helmet.
99–103 But I . . . lords The King exercises his power more forcefully than his opening lines would lead us to expect. In Holinshed's account, the Percys of their own accord arrive to challenge the King.
105–6 For . . . utterèd The King adapts a common proverb 'Nothing is well said or done in a passion' (Tilley N 307).

Act 1, Scene 2
[1.2] The dialogue does not specify the loca-

tion. Most editors have assumed it to be the Prince's apartments in London, but some productions have erroneously treated this as the first of the tavern scenes. Both the general atmosphere and the predominant use of prose create strong contrasts with the opening scene.
   0 SD The two characters may enter together or from opposite sides of the stage. Falstaff can be spruce and ready for action, or, in a staging popular since the early nineteenth century, he can be discovered asleep by the Prince. He may even sit down immediately on a vacant 'throne' and address the Prince in mimicry of Henry IV. To present a sleeping Falstaff ignores the stage direction but anticipates his nap behind the arras 2.4.443 ff.
   1 Now . . . lad? A natural question, perhaps with the additional sense, 'What's up?' (if Falstaff is not discovered asleep). His tone can also suggest that he is thirsty, or hung over – or that, half-awake, he is reproving the Prince with mock seriousness. His nine monosyllables have a simplicity lacking in the Prince's first speech, a long aggressive response.

PRINCE Thou art so fat-witted with drinking of old sack, and unbutton-
ing thee after supper, and sleeping upon benches after noon, that
thou hast forgotten to demand that truly which thou wouldst truly
know. What a devil hast thou to do with the time of the day? Unless   5
hours were cups of sack, and minutes capons, and clocks the tongues
of bawds, and dials the signs of leaping-houses, and the blessed sun
himself a fair hot wench in flame-coloured taffeta, I see no reason
why thou shouldst be so superfluous to demand the time of the day.

FALSTAFF Indeed, you come near me now, Hal, for we that take purses   10
go by the moon and the seven stars, and not 'by Phoebus, he, that
wandering knight so fair'. And I prithee, sweet wag, when thou art
king, as God save thy grace – majesty, I should say, for grace thou
wilt have none –

11–12 'by . . . fair'] *Humphreys;* by . . . faire QqF   13 king] Qq2–5, F; a king Q1

2–9 **Thou art . . . day** 'This comic onslaught . . .
with its tight logical framework and its figures
of climax . . . [is a] superlative instance of high
symmetricality combined with flexibility' (Jonas
Barish, 'Mixed verse and prose in Shakespearean
comedy', *English Comedy*, ed. Michael Cordner
et al., 1994, p. 66.) Many find in this speech, however, a parodoxical effect of improvising, an apparent absence of order.

2 **fat-witted** thick-witted.

2 **sack** General name for white wines imported
from Spain and the Canary Islands. 1.2.92 indicates that Falstaff adds sugar to his sack.

4 **forgotten** neglected, not bothered to (*OED*
Forget sv *v* 4).

5–9 **What a devil . . . time of the day**
Hal attacks Falstaff's supposed indifference to all
clock time.

6 **capons** castrated cocks, big and fat (like Falstaff). The frequent association of Falstaff with
capons, his favourite food, emphasises his gluttony
and his size, and ironically glances at his alleged
lechery.

7 **dials** watches or clock faces; also sundials
which 'tell the hour of the day, by means of the
sun's shadow' (*OED sb*[1] 1).

7 **leaping-houses** brothels, clearly identified
by signs comparable to the signs of taverns or ale-
houses. Stow, *Survey*, describes the signs of the
former 'stewhouses' in Southwark as 'not hanged
out, but painted on the walles' (II, 55). Compare *Ado* 1.1.253–4, 'hang me up at the door of
a brothel-house for the sign of blind Cupid'.

8 **hot wench in flame-coloured taffeta**
Taffeta is a silk fabric associated with dressing to attract attention. Prostitutes might wear
flame-coloured taffeta for ostentatious petticoats
or gowns (compare *AWW* 2.2.22). The colour

suggests passion, but also hell, the punishment
for lechery, and perhaps the torment of venereal
disease. Hal's reference to 'the blessed sun himself' as an exhibitionist 'wench' contrasts with his
later appropriation of the sun/son analogy at 1 57.

9 **superfluous** needlessly concerned, with a
pun on self-indulgent, overflowing.

10 **come near me** A phrase borrowed from
fencing. Although it is often glossed as 'score a
point', it literally means 'just miss me' or 'almost
hit me' – an important distinction for Falstaff's
first line spoken in this duel of wits in which he
proves so elusive an opponent.

11 **go by** (1) are guided by the light of, (2) tell
the time by.

11 **seven stars** constellation of the Pleiades and
perhaps the name of an inn.

11–12 **by Phoebus . . . fair** Warburton (1747)
thought this phrase might come from a lost ballad. Steevens (1785) detected a possible allusion to
the wandering knight of the sun in *The Mirror of
Knighthood*, a romance translated in 1578 by Margaret Tyler. Douce (*Illustrations of Shakespeare*,
1807) suggested a reference to *The Voyage of the
Wandering Knight*, translated in 1581 by William
Goodyear (cited by Hemingway).

11 **Phoebus** A name for Apollo, god of the sun.

12 **wag** Affectionate tag for a mischievous
youth. It shows the intimacy that the Prince allows
Falstaff.

12–13 **when thou art king** The first of Falstaff's many hopeful allusions to the future. The
fact that he so often refers to favours he will be
granted when Hal rules should refute the arguments of many critics that Falstaff cares only for
the present.

13 **grace** A quibble which may well include
four meanings: (1) political majesty, (2) a state of

PRINCE What, none?   15

FALSTAFF No, by my troth, not so much as will serve to be prologue to
an egg and butter.

PRINCE Well, how then? Come, roundly, roundly.

FALSTAFF Marry then, sweet wag, when thou art king let not us that are
squires of the night's body be called thieves of the day's beauty. Let   20
us be Diana's foresters, gentlemen of the shade, minions of the
moon. And let men say we ' be men of good government, being
governed as the sea is, by our noble and chaste mistress the moon,
under whose countenance we steal.

PRINCE Thou sayest well, and it holds well too, for the fortune of us   25
that are the moon's men doth ebb and flow like the sea, being
governed as the sea is, by the moon. As for proof now: a purse of
gold most resolutely snatched on Monday night, and most disso-
lutely spent on Tuesday morning, got with swearing 'Lay by!', and
spent with crying 'Bring in!', now in as low an ebb as the foot of the   30
ladder, and by and by in as high a flow as the ridge of the gallows.

---

27 proof now:| *Collier*, proofe. Now QqF; proof now, *Wilson*

---

spiritual grace, (3) refinement, and (4) the bless-
ing before a meal, the meaning made explicit in
Falstaff's next speech.

17 an egg and butter a simple informal meal,
therefore not requiring that an elaborate grace be
said before it.

18 roundly plainly, without deception or cir-
cumlocution (*OED* 4); (the Prince may glance at
Falstaff's rotund shape).

19 Marry An oath (by the Virgin Mary), so
mild that it remained when others were deleted
from F, in response to the 1606 Act 'to Restraine
Abuses of Players', forbidding profanity onstage.
See Textual Analysis, pp. 219–20.

19–20 let not ... beauty Falstaff absorbs Hal's
attack, rather than refuting it. Punning on night
as knight (a common pun even though the 'k' was
probably pronounced, Cercignani, 320), on body
as bawdy, and on beauty as booty, he asserts that
those who must serve at night should not be criticised for wasting time during the day.

20–2 squires . . . moon Falstaff invents par-
odic titles for officers in the government of the
future king.

20 squires of the night's body Squires of the
body were personal attendants to knights in great
medieval households. There is also a punning allusion to prostitutes whose bodies often are squired
at night.

21 Diana's foresters Servants to the goddess
of the moon, of the hunt, and (ironic in this context) of chastity. For the bawdy sense, see *MM*
4.3.161–2, 'he's a better woodman than thou tak'st
him for'.

21 gentlemen of the shade Suggesting shady
dealings, as in 'gentlemen of the road' for highwaymen. Wilson notes the title of members of
the royal household, 'Gentlemen of the Chamber',
and points out that in *FV*, the Prince promises an
annual pension to all highwaymen (469–74).

21 minions servants or lovers, compare 1.1.82.

22 government (1) discipline or conduct, (2)
the regime in which offices are held.

24 countenance A quibble: (1) face, (2) patronage or protection. Compare 126–7 below.

24 steal (1) rob, (2) go stealthily.

25 it holds well what you say is valid, it applies
(*OED* sv *v* 23c, citing this example).

29 Lay by The equivalent of 'Stand and deliver'
or 'Drop your weapons.'

30 Bring in Order for service in a tavern.

30–1 now . . . gallows According to the
proverb, 'He that is at low ebb at Newgate may
soon be afloat at Tyburn' (Dent E 56). Both low
and high tide, as metaphors for the fortunes of a
thief, bring disaster.

31 ladder At low tide it reaches down into the
water, at high, it leads up to the scaffold.

31 ridge the crossbar for the hangman's rope.

FALSTAFF By the Lord thou sayest true, lad – and is not my Hostess of
    the tavern a most sweet wench?
PRINCE As the honey of Hybla, my old lad of the castle.
    And is not a buff jerkin a most sweet robe of durance?   35
FALSTAFF How now, how now, mad wag? What, in thy quips and thy
    quiddities? What a plague have I to do with a buff jerkin?
PRINCE Why, what a pox have I to do with my Hostess of the tavern?
FALSTAFF Well, thou hast called her to a reckoning many a time and
    oft.   40
PRINCE Did I ever call for thee to pay thy part?
FALSTAFF No, I'll give thee thy due, thou hast paid all there.
PRINCE Yea, and elsewhere, so far as my coin would stretch, and where
    it would not, I have used my credit.
FALSTAFF Yea, and so used it that were it not here apparent that thou   45
    art heir apparent – but I prithee, sweet wag, shall there be gallows
    standing in England when thou art king? And resolution thus

32 **thou sayest true lad,** Falstaff apparently accepts the Prince's insinuation, but quickly changes the subject.

34 **As the honey of Hybla** Hybla is a town in Sicily famous for its honey. The Prince adopts the common phrase 'as sweet as honey' (Dent H544) giving it more resonance through alliteration.

34 **my old lad of the castle** Echoing 'my Hostess of the tavern', with word-play on Sir John Oldcastle, the name given to the Falstaff character in the first version of the play. 'Old lad of the castle' was also a familiar phrase (Dent C124.1). Humphreys suggests an allusion to 'one of Southwark's principal brothels . . . called The Castle' (mentioned by Stow, *Survey*, II, 55), and cites G. R. Owst's observation that a tavern in homiletic works was often called 'the devil's castle' (*Literature and Pulpit in Medieval England*, 1961, p. 438.) On the change from 'Oldcastle' to Falstaff, see Introduction, pp. 5–6, 29–30 and Textual Analysis, p. 220.

35 **buff jerkin** close-fitting leather jacket worn by an arresting officer. Ian Donaldson, 'Falstaff's buff jerkin', *SQ* 37 (1986), 100–1, suggests that 'buff' may refer to human skin, initiating a sexual joke continued in 'sweet robe'. The Prince mocks Falstaff's praise for the Hostess by implying that she is a '*bona roba*' or prostitute.

35 **durance** (1) long wearing quality, (2) imprisonment (here for stealing), (3) sturdy fabric.

37 **quiddities** quibbles, subtleties (*OED* 2); literally 'subtle definitions', the 'what-ness of a thing'.

38 **what a pox** Echoes Falstaff's 'What a plague'. Because pocks/pox can mean 'plague' there is probably an allusion to venereal disease, prompted by insinuations about the Hostess.

39 **reckoning** (1) payment of the tavern bill, (2) an account for herself, and (3) by innuendo, sexual encounter. Bevington notes that this exchange continues to build through puns on payment and sexuality ('pay thy part', 41, 'paid all there', 42, 'coin would stretch', 43). Dent, p. xviii, uses this passage as a primary example of how recognising a proverb, 'Oft counting makes good friends' (C706) can throw new light on the text: 'For me, at least, this clarifies the jest in what has otherwise seemed a pointless line.'

44 **credit** (1) financial solvency, based on confidence that debts will be paid, as in 169, (2) good name (*OED* sv *sb* 5b).

45–9 **Yea . . . thief** Falstaff repeats for the third time 'when thou art king' and his anxiety about future legal consequences. In sharp contrast to Shakespeare's Prince Hal, the Prince in *FV* (455–6), claims, 'When I am King, we will have no such things' (as prisons).

45–6 **were . . . heir apparent** The obvious pun may cloak a warning against the loss of reputation.

47–8 **resolution thus fubbed** courage so cheated or robbed.

fubbed as it is with the rusty curb of old Father Antic the law? Do
not thou when thou art king hang a thief.

PRINCE No, thou shalt. 50

FALSTAFF Shall I? O rare! By the Lord, I'll be a brave judge!

PRINCE Thou judgest false already! I mean thou shalt have the hanging
of the thieves, and so become a rare hangman.

FALSTAFF Well, Hal, well! And in some sort it jumps with my humour
– as well as waiting in the court, I can tell you. 55

PRINCE For obtaining of suits?

FALSTAFF Yea, for obtaining of suits, whereof the hangman hath no
lean wardrobe. 'Sblood, I am as melancholy as a gib cat, or a lugged
bear.

PRINCE Or an old lion, or a lover's lute. 60

FALSTAFF Yea, or the drone of a Lincolnshire bagpipe.

PRINCE What sayest thou to a hare, or the melancholy of Moorditch?

FALSTAFF Thou hast the most unsavoury similes, and art indeed the
most comparative rascalliest sweet young prince. But Hal, I prithee

---

48 law?] F; law, Qq1, 2; law: Qq3–5   63 similes] Q5; smiles Qq1–4, F

48 old Father Antic the law Falstaff carica-
tures authority as a grotesque old buffoon named
for Antic, a clown in earlier Tudor drama and a
figure for death in *R2* (3.2.162).

51 brave excellent, as well as courageous or
stylish.

52 judgest (1) pass sentence, (2) choose a meaning.

52–3 thou shalt . . . thieves Proverbial: 'The
great thieves hang the little ones' (Dent T119). In
FV, the Prince promises to make his henchman
Ned Chief Justice (459–61).

54 jumps with my humour fits my temperament or mood. Compare 156.

55 waiting in the court 'Court' means royal
court as well as court of justice. Falstaff rejects the
role of petitioner or plaintiff waiting for his 'suit'
or plea to be dealt with.

57–8 Yea . . . wardrobe Public executioners
received as perquisites the clothing ('suits') of
those they hanged.

58 'Sblood Literally, 'by Christ's blood', but
used loosely like 'zounds' ('God's wounds').

58–62 melancholy . . . Moorditch Falstaff
and Hal compete, returning, as if they were tennis
balls, similes of melancholy, a condition of gloom
which might be temporary or chronic.

58 gib cat A male or tom-cat, not necessarily castrated (*OED sb*¹ 2). Gib is a diminutive of
Gilbert, a common name for a cat.

58 lugged baited. A local allusion because bear-
baiting was a rival attraction to the theatre on

Bankside. The chained bear is a melancholy
object.

60 lover's lute In *Ado*, Claudio contrasts
the sad pensive mood frequently connoted by
lute music to Benedick's earlier jesting humour
(3.2.59–60).

61 drone . . . bagpipe Davison suggests that
'Shakespeare has in mind the drone of a long-
winded speaker' or 'windbag', a meaning not
recorded for 'bagpipe' until 1603. English bagpipes were apparently linked in Elizabethan times
to Lancashire and Lincolnshire (Humphreys).

62 hare Dent (H151) cites the proverbial belief
that eating the hare's flesh caused melancholy.
The hare is commonly contrasted to the lion's
active and courageous temper. Turberville, *Booke
of Hunting*, 1575, p. 160, says the hare is one of the
'moste melancholike beastes that is'.

62 Moorditch A narrow, filthy ditch (remain-
ing from the moat around the walls) between Bish-
opsgate and Moorgate, north of the City of London. It had been widened and cleaned in 1595,
but was 'never the better' (Stow, *Survey*, I, 20). Its
proximity to Bedlam, the madhouse, would add to
its associations with melancholy (Sugden).

64 comparative one who makes witty comparisons. The King uses the word to describe trivial
mockers, 3.2.67.

64–9 But Hal . . . too Falstaff imitates 'the

trouble me no more with vanity. I would to God thou and I knew   65
where a commodity of good names were to be bought. An old lord of
the Council rated me the other day in the street about you, sir, but
I marked him not, and yet he talked very wisely, but I regarded him
not, and yet he talked wisely – and in the street too.

PRINCE Thou didst well, for wisdom cries out in the streets and no man   70
regards it.

FALSTAFF O, thou hast damnable iteration, and art indeed able to
corrupt a saint. Thou hast done much harm upon me, Hal, God
forgive thee for it. Before I knew thee, Hal, I knew nothing, and now
am I, if a man should speak truly, little better than one of the wicked.   75
I must give over this life, and I will give it over. By the Lord, an I do
not I am a villain. I'll be damned for never a king's son in Christendom.

PRINCE Where shall we take a purse tomorrow, Jack?

FALSTAFF Zounds, where thou wilt, lad, I'll make one; an I do not, call   80
me villain and baffle me.

PRINCE I see a good amendment of life in thee, from praying to purse-
taking.

FALSTAFF Why Hal, 'tis my vocation, Hal. 'Tis no sin for a man to
labour in his vocation.   85

---

70 wisdom . . . and] Qq; *not in* F   73 upon] Q1; unto Qq2–5, F   76 an] QqF (and), *Pope*

Scriptural style of the sanctimonious Puritan'
(Hemingway), initiating another serious concern,
repentance. Other examples include 'little better
than one of the wicked', 75, and 'I must give over
this life', 76. Hal takes up this theme in his soliloquy that concludes this scene. Compare 76 and
note.

65 trouble me no more with vanity Falstaff pretends that he has been corrupted by
the Prince's frivolity. Bevington observes that the
term 'vanity' is 'repeatedly associated with Falstaff as Hal's companion'.

66 commodity supply.

66 names reputations.

67 rated scolded.

70 wisdom . . . streets The Prince echoes
Proverbs 1.20: 'Wisdome cryeth without; she
uttereth her voyce in the stretes', and 1.24:
'Because I have called, and ye refused: I have
stretched out mine hand, and none wolde regarde.'
He mocks Falstaff by implying that he is immune
to wisdom.

72 damnable iteration It was commonly
thought that the Devil was a sophisticated theologian and could glibly quote Scripture. Distorting
this sense, Falstaff jokingly accuses Hal of repeat-

ing but twisting biblical allusion in order to lead
him to damnation.

73 corrupt a saint This self-praise is a comic
forerunner of the way the hypocrite Angelo identifies himself in *MM* 2.2.179–80: 'Oh cunning
enemy, that to catch a saint, / With saints dost
bait thy hook!'

76 I must give over this life A canting parody
in advance of Hal's programme for self-reform,
155 ff. The Wycliffites and Lollards, with whom
the historical Oldcastle was associated, anticipated
the Protestant Reformers in their emphasis on personal faith and salvation.

76 an if.

77 villain one who (1) has no principles or honour, (2) is of low birth.

80 Zounds God's wounds; a particularly strong
oath. Compare ''Sblood', 58.

80 make one be one of the participants.

81 baffle Literally, to disgrace a perjured
knight who has lost his honour by hanging him
– or his shield – upside down. Compare Spenser,
The Faerie Queene VI, vii, 27.

82 amendment of life reformation.

84–5 'Tis no sin . . . vocation Alluding ironi-

Enter POINS

Poins! Now shall we know if Gadshill have set a match. O, if men
were to be saved by merit, what hole in hell were hot enough for
him? This is the most omnipotent villain that ever cried 'Stand!' to
a true man.

PRINCE Good morrow, Ned.   90

POINS Good morrow, sweet Hal. What says Monsieur Remorse? What
says Sir John Sack, and Sugar Jack? How agrees the devil and thee
about thy soul, that thou soldest him on Good Friday last, for a cup
of Madeira and a cold capon's leg?

PRINCE Sir John stands to his word, the devil shall have his bargain, for   95
he was never yet a breaker of proverbs. He will give the devil his
due.

POINS Then art thou damned for keeping thy word with the devil.

PRINCE Else he had been damned for cozening the devil.

POINS But my lads, my lads, tomorrow morning, by four o'clock early   100
at Gad's Hill, there are pilgrims going to Canterbury with rich

---

85 SD] Qq; *not in* F   86 Poins! Now] *Theobald;* Poynes nowe Q; Pointz. |*taken as a speech heading*| Now Qq4,5, F
86 match] Qq; Watch F   92 Sack, and Sugar Jack?] Qq1–4 *subst.;* Sacke and Sugar: Jacke? F; Sack-and-Sugar? Jack! *Rowe*

---

cally to 1 Cor. 7.20, 'Let every man abide in the same vocation wherein he was called.' This was a favourite text of Protestant preachers, urging hard work and conformity to the social order.

86 Poins See Collation for the confusion of speakers in Qq4, 5, F.

86 Gadshill See List of Characters for the confusion of the character and the location, Gad's Hill (101 below).

86 set a match thieves' cant, meaning 'plan a robbery'. In 2.2.40, Gadshill is 'our setter'.

87 by merit i.e. by good works, not faith alone. Falstaff finds it opportune here to side against Lutheran theology in the Reformation controversy over salvation. Luther maintained that man could only be saved by faith and God's grace.

88 omnipotent almighty, a comic exaggeration.

88 Stand The cry with which the highwayman stops his victim.

89 true honest.

91 Monsieur Remorse Continuing the mockery of Puritan piety. In giving Falstaff a fictive name, Poins shows familiarity with Falstaff's pretence of repentance.

92 Sir John Sack, and Sugar Jack 'Jack' is the familiar diminutive of John, while sack and sugar

is Sir John's favourite drink. Poins' word-play touches on 'jack' as a common term for 'knave' (i.e. a social inferior) and for a drinking vessel. 'Sack' may quibble on the sackcloth worn by a penitent (Monsieur Remorse). Q punctuation, followed here, creates a more balanced antithesis; if Poins pauses instead after 'John' or 'Sugar', he can alter the play of meaning within the line (i.e. 'after all, you are only Jack').

93 Good Friday The strictest fast-day.

95–9 Sir John . . . devil Promise-keeping was essential to the knightly code. Hal and Poins enjoy using it to trap Falstaff (if one accepts their logic) in hell.

96 breaker of proverbs A proverbial saying (Dent P 615.1), applied to someone who breaks the rules taught by proverbs.

96 devil The insistent allusions to damnation keep an audience aware of the Morality-drama features of the play. See Introduction, pp. 10 ff.

99 cozening cheating.

101 Gad's Hill Two miles north-west of Rochester in Kent on the road to London. It was notorious for robberies.

101 pilgrims A major route for pilgrims going to the shrine of St Thomas at Canterbury crossed Gad's Hill. Those actually robbed in 2.2 are simply called Travellers.

offerings and traders riding to London with fat purses. I have
vizards for you all; you have horses for yourselves. Gadshill lies
tonight in Rochester. I have bespoke supper tomorrow night in
Eastcheap. We may do it as secure as sleep. If you will go, I will stuff   105
your purses full of crowns. If you will not, tarry at home and be
hanged.

FALSTAFF Hear ye, Yedward, if I tarry at home and go not, I'll hang
you for going.

POINS You will, chops?   110

FALSTAFF Hal, wilt thou make one?

PRINCE Who I? Rob? I, a thief? Not I, by my faith.

FALSTAFF There's neither honesty, manhood, nor good fellowship in
thee, nor thou camest not of the blood royal, if thou darest not stand
for ten shillings.   115

PRINCE Well then, once in my days I'll be a madcap.

FALSTAFF Why, that's well said.

PRINCE Well, come what will, I'll tarry at home.

FALSTAFF By the Lord, I'll be a traitor then, when thou art king.

PRINCE I care not.   120

POINS Sir John, I prithee leave the Prince and me alone. I will lay him
down such reasons for this adventure that he shall go.

FALSTAFF Well, God give thee the spirit of persuasion, and him the
ears of profiting, that what thou speakest may move, and what he
hears may be believed, that the true prince may – for recreation sake   125

---

110 chops?] Q7; chops. Qq1–5, F, Q6   123 God give . . . him] Qq; maist thou have . . . he F

103 **vizards** masks.
104 **bespoke** ordered.
105 **Eastcheap** District of the City of London,
named after Great Eastcheap Street, and the setting for the tavern scenes, 2.4 and 3.3. In *FV* the
Prince himself proposes a meeting there. Shakespeare never names the tavern – traditionally
called 'The Boar's Head'. Compare 2.4.12.
106 **crowns** Coins valued at five shillings each.
Ironic parallels between stealing kingdoms and
stealing money, as well as between rulers and coins,
become more explicit at 114–15. Contrast the plan
of the Prince to reveal himself as 'bright metal',
172.
108 **Yedward** Dialect form of Edward.
108–9 **hang you** turn state's evidence and get
you hanged. Clearly a jest.
110 **chops** fat or bloated cheeks (*OED* sv *sb*² 3).
114 **royal** A quibble on the coin of that name,

then worth ten shillings. Compare *2H4* 1.2.23.
114–15 **stand for** (1) fight for, (2) be worth ten
shillings.
116 **madcap** reckless, wildly impulsive person
(*OED*), alluding to a proverb, Dent D121.1, 'to be
mad once in one's days'.
122 **adventure** daring feat. Compare 1.1.92
and note.
123–7 **Well . . . countenance.** Falstaff parodies
the emphasis on inspiration and spiritual recep-
tiveness in Puritan preaching. His speech takes the
form of a 'collect' or prayer used at the conclusion
of a service and aptly leads to his exit-line (Bevington, citing Peter Milward, *Shakespeare's Religious
Background*, 1973, pp. 107–8 on the prayer, and
Richmond Noble, *Shakespeare's Biblical Knowledge and use of the Book of Common Prayer*, 1935,
p. 171 on the service).

– prove a false thief, for the poor abuses of the time want countenance. Farewell, you shall find me in Eastcheap.

PRINCE Farewell, the latter spring! Farewell, All-hallown summer!

[*Exit Falstaff*]

POINS Now my good sweet honey lord, ride with us tomorrow. I have
a jest to execute that I cannot manage alone. Falstaff, Peto,   130
Bardolph, and Gadshill shall rob those men that we have already
waylaid – yourself and I will not be there. And when they have the
booty, if you and I do not rob them – cut this head off from my
shoulders.

PRINCE How shall we part with them in setting forth?   135

POINS Why, we will set forth before or after them, and appoint them a
place of meeting – wherein it is at our pleasure to fail – and then will
they adventure upon the exploit themselves, which they shall have
no sooner achieved but we'll set upon them.

PRINCE Yea, but 'tis like that they will know us by our horses, by our   140
habits, and by every other appointment to be ourselves.

POINS Tut, our horses they shall not see, I'll tie them in the wood. Our
vizards we will change after we leave them. And, sirrah, I have cases
of buckram for the nonce, to immask our noted outward garments.

PRINCE Yea, but I doubt they will be too hard for us.   145

POINS Well, for two of them, I know them to be as true-bred cowards as
ever turned back, and for the third, if he fight longer than he sees
reason, I'll forswear arms. The virtue of this jest will be the incom-

128 the] QqF; thou *Pope*   128 SD *Exit Falstaff*] F2; *not in* QqF   130–1 Peto, Bardolph] *Bevington;* Harvey, Rossill QqF;
Bardolph, Peto *Theobald;* Harvey, Russell *Oxford*   135 How] Qq; But how F   140 Yea, but] Qq (Yea but); I, but F
145 Yea, but] Qq; But F

126–7 poor . . . countenance Falstaff refers
to complaints that the nobility are not sufficiently
generous; he may also be asking them, perhaps
hypocritically, to prevent disorder by helping the
poor.

128 All-hallown summer Like 'latter spring',
referring to Falstaff's youthful behaviour in old
age, unseasonal warm weather sometimes occurring about 1 November, All Hallows or All Saints'
Day.

129 sweet honey Terms of endearment
addressed to both sexes. Compare 'Sugar Jack',
92 above.

130–1 Peto, Bardolph For a detailed analysis of how the names of Falstaff's companions,
Bardolph and Peto, were presumably altered from
Rossill and Harvey when Oldcastle was changed
to Falstaff, see Melchiori p. 5 and pp. 9–15.

132 waylaid set an ambush for.

135–53 How shall . . . Farewell Hal plays the
straight man, thereby learning the details of Poins'
plan, but delaying our insight about his own character.

137 at our pleasure our choice.

141 habits clothing.

141 appointment piece of equipment, accou-
trement.

143 sirrah A familiar form of 'sir', used when
addressing underlings and children, but also, as
here, comrades (Kittredge).

143–4 cases . . . nonce coarse cloth suits or
overalls for the occasion.

145 doubt fear.

148–9 incomprehensible (1) beyond limits or
bounds, (2) beyond understanding. The meaning
'uncatchable', not cited by *OED* before 1607, may
also be suggested; to 'comprehend' is to seize or
entrap (*OED v* 1).

prehensible lies that this same fat rogue will tell us when we meet at
supper. How thirty at least he fought with, what wards, what blows,   150
what extremities he endured, and in the reproof of this lives the jest.

PRINCE Well, I'll go with thee. Provide us all things necessary and meet
me tomorrow night in Eastcheap. There I'll sup. Farewell.

POINS Farewell, my lord.   *Exit Poins*

PRINCE I know you all, and will a while uphold   155
The unyoked humour of your idleness.
Yet herein will I imitate the sun,
Who doth permit the base contagious clouds
To smother up his beauty from the world,
That when he please again to be himself,   160
Being wanted, he may be more wondered at
By breaking through the foul and ugly mists
Of vapours that did seem to strangle him.
If all the year were playing holidays,
To sport would be as tedious as to work;   165
But when they seldom come, they wished-for come,
And nothing pleaseth but rare accidents.
So when this loose behaviour I throw off,
And pay the debt I never promisèd,
By how much better than my word I am,   170

---

151 lives] Q1; lyes Qq2–5, F

149 this same fat rogue Falstaff. According to
OED, 'rogue' (sv *sb*) is one of 'the numerous canting words introduced about the middle of the 16th
cent. to designate the various kinds of beggars and
vaga-bonds . . .'. Shakespeare uses 'rogue' fourteen times in *1H4*, twice as often as in any other
play except *2H4* (thirteen).

150 wards stances for defence or methods of
parrying attack in fencing.

151 reproof disproof, with the additional sense
'reprimand' perhaps implied (*OED sv sb*[1] 5 and 3).
Compare 3.2.23.

153 tomorrow night They of course plan to
meet in the morning at Gad's Hill, but the mind
and tongue of the Prince (or of his creator) leap
ahead to the more exciting aftermath of the robbery.

155 I know you all Although only Poins has
just departed, 'you all' refers generally to Prince
Hal's companions. Its sense may even extend
to all the people in the audience and in the
realm. Johnson comments on the Prince's speech
here as 'a natural picture of a great mind offer-

ing excuses to itself and palliating those follies
which it can neither justify nor forsake' (*Johnson on Shakespeare, The Yale Edition*, vol. VII ed.
Arthur Sherbo, 1968, p. 458). For detailed discussion of this soliloquy, its implications, and possible staging, see Introduction, pp. 10–12, 42 and
illustration 2.

156 unyoked humour unrestrained inclination.

157 sun Often used as a symbol for royalty.

158 contagious clouds 'Pestilence was
thought to be generated in fog, mist, and cloud'
(Kittredge).

161 Being wanted . . . more wondered at For
strikingly similar cynicism about creating a reputation for virtue, compare Cressida's soliloquy,
Tro. 1.2.282–95.

161 wanted missed.

163 strangle stifle or quench (a fire) (*OED sv v*
3a). Compare *Mac.* 'dark night strangles the trav-
elling lamp' (2.4.7).

167 rare accidents exceptional events which
are also unexpected.

By so much shall I falsify men's hopes.
And like bright metal on a sullen ground,
My reformation, glitt'ring o'er my fault,
Shall show more goodly, and attract more eyes
Than that which hath no foil to set it off.   175
I'll so offend, to make offence a skill,
Redeeming time when men think least I will.   *Exit*

[**1.3**] *Enter the* KING, NORTHUMBERLAND, WORCESTER, HOTSPUR,
SIR WALTER BLUNT, *with others*

KING My blood hath been too cold and temperate,
    Unapt to stir at these indignities,
    And you have found me – for accordingly
    You tread upon my patience. But be sure
    I will from henceforth rather be myself,   5
    Mighty, and to be feared, than my condition
    Which hath been smooth as oil, soft as young down,
    And therefore lost that title of respect,
    Which the proud soul ne'er pays but to the proud.
WORCESTER Our house, my sovereign liege, little deserves   10

---

175 foil] Qq1–3 (foile); soile Qq4, 5; soyle F   177 SD] Qq; *not in* F   Act 1, Scene 3   1.3] *Scana Tertia*. F; *not in* Qq

171 hopes expectations. 'Hope' for Elizabethans could be much more ambivalent than for the modern audience. In the primary meaning (*OED* sv *sb*¹ 1a), expectation and desire are combined; in a second sense, there is no implication of desire.

172 bright metal See 106 n. above.

172 sullen ground dark background serving as a foil (175), as on a damascened sword.

175 foil That which makes another thing look better by a contrast in colour or quality (*OED* sv *sb*¹ 6).

176 skill A piece of good strategy and an art (not a vice or crime).

177 Redeeming time (1) Paying back time, as in 'redeeming a debt', (2) Making amends for lost time, (3) Making the best use of time as in 'walke circumspectly, not as fooles, but as wise, / Redeeming the time: for the dayes are evil' (Eph. 5.15–16). Compare Col. 4.5.

Act 1, Scene 3
[1.3] No explicit time or place is designated

in the dialogue. The Council meeting was proposed at 1.1.102–3 for Windsor, where Holinshed also locates it. Some time must have passed after 1.1. This may now well be 'Wednesday next' (1.1.102).

0 SD In contrast to 1.1, where the King dominates his reliable followers, this second court scene gives prominence to three men whom the King distrusts.

1–9 My blood . . . to the proud Starting with his first word, using five first-person pronouns or adjectives, King Henry shows much greater confidence than he did in opening the play. No longer 'wan with care', he forcefully moves in five lines from past to present to future. See Introduction, p. 9.

3 found found me so.

5 myself my royal self.

6 condition natural disposition, as in 'blood', 1 above. Compare 3.1.175.

10 house An extended alliance of the Percy family with their followers.

The scourge of greatness to be used on it,
And that same greatness too which our own hands
Have helped to make so portly.
NORTHUMBERLAND   My lord –
KING Worcester, get thee gone, for I do see
        Danger and disobedience in thine eye.   15
        O sir, your presence is too bold and peremptory,
        And majesty might never yet endure
        The moody frontier of a servant brow.
        You have good leave to leave us. When we need
        Your use and counsel we shall send for you.   20

                                        Exit Worcester

[*To Northumberland*] You were about to speak.
NORTHUMBERLAND   Yea, my good lord.
        Those prisoners in your highness' name demanded,
        Which Harry Percy here at Holmedon took,
        Were, as he says, not with such strength denied
        As is delivered to your majesty.   25
        Either envy therefore, or misprision,
        Is guilty of this fault, and not my son.
HOTSPUR My liege, I did deny no prisoners.
        But I remember when the fight was done,
        When I was dry with rage and extreme toil,   30
        Breathless and faint, leaning upon my sword,
        Came there a certain lord, neat and trimly dressed,
        Fresh as a bridegroom, and his chin new reaped
        Showed like a stubble-land at harvest-home.

---

13 helped] Qq (holpe)   20 SD *Exit Worcester*] Qq; *not in* F   21 SD *To Northumberland*] Rowe; *not in* QqF   22 name] Qq;
not in F   25 is] Qq1–4; he Q5; was F   26 Either envy therefore] Qq; Who either through envy F   27 Is] Qq; Was F

11 scourge The action, agent, and instrument
of extreme punishment. Compare 3.2.7 and n.
13 portly stately, imposing, (with a hint of criticism). In *R2*, Northumberland and Worcester
were Henry's strongest supporters.
16 peremptory obstinate.
18 moody . . . brow frowning forehead of a servant. Henry compares the angry brows to a fort's
rampart, objecting to such hostility from an ally.
In calling Worcester 'servant', he exaggerates the
inferior status of a subject.

19 good leave full permission.
25 delivered reported.
26 envy malice.
26 misprision misunderstanding.
32 neat foppish, exquisite.
33–4 new reaped . . . harvest-home His
fresh shaved chin contrasts with the soldiers'
rough beards, the image implying that their work,
unlike the harvest, is not yet finished.

He was perfumèd like a milliner,   35
And 'twixt his finger and his thumb he held
A pouncet-box, which ever and anon
He gave his nose, and took't away again –
Who therewith angry, when it next came there,
Took it in snuff. And still he smiled and talked;   40
And as the soldiers bore dead bodies by,
He called them untaught knaves, unmannerly,
To bring a slovenly unhandsome corpse
Betwixt the wind and his nobility.
With many holiday and lady terms   45
He questioned me, amongst the rest demanded
My prisoners in your majesty's behalf.
I then, all smarting with my wounds being cold,
To be so pestered with a popinjay,
Out of my grief and my impatience   50
Answered neglectingly, I know not what,
He should, or he should not, for he made me mad
To see him shine so brisk, and smell so sweet,
And talk so like a waiting-gentlewoman
Of guns, and drums, and wounds, God save the mark!   55
And telling me the sovereignest thing on earth
Was parmacity for an inward bruise,
And that it was great pity, so it was,
This villainous saltpetre should be digged
Out of the bowels of the harmless earth,   60

---

52 or he| Qq; or F   59 This| Qq; That F

35 milliner dealer in bonnets and gloves, often perfumed; an occupation for men in earlier times. The analogy suggests effeminacy, as at 45 and 54 below.

37 pouncet-box a small box with a perforated lid, which held aromatic herbs or snuff. The term is not recorded before this example (*OED*).

39 Who i.e. the nose, suggesting a personification, as of the sun at 1.2.158 and the river at 1.3.103.

40 Took it in snuff Inhaled, and (with a pun) took offence (*OED* Snuff *sb*¹ 4).

45 holiday and lady terms dainty, lady-like expressions, not workaday words.

46 questioned 'interrogated' and perhaps also insisted on talking.

49 popinjay parrot, a prattler with gaudy plumes who only repeats imitatively. The explosive alliteration displays Hotspur's impatience.

50 grief pain (*OED* sv *sb* 6)

51 neglectingly negligently (first citation in *OED*).

55 God save the mark An expression of indignation, but normally (Dent G179.1) a common formula for apology and deprecation, 'Mark' probably refers to the sign of the cross, used to ward off evil. Hotspur may be parroting one of the messenger's 'lady terms'.

57 parmacity A variant form of spermaceti, fatty substance from the sperm whale used as medicine.

59 saltpetre Chief ingredient in gunpowder, also used as medicine.

> Which many a good tall fellow had destroyed
> So cowardly, and but for these vile guns
> He would himself have been a soldier.
> This bald unjointed chat of his, my lord,
> I answered indirectly, as I said,   65
> And I beseech you, let not his report
> Come current for an accusation
> Betwixt my love and your high majesty.
> BLUNT The circumstance considered, good my lord,
> Whate'er Lord Harry Percy then had said   70
> To such a person, and in such a place,
> At such a time, with all the rest retold,
> May reasonably die, and never rise
> To do him wrong, or any way impeach
> What then he said, so he unsay it now.   75
> KING Why, yet he doth deny his prisoners,
> But with proviso and exception,
> That we at our own charge shall ransom straight
> His brother-in-law, the foolish Mortimer,
> Who, on my soul, hath wilfully betrayed   80
> The lives of those that he did lead to fight
> Against that great magician, damned Glendower,
> Whose daughter, as we hear, that Earl of March
> Hath lately married. Shall our coffers then
> Be emptied to redeem a traitor home?   85

61 Which The saltpetre, 59; gunpowder has destroyed many a brave man.

61 tall strong in combat.

64 bald empty, trivial.

65 indirectly without paying attention. Compare 'neglectingly', 51 and note.

67 come current (1) be accepted at face value, (2) rush in, like a flood.

70 had said may have said.

72 retold Compare 1.1.46, the only other use in the play.

74–5 or . . . now i.e. or provide legal grounds for accusation, unless he refuses to retract it now.

76 yet still (spoken emphatically).

77 But . . . exception i.e. except on the condition or stipulation ('proviso').

78 ransom The ruler had a duty to free his agents and officers.

78 straight at once, immediately.

79 brother-in-law The historical Hotspur married Elizabeth (called Kate by Shakespeare) who was elder sister to Lord Edmund Mortimer (1376–1409), Glendower's captive and son-in-law. See 2.3.75 and List of Characters.

82 great magician, damned Glendower The King is understandably angry at this Welshman who has defeated him personally three times and won over Mortimer, his representative. Compare 3.1.60–3. For a fuller discussion, see Appendix, pp. 231–2.

83 Earl of March i.e. Mortimer. Shakespeare confused this Edmund Mortimer with his brother Roger's son, Edmund, heir to the throne. The older Edmund Mortimer was in fact never Earl of March. See List of Characters.

85 redeem In association with 'coffers', the commercial sense 'buy back' applies. For the wide range of meanings crucial to the play, see 1.2.177 and note. As with 'ransom' 78 above, spiritual and financial meanings become ironically intertwined.

> Shall we buy treason, and indent with fears
> When they have lost and forfeited themselves?
> No, on the barren mountains let him starve.
> For I shall never hold that man my friend
> Whose tongue shall ask me for one penny cost   90
> To ransom home revolted Mortimer.

HOTSPUR   Revolted Mortimer!
> He never did fall off, my sovereign liege,
> But by the chance of war. To prove that true
> Needs no more but one tongue for all those wounds,   95
> Those mouthèd wounds, which valiantly he took,
> When on the gentle Severn's sedgy bank,
> In single opposition, hand to hand,
> He did confound the best part of an hour
> In changing hardiment with great Glendower.   100
> Three times they breathed, and three times did they drink
> Upon agreement of swift Severn's flood,
> Who then affrighted with their bloody looks
> Ran fearfully among the trembling reeds,
> And hid his crisp head in the hollow bank   105
> Bloodstained with these valiant combatants.
> Never did bare and rotten policy
> Colour her working with such deadly wounds,
> Nor never could the noble Mortimer
> Receive so many, and all willingly.   110

---

94 war.] Qq2–5, F; war, Q1   95 tongue for] *Hanmer;* tongue: for Qq; tongue. For F   107 bare] Qq; base F

---

86 Shall . . . fears Make a binding contract with those who (1) are cowards, (2) threaten us.

88 No . . . starve According to Thomas Phaer in *A Mirror for Magistrates*, the Prince of Wales chased Glendower 'to the mountaynes, where he miserably dyed for lacke of foode' (Bullough, p. 197). Shakespeare turns a probability into a wish and changes its human object.

93 fall off (1) leave our party, (2) change allegiance.

96 mouthèd gaping. See *JC* 3.1.259–60: 'wounds . . . / Which like dumb mouths do ope their ruby lips'. The association of wounds with mouths is conventional.

97 Severn A river which divides England from south-eastern Wales. See 3.1.70–1.

97 sedgy bordered with reeds and rushes.

98 single opposition man-to-man.

99 confound spend (*OED* sv *v* 1e, citing this

line). For a vivid contrast, see 'fought a long hour', 5.4.140 and n.

100 changing hardiment exchanging hard and courageous blows.

101 breathed paused for breath.

102 flood river.

103 Who The river is personified in this rhetorically elaborate passage. Compare 39 above.

105 crisp Continuing the personification of the river, here seen as wavy-haired because of its rippled or curled surface.

107–8 Never . . . wounds i.e. these dreadful wounds prove that Mortimer was loyal, because a deceiver (the King's accusation) cannot counterfeit such wounds.

107 bare poor, beggarly. Compare 3.2.13 and note.

107 policy cunning, trickery, expedience.

108 Colour Disguise (and make coloured).

Then let not him be slandered with revolt.

KING   Thou dost belie him, Percy, thou dost belie him,
He never did encounter with Glendower.
I tell thee, he durst as well have met the devil alone
As Owen Glendower for an enemy.   115
Art thou not ashamed? But sirrah, henceforth
Let me not hear you speak of Mortimer.
Send me your prisoners with the speediest means –
Or you shall hear in such a kind from me
As will displease you. My Lord Northumberland: 120
We license your departure with your son.
Send us your prisoners, or you will hear of it.

                        Exit King [, *with Blunt and train*]

HOTSPUR And if the devil come and roar for them
I will not send them. I will after straight
And tell him so, for I will ease my heart,   125
Albeit I make a hazard of my head.

NORTHUMBERLAND What? Drunk with choler? Stay, and pause a while,
Here comes your uncle.

                        Enter WORCESTER

HOTSPUR   Speak of Mortimer?
Zounds, I will speak of him, and let my soul
Want mercy if I do not join with him.   130
Yea, on his part I'll empty all these veins
And shed my dear blood, drop by drop in the dust,
But I will lift the down-trod Mortimer

---

114 I tell thee,] *As* QqF; *deleted by Pope; as a separate line,* Steevens   122 SD *with Blunt and train*] Capell *subst.; not in*
QqF   126 Albeit I make a] Qq; Although it be with F   131 Yea, on his part] Qq; In his behalfe F   133 down-trod] Qq;
downfall F

111 **slandered** accused or discredited. 'Slander' often connotes deliberate malice and falsehood in Shakespeare's plays. C. T. Onions' influential *A Shakespeare Glossary* (1911; enlarged
edn 1966) misleadingly confines its senses to
'reproach' or 'bring disgrace upon'.

112–22 **Thou . . . it** Henry dishonours Hotspur by denying his word and by referring to him
as 'thou', 'thee', 'sirrah', and 'your son'.

112 **belie** misrepresent.

114 **I . . . alone** QqF print these thirteen syllables
as one line.

121 **We . . . son** A command thinly disguised
as a permission.

123 **if the devil come and roar** This echoes
1 Pet. 5.8: 'Your adversarie the devil, as a roaring lyon walketh about, seeking whome he may
devoure.'

124 **will after straight** will follow him at once.

126 **Albeit** Although (literally, 'although it
be that'). Compare *Cym.* 2.3.55–6: 'A worthy fellow, / Albeit he comes on angry purpose now.'

127 **choler** anger, a humour or physical condition caused by excessive bile.

130 **Want mercy** Be damned.

133 **But** i.e. even if I have to bleed to death
(131–2).

As high in the air as this unthankful King,
As this ingrate and cankered Bullingbrook.   135
NORTHUMBERLAND Brother, the King hath made your nephew mad.
WORCESTER Who struck this heat up after I was gone?
HOTSPUR He will forsooth have all my prisoners,
          And when I urged the ransom once again
          Of my wife's brother, then his cheek looked pale,   140
          And on my face he turned an eye of death,
          Trembling even at the name of Mortimer.
WORCESTER I cannot blame him. Was not he proclaimed,
          By Richard that dead is, the next of blood?
NORTHUMBERLAND He was, I heard the proclamation.   145
          And then it was, when the unhappy King –
          Whose wrongs in us God pardon! – did set forth
          Upon his Irish expedition;
          From whence he, intercepted, did return
          To be deposed, and shortly murderèd.   150
WORCESTER And for whose death we in the world's wide mouth
          Live scandalised and foully spoken of.
HOTSPUR But soft, I pray you, did King Richard then
          Proclaim my brother Edmund Mortimer
          Heir to the crown?
NORTHUMBERLAND   He did, myself did hear it.   155
HOTSPUR Nay then, I cannot blame his cousin King,
          That wished him on the barren mountains starve.
          But shall it be that you that set the crown
          Upon the head of this forgetful man,

---

135 Bullingbrook] QqF (Bullingbrooke); Bolingbroke, *Pope*   143 not he] Qq; he not F   157 starve] Qq; starv'd F

135 ingrate ungrateful.
135 cankered diseased, ulcerated, wormy. Hotspur may insinuate the King's inferior stock or lineage, as in his reference to the 'canker' or wild rose at 174 below.
135 Bullingbrook Hotspur rudely insists upon the name used before the King assumed the crown. See List of Characters.
138 forsooth 'truly' in normal usage, but here used to show impatience.
141 an eye of death a look (1) showing 'mortal fear' (Kittredge) as well as (2) 'menacing death' (Johnson).
143–4 Was not . . . blood? Worcester's question presents Henry's power as illegitimate. By inference this explains his hostility to Hotspur (and his fellow former main supporters) as char-

acteristic of his treacherous nature. For an analysis of how Shakespeare develops this sequence from Holinshed, see Introduction, p. 8 and Appendix, pp. 231–2.
145 He Mortimer.
146 unhappy unlucky.
147 in us inflicted by us.
148 his Irish expedition While Richard suppressed a rebellion in Ireland, Bullingbrook returned from exile and seized power. See *R2* 2.3 and 3.1.
149 intercepted interrupted.
152 scandalised disgraced.
153 soft slow down.
154 brother brother-in-law. Compare 79 above and n.

And for his sake wear the detested blot   160
Of murderous subornation – shall it be
That you a world of curses undergo,
Being the agents, or base second means,
The cords, the ladder, or the hangman rather?
O pardon me, that I descend so low,   165
To show the line and the predicament
Wherein you range under this subtle King!
Shall it for shame be spoken in these days,
Or fill up chronicles in time to come,
That men of your nobility and power   170
Did gage them both in an unjust behalf –
As both of you, God pardon it, have done –
To put down Richard, that sweet lovely rose,
And plant this thorn, this canker Bullingbrook?
And shall it in more shame be further spoken,   175
That you are fooled, discarded, and shook off
By him for whom these shames ye underwent?
No, yet time serves wherein you may redeem
Your banished honours, and restore yourselves
Into the good thoughts of the world again: 180
Revenge the jeering and disdained contempt
Of this proud King, who studies day and night
To answer all the debt he owes to you,
Even with the bloody payment of your deaths.
Therefore, I say –
WORCESTER   Peace, cousin, say no more.   185
And now I will unclasp a secret book,
And to your quick-conceiving discontents

---

160 wear] Qq; wore F

160 **detested blot** hated stain or blemish, physical or moral.
   161 **murderous subornation** aiding the killer.
   163 **base second means** shameful instruments.
   166 **the line and the predicament** Hotspur underscores the lowered status of his father
and uncle. 'Line', signifying rank, status, is pun-
ningly related to 'cords' and the hangman's rope,
164. 'Predicament' means dangerous situation
(*OED*3).
   167 **range** (1) are ranked, (2) are permitted to
move (i.e. despite restriction).
   167 **subtle** cunning.
   171 **gage them** pledge their 'nobility and
power' (170).

171 **behalf** interest, cause.
   174 **canker** the dog-rose, an inferior category
as opposed to 'that sweet lovely rose', Richard, in
173. Also, as canker worm, it recalls 135. Compare
Ham. 5.2.69.
   181 **disdained** disdainful. This grammatical
form, '-ed' (compare 'hated'), is an alternative to
the '-ful' form.
   183 **answer** discharge.
   183–4 **debt ... deaths** Word-play, more forcefully used by Falstaff at 5.1.127.
   186 **unclasp ... book** Literally, 'reveal a plot'.
Expensively produced Bibles and missals often
had clasps.

I'll read you matter deep and dangerous,
As full of peril and adventurous spirit
As to o'er-walk a current roaring loud   190
On the unsteadfast footing of a spear.

HOTSPUR If he fall in, good night, or sink, or swim!
Send danger from the east unto the west,
So honour cross it from the north to south,
And let them grapple. O, the blood more stirs   195
To rouse a lion than to start a hare!

NORTHUMBERLAND Imagination of some great exploit
Drives him beyond the bounds of patience.

[HOTSPUR] By heaven, methinks it were an easy leap
To pluck bright honour from the pale-faced moon,   200
Or dive into the bottom of the deep,
Where fathom-line could never touch the ground,
And pluck up drownèd honour by the locks,
So he that doth redeem her thence might wear
Without corrival all her dignities.   205
But out upon this half-faced fellowship!

WORCESTER He apprehends a world of figures here,

---

199 SH HOTSPUR] Q5, F; *not in* Qq0–4

191 footing of a spear Humphreys explains this as referring to the 'perilous bridge' or 'sword-bridge' of medieval romances such as the *Mabino-gion* and *Erec and Enid*.

192 If . . . swim Hotspur's impetuousness is apparent in this outburst: 'good night' suggests 'that's the end of him, he's had it'.

192 or sink, or swim This ambiguous phrase may refer only to an adversary or to both the adversary and Hotspur. In the literal sense, 'he's doomed, whether he sinks quickly or delays it by swimming (and who cares?)'; alternatively, both the speaker and his opponent are stimulated by the challenge of 'danger', the 'footing of a spear'.

194 So Provided that.

196 rouse . . . start Hunting terms: 'to start' applies to small animals, 'to rouse', to bigger game. Hotspur's 'lion' is of course the King.

199 From this line to the end of 2.2, Q0 provides the primary text.

199 SH HOTSPUR Qq0–4 do not provide a new speaker here, but it is hard to imagine a reader who would not readily accept the emendation from Q5. Editors agree that Q0 simply omitted a speech heading.

199–206 By heaven . . . fellowship Hotspur

reveals both his commitment to honourable acts and his recklessness. The accelerated pace makes these heroic acts absurd. Hotspur's own splendid sense of humour perhaps contributes to the feeling that he mocks himself as well as others. Parody in this play is often linked to political subversion.

202 fathom-line Used to test the depth of the sea, measured in fathoms (*OED* Fathom sv *sb* 6). A fathom is roughly 6 feet or 1.9 metres.

204 redeem save, restore.

205 Without corrival i.e. without sharing. 'Corrival' can mean (1) a rival in loving honour, here personified as female, (2) a competitor whose claims are equal.

205 dignities favours of the rescued 'honour'; also titles, as in 5.4.78.

206 half-faced partial, imperfect. Usually said of a coin, having a profile stamped on it (*OED a* 1). The term suggests that Hotspur must be the sole hero, shared honour being only a flat, partial glory.

207 apprehends perceives, recognises (*OED v* 8).

207 figures Both (1) the images in Hotspur's speech, and (2) appearances rather than 'form' (Johnson).

    But not the form of what he should attend.

    Good cousin, give me audience for a while.

HOTSPUR I cry you mercy.

WORCESTER   Those same noble Scots   210

    That are your prisoners –

HOTSPUR   I'll keep them all!

    By God he shall not have a scot of them,

    No, if a Scot would save his soul he shall not.

    I'll keep them, by this hand!

WORCESTER   You start away,

    And lend no ear unto my purposes.   215

    Those prisoners you shall keep –

HOTSPUR   Nay, I will. That's flat!

    He said he would not ransom Mortimer,

    Forbade my tongue to speak of Mortimer,

    But I will find him when he lies asleep,

    And in his ear I'll holla 'Mortimer!'   220

    Nay, I'll have a starling shall be taught to speak

    Nothing but 'Mortimer', and give it him

    To keep his anger still in motion.

WORCESTER Hear you, cousin, a word.

HOTSPUR All studies here I solemnly defy,   225

    Save how to gall and pinch this Bullingbrook.

    And that same sword-and-buckler Prince of Wales –

    But that I think his father loves him not

    And would be glad he met with some mischance –

    I would have him poisoned with a pot of ale.   230

WORCESTER Farewell, kinsman. I'll talk to you

---

209 a while.] Qq; a-while, / And list to me F   210–11 Those . . . Scots / That . . . prisoners] F; *as one line*, Qq
220 holla] F; hollow Qq–2; hollo Qq3–4; hallow Q5; holler *Bevington*

208 **form** principle or idea.
212 **a scot** a small payment.
214 **start** Compare 196 and n. above.
220 **holla** shout.
221–2 **Nay . . . 'Mortimer'** Compare Hotspur's reference to the popinjay, 49 above, and Lady Percy's 'paraquito' at 2.3.79. Humphreys notes that 'Elizabethan texts have many talking starlings', e.g. Florio's *Montaigne* ii, xii, 267 ('An Apologie of Raymond Sebond'), 'We teach Blacke-birds, Starlins . . . to chat'; and Drayton, *The Owle*, line 634, 'Like a *Starling*, that is taught to prate'.
223 **still** continually.
225 **studies** occupations.

225 **defy** renounce.
226 **gall and pinch** irritate, harass. These verbs suggest that he does not take his foe very seriously.
227 **sword-and-buckler** Hotspur accuses Hal of vulgarity. By 1590, the sword and small round shield or buckler were left to servants and swaggerers. Gentlemen used the rapier and dagger. *OED* (Sword sv *sb* 6d) cites this line and Porter, *Two Angry Women of Abington*, 1599, p. 61, 'a good sword and buckler man, will be spitted like a cat or a conney'.
230 **pot of ale** Another slap at Hal's plebeian tastes. By *2H4*, Hal is growing tired of small beer (2.2.5–11).

When you are better tempered to attend.

NORTHUMBERLAND Why, what a wasp-stung and impatient fool
Art thou to break into this woman's mood,
Tying thine ear to no tongue but thine own!   235

HOTSPUR Why, look you, I am whipped and scourged with rods,
Nettled, and stung with pismires, when I hear
Of this vile politician Bullingbrook.
In Richard's time – what do you call the place?
A plague upon it, it is in Gloucestershire.   240
'Twas where the madcap Duke his uncle kept –
His uncle York – where I first bowed my knee
Unto this king of smiles, this Bullingbrook –
'Sblood, when you and he came back from Ravenspurgh –

NORTHUMBERLAND At Berkeley Castle.

HOTSPUR   You say true.   245
Why, what a candy deal of courtesy
This fawning greyhound then did proffer me!
'Look when his infant fortune came to age',
And 'gentle Harry Percy', and 'kind cousin'.
O, the devil take such cozeners – God forgive me!   250
Good uncle, tell your tale. I have done.

WORCESTER Nay, if you have not, to it again,
We will stay your leisure.

HOTSPUR   I have done, i'faith.

---

233 wasp-stung] Qq–1; waspe-tongue Qq2–5; Waspe-tongu'd F   236 Why, look you,] Q1 (Why, looke you,); Why looke you? Q0   236 whipped] Qq1–5, F (whipt); whip Q0

233 wasp-stung irritable, impatient.
234 this woman's mood In this play, women and most references to women occur in the worlds of the rebels and the tavern. Such references are strangely absent from the scenes at court. See Introduction, pp. 12–13, 15, 16.
237 Nettled Irritated, stung with nettles.
237 pismires ants.
238 politician A noun almost always contemptuous or sinister in Elizabethan usage. Compare *Lear* 4.6.171.
239–44 In Richard's time . . . Ravenspurgh – Q0's punctuation using commas suggests the startling breaks in the consciousness of the speaker.
241 madcap Duke Edmund Langley, Duke of York, as described in Holinshed. He does not show such a trait in *R2* or in *Woodstock*.
241 kept lived.
244 'Sblood This oath in the Q version lends an extra syllable to Hotspur's otherwise regular line,

thereby conveying his 'impatience with his faulty memory' (Bevington).
244 Ravensburgh In Yorkshire, where Bullingbrook landed in 1399 when he returned from exile.
245 Berkeley Castle In Gloucestershire northeast of Bristol; hundreds of miles to the south and west of Ravensburgh.
246 candy deal sugary or flattering lot.
247 fawning greyhound Shakespeare's clustered images of dogs, of licking candy, and of melting, are 'called up inevitably by the thought of false friends or flatterers' (Spurgeon, *Shakespeare's Imagery and What It Tells Us*, 1935, p. 195). Humphreys comments, 'The image-cluster may be Shakespearean, but its parts are popular tags.'
248 Look when When.
250 cozeners cheats (with a pun on cousins).
253 stay wait for.

WORCESTER Then once more to your Scottish prisoners.
    Deliver them up without their ransom straight,   255
    And make the Douglas' son your only mean
    For powers in Scotland, which, for divers reasons
    Which I shall send you written, be assured
    Will easily be granted. [*To Northumberland*] You my lord,
    Your son in Scotland being thus employed,   260
    Shall secretly into the bosom creep
    Of that same noble prelate well-beloved,
    The Archbishop.
HOTSPUR   Of York, is it not?
WORCESTER True, who bears hard
    His brother's death at Bristol, the Lord Scroop.   265
    I speak not this in estimation,
    As what I think might be, but what I know
    Is ruminated, plotted, and set down,
    And only stays but to behold the face
    Of that occasion that shall bring it on.   270
HOTSPUR I smell it! Upon my life it will do well!
NORTHUMBERLAND Before the game is afoot thou still let'st slip.
HOTSPUR Why, it cannot choose but be a noble plot;
    And then the power of Scotland, and of York,
    To join with Mortimer, ha?
WORCESTER   And so they shall.   275
HOTSPUR In faith it is exceedingly well aimed.
WORCESTER And 'tis no little reason bids us speed,
    To save our heads by raising of a head.
    For, bear ourselves as even as we can,

---

259 granted. You my lord] *Hanmer subst.;* granted you my lord Qq0, 1, 4*;* granted you, my Lord Qq2, 3, 5, F   259 SD
To Northumberland] *Theobald; not in* QqF   271 I smell it! Upon . . . do well] Qq; I smell it: / Upon . . . do wondrous
well F

255 **straight** immediately.
256 **the Douglas' son** The Earl of Fife, mistakenly called son of Douglas. The definite article used before 'Douglas' indicates the headship of a distinguished Scottish family (Humphreys).
256 **mean** means, instrument. Worcester takes it for granted that sons (including Hotspur) should be the instruments of feudal politics.
261 **into . . . creep** insinuate himself into the confidence.
264–5 **who . . . Scroop** William Scroop, Earl of Wiltshire and Lord Treasurer under Richard II, was executed by Bullingbrook at Bristol in 1399

with Richard's other favourites (*R2* 3.2.141–2). He was the cousin of the Archbishop of York, Richard Scroop, not his brother. Holinshed confuses the relationship.
266 **estimation** conjecture.
271 **smell** Like hounds finding the scent of a quarry in a hunt.
272 **thou still let'st slip** Northumberland, picking up the hunting metaphor in 'smell', scolds his son for releasing the dogs prematurely.
278 **head** army of family, retainers, and followers.
279 **even** (1) carefully, (2) justly.

> The King will always think him in our debt,   280
> And think we think ourselves unsatisfied,
> Till he hath found a time to pay us home.
> And see already how he doth begin
> To make us strangers to his looks of love.

HOTSPUR   He does, he does, we'll be revenged on him.   285

WORCESTER   Cousin, farewell. No further go in this
> Than I by letters shall direct your course.
> When time is ripe, which will be suddenly,
> I'll steal to Glendower and Lord Mortimer,
> Where you, and Douglas, and our powers at once,   290
> As I will fashion it, shall happily meet
> To bear our fortunes in our own strong arms,
> Which now we hold at much uncertainty.

NORTHUMBERLAND   Farewell, good brother. We shall thrive, I trust.

HOTSPUR   Uncle, adieu. O, let the hours be short,   295
> Till fields, and blows, and groans applaud our sport!

Exeunt

[**2.1**]   *Enter a* CARRIER *with a lantern in his hand*

FIRST CARRIER   Heigh-ho! An it be not four by the day I'll be hanged.
Charles' Wain is over the new chimney, and yet our horse not
packed. What, Ostler!

---

289 Lord] *Rowe;* Lo: Qq0, 1; loe Qq2–5, F   292 bear our] Qq1–5, F; beare out Q0   296 SD *Exeunt*] Qq; *exit* F   Act 2,
Scene 1   2.1] *Actus Secundus. Scena Prima.* F; *not in* Qq

282 pay us home pay us back (with the punning implication 'give us a fatal blow').
288 suddenly at once.
290 at once altogether.
296 fields battlefields.
296 sport Hotspur treats battle as a diversion or amusement, like hunting. Compare the Prince's view of playing as strategic political work, 1.2.164 ff. Both young men have a sense of humour, in contrast to their fathers, who see playfulness as mere weakness.

Act 2, Scene 1
[**2.1**] In the fictional narrative, this scene is set at dawn in an innyard, presumably on the London-Canterbury road near Gad's Hill. The costumes and language immediately establish a contrast with the preceding court scene.

0 SD CARRIER Produce and goods were brought on pack-horses, 2–3, to London by the carriers in their panniers and baskets.
0 SD lantern The play would originally have been performed at an arena playhouse in daylight. The lantern conventionally signifies that the action takes place at night or near daybreak.
1 by the day towards morning.
2 Charles' Wain An old name, derived from Charlemagne's wagon, for the constellation known as the Plough.
2 horse horses. 'Horse' was used in both plural and singular forms.
3 packed loaded.
3 Ostler Groom, stable-boy.

OSTLER [*Within*] Anon, anon.

FIRST CARRIER I prithee, Tom, beat Cut's saddle, put a few flocks in   5
the point; poor jade is wrung in the withers, out of all cess.

Enter another CARRIER

SECOND CARRIER Peas and beans are as dank here as a dog, and that is
the next way to give poor jades the bots. This house is turned upside
down since Robin Ostler died.

FIRST CARRIER Poor fellow never joyed since the price of oats rose, it   10
was the death of him.

SECOND CARRIER I think this be the most villainous house in all
London road for fleas, I am stung like a tench.

FIRST CARRIER Like a tench! By the mass, there is ne'er a king Christian could be better bit than I have been since the first cock.   15

SECOND CARRIER Why, they will allow us ne'er a jordan, and then we
leak in your chimney, and your chamber-lye breeds fleas like a loach.

4 SD *Within*] *Theobald; not in* QqF 12 be] Qqo–4; to be Q5; is F 14 By the mass] Qq; *not in* F 14–15 Christian] Qq
(christen); in Christendome F 16 ne'er] Qq (nere); ne're F

4 Anon Just a minute.

5 Tom This seems to be the name of the Ostler.
The First Carrier is addressed at line 36 as Mugs,
which may be a nickname. On the variable identification of secondary characters, see Textual Analysis, pp. 221 ff.

5 beat smooth by beating to make it less lumpy
and more comfortable.

5 Cut The name of this horse. Cut was also the
common word for a work-horse, referring either
to its having a docked tail or to its being gelded.

5–6 put . . . point stuff wool into the pommel
of the saddle.

6 jade nag, old horse.

6 wrung . . . withers rubbed or bruised on the
ridge between the shoulder-blades.

6 out of all cess excessively.

**7 Peas and beans are as dank here as a
dog** i.e. the horses' fodder is as 'damp as can be'
(Bevington). Compare Dent D433–41 for sayings
which use 'dog' to intensify conditions (such as
'sick as a dog', 'dog-tired').

7 dank unwholesomely damp and cold.

8 next quickest.

8 bots parasitic maggots in horses' intestines.
These were 'little short wormes with great red
heads, and long small white Tailes', according
to G. Markham, *Maister-Peece of Farriery*, 1615,
chap. 74, as noted by Humphreys who observes
that they are hatched from eggs on the leaves that
the horse eats.

8 house inn.

8–9 turned upside down badly run, disor-
dered.

10 price of oats rose Because of many poor
harvests, the price almost tripled between 1593
and 1596, after which it fell. England experienced
severe periods of dearth in the last decade of the
sixteenth century. See D. M. Palliser, *The Age of
Elizabeth*, 1983, chaps. 4 and 5.

13 tench fish, the spotted markings of which
may have suggested flea-bites. Humphreys suggests that it was, like the loach, 17, thought to
breed parasites.

14 By the mass A gentle, old-fashioned oath,
nevertheless dropped in the Folio.

14–15 king Christian king in Christendom,
implying that kings 'have the best of everything'
(Kittredge).

15 first cock Conventionally midnight: the second cock came at 3 a.m., the third, an hour before
dawn.

16 jordan chamber-pot.

17 leak urinate.

17 your Used to refer to something commonly
known, not necessarily possessed. See Abbott 221.

17 chimney fireplace.

17 chamber-lye urine.

17 loach A small freshwater fish, popularly
thought to breed lice.

FIRST CARRIER What, Ostler! Come away, and be hanged, come away!

SECOND CARRIER I have a gammon of bacon, and two races of ginger,
     to be delivered as far as Charing Cross.   20

FIRST CARRIER God's body! The turkeys in my pannier are quite
     starved. What, Ostler! A plague on thee, hast thou never an eye in
     thy head? Canst not hear? An 'twere not as good deed as drink to
     break the pate on thee, I am a very villain. Come and be hanged!
     Hast no faith in thee?   25

Enter GADSHILL

GADSHILL Good morrow, carriers, what's o'clock?

(FIRST) CARRIER I think it be two o'clock.

GADSHILL I prithee lend me thy lantern, to see my gelding in the stable.

FIRST CARRIER Nay, by God, soft! I know a trick worth two of that,
     i'faith.   30

GADSHILL I pray thee lend me thine.

SECOND CARRIER Ay, when? Canst tell? Lend me thy lantern, quoth
     he! Marry I'll see thee hanged first.

GADSHILL Sirrah carrier, what time do you mean to come to London?

SECOND CARRIER Time enough to go to bed with a candle, I warrant   35

27 SH FIRST] *Hanmer subst.; Car.* QqF   29 by God, soft!] Qq; soft I pray ye F   31 pray thee] Qq0-2; prethee Qq3-5, F

18 **Come . . . hanged** Come on, blast you (see
Dent H130.1).
   19 **gammon of bacon** ham.
   19 **races** roots of ginger, used both medicinally
and as a spice. They recall the complaint in *FV* by
the carrier: he 'hath taken the great rase of ginger,
that bouncing Bess with the jolly buttocks should
have had' (302–4).
   20 **Charing Cross** A familiar landmark
between the City (London) and Westminster,
located towards the west end of the Strand near its
junction with Whitehall. The stone cross, erected
in 1294 (to commemorate the last spot where the
body of Eleanor, queen of Edward I, had rested on
the way to Westminster) was in ruinous condition
by 1596–7 (Sugden; compare Stow, *Survey*, 11,
100–1).
   21 **God's body** Another oath omitted from the
Folio.
   21 **pannier** Either of a pair of large baskets used
to carry provisions.
   22–3 **hast . . . head** Dent E248.1 lists this
proverbial expression.
   22 **never** not (intensified).
   23 **as good deed as drink** Proverbial expression (Dent D183.1), playfully equating good deeds
and self-indulgence. Falstaff repeats it at 2.2.18.
See Dent's Introduction, p. xxiv, on how this

phrase helped establish his criteria for describ-
ing sayings as proverbial, '[even though] . . . there
are no known instances outside Shakespeare until
Sir Wilfull Witwood in Congreve [1700]. It is difficult otherwise to account for Falstaff's sharing
the whole of an expression with the First Carrier,
and the bulk of it with Sir Andrew Aguecheek [*TN*
2.3.126].'
   24 **break . . . thee** i.e. 'crack your skull', an
exaggerated threat referring to a blow that draws
blood but need not actually cause a fracture.
   24 **very** true.
   25 **faith** trustworthiness.
   27 **two o'clock** The Carrier, in the first line
of this scene, declared that it was four o'clock.
Unless there is a textual error, this reply indicates
that he does not sufficiently trust Gadshill even to
tell him the correct time, much less to lend him
his lantern.
   29 **soft** wait a minute.
   29 **I know . . . that** i.e. 'You can't fool me', a
familiar saying (Dent T518).
   32 **Ay, when? Canst tell?** Proverbial denial
(Dent T88), to the effect of 'You haven't got a
hope!'
   35 **Time . . . candle** Evasive and contemptuous
reply.
   35 **warrant** assure.

thee! Come, neighbour Mugs, we'll call up the gentlemen, they will
along with company, for they have great charge.

Exeunt [Carriers]

GADSHILL What ho! Chamberlain!

Enter CHAMBERLAIN

CHAMBERLAIN 'At hand, quoth pick-purse.'

GADSHILL That's even as fair as 'At hand, quoth the chamberlain', for   40
thou variest no more from picking of purses than giving direction
doth from labouring. Thou layest the plot how.

CHAMBERLAIN Good morrow, Master Gadshill. It holds current that I
told you yesternight. There's a franklin in the Weald of Kent hath
brought three hundred marks with him in gold – I heard him tell it   45
to one of his company last night at supper, a kind of auditor, one that
hath abundance of charge too, God knows what. They are up already, and call for eggs and butter. They will away presently.

GADSHILL Sirrah, if they meet not with Saint Nicholas' clerks, I'll give
thee this neck.   50

CHAMBERLAIN No, I'll none of it, I pray thee keep that for the hangman, for I know thou worshippest Saint Nicholas, as truly as a man
of falsehood may.

GADSHILL What talkest thou to me of the hangman? If I hang, I'll make

37 SD *Carriers*] *Rowe; not in* QqF   38 SD *Enter* CHAMBERLAIN] *Kittredge; after 37,* QqF   44 Weald] Qo (wild)*; wilde*
Qq1–5, F   51 pray thee] Qq*; prythee* F

36–7 will . . . charge prefer to travel with a
group because they have valuables or baggage.

38 Chamberlain Servant in charge of guests'
rooms at an inn. Harrison, *The Description of
Britain* (Holinshed, 1, 414–15), criticises the dishonesty of inn servants, who give 'warning to such
od ghests as hant the house and are of [their] con-
federacie, to the utter undoing of manie an honest
yeoman as he iournieth by the waie'.

39 At hand, quoth pick-purse 'Here I am',
a popular tag, which is ironically apt from the
crooked Chamberlain to the thief Gadshill.

40 even as fair as 'as good as saying'.

41–2 thou variest . . . labouring you are no
more different from an actual pickpocket than is
an overseer from his labourers, i.e. you are both
responsible for the work.

42 Thou layest the plot how You supervise
the labour, plan the crime.

44 franklin A rich yeoman, one who holds his
own land and ranks just below the gentry.

44 Weald The area lying between the North
and South Downs, a rich agricultural district, for-
merly wooded.

45 three hundred marks two hundred
pounds. A mark was worth 13s.4d., or two-thirds
of a pound. It was not a coin.

46 auditor A royal officer who examined the
accounts of receivers, sheriffs, and other officers
of the crown.

48 eggs and butter see 1.2.17 and note.

48 presently at once.

49 Saint Nicholas' clerks Slang for highwaymen. St Nicholas, the popular patron saint of wandering scholars, travellers, and children, became,
probably through the suggestion of the popular
name 'Old Nick' for the Devil, the protector of
thieves and masterless men as well. In the legend which is the subject of the miracle play *Ludus
Super Iconia Sancti Nicolai* (ed. Pollard, *English
Miracle Plays*, Appendix 11), the saint causes robbers to restore a treasure (cited by Hemingway).
Compare 5.4.112 and n. on 'termagant'. The cant
term 'nick' meant cheat or defraud (*OED* sv *v*²
11).

49–50 give . . . neck you can hang me, 'neck'
offering a pun on 'nick'.

54 What Why.

a fat pair of gallows. For if I hang, old Sir John hangs with me, and   55
thou knowest he is no starveling. Tut, there are other Troyans that
thou dreamest not of, the which for sport sake are content to do the
profession some grace, that would, if matters should be looked into,
for their own credit sake make all whole. I am joined with no foot-
landrakers, no long-staff sixpenny strikers, none of these mad   60
mustachio purple-hued maltworms, but with nobility and tranquillity, burgomasters and great oneyres, such as can hold in, such as
will strike sooner than speak, and speak sooner than drink, and drink
sooner than pray. And yet, zounds, I lie, for they pray continually to
their saint the commonwealth, or rather not pray to her, but prey on   65
her, for they ride up and down on her, and make her their boots.

62 oneyres] Qq0, 1; Oneyers Qq2–5, F; Oneraires *conj. Pope;* One-eyers *conj. Pope²*; Moneyers *Theobald;* owners
Hanmer; one-yers *Johnson*   65 prey] Q5, F; pray Qq0–4

56 starveling one emaciated from lack of food
(*OED* sv *sb* a).
56 Troyans Trojans, cant term for good companions, like Hal's 'Corinthian', 2.4.10, and the
Page's reference to 'Ephesians . . . of the old
church', *2H4* 2.2.150. In *Wiv.* 4.5.18, the tavern
host is termed an 'Ephesian'.
57 the which who.
57–8 do . . . grace favour the profession.
58 looked into subjected to criminal investigation.
59 for . . . whole for the sake of their own reputation, make sure there was no trouble.
59–60 foot-landrakers wandering footpads,
who presumably cannot afford a horse. To 'rake'
is to wander (*OED v²* 1).
60 long-staff sixpenny strikers cut-price
thieves who will rob for a mere sixpence. They
use long poles with an iron hook on the end to
pull men from their horses. 'Strike' is a cant term
for picking pockets.
61 mustachio Fierce moustaches supposedly
indicated valour.
61 purple-hued maltworms heavy drinkers
with purple faces. Compare Falstaff on Bardolph's
purple face, 3.3.23–5, and his description of Bardolph's face in *2H4* 2.4.333–4: 'Lucifer's privy-
kitchen, where he doth nothing but roast maltworms'. These worms infest the malt used to brew,
and hence those who drink it. Compare allusions
to other parasites in 'bots', 8, 'tench', 13, 'fleas',
13, 17, and 'loach', 17. Analogies between animal and human parasites are latent throughout the
scene.
61–2 tranquillity An invented meaning which
may travesty pretentious diction. Compare *TN*
2.3.26, 'I did impeticos thy gratillity.'

62 burgomasters chief magistrates of a town.
62 oneyres 'honeyers', probably an invented
word. If 'honey' is spelled without an 'h' (*OED*
sb variant) like 'Ebrew' (2.4.152) and employed
as a verb meaning to use terms of endearment
or to flatter (*OED* sv *v* 2–3), it is possible to
suppose that Gadshill characterises as 'honeyers' the Prince's followers, both for their flattery (i.e. 'good sweet honey lord', 1.2.129) and
for their wenching (as in *Ham.* 3.4.93), with a
glance at Falstaff's taste for sugared sack. The
King compares common popularity to a surfeit
of honey at 3.2.69–71. As the Collation indicates, the word has been extensively discussed
and amended. Johnson suggested that Gadshill
gives a 'cant termination' to 'great ones' 'as we
say privateer, auctioneer'. Malone suggested 'ony-
ers', derived from the abbreviation 'o.ni.' (*oner-*
atur, nisi habeat sufficientem exonerationem), a term
used by the royal treasury to identify revenue
collected by sheriffs but owed to the crown.
Other proposed emendations include seigniors,
junkers, mynheers, wonyers, one-ers. Davison
proposes 'Oyeas', Jowett (*Textual Companion*),
'Oiezres' or court officials, West, 'younker'
(compare 3.3.63).
62 hold in A multiple pun: (1) keep a secret,
(2) stick together, (3) continue to pursue a
quarry.
63 strike . . . drink are as ready to knock down
a victim as to speak; 'sooner' implies preference
or choice (*OED* Soon *adv* 11b). 'To speak to or
with a victim was thieves' cant for holding him
up' (Humphreys).
66 make her their boots use her for their
financial advantage, with a pun on booty and a
sexual slur.

CHAMBERLAIN What, the commonwealth their boots? Will she hold
 out water in foul way?

GADSHILL She will, she will, justice hath liquored her. We steal as
 in a castle, cock-sure. We have the receipt of fern-seed, we walk   70
 invisible.

CHAMBERLAIN Nay, by my faith, I think you are more beholding to the
 night than to fern-seed for your walking invisible.

GADSHILL Give me thy hand, thou shalt have a share in our purchase,
 as I am a true man.   75

CHAMBERLAIN Nay, rather let me have it as you are a false thief.

GADSHILL Go to, *homo* is a common name to all men. Bid the ostler
 bring my gelding out of the stable. Farewell, you muddy knave.

[Exeunt]

[2.2] *Enter* PRINCE, POINS, *and* PETO [*with* BARDOLPH]

POINS Come, shelter, shelter! I have removed Falstaff's horse, and he
 frets like a gummed velvet.

74 purchase] Qq,; purpose F   78 my] Qq,; the F   78 SD *Exeunt*] F; *not in* Qq   Act 2, Scene 2   2.2] *Scæna Secunda.* F;
not in Qq   0 SD *and* PETO *with* BARDOLPH] *Bevington subst.; and Peto Etc.* Qq0–5 *and Peto* F; *Bardolph and Peto, at
some distance* / *Malone*

67–8 Will . . . way Literally, 'can she (like boots)
keep your feet dry on a wet muddy road?', can she
help you in need?

69 justice hath liquored her the authorities
have (1) given her a protective coat to keep out legal
prosecution (58–9 above and notes), (2) made her
drunk.

70 in a castle in complete security, echoing the
commonplace, 'as safe as in a castle' (Dent C122.1).
Perhaps, in an earlier version of the text, this was
a reference to Oldcastle (Kittredge).

70 receipt of fern-seed recipe for making one-
self invisible. Small fern-seeds were believed to
become visible only on St John's or Midsummer
Eve, 23 June. Anyone who picked them then and
carried them later on would also become invisible.

74 purchase plunder, a euphemism for booty.

75 true man one who keeps his word; taken by
the Chamberlain, 76, as a claim to general honesty.
Compare thieves 'true one to another', 2.2.22–3.

77 homo . . . all men The Latin word for 'man'
includes all humanity; therefore, a thief must be 'a
true man'. Gadshill's term may derive from Lily
and Colet's *Shorte Introduction of Grammar* (1549).

78 muddy dull-witted or muddled, with a

suggestion of dishonesty (as in 'foul', 68).

Act 2, Scene 2

[2.2] The opening lines indicate a brief passage
of time and a change of location, but closely follow
the narrative thread of the last scene. It is still too
dark for the thieves gathered at Gad's Hill to see
one another clearly; Poins identifies the 'setter' by
his voice, 40–1. Between the two robberies, 75 SD,
the unlocalised Elizabethan stage makes possible
the illusion of movement along a road.

0 SD *with* BARDOLPH Not named in stage
directions of QqF, but Q0 and Q1 have '&c'
which implies Bardolph because no other character becomes relevant in the ensuing sequence.
Falstaff cries out to Bardolph and Peto at 17, as
if they were both nearby. When they enter with
the Prince and Poins, they are presumably aware
of the first joke, that being played with Falstaff's
horse.

2 frets like a gummed velvet is irritated,
chafes. Proverbial (Dent T8); velvet wore quickly
or 'fretted' when treated with gum to give it gloss
or an appearance of firmness.

PRINCE Stand close!

[They retire]

Enter FALSTAFF

FALSTAFF Poins! Poins, and be hanged! Poins!

PRINCE [*Coming forward*] Peace, ye fat-kidneyed rascal, what a brawling   5
dost thou keep!

FALSTAFF Where's Poins, Hal?

PRINCE He is walked up to the top of the hill. I'll go seek him.

[He steps to one side]

FALSTAFF I am accursed to rob in that thief's company. The rascal hath
removed my horse and tied him I know not where. If I travel but   10
four foot by the square further afoot, I shall break my wind. Well, I
doubt not but to die a fair death for all this, if I scape hanging for
killing that rogue. I have forsworn his company hourly any time this
two-and-twenty years, and yet I am bewitched with the rogue's
company. If the rascal have not given me medicines to make me love   15
him, I'll be hanged. It could not be else. I have drunk medicines.
Poins! Hal! A plague upon you both! Bardolph! Peto! I'll starve ere
I'll rob a foot further – an 'twere not as good a deed as drink to turn
true man, and to leave these rogues, I am the veriest varlet that ever
chewed with a tooth. Eight yards of uneven ground is threescore-   20

---

3 SD. I *They retire* | *Dyce; not in* QqF   5 SD *Coming forward* | *Dyce; not in* QqF   8 SD *He steps to one side* | *Bevington subst.;
not in* QqF   11 square | QqF (squire)   14 two-and-twenty | F; xxii Qq0–4; 22 Q5   17 Bardolph | F; Bardol Qo; Bardoll
Qq1–5 (*throughout, with variation of spelling*)

---

3 Stand close Hide.

3 SD.1 *They retire* The fluid staging of the jokes
in this scene calls for several conjectured directions not provided by QqF. With a platform stage,
the audience (unlike Falstaff) may be able to see
the characters who hide. See Textual Analysis,
pp. 221–2, on how stage directions and dialogue
leave open options for several entrances and exits.

5 fat-kidneyed fat-gutted.

5 rascal knave. As a term for lean young deer
that are unsuitable for hunting, 'rascal' may suggest that a fat old man makes an absurd highway
robber.

5 brawling clamour.

6 keep make.

10–11 but . . . square exactly four feet. A square
(variant spelling for obsolete 'squire') is a measur-
ing instrument. Humphreys cites Spenser, *The
Faerie Queene*, 11, i, 57, 'Temperance . . . with
golden squire / . . . can measure out a meane.'

11 break my wind (1) pant or wheeze, (2) fart.

11–12 I doubt not but to I expect to.

12 die . . . this die honourably, in spite of all
this torment.

13 I have . . . company Falstaff at first may
refer here to Poins, but the next four lines are taken
by many to refer to the Prince. See Introduction,
pp. 33–4.

15 medicines love potions. Compare *Oth.*
1.3.60–1: 'She is abus'd, stol'n from me, and corrupted / By spells and medicines bought of moun-
tebanks.'

17 starve die (the original sense), but almost
certainly suggesting death by hunger (*OED* sv *v*
4a).

18 as good . . . drink On this proverbial phrase,
compare 2.1.23 and n.

18–19 turn true man reform. Falstaff puns on
the paradoxes of truth among false men that were
initiated in 2.1.

19 veriest truest, most authentic.

19 varlet servant or groom; in chivalry, the
attendant on a knight.

and-ten miles afoot with me, and the stony-hearted villains know it
well enough. A plague upon it when thieves cannot be true one to
another!

They whistle

Whew! A plague upon you all. Give me my horse you rogues, give
me my horse and be hanged!   25

PRINCE [*Coming forward*] Peace, ye fat-guts, lie down, lay thine ear
    close to the ground and list if thou canst hear the tread of travellers.

FALSTAFF Have you any levers to lift me up again, being down?
    'Sblood, I'll not bear my own flesh so far afoot again for all the coin
    in thy father's exchequer. What a plague mean ye to colt me thus?   30

PRINCE Thou liest, thou art not colted, thou art uncolted.

FALSTAFF I prithee good Prince, help me to my horse, good king's son.

PRINCE Out ye rogue, shall I be your ostler?

FALSTAFF Hang thyself in thine own heir-apparent garters! If I be
    taken, I'll peach for this. An I have not ballads made on you all, and   35
    sung to filthy tunes, let a cup of sack be my poison. When a jest is so
    forward – and afoot too – I hate it!

Enter GADSHILL

GADSHILL Stand!

FALSTAFF So I do, against my will.

POINS [*Coming forward with Bardolph and Peto*] O, 'tis our setter, I know   40
    his voice. Bardolph, what news?

26 SD *Coming forward*] Dyce; *not in* QqF   29 my own] Qo (my owne); mine owne Qq1–5, F   40 SD *Coming forward with Bardolph and Peto*] Dyce; *not in* QqF   41 Bardolph, what news?] QqF *subst.*; *Bardolph.* What news? *Var. 1773, conj. Johnson, Bevington (taking Bardolph as a speech heading)*

22–3 **A plague . . . another** The proverb, 'Thieves are never rogues among themselves' (Dent T121a) is revised in order to proclaim that thieves should be more loyal than honest men.

24 **Whew** Perhaps a comic response to the preceding stage direction. Wilson thinks Falstaff may mock the whistling of the others, while Davison infers that Falstaff, out of breath, is laughable in his attempts to whistle. Alternatively, he expresses disgust or makes a noise indicating that he pauses for breath – a repeated motif.

30 **exchequer** treasury; it holds funds collected by sheriffs and other royal officers (*OED* sv *sb* 4).

30 **colt** trick, cheat.

33 **shall . . . ostler** For the sake of a pun, Hal mistakes Falstaff's meaning, interpreting his 'help me' as a request for aid to mount, rather than to find, his horse. In a literal sense, Hal suggests that he would help, but only as a servant, not as a friend or companion.

34 **Hang . . . garters** As heir apparent, the Prince of Wales belonged to the Order of the Garter. Falstaff answers Hal with another outrageous pun, based on a proverbial saying (Dent G42).

35 **peach** inform against an accomplice (*OED* sv *v* 2, citing this example).

35 **ballads . . . all** It was a common practice to shame or mock one's enemies by hiring a writer whose verses would be set to familiar music. In *Ant.* Cleopatra fears that 'scald rhymers [will] / Ballad's out a' tune' (5.2.215–16).

37 **forward** (1) presumptuous, insulting his dignity, (2) advanced (i.e. the plot to rob the travellers).

37 SD Some editions bring Bardolph and Peto on here with Gadshill rather than at the beginning of the scene, but see 0 SD n. above.

40 **setter** Thieves' term for one who sets up the victim or who gathers information (*OED* sv *sb*[1] 7a).

41–3 **Bardolph, what . . . exchequer** There is nothing improbable in Qo's giving to Poins,

BARDOLPH Case ye, case ye, on with your vizards, there's money of the
    King's coming down the hill. 'Tis going to the King's exchequer.
                          [They put on visors]

FALSTAFF You lie, ye rogue, 'tis going to the King's tavern.

GADSHILL There's enough to make us all –   45

FALSTAFF To be hanged.

PRINCE Sirs, you four shall front them in the narrow lane. Ned Poins
    and I will walk lower – if they scape from your encounter, then they
    light on us.

PETO How many be there of them?   50

GADSHILL Some eight or ten.

FALSTAFF Zounds, will they not rob us?

PRINCE What, a coward, Sir John Paunch?

FALSTAFF Indeed, I am not John of Gaunt your grandfather, but yet no
    coward, Hal.   55

PRINCE Well, we leave that to the proof.

POINS Sirrah Jack, thy horse stands behind the hedge. When thou
    need'st him, there thou shalt find him. Farewell, and stand fast!

FALSTAFF Now cannot I strike him, if I should be hanged.

PRINCE [*Aside to Poins*] Ned, where are our disguises?   60

POINS Here, hard by, stand close.

                     [Exeunt Prince and Poins]

FALSTAFF Now, my masters, happy man be his dole, say I. Every man
    to his business.

               Enter the TRAVELLERS

---

42 SH BARDOLPH] QqF; *Gadshill Johnson, Bevington*   47 Poins] Qq; *not in* F   60 SD *Aside to Poins*] *Collier; not in*
QqF   61 SD *Exeunt Prince and Poins*] *Malone; not in* QqF

'Bardoll, what news?' and the following lines 'Case
ye . . . exchequer' to Bardolph, who can have
been lurking observantly to the side or just offstage. Bevington, however, assigns 'What news?'
to Bardolph and the reply 'Case . . . exchequer' to
Gadshill. He argues that the QO compositor mis-
took 'Bardoll', intended as a speech heading before
'what news', and wrongly attributed to Poins as a
speech, 'Bardoll [F: Bardolfe], what newes'. See
Textual Analysis, p. 222.
    42 Case ye Put on your masks.
    42 vizards masks.
    51 eight or ten See 63 SD and n. below.
    54 John of Gaunt A quick countering of 'Sir
John Paunch', with a pun on the name of the

Prince's grandfather, implying as an insult that
Hal inherits his thinness. Compare the exchange
between the Prince and Falstaff at 2.4.201–6.
    61 SD *Exeunt Prince and Poins* QqF give no
'*Exeunt*' but specify at 75 that they '*Enter*'. Here
they may simply stand aside.
    62 happy . . . dole A familiar expression (Dent
M158), with the basic sense, 'may happiness be our
lot'.
    63 SD TRAVELLERS QqF do not indicate
any specific number. Hal later says that he saw
'you four set on four' (2.4.210). Mahood, *Bit Parts*,
shows that playtexts frequently leave indeterminate the precise numbers of 'nonentities', depending upon the supernumeraries available (pp. 8–11).

[FIRST] TRAVELLER Come, neighbour, the boy shall lead our horses
    down the hill. We'll walk afoot a while and ease our legs.   65
THIEVES Stand!
[SECOND] TRAVELLER Jesus bless us!
FALSTAFF Strike, down with them, cut the villains' throats! Ah,
    whoreson caterpillars, bacon-fed knaves, they hate us youth! Down
    with them, fleece them!   70
[FIRST] TRAVELLER O, we are undone, both we and ours for ever!
FALSTAFF Hang ye, gorbellied knaves, are ye undone? No, ye fat chuffs,
    I would your store were here! On, bacons, on! What, ye knaves,
    young men must live! You are grandjurors, are ye? We'll jure ye,
    faith.   75

Here they rob them and bind them

Exeunt

Enter the PRINCE *and* POINS [*, disguised*]

PRINCE The thieves have bound the true men. Now, could thou and I
    rob the thieves, and go merrily to London, it would be argument for
    a week, laughter for a month, and a good jest for ever.
POINS Stand close, I hear them coming.

[*They retire*]

Enter the thieves again

FALSTAFF Come, my masters, let us share, and then to horse before   80
    day. An the Prince and Poins be not two arrant cowards there's no
    equity stirring. There's no more valour in that Poins than in a wild
    duck.

As they are sharing the PRINCE *and* POINS *set upon them*

---

64 SH FIRST] *Capell; not in* QqF   67 SECOND] *Dyce²; not in* QqF   67 Jesus] Qq; Jesu F   71 SH FIRST] *Capell; not in*
QqF   75 SD.3 *disguised*] *Cam.; not in* QqF   79 SD.1 *They retire*] *Dyce; not in* QqF   83 SD *As . . . them*] QqF *subst.* (QqO, 1
print with 85 SD *in four lines to the right of 84–5*)

69 whoreson vile, wretched.
69 caterpillars extortioners who prey upon
the commonwealth like parasitic worms. Compare 2.1.64–6. Bullingbrook describes the King's
councillors as caterpillars in *R2* 2.3.166; the allegation occurs frequently in feudal justifications of
rebellion. Falstaff deflects his own failings onto
his opponents.
69 bacon-fed knaves overfed bumpkins.
69 us youth A deliberate comic absurdity, at
least for Falstaff; strife between generations is
often treated seriously in other contexts.

72 gorbellied pot-bellied, corpulent (*OED*).
72 chuffs wealthy miserly yeomen or citizens.
73 your store 'all you possess' (Kittredge).
74 grandjurors Only men of standing or
wealth, normally landowners, could serve on a
grand jury (*OED* Jury sv *sb* 2 b).
74 jure ye A pun on 'jury' used as a threat:
'We'll dose you with your own medicine!'
77 argument subject-matter of discussion or
discourse (*OED* sv *sb* 6).
81–2 no equity stirring no measure of justice
in the world.

PRINCE Your money!

POINS Villains!   85

> *They all run away, and Falstaff after a blow or two runs away too,*
> *leaving the booty behind them*

PRINCE Got with much ease. Now merrily to horse.
The thieves are all scattered and possessed with fear
So strongly that they dare not meet each other.
Each takes his fellow for an officer!
Away, good Ned! Falstaff sweats to death,   90
And lards the lean earth as he walks along.
Were it not for laughing I should pity him.

POINS How the fat rogue roared!

> *Exeunt*

[2.3] *Enter* HOTSPUR [*alone,*] *reading a letter*

[HOTSPUR] '*But for mine own part, my lord, I could be well contented to be*
there, in respect of the love I bear your house.'
He could be contented! Why is he not then? In respect of the love he
bears our house. He shows in this he loves his own barn better than
he loves our house. Let me see some more.   5
'*The purpose you undertake is dangerous,*'
Why, that's certain. 'Tis dangerous to take a cold, to sleep, to drink.
But I tell you, my lord fool, out of this nettle, danger, we pluck this
flower, safety.

85 SD.1 *and Falstaff . . . too*] Qq; *not in* F   86–92 Got . . . him] *As verse, Pope; as prose,* QqF   93 fat] Qo; *not in* Qq1–5, F
Act 2, Scene 3   2.3] *Scæna Tertia.* F; *not in* Qq   o SD *alone*] *solus* QqF   1 SH HOTSPUR | *Capell; not in* QqF   3 respect
of] F; the respect of Qq1–5

86–92 Got . . . him Printed as prose in QqF but
most editors follow Pope in having Hal implicitly assert his royal stature by returning to verse.
Compare 1.2.155–77, 3.3.162–71, and 5.3.38–52.

89 takes . . . officer mistakes for a constable. In
a familiar proverb, 'The thief does fear each bush
an officer' (Dent T112).

91 lards fattens (*OED* sv v 2, this example), as
if Falstaff were sweating his own fat rather than
drops of water. The verb suggests meat cooking
on a spit.

Act 2, Scene 3
[2.3] The Percy plot is now well advanced. The
letter that Hotspur reads is a response to 'certeine
articles' (Holinshed) and letters circulated by the
conspirators. It reflects, but modifies, Holinshed's
report that 'when the matter came to triall, the
most part of the confederates abandoned them'
(III, 23).

In the Elizabethan theatre, audiences first see a
single actor in an unlocalised setting. The entries
of Lady Percy and the servants create a domestic
atmosphere.

The text of this edition from the beginning of
this scene to the end of the play is based upon Q1.
See Textual Analysis, pp. 219–21.

o SD The scene begins in mid-argument
between Hotspur and the absent, never to be identified writer of the letter.

2 *house* family. Compare 1.3.10 and n.

7 'Tis . . . drink Hotspur mocks what he considers the writer's great timidity.

7 take a cold catch a cold.

8–9 out . . . safety An adaptation of the
proverbs, 'Danger itself the best remedy for
danger' (Dent D30) and 'To pluck a flower from
among nettles' (Dent F388.1).

'*The purpose you undertake is dangerous, the friends you have named*   10
uncertain, the time itself unsorted, and your whole plot too light, for the
counterpoise of so great an opposition.'
Say you so, say you so? I say unto you again, you are a shallow
cowardly hind, and you lie. What a lack-brain is this! By the Lord,
our plot is a good plot, as ever was laid, our friends true and   15
constant. A good plot, good friends, and full of expectation. An
excellent plot, very good friends. What a frosty-spirited rogue is
this! Why, my Lord of York commends the plot, and the general
course of the action. Zounds, an I were now by this rascal I could
brain him with his lady's fan. Is there not my father, my uncle, and   20
myself? Lord Edmund Mortimer, my Lord of York, and Owen
Glendower? Is there not besides the Douglas? Have I not all their
letters to meet me in arms by the ninth of the next month, and are
they not some of them set forward already? What a pagan rascal is
this, an infidel! Ha! You shall see now in very sincerity of fear and   25
cold heart will he to the King, and lay open all our proceedings! O,
I could divide myself, and go to buffets, for moving such a dish of
skim milk with so honourable an action! Hang him, let him tell the
King, we are prepared. I will set forward tonight.

Enter his LADY

How now, Kate? I must leave you within these two hours.   30
LADY PERCY O my good lord, why are you thus alone?
        For what offence have I this fortnight been
        A banished woman from my Harry's bed?

14 By the Lord] Qq; I protest F   19 Zounds, an] Qq (Zoundes and); By this hand if F

11 *unsorted* not well chosen.
12 *counterpoise* a balancing force or weight
(*OED* sv *sb* 1).
14 **hind** (1) menial servant (*OED* sv *sb²* 1), (2)
rustic or boor (*OED* sv *sb²* 3).
14–17 **By . . . friends** Hotspur's misguided
enthusiasm mounts despite the reasonable objections that have been raised.
15 **friends** allies, supporters.
16 **full of expectation** extremely promising.
18–19 **my Lord . . . action** In Holinshed,
Richard Scroop, Archbishop of York, is said to
have written the 'articles' that attempt to justify
the Percy cause.
20 **brain . . . lady's fan** Hotspur follows up
his claim that the writer is a lack-brain, 14, by this
threat to use an almost weightless weapon.
24 **pagan** Like 'infidel', 25, one who resists the
established faith.

26 **will he** he will go.
27 **divide . . . buffets** split into two parts and
set each to cuffing the other. Hotspur anticipates
Lady Percy's diagnosis of his condition, 50 below.
27 **moving** urging.
30 **Kate** See List of Characters and 1.3.79. n.
31–58 **O my . . . loves me not** Kate's long first
speech and the following dialogue are often compared to the exchanges between Portia and Brutus,
JC 2.1.233 ff. Both women are shrewd observers of
their husbands, but Kate communicates her anxiety in a jesting manner. Hotspur does not respond
to her direct questions, perhaps because he wishes
to tease her, perhaps because he is too preoccupied.
33 **banished woman** Sexual activity supposedly diminished a man's energy and physical
strength – a notion still current among some sports
managers and journalists.

Tell me, sweet lord, what is't that takes from thee
Thy stomach, pleasure, and thy golden sleep?   35
Why dost thou bend thine eyes upon the earth,
And start so often when thou sittest alone?
Why hast thou lost the fresh blood in thy cheeks,
And given my treasures and my rights of thee
To thick-eyed musing, and curst melancholy?   40
In thy faint slumbers I by thee have watched
And heard thee murmur tales of iron wars,
Speak terms of manage to thy bounding steed,
Cry 'Courage! To the field!' and thou hast talked
Of sallies, and retires, of trenches, tents,   45
Of palisadoes, frontiers, parapets,
Of basilisks, of cannon, culverin,
Of prisoners' ransom, and of soldiers slain,
And all the currents of a heady fight.
Thy spirit within thee hath been so at war,   50
And thus hath so bestirred thee in thy sleep,
That beads of sweat have stood upon thy brow
Like bubbles in a late-disturbèd stream,
And in thy face strange motions have appeared,
Such as we see when men restrain their breath   55
On some great sudden hest. O, what portents are these?
Some heavy business hath my lord in hand,
And I must know it, else he loves me not.

---

41 thy] Qq1–3; my Qq4–5, F   42 thee] Qq2–5, F; the Q1   48 ransom] QqF (ransome); ransom'd *Dyce²*, *conj. Capell*

---

35 stomach appetite.

35 golden precious (*OED* sv *a* 4a).

39 my treasures and my rights Kate expresses how much pleasure she has taken in the exercise of the more formal 'rights' that are owed to a wife.

40 thick-eyed dim-sighted, related to 'bend thine eyes upon the earth', 36. These acute observations create an image that contrasts sharply with her husband's confident rhetoric.

40 curst waspish, cross, bad-tempered.

41 faint light.

41 watched (1) kept awake (*OED* sv *v* 1b), (2) been on the lookout.

42 iron wars Figurative description of battle.

43 manage The art of training and managing horses (*OED* sv *sb* 1).

45 sallies sudden rushes towards an enemy from a besieged position.

45 retires retreats.

46 palisadoes Variant of palisades, fences made out of stakes and used for enclosure or defence.

46 frontiers ramparts. Compare 1.3.18.

46 parapets defences made of earth or stone, raised on the ground or on a rampart, literally breast-high (*OED* 1).

47 basilisks The largest cannons, named for a fabulous monster, the basilisk or cockatrice, which was hatched by a serpent from a cock's egg. Its breath or gaze was supposedly fatal.

47 culverin A small cannon originally used as a handgun. Its name derives from French 'coulcuvre', snake. 'Names of reptiles were frequently applied to early cannon' (*OED* 1).

49 currents movements.

49 heady violent.

54 motions (1) commotions, (2) expressions.

56 hest behest, injunction.

57 heavy grave.

HOTSPUR What ho!

[*Enter a* SERVANT]

Is Gillams with the packet gone?

SERVANT He is, my lord, an hour ago.   60

HOTSPUR Hath Butler brought those horses from the sheriff?

SERVANT One horse, my lord, he brought even now.

HOTSPUR What horse? A roan, a crop-ear is it not?

SERVANT It is, my lord.

HOTSPUR   That roan shall be my throne.

Well, I will back him straight. O Esperance!   65

Bid Butler lead him forth into the park.

[*Exit Servant*]

LADY PERCY But hear you, my lord.

HOTSPUR What sayest thou, my lady?

LADY PERCY What is it carries you away?

HOTSPUR Why, my horse, my love, my horse.   70

LADY PERCY Out, you mad-headed ape!

A weasel hath not such a deal of spleen

As you are tossed with. In faith,

I'll know your business, Harry, that I will.

I fear my brother Mortimer doth stir   75

---

59 SD *Enter a* SERVANT] *Capell; after 58, Dering MS.; not in* QqF   63 A roan] Qq3–5, F; Roane Qq1, 2   65–6 Well . . .
park] *As verse,* Pope; *as prose,* QqF   66 SD *Exit Servant*] *Dering MS., Hanmer; not in* QqF   71–7 Out . . . go] *As verse,*
Capell; *as prose,* QqF   73 In faith] Qq; In sooth F

---

59 packet dispatch or message (about the conspiracy, we infer).

59, 61 Gillams, Butler Why Shakespeare chooses to name these servants who never appear has not received clear explanation. The names may provide evidence of the closeness of Q1 to an unrevised authorial manuscript. Compare the use of names: Tom, Cut, Robin Ostler, and Mugs in the short sequence 2.1.5–36.

61 sheriff high officer in a shire who represents the king. This sheriff apparently supports the locally powerful Percy family.

63 A roan A horse either named for or described by its colours, reddish brown mottled with white or grey. Hal mocks Hotspur's preference for this horse at 2.4.92.

64–82 That roan . . . true Editors generally follow Pope in arranging the lines as verse; QqF print this passage as prose. With the emendation from Q3, 'A roan', verse can begin one line earlier at 63.

65 back him mount him.

65 Esperance 'Esperance' or 'Esperance ma comforte' (Hope, my comfort) was the Percy motto. Compare 5.2.96.

67–71 But . . . ape Five consecutive short lines, mostly in monosyllables, capture the quick repartee of Hotspur and Kate.

69 What . . . away (1) Why are you going? (2) What (passion) sweeps you away?

72 weasel 'As angry as a weasel' (Dent W211.1) was a common comparison.

72 spleen a capricious humour, marked by sudden, contradictory emotions and thought to be caused, like more violent tempers, by the organ of the body called the spleen. Compare 3.2.125 and 5.2.19, 'A hare-brained Hotspur, governed by a spleen'.

75 my brother Mortimer Historically, Lord Edmund Mortimer, captured by Glendower, was her younger brother; the heir presumptive was her nephew. See 1.3.79 n. and List of Characters for Shakespeare's conflation of the two.

   About his title, and hath sent for you
   To line his enterprise. But if you go –
HOTSPUR So far afoot I shall be weary, love.
LADY PERCY Come, come, you paraquito, answer me
   Directly unto this question that I ask.   80
   In faith, I'll break thy little finger, Harry,
   And if thou wilt not tell me all things true.
HOTSPUR Away,
   Away you trifler! Love! I love thee not,
   I care not for thee, Kate; this is no world   85
   To play with mammets, and to tilt with lips.
   We must have bloody noses, and cracked crowns,
   And pass them current too. God's me! My horse!
   What say'st thou, Kate? What wouldst thou have with me?
LADY PERCY Do you not love me? Do you not indeed?   90
   Well, do not then, for since you love me not
   I will not love myself. Do you not love me?
   Nay, tell me if you speak in jest or no?
HOTSPUR Come, wilt thou see me ride?
   And when I am a-horseback I will swear   95
   I love thee infinitely. But hark you, Kate,
   I must not have you henceforth question me
   Whither I go, nor reason whereabout.
   Whither I must, I must. And, to conclude,
   This evening must I leave you, gentle Kate.   100
   I know you wise, but yet no farther wise

79–82 Come . . . true] *As verse, Pope; as prose,* QqF 81 In faith] Qq; Indeede F 93 you speak] Qq; thou speak'st F 98, 99 Whither] Qq; Whether F

76 **title** claim to the crown.

77 **line** strengthen, reinforce (as in lining a garment).

79 **paraquito** A small parrot, used as a term of endearment, but also suggesting excessive talk. Compare 'popinjay' 1.3.49 and n.

83–4 **Away . . . not** Hotspur facetiously replies to Kate's demand at 58: because he cannot tell her his business, it follows that he does not love her.

86 **mammets** dolls or puppets, and, by implication, his wife as a sexual partner. The original meaning, idols or false gods, (from Mahomet or Mohammed) tinges Hotspur's gibe with a charge

of false belief. Compare 'pagan' and 'infidel', 24–5.

86 **tilt with lips** Literally, to joust with lips. This may imply that (1) both tournaments and kissing are idle sports or games in time of war, (2) only sexual play is inappropriate.

87 **crowns** (1) heads, (2) coins, valued at five shillings, still used in sixteenth-century England.

88 **pass them current** (1) use them as valid currency despite their being cracked, (2) use them frequently, i.e. crack many heads.

88 **God's me** God save me, an oath that escaped purging in the Folio.

98 **reason whereabout** examine my purpose.

Than Harry Percy's wife. Constant you are,
But yet a woman. And for secrecy,
No lady closer, for I well believe
Thou wilt not utter what thou dost not know.   105
And so far will I trust thee, gentle Kate.
LADY PERCY How? So far?
HOTSPUR Not an inch further. But hark you, Kate,
Whither I go, thither shall you go too.
Today will I set forth, tomorrow you.   110
Will this content you, Kate?
LADY PERCY   It must, of force.

Exeunt

[**2.4**] *Enter* PRINCE *and* POINS

PRINCE Ned, prithee come out of that fat room, and lend me thy hand
    to laugh a little.
POINS Where hast been, Hal?
PRINCE With three or four loggerheads, amongst three or fourscore
    hogsheads. I have sounded the very base string of humility. Sirrah,   5
    I am sworn brother to a leash of drawers, and can call them all by

---

104 well] Qq1–3; wil Q4; will Q5, F   106 far will] Qq1–4; farewill Q5; farre wilt F   Act 2, Scene 4   2.4] *Scena quarta.*
F; *not in* Qq

103 But yet a woman Hotspur's unwillingness to trust his wife balances his misplaced confidence in 'a dish of skim milk', 27–8 above.
105 Thou . . . know Humphreys traces this 'venerable jest' back to Seneca, *Controversiae*, II, xiii, 12. Compare Dent W649, S196, W706.1.
109 Whither . . . too An echo of Ruth's refusal to abandon Naomi, in Ruth 1.16 (Davison).
111 of force of necessity.

Act 2, Scene 4
[**2.4**] This first tavern scene, as it is conventionally and accurately known, takes place in Eastcheap, 12 below. The inn, never explicitly named in the text, has traditionally been identified as the Boar's Head, which stood on the north side of Great Eastcheap. This street, noted for its meat-markets, provides an appropriate background for numerous references to food and feasting. Both neighbourhood and tavern are closely associated with Falstaff. In *2H4* 2.2.146–7, Prince Hal asks, 'Doth the old boar feed in the old frank?'

Tables, chairs, and drinking vessels provide the only props needed.
1 fat (1) filled with dense, cloying air (*OED sv a* 7c), (2) vat, a large cask in which to ferment or store beer or cider; distinct from the 'hogsheads' among which Hal has been drinking, 5 below.
1 lend . . . hand give me your support, i.e. lend a helping hand (*OED sv v*² 2e).
4 loggerheads blockheads, the drawers, 6, who invite some of the guests into their cellar to drink among the casks.
4–5 amongst . . . hogsheads i.e. in the cellar. Dekker in *Guls Horne-booke* (1609), ed. Grosart, II, 260, advises gallants 'to accept of the courtesie of the Cellar when tis offered you by the drawers' (cited by Humphreys).
5 humility (1) 'freedom from pride or arrogance' (Hemingway), (2) humble or low condition (*OED* 2).
6 leash set of three; a hunting term, often used for dogs.
6 drawers tapsters.

their Christian names, as Tom, Dick, and Francis. They take it
already upon their salvation that though I be but Prince of Wales yet
I am the king of courtesy, and tell me flatly I am no proud Jack like
Falstaff, but a Corinthian, a lad of mettle, a good boy – by the Lord,   10
so they call me! – and when I am King of England I shall command
all the good lads in Eastcheap. They call drinking deep 'dyeing
scarlet', and when you breathe in your watering they cry 'Hem!' and
bid you 'Play it off!' To conclude, I am so good a proficient in one
quarter of an hour that I can drink with any tinker in his own   15
language during my life. I tell thee, Ned, thou hast lost much
honour that thou wert not with me in this action. But, sweet Ned –
to sweeten which name of Ned I give thee this pennyworth of sugar,
clapped even now into my hand by an underskinker, one that never
spake other English in his life than 'Eight shillings and sixpence',   20
and 'You are welcome', with this shrill addition, 'Anon, anon, sir!
Score a pint of bastard in the Half-moon!', or so. But Ned, to drive
away the time till Falstaff come – I prithee do thou stand in some by-
room while I question my puny drawer to what end he gave me the
sugar. And do thou never leave calling 'Francis!', that his tale to   25

---

7 Christian] Q5; christen Qq1–4; *not in* F   8 salvation] Qq; confidence F   10–11 by . . . me] Qq; *not in* F

7 Christian names Dekker, *Guls Horne-booke*,
11, 256, mockingly recommends, 'Your first com-
plement shall be to grow most inwardly acquainted
with the drawers, to learne their names, as *Jack*,
and *Will*, and *Tom*' (Humphreys).
   9 king best example (Dent K65.1).
   9 Jack Fellow or knave, as well as Falstaff's
nickname.
   10 Corinthian Drinking companion; the
ancient Greek city of Corinth was notorious for
dissipation and wenching. Compare 'Troyans'
2.1.56 and n.
   10 mettle courageous temperament (*OED* sv
sb 3, this example); originally a figurative use of
'metal'. Compare 290.
   12–13 dyeing scarlet What happens to the
complexions of deep drinkers; compare 'purple-
hued malt worms' 2.1.61. The phrase derives from
the practice of mixing urine into dyes, thereby
making them colour-fast on fabric. 'Topers' urine
was supposed to make the best scarlet dye' (Wilson).
   13 breathe in your watering pause for breath
while drinking, a sign of inexperience. 'Breathe' is
used repeatedly in *1H4* to signal pauses in vigorous combat; see 1.3.101 and 207 below.
   13 Hem 'Clear your throat' (Wilson) and keep
on drinking.

   14 Play it off 'Finish up'.
   15–16 tinker . . . language These craftsmen,
often itinerant menders of metal utensils, were
known as great drinkers who often used a canting language. For an account of how the Prince
masters the languages of England, see Joan Web-
ber, 'The renewal of the king's symbolic role
from *Richard II to Henry V*', *TSLL* 4 (1963),
530–8.
   17 action military venture, as at 2.3.19 and 28,
but said in jest.
   18 to sweeten . . . sugar i.e. to compliment you
by making your (plain) name more appetising.
   19 clapped pressed.
   19 underskinker subordinate tapster.
   21 Anon, anon (1) 'Right away' (2) 'In a
minute'.
   22 Score Charge to a bill, reckon up.
   22 bastard Sweet Spanish wine, often adulter-
ated.
   22 Half-moon A room in the tavern, like 'Pomgarnet', 31.
   23–4 by-room side room.
   24 puny (1) junior or inferior in rank, like an
'underskinker', 19, (2) raw, inexperienced (not
necessarily small or thin).

me may be nothing but 'Anon'. Step aside, and I'll show thee a precedent.

[Poins withdraws]

POINS [*Within*] Francis!
PRINCE Thou art perfect.
POINS [*Within*] Francis!   30

Enter [FRANCIS, *a*] *Drawer*

FRANCIS Anon, anon, sir. Look down into the Pomgarnet, Ralph!
PRINCE Come hither, Francis.
FRANCIS My lord?
PRINCE How long hast thou to serve, Francis?
FRANCIS Forsooth, five years, and as much as to –   35
POINS [*Within*] Francis!
FRANCIS Anon, anon, sir.
PRINCE Five year! By'r lady, a long lease for the clinking of pewter. But
   Francis, darest thou be so valiant as to play the coward with thy
   indenture, and show it a fair pair of heels, and run from it?   40
FRANCIS O Lord, sir, I'll be sworn upon all the books in England, I
   could find in my heart –
POINS [*Within*] Francis!
FRANCIS Anon, sir.
PRINCE How old art thou, Francis?   45
FRANCIS Let me see, about Michaelmas next I shall be –
POINS [*Within*] Francis!

---

27 precedent] F (President), *Pope*; present Qq   27 SD *Poins withdraws*] *Theobald subst.; not in* QqF   28 SD, 30 SD.1 *Within*] *Dyce; not in* QqF   30 SH POINS] Qq4, 5, F; *Prin.* Qq1–3 *subst.*   30 SD.2 FRANCIS, a] *Rowe; not in* QqF   36, 43, 47, 54, 68 SD *Within*] *Capell; not in* QqF

27 **precedent** example (of how the drawer speaks English). This reading from F appears to correct the Qq version, 'present'; it could be an editorial intervention, rather than evidence that F relies on the authority of a manuscript or prompt-book. See Textual Analysis, p. 226.
27 SD *Poins withdraws* Poins has no exit in QqF, but he enters at line 74. He may simply retire to the rear or to the side of the stage.
31 **Look down into** Go down and look into.
31 **Pomgarnet** Pomegranate. Another tavern room given a name, like the Bunch of Grapes in *MM* 2.1.128–9.
34 **to serve** i.e. as an apprentice; the normal length of service was seven years. Francis would

probably be fourteen to sixteen if he has served for two years.
38 **By'r lady** By Our Lady (the Virgin Mary).
38 **lease** term.
40 **indenture** contract; compare 1.3.86, where 'indent' is used figuratively. The rebels draw up 'indentures' at 3.1.76, 135, and 253.
40 **show . . . heels** A common saying (Dent P31). The Prince may be going on to tempt Francis with employment in his own household (Wilson); compare Gobbo's decision to serve a new master in *MV* 2.2.1–32.
41 **books** Bibles or prayer-books.
46 **Michaelmas** 29 September, the feast of Michael the Archangel; also a quarter-day (annual dates, on which quarterly charges fall due).

FRANCIS Anon, sir – pray stay a little, my lord.

PRINCE Nay but hark you, Francis, for the sugar thou gavest me, 'twas
a pennyworth, was't not?   50

FRANCIS O Lord, I would it had been two!

PRINCE I will give thee for it a thousand pound – ask me when thou wilt,
and thou shalt have it.

POINS [*Within*] Francis!

FRANCIS Anon, anon.   55

PRINCE Anon, Francis? No, Francis, but tomorrow, Francis. Or
Francis, a-Thursday. Or indeed Francis, when thou wilt. But
Francis!

FRANCIS My lord?

PRINCE Wilt thou rob this leathern-jerkin, crystal-button, not-pated,   60
agate-ring, puke-stocking, caddis-garter, smooth-tongue Spanish
pouch?

FRANCIS O Lord, sir, who do you mean?

PRINCE Why then your brown bastard is your only drink. For look you,
Francis, your white canvas doublet will sully. In Barbary, sir, it   65
cannot come to so much.

FRANCIS What, sir?

POINS [*Within*] Francis!

PRINCE Away, you rogue, dost thou not hear them call?

*Here they both call him; the Drawer stands amazed,
not knowing which way to go*

48 **stay a little** wait for a moment.

60 **rob** i.e. steal your own services, which belong
to your master, by running away.

60–2 **leathern-jerkin . . . Spanish pouch** Hal
reels off this burlesque of the vintner and his
apparel in order to confuse Francis and to satirise
innkeepers.

60 **not-pated** with close-cropped hair (*OED*
Not sv *a* 1), as worn by Chaucer's Yeoman (Prologue, *Canterbury Tales*, 109). It was a common
style for lower and middle classes.

61 **agate-ring** Probably a seal-ring (and status-
symbol) carved from an agate. Compare 3.3.64.

61 **puke**– of dark grey or blue-black wool. Gentlemen wore light-coloured silk stockings.

61 **caddis-garter** gartered with coarse worsted
tape or yarn.

61 **smooth-tongue** flattering, but also articulate speaker, (which Francis might resent). This
suggestion of glibness provides a jolting break in
a series of sharply visualised traits.

61–2 **Spanish pouch** Vintners commonly
wore pouches of Spanish leather (Humphreys).

62 To replace this QQF punctuation with a
dash, as do many editors, suggests that Francis,
in the next line, interrupts his Prince. That seems
unlikely, however befuddled the drawer might be.

64–6 **Why . . . much** The Prince's 'humbug
style' (Gentleman, 1773) serves to baffle Francis.
Hal may imply that he has offered Francis adventure in Barbary, as well as a new position in his
own household, 38–40; because Francis has not
seized this chance, he may be better off in the tavern than seeking his fortune. Heroic apprentices
would soon be celebrated in Thomas Deloney's
tales of shoemakers in *The Gentle Craft* (1598).
Compare the questing heroes of Thomas Heywood's *The Four Prentices of London* (1615, but
probably written by 1594).

65 **Barbary** Northern Africa.

Enter VINTNER

VINTNER What, standest thou still and hearest such a calling? Look to   70
the guests within.

[*Exit Francis*]

My lord, old Sir John with half-a-dozen more are at the door. Shall
I let them in?

PRINCE Let them alone a while, and then open the door.

[*Exit Vintner*]

Enter POINS

Poins!   75

POINS Anon, anon, sir.

PRINCE Sirrah, Falstaff and the rest of the thieves are at the door. Shall
we be merry?

POINS As merry as crickets, my lad. But hark ye, what cunning match
have you made with this jest of the drawer? Come, what's the issue?   80

PRINCE I am now of all humours that have showed themselves humours
since the old days of goodman Adam to the pupil age of this present
twelve o'clock at midnight.

[*Enter* FRANCIS]

What's o'clock, Francis?

FRANCIS Anon, anon, sir.   [*Exit*]   85

PRINCE That ever this fellow should have fewer words than a parrot,
and yet the son of a woman! His industry is up-stairs and down-
stairs, his eloquence the parcel of a reckoning. I am not yet of

---

71 SD *Exit Francis*] Johnson (*Exit Drawer*); not in QqF   74 SD.1 *Exit Vintner*] Theobald (*after 75*); not in QqF   74 SD.2
Enter POINS] QqF (*after 76*)   83 SD *Enter* FRANCIS] Malone (*Re-enter Francis, with wine*); not in QqF   84 o'] QqF (a)   85
SD *Exit*] Collier; not in QqF

69 SD.3 VINTNER Innkeeper, literally wine-
merchant.

74 Let . . . door Hal shows his eagerness to
stage-manage the situation by controlling its timing.

74 SD.2 *Enter* POINS Compare 27 SD above.
If he has left the stage, Poins can enter by one door
as the Vintner leaves by the other.

79 my lad Poins, like Falstaff, feels free to
address the Prince informally. Because the Prince
does not object, one might infer that he takes such
playful intimacy for granted.

79–80 what cunning . . . drawer? i.e. what
sort of a witty contest have you turned this joke
into? Poins may be tactfully calling attention to
the energy that Hal is expending on so easy a trick.
He invokes the model of winning and losing in a

context where battles of wits seem irrelevant.

80 what's the issue? (1) what's the outcome?
(2) what's your purpose?

81–3 I am . . . midnight 'I am in the mood to
indulge any fancy that any man has ever had since
the creation' (Kittredge). Hal either evades Poins'
question or suggests that he is now too 'humorous'
to worry about 'issues'.

82 goodman Title given to a yeoman or a
farmer. The Prince speaks of Adam as if he were
a neighbour.

82 pupil A minor or a ward. Midnight is treated
as the beginning (youth) of a new day.

88 parcel of a reckoning item in a bill.

88–9 I am . . . mind This sudden shift of subject in mid-speech alerts the actor to the instability

Percy's mind, the Hotspur of the north, he that kills me some six or
seven dozen of Scots at a breakfast, washes his hands, and says to his   90
wife, 'Fie upon this quiet life, I want work.' 'O my sweet Harry',
says she, 'how many hast thou killed today?' 'Give my roan horse a
drench', says he, and answers, 'Some fourteen', an hour after, 'a
trifle, a trifle'. I prithee, call in Falstaff. I'll play Percy, and that
damned brawn shall play Dame Mortimer his wife. 'Rivo!' says the   95
drunkard. Call in Ribs, call in Tallow!

Enter FALSTAFF [, GADSHILL, BARDOLPH, *and* PETO;
followed by FRANCIS, *with wine*]

POINS Welcome, Jack, where hast thou been?
FALSTAFF A plague of all cowards, I say, and a vengeance too, marry
and amen! Give me a cup of sack, boy. Ere I lead this life long, I'll
sew nether-stocks, and mend them and foot them too. A plague of   100
all cowards! Give me a cup of sack, rogue. Is there no virtue extant?
He drinks
PRINCE Didst thou never see Titan kiss a dish of butter – pitiful–

---

96 SD.1 GADSHILL . . . PETO] *Theobald; not in* QqF   96 SD.2 *followed . . . wine*] *Dering MS., Dyce; not in* QqF   100
and foot them] Qq; *not in* F   102 Titan!] *Warburton;* Titan QqF

of the Prince's mood. He mocks Hotspur's single-
minded attitude as opposed to his own 'all
humours'. The leap with no transition from Francis to Hotspur (in this, the Prince's first explicit
reference to his rival) may suggest an undercur-
rent that unexpectedly links the tapster and the
rebel.

89 kills me The ethical dative 'me' makes the
slaughter of Scots sound absurdly practical.

91–4 Fie . . . trifle A shrewd imitation of Hotspur's style, capturing his long-delayed responses
and his exasperated understatements.

93 drench (1) drink, (2) dose of medicine.

94 I'll play Percy An intriguing promise never
enacted.

95 brawn (1) the meat of the boar, (2) the flesh
most suitable for roasting.

95 Rivo A cry of uncertain origin used in drinking bouts; perhaps from Italian '*riviva*', meaning
'Another toast!' (Davison).

96 Ribs . . . Tallow Meat (on bones) . . .
coarse, hard fat, dripping, or gravy. Wilson, *Fortunes*, p. 27, notes that these terms 'recall the chief
stock-in-trade of the victuallers and butchers of
Eastcheap'.

98 of on.

100 nether-stocks stockings or hose. Falstaff

pretends to humble virtue, like that of the honest
citizen in Jonson's *The Alchemist* who 'sate up a
mending my wifes stockings' (5.1.35).

100 foot make feet for. Bevington links this
vision of tedious labour to Falstaff's discomfort
'afoot'.

102–4 Didst . . . compound The Prince
invents a riddle which refers to Falstaff's excessive
drinking and/or to his sweating. It further hints
at his contradictory nature. The sun (Titan) over-
powers and melts the dish of butter, which may
(to ludicrous effect) identify with butter the helpless mortals loved by the gods of classical myths.
Within this scenario, there are several possible
meanings: (1) Falstaff is the sun, the cup of sack,
his butter; (2) Falstaff, incongruously, is both sun
and butter, huge and red-faced (the Titans were
rebellious giants), but in process of dissolution;
(3) The Prince is the sun, perpetrator of the joke
that has caused Falstaff (the butter) to sweat his
own fat (2.2.90–1) or 'Tallow' (96 above). 'To melt
like butter before the sun' was a common saying
(Dent B780).

The second 'Titan' has been considered by
some editors to be a printer's error; Theobald proposed 'butter'. 'Pitiful' could mean compassionate
or tender.

hearted Titan! – that melted at the sweet tale of the sun's? If thou
didst, then behold that compound.

FALSTAFF You rogue, here's lime in this sack too. There is nothing but   105
roguery to be found in villainous man, yet a coward is worse than a
cup of sack with lime in it. A villainous coward! Go thy ways, old
Jack, die when thou wilt. If manhood, good manhood, be not forgot
upon the face of the earth, then am I a shotten herring. There lives
not three good men unhanged in England, and one of them is fat,   110
and grows old. God help the while, a bad world I say. I would I were
a weaver: I could sing psalms – or anything. A plague of all cowards,
I say still.

PRINCE How now, woolsack, what mutter you?

FALSTAFF A king's son! If I do not beat thee out of thy kingdom with a   115
dagger of lath, and drive all thy subjects afore thee like a flock of
wild geese, I'll never wear hair on my face more. You, Prince of
Wales!

PRINCE Why, you whoreson round man, what's the matter?

FALSTAFF Are not you a coward? Answer me to that – and Poins there?   120

---

103 sun's] *Cam.;* soanes Qq1, 2; sunne Qq3–5, F   112 psalms – or anything] Qq; all manner of songs F

---

104 compound (1) mixture, (2) a substance in
which the elements composing it retain their distinctive (and in this case mismatched) qualities.
Both meanings antedate *OED*'s earliest examples.

105 lime Alkaline substance (i.e. calcium oxide,
not lime juice), used by vintners to make wine dry
and sparkling. Humphreys cites Elyot's *Ortho-
epia Gallica* 11, 40 on this practice, regarded as
worse than watering the wine: 'nothing is more
hurtfull to mens bodies . . . for thence proceed
infinit maladies, and specially the goutes'.

105–6 There . . . man Adapting a proverbial
saying, 'There is no faith (trust, honesty) in man'
(Dent F34), Falstaff returns to his theme of truth
among thieves. Compare 2.2.18 ff.

109 shotten herring one thin and emaciated
because it had shot or spawned its roe. Falstaff,
the festive, meaty, carnival figure, contrasts his
bulk with that of a popular Lenten food, simultaneously mocking the thin Prince Hal. Compare
'soused gurnet' 4.2.11.

110 good (1) brave, (2) virtuous.

111 the while these bad times.

111–12 I would . . . psalms Weavers were
noted for singing at work; they may often have
been pious immigrants from the Low Countries

to East Anglia. (See Peter Milward, *Shakespeare's
Religious Background*, 1973, p. 153). Compare *TN*
2.3.58–9: 'a catch that will draw three souls out of
one weaver'.

112 or anything i.e. as if weaving or sewing,
100, were the most extreme renunciations imag-
inable.

114 woolsack (1) a large bale or bag made of
wool, (2) an incongruous 'compound' (104) of
stuffing and wine.

114 mutter An implicit stage direction: Falstaff may be talking to himself.

116 dagger of lath A stage property of the
Morality-play Vice, a role attributed to Falstaff at
375 below. For the absurd uproar associated with
the Vice, compare *TN* 'the old Vice . . . / Who
with dagger of lath / In his rage and his wrath /
Cries, ah, ha! to the devil' (4.2.124–8). On uses of
Morality-play conventions in *1H4*, see Introduction, p. 10 ff. Falstaff's weapon may be 'a traditional apprentice's play-sword made of wood', i.e.
'a false staff', according to David Wiles, *Shakespeare's Clown*, 1987, pp. 121–2.

117 I'll . . . more Perhaps a 'gibe at Hal's hair-
less chin' (Wilson).

POINS Zounds, ye fat paunch, an ye call me coward by the Lord I'll stab
    thee.

FALSTAFF I call thee coward? I'll see thee damned ere I call thee cow-
    ard, but I would give a thousand pound I could run as fast as thou
    canst. You are straight enough in the shoulders, you care not who   125
    sees your back. Call you that backing of your friends? A plague
    upon such backing, give me them that will face me! Give me a cup
    of sack! I am a rogue if I drunk today.

PRINCE O, villain! Thy lips are scarce wiped since thou drunk'st last.

FALSTAFF All is one for that. (*He drinks.*) A plague of all cowards, still   130
    say I.

PRINCE What's the matter?

FALSTAFF What's the matter? There be four of us here have taken a
    thousand pound this day morning.

PRINCE Where is it, Jack, where is it?   135

FALSTAFF Where is it? Taken from us it is. A hundred upon poor four
    of us.

PRINCE What, a hundred, man?

FALSTAFF I am a rogue if I were not at half-sword with a dozen of them
    two hours together. I have scaped by miracle. I am eight times   140
    thrust through the doublet, four through the hose, my buckler cut
    through and through, my sword hacked like a handsaw – *ecce*
    signum! I never dealt better since I was a man. All would not do. A
    plague of all cowards! Let them speak. If they speak more or less
    than truth, they are villains and the sons of darkness.   145

[PRINCE] Speak, sirs, how was it?

---

121 SH POINS] Qq1–4; *Prin.* Q5, F   130 All is] Qq1, 2; *All's* Qq3–5, F   146 SH PRINCE] *Prince Henry* F, *Dering MS.*;
Gad Qq

126 **backing** (1) supporting, (2) turning to flee.

129 **O, villain . . . last** A particularly apposite
twist to the saying, 'You licked not your lips since
you lied last' (Dent L329, Appendix C).

133–4 **a thousand pound** Perhaps an echo of
FV, 86; Shakespeare's robbers have stolen only
300 marks (436), or a mere 200 pounds. For use
of the phrase as hyperbole, compare 52 and 124
above. The sum is repeatedly associated with Falstaff and his expenses in this play, in *2H4* and in
Wiv.

139 **at half-sword** (1) fighting at close quarters
(*OED* 2), (2) fighting with short swords (*OED* 1).

141 **buckler** A small round shield, in Shakespeare's day considered more suitable for servants and rowdies. Falstaff's 'claim to sturdy old-
fashioned manhood . . . extends also to his choice

of weapons' (Humphreys). Compare Hotspur's
remark at 1.3.227 and n.

142–3 *ecce signum* behold the proof (or sign);
an implied stage direction using a familiar saying (Dent S443), perhaps suggested by 'miracle'
in 140. If the phrase is a corruption of '*ecce lignum*
crucis' in the Good Friday service (Cowl and Morgan), it would support Falstaff's pose as a virtuous
outlaw.

143 **All would not do** Even my bravery was
not enough.

145 **sons of darkness** A biblical echo, 1 Thess.
5.5: 'Ye are all the children of light . . . we are not
of the night nether of darkenes.'

146, 147, 149, 153 SHS Q gives 146 to 'Gad',
and the other three lines to 'Ross.' (for Rossill), as
Bardolph was originally called. For an account of

[BARDOLPH] We four set upon some dozen –

FALSTAFF Sixteen at least, my lord.

[BARDOLPH] And bound them.

PETO No, no, they were not bound.   150

FALSTAFF You rogue, they were bound, every man of them, or I am a
    Jew else: an Ebrew Jew.

[BARDOLPH] As we were sharing, some six or seven fresh men set upon
    us –

FALSTAFF And unbound the rest, and then come in the other.   155

PRINCE What, fought you with them all?

FALSTAFF All? I know not what you call all, but if I fought not with fifty
    of them I am a bunch of radish. If there were not two or three and
    fifty upon poor old Jack, then am I no two-legg'd creature.

PRINCE Pray God you have not murdered some of them.   160

FALSTAFF Nay, that's past praying for, I have peppered two of them.
    Two I am sure I have paid, two rogues in buckram suits. I tell thee
    what, Hal, if I tell thee a lie, spit in my face, call me horse. Thou
    knowest my old ward – here I lay, and thus I bore my point. Four
    rogues in buckram let drive at me –   165

PRINCE What, four? Thou saidst but two even now.

FALSTAFF Four, Hal, I told thee four.

POINS Ay, ay, he said four.

FALSTAFF These four came all afront, and mainly thrust at me. I made
    me no more ado, but took all their seven points in my target, thus! 170

PRINCE Seven? Why, there were but four even now.

147, 149, 153 SH BARDOLPH] *Dering MS., Collier (Bard.); Ross.* QQ; *Gad.* F   150 SH PETO] QQF; *Bard./ Dering
MS.*   160 SH PRINCE] QQ1–4 *subst.; Poines.* Q5, F

the textual confusion surrounding the robbery and
its aftermath, see Textual Analysis, p. 223.

  152 Ebrew Jew i.e. an authentic one (compare
'the veriest varlet' 2.2.19); perhaps also a clumsily
comic repetition or intensifier. At a time when no
Jews could publicly practise their religion in England, casual equations of Jews with knaves, though
indefensible, were common. Compare Benedick's
vow (*Ado* 2.3.263).

  155 other all the others.

  158 a bunch of radish Radishes could signify excessive leanness. See 'shotten herring' 109
and note. In *2H4* Falstaff compares Shallow to a
'fork'd redish' (3.2.311). According to Elyot, *Castle of Health*, 1539, p. 35, 'Radyshe rootes have the
vertu to extenuate or make thin' (Wilson).

  158–9 three and fifty Many editors consider

this an allusion to the fifty-three Spanish ships
that opposed the *Revenge* in 1591.

  161 peppered trounced, severely injured.

  162 paid killed, settled with.

  163 call me horse A common expression of
contempt; compare *TN* 2.3.186–7, 'If thou hast
her not i'th'end, call me cut' (i.e. horse, with a
docked tail). Falstaff also plays on 'no two-legg'd
creature', 159.

  164 ward position of defence.

  164 here . . . point this is how I stood and how
I pointed my sword. Falstaff acts out his words.

  169 afront abreast.

  169 mainly mightily.

  170 target light shield (the 'buckler', 141). It
would be quite a feat for seven armed men abreast
to strike it at once.

FALSTAFF In buckram?

POINS Aye, four, in buckram suits.

FALSTAFF Seven, by these hilts, or I am a villain else.

PRINCE Prithee let him alone, we shall have more anon.   175

FALSTAFF Dost thou hear me, Hal?

PRINCE Ay, and mark thee too, Jack.

FALSTAFF Do so, for it is worth the listening to. These nine in buckram
    that I told thee of –

PRINCE So, two more already.   180

FALSTAFF Their points being broken –

POINS Down fell their hose.

FALSTAFF – began to give me ground. But I followed me close, came in,
    foot and hand, and, with a thought, seven of the eleven I paid.

PRINCE O monstrous! Eleven buckram men grown out of two!   185

FALSTAFF But as the devil would have it, three misbegotten knaves in
    Kendal green came at my back and let drive at me, for it was so dark,
    Hal, that thou couldst not see thy hand.

PRINCE These lies are like their father that begets them, gross as a
    mountain, open, palpable. Why, thou clay-brained guts, thou   190
    knotty-pated fool, thou whoreson obscene greasy tallow-catch –

FALSTAFF What, art thou mad? Art thou mad? Is not the truth the truth?

---

177 too, Jack | Qq2–5, F *subst.;* to iacke Q1   191 -catch | QqF; chest *Dering MS. (orig.* catch, *then altered); ketch Hanmer;*
keech *Var. 1778;* cake *Cowl and Morgan*

174 hilts sword handle. Because it had three
parts – a knob on the end, a handle, and a hand-
guard – the 'hilt' could be referred to as both
singular and plural. Its cross-like shape made it
appropriate for swearing an oath on. Compare
Ham. 1.5.147.
177 mark (1) pay attention to, (2) keep count
(Wilson).
181–2 Their points . . . hose An aggressive
quibble on points as (1) swords (or their sharp
ends), (2) the laces used to attach stockings to the
doublet.
183 followed me followed; ('me' is an ethical
dative, as in 89).
183–4 came . . . hand pursued closely. Here the
common phrase expresses the lunging of sword-
play; it may also suggest 'in close attendance', as
if ready to 'wait upon one hand and foot' (*OED*
Foot *sv sb* 30b).
184 with a thought as quick as thought.
186 misbegotten illegally engendered. Falstaff is prompted by the Prince's exclamation, 185.
187 Kendal green Cloth associated with

Kendal in Westmoreland (now Cumbria), commonly worn by foresters, servants, country people,
and thieves in disguise. Compare Robert Armin's
Nest of Ninnies (1608, probably echoing Falstaff),
ed. Collier, p. xvi: 'Truth, in plaine attire, is the
easier knowne: let fixion [fiction] maske in Kendall
greene' (cited by Humphreys).
189 father Falstaff. The Prince alludes to the
saying that the Devil is the father of lies (Dent
D241.1 and F92).
190 clay-brained dull-witted.
191 knotty-pated block-headed; compare loggerheads, 4.
191 obscene disgusting.
191 tallow-catch A pan or tub to catch the fat
which drips from roasting meat. This QqF reading
echoes references to 'lard', 'tallow', and 'butter'.
The emendation 'keech', adopted by many editors, does correspond to the Prince's adjectives. A
'keech' is the fat of a slaughtered animal, rolled up
by the butcher into a lump (*OED sv sb* 1).
192 Is not . . . truth? A proverbial expression
(Dent T581).

PRINCE Why, how couldst thou know these men in Kendal green when
    it was so dark thou couldst not see thy hand? Come, tell us your
    reason. What sayest thou to this?   195
POINS Come, your reason, Jack, your reason!
FALSTAFF What, upon compulsion? Zounds, an I were at the strappado,
    or all the racks in the world, I would not tell you on compulsion.
    Give you a reason on compulsion? If reasons were as plentiful as
    blackberries, I would give no man a reason upon compulsion, I.   200
PRINCE I'll be no longer guilty of this sin. This sanguine coward, this
    bed-presser, this horse-back-breaker, this huge hill of flesh –
FALSTAFF 'Sblood, you starveling, you elf-skin, you dried neat's-
    tongue, you bull's-pizzle, you stock-fish! O for breath to utter what
    is like thee! You tailor's-yard, you sheath, you bow-case, you vile   205
    standing tuck!

---

203 elf-skin] Qq1, 2 (elʃ skin); elfskin Qq3–5; elfe-skin F; eel-skin *Hanmer*

197 strappado A kind of torture in which the
victim was lifted, then let down by ropes that tied
his hands behind his back, often dislocating his
shoulders. He could also be dropped suddenly,
fracturing many other bones.
  198 racks Instruments of torture consisting of
a frame, with rollers at each end, on which the
victim was stretched.
  199 reason on compulsion Wilson notes that
'reasons' or opinions were at that time often
'extracted by the "compulsion" of torture'.
  199–200 If reasons ... blackberries As cheap
as blackberries was a common saying (Dent B442).
Falstaff puns on 'raisins', pronounced much like
'reasons' (Cercignani, 235).
  201 this sin i.e. failing to challenge Falstaff's
lies.
  201 sanguine coward 'A comic contradiction
in terms' (Davison). Because of his red face and
robust size, Falstaff looks like a man of sanguine
temperament, which is normally associated with
courage.
  203 starveling emaciated person, in contrast
to Falstaff.
  203 elf-skin Falstaff compares the thin Prince
'to the thinnest thing he could think of ... a fairy's
skin' (Wright, ed. 1897). Qq1, 2 read 'elʃ skin'.
Wilson, Humphreys, and Bevington follow Hanmer by emending to 'eel-skin', which anticipates
three more comparisons to fish or flesh (Hemingway) and appears in other work by Shakespeare,
notably in *2H4* 3.2.325–6 when Falstaff says of
the 'starved justice' Shallow, 'you might have
thrust him and all his apparel into an eel-skin'.

The emendation proposed by Evans to 'elshin' or
'elsin' – a shoemaker's awl – would apply more
to a tall than a thin man. Davison convincingly
suggests that a compositor could easily mistake
part of a ligatured long 's' (ʃ) for an 'f', producing elʃ skin; if 'eelskin' were intended, however,
the compositor has made a 'complex sequence of
errors'.
  203–4 neat's-tongue ox's tongue.
  204 bull's-pizzle penis, dried (like the tongue)
for use as a whip.
  204 stock-fish dried cod. Falstaff ascribes to
the Prince a dryness and sexual inadequacy more
common to old age. Compare *MM* 3.2.109: 'he was
begot between two stock-fishes'. Coleman, p. 216,
refers to the statement by Lechery in Marlowe,
Doctor Faustus, 2.2.708–9, 'I am one that loves an
inch of raw Mutton, better than an ell of fryde
Stockfish.'
  205 tailor's yard yard-stick, again suggesting
thinness and perhaps a lack of virility.
  205 sheath empty case or cover, a retort to Hal's
many gibes about Falstaff's weight, and possibly
an allusion to female genitals.
  205 bow-case Long thin case for unstrung
bows; perhaps a figure for sexual impotence.
  206 standing tuck A very small dagger that has
gone stiff, losing its temper and resilience (*OED*
Standing *ppl a* 8). Falstaff's sexual slur is both devastating and unusual, when he twists the more conventional bawdy sense of 'stand' from the desirable (male erection) to the undesirable (military
unreadiness).

PRINCE Well, breathe a while, and then to it again, and when thou hast
   tired thyself in base comparisons hear me speak but this.

POINS Mark, Jack!

PRINCE We two saw you four set on four, and bound them and were   210
   masters of their wealth – mark now how a plain tale shall put you
   down. Then did we two set on you four, and, with a word, out-faced
   you from your prize, and have it, yea, and can show it you here in
   the house. And Falstaff, you carried your guts away as nimbly, with
   as quick dexterity, and roared for mercy, and still run and roared, as   215
   ever I heard bull-calf. What a slave art thou to hack thy sword as
   thou hast done, and then say it was in fight! What trick, what device,
   what starting-hole canst thou now find out, to hide thee from this
   open and apparent shame?

POINS Come, let's hear Jack, what trick hast thou now?   220

FALSTAFF By the Lord, I knew ye as well as he that made ye. Why, hear
   you, my masters, was it for me to kill the heir apparent? Should I
   turn upon the true prince? Why, thou knowest I am as valiant as
   Hercules. But beware instinct. The lion will not touch the true
   prince. Instinct is a great matter. I was now a coward on instinct. I   225
   shall think the better of myself, and thee, during my life – I for a
   valiant lion, and thou for a true prince. But by the Lord, lads, I am
   glad you have the money! Hostess, clap to the doors! Watch tonight,
   pray tomorrow! Gallants, lads, boys, hearts of gold, all the titles of
   good fellowship come to you! What, shall we be merry? Shall we   230
   have a play extempore?

215 run] Qq; ranne F   **225** now] Q1; *not in* Qq2–5, F

210 set . . . bound The shift in mood to the indicative past is a common usage.

212 with a word (1) with only a word, quickly, (2) with a brief shout.

218 starting-hole bolt-hole, a hiding place for a hunted animal, criminal, or enemy (*OED*).

219 apparent clear, undeniable.

221 I . . . ye A forceful use of a familiar expression (Dent K170.1). In addition to providing a climactic escape for Falstaff from a long sequence of traps, it may ironically glance at how little the Prince's biological father does know him.

222 my masters gentlemen (*OED* sv *sb*¹ 21), a courteous address that need not imply superiority.

224 Hercules One of the most familiar heroes or demigods from Greek mythology, noted for his extraordinary strength and courage.

224–5 The lion . . . prince A belief expressed in many Elizabethan texts, which can be traced back to Pliny. Topsell's *Historie of Foure-footed beastes*

mentions an English lion 'which by evident token was able to distinguish betwixt the King, Nobles, and vulgar sort of people' (1658 edn, p. 370, cited by Humphreys).

225–7 I shall . . . true prince Falstaff continues to quibble on different meanings of 'true'.

228 clap to shut noisily or slam (*OED* sv *v*¹ 4b).

228 Watch (1) Keep guard, (2) Carouse. An ironic echo of Lady Percy, 2.3.41, as well as of Matt. 26.41, 'Watch, and pray, that ye enter not into temptation.' Compare Mark 14.38.

229 pray The pun on 'prey' repeats Gadshill's joke about predators at 2.1.64–6.

231 play extempore Professional theatre was prohibited at this time in inns under jurisdiction of the City of London; scenes without written texts often served as substitutes. See Glynne Wickham, *Early English Stages 1300–1660*, vol. II, *1576–1660, Part II*, 1972, pp. 22, 99.

PRINCE Content, and the argument shall be thy running away.

FALSTAFF Ah, no more of that Hal, an thou lovest me.

Enter HOSTESS

HOSTESS O Jesu, my lord the Prince!

PRINCE How now, my lady the Hostess, what sayest thou to me?   235

HOSTESS Marry my lord, there is a nobleman of the court at door would speak with you. He says he comes from your father.

PRINCE Give him as much as will make him a royal man and send him back again to my mother.

FALSTAFF What manner of man is he?   240

HOSTESS An old man.

FALSTAFF What doth gravity out of his bed at midnight? Shall I give him his answer?

PRINCE Prithee do, Jack.

FALSTAFF Faith, and I'll send him packing.   *Exit*   245

PRINCE Now sirs, by'r lady, you fought fair, so did you, Peto, so did you, Bardolph. You are lions too, you ran away upon instinct, you will not touch the true prince, no, fie!

BARDOLPH Faith, I ran when I saw others run.

PRINCE Faith, tell me now in earnest, how came Falstaff's sword so   250
hacked?

PETO Why, he hacked it with his dagger, and said he would swear truth out of England but he would make you believe it was done in fight, and persuaded us to do the like.

BARDOLPH Yea, and to tickle our noses with spear-grass, to make them   255
bleed, and then to beslubber our garments with it, and swear it was the blood of true men. I did that I did not this seven year before: I blushed to hear his monstrous devices.

---

246 by'r lady] Qq (birlady), *Pope;* not in F   247 lions too,] Q1 *corr.* (lions to,) *Huntington Library copy;* lions, to Q1 *uncorr. British Museum and Trinity College Cambridge copies*   255 SH BARDOLPH] Q1, F (*Bar.*); *Car.* Qq2–5

232 **argument** plot of the story.

233 **no more . . . an thou lovest me** Many actors playing Falstaff assume, despite the literal sense of 'an' as 'if', that Hal does love him, while others convey doubt. On the varied feelings of the Prince for Falstaff in recent productions, see Introduction, pp. 56, 59, 60–1; on their 'friendship', see Introduction, pp. 32–4. Falstaff's evocative line employs a familiar saying (Dent M1154.1).

233 SD HOSTESS See List of Characters for some of the variations in her later parts in *2H4*, *H5*, and *Wiv.*

236, 238 **nobleman, royal man** Hal puns on

the value of coins and on social rank. See 1.2.114–15.

242 **gravity** Falstaff seems to invent a Morality-play character, one of over-earnest age.

252–3 **swear . . . England** 'swear so many false oaths that Truth would flee the country . . . in horror' (Kittredge).

253 **but he would** i.e. if that is what he must do to.

255–7 **tickle . . . men** An echo of *FV* 1426–30, where Dericke tells how he made himself appear to be wounded in Henry V's French campaign so that he would not have to fight in battle.

257 **that** something.

PRINCE O villain, thou stolest a cup of sack eighteen years ago, and wert
taken with the manner, and ever since thou hast blushed extempore.   260
Thou hadst fire and sword on thy side, and yet thou ran'st away.
What instinct hadst thou for it?

BARDOLPH My lord, do you see these meteors? Do you behold these
exhalations?

PRINCE I do.   265

BARDOLPH What think you they portend?

PRINCE Hot livers, and cold purses.

BARDOLPH Choler, my lord, if rightly taken.

PRINCE No, if rightly taken, halter.

Enter FALSTAFF

Here comes lean Jack, here comes bare-bone. How now my sweet   270
creature of bombast, how long is't ago, Jack, since thou sawest thine
own knee?

FALSTAFF My own knee? When I was about thy years, Hal, I was not an
eagle's talon in the waist – I could have crept into any alderman's
thumb-ring. A plague of sighing and grief, it blows a man up like a   275

---

269 SD *Enter* FALSTAFF | F; *after 268*, Qq   274 talon] QqF (talent)

---

260 taken with the manner A common legal
expression (Dent M633) meaning caught in the
act. By turning Bardolph's face red, the sack has
betrayed his crime.

260 blushed extempore All blushing is
unplanned or spontaneous. The Prince mocks
Bardolph's pretence of sincerity, 257–8, by jesting
that he has been turning on this blush for eighteen
years.

261 fire and sword i.e. invincible military
might. The fire comes from Bardolph's complex-
ion.

264 exhalations fiery meteors, as in *Rom.*
3.5.13, 'It is some meteor that the sun [exhal'd]'.
In some productions, Bardolph points to his face
to signify ominous portents in the heavens.

267 Hot livers, and cold purses Drink will
heat the liver, i.e. (1) the seat in the body of courage
and love, (2) one who lives. Paying for the drink
will empty the purse.

268 Choler A temperament dominated by
anger. Bardolph tries to pretend that his face shows
his wrathful nature.

268 rightly taken correctly interpreted.

269 No . . . halter The Prince manages to pun
on three of his five words: rightly (justly), taken
(arrested), and halter (choler, collar, the hangman's noose).

269 SD In some productions, Bardolph leaves
when Falstaff enters. QqF provide no exits for
Bardolph, the Hostess or Francis – none of
whom speaks until Bardolph enters 'running' at
399 below, soon followed by the Hostess, 403.
Although confused and informal movement seems
appropriate for a tavern late at night, Shakespeare
probably left the movements of these two actors
to be worked out in rehearsal. They might have
remained visible to the audience while they listened to Hal and Falstaff.

271 bombast (1) cotton stuffing (*OED* sv *sb*
2b), (2) inflated language (*OED* sv *sb* 3).

274 talon claw. The QqF spelling 'talent' was
one of several variants. Compare, 'If a talent be a
claw', *LLL* 4.2.63.

274–5 alderman's thumb-ring Worn on the
thumb, it might be decorated with a seal and used
to stamp documents. (First reference in *OED*.) An
alderman was the chief officer of a London ward.

275–6 it . . . bladder i.e. it turns a man into
a windbag. Animal bladders, used as containers,
floats, or in bagpipes (see 1.2.61 and *OED* 3), could
signify frivolity; compare *H8* 3.2.359, 'little wanton boys that swim on bladders' (as in Brueghel's
carnivalesque painting *Children's Games*). This
parody of renunciation, Bevington notes, distorts
the received belief that grief, by making the heart

bladder. There's villainous news abroad. Here was Sir John Bracy
from your father. You must to the court in the morning. That same
mad fellow of the north, Percy, and he of Wales that gave Amamon
the bastinado, and made Lucifer cuckold, and swore the devil his
true liegeman upon the cross of a Welsh hook – what a plague call   280
you him?

POINS   O, Glendower.

FALSTAFF   Owen, Owen, the same. And his son-in-law Mortimer, and
     old Northumberland, and that sprightly Scot of Scots, Douglas,
     that runs a-horseback up a hill perpendicular –   285

PRINCE   He that rides at high speed, and with his pistol kills a sparrow
     flying.

FALSTAFF   You have hit it.

PRINCE   So did he never the sparrow.

FALSTAFF   Well, that rascal hath good mettle in him, he will not run.   290

PRINCE   Why, what a rascal art thou then, to praise him so for running!

FALSTAFF   A-horseback, ye cuckoo, but afoot he will not budge a foot.

PRINCE   Yes, Jack, upon instinct.

FALSTAFF   I grant ye, upon instinct. Well, he is there too, and one
     Mordake, and a thousand blue-caps more. Worcester is stolen away   295
     tonight. Thy father's beard is turned white with the news. You may
     buy land now as cheap as stinking mackerel.

PRINCE   Why then, it is like if there come a hot June, and this civil

---

292 afoot] Qq2, 3; a foote Qq1, 4, 5, F

---

contract, withdraws heat, blood, and colour from
the body.

276 Bracy The chronicles and other sources
do not mention this name.

278 Amamon A major devil. Reginald Scot,
Discovery of Witchcraft (1584), identifies him as
'king of the east' (xv, 3) and 'king Baell' or
Amoiman (xv, 19) (cited by Humphreys).

279 bastinado A blow with a stick or club,
especially on the soles of the feet (*OED* sv *sb* 1).

279 made . . . cuckold gave him his horns by
seducing his wife.

279–80 swore . . . Welsh hook made him swear
allegiance as a vassal upon a billhook, a hooked
staff used as a rustic weapon which had no hilt,
and therefore no cross upon which to swear. Falstaff travesties Glendower's reputation for supernatural powers.

290 mettle . . . run Pun on mettle as (1) courageous temperament, (2) metal which dissolves if
poorly made. 'Mettle', like QqF 'mettall', is a variant spelling of 'metal'. Compare 10 above.

292 cuckoo witless repeater, who misses the
figurative sense of 'run', 290, and remembers
the literal one, 285. Compare 'ape', 2.3.71, and
'paraquito', 2.3.79.

292 afoot in hand-to-hand combat (Bevington). Compare 'foot and hand', 184 above.

295 Mordake Earl of Fife. For Shakespeare's
misidentification of him as Douglas' son, see
1.1.71 and n.

295 blue-caps Scottish soldiers wearing blue
hats.

297 as cheap . . . mackerel extremely inexpensive, almost for nothing. This fish has gone
bad, but it cost very little even when fresh.

298–9 it is . . . hob-nails 'Given the heat of
summer, and the excitements of civil war, the girls
won't resist us at all' (Humphreys). This reading
omits the dark weight of 'hob-nails', used to protect heavy boots (*OED* sv *sb* 1). As 'booty', the
Prince implies, the maidens will have no power to
resist attack. Compare 2.1.66 and n.

298 like likely, probable.

buffeting hold, we shall buy maidenheads as they buy hob-nails, by
the hundreds.   300

FALSTAFF By the mass, lad, thou sayest true, it is like we shall have
good trading that way. But tell me, Hal, art not thou horrible
afeard? Thou being heir apparent, could the world pick thee out
three such enemies again, as that fiend Douglas, that spirit Percy,
and that devil Glendower? Art thou not horribly afraid? Doth not   305
thy blood thrill at it?

PRINCE Not a whit, i'faith, I lack some of thy instinct.

FALSTAFF Well, thou wilt be horribly chid tomorrow when thou
comest to thy father. If thou love me, practise an answer.

PRINCE Do thou stand for my father and examine me upon the particu-   310
lars of my life.

FALSTAFF Shall I? Content! This chair shall be my state, this dagger my
sceptre, and this cushion my crown.

PRINCE Thy state is taken for a joint-stool, thy golden sceptre for a
leaden dagger, and thy precious rich crown for a pitiful bald crown.   315

FALSTAFF Well, an the fire of grace be not quite out of thee, now shalt
thou be moved. Give me a cup of sack to make my eyes look red,
that it may be thought I have wept, for I must speak in passion, and
I will do it in King Cambyses' vein.

PRINCE Well, here is my leg.   320

FALSTAFF And here is my speech. Stand aside, nobility.

HOSTESS O Jesu, this is excellent sport, i'faith.

---

299 buffeting fighting, with a sense of blows struck in hand-to-hand combat.

299 hold takes place.

304 spirit devil, as well as the embodiment of courage.

306 thrill shiver as if cold.

310–11 Do thou . . . life Perhaps suggested by *FV* 386–416 where Dericke the clown pretends to be the Prince and John Cobler, the Lord Chief Justice.

312 state royal throne, a basic prop on the Elizabethan stage.

314–15 Thy state . . . crown The Prince playfully reverses the process of theatrical illusion (in which a 'stool' would normally be 'taken for', or believed to be, a throne) both to mock the power of illusion and to imply its fragility.

314 joint-stool stool well made by a joiner or skilled craftsman, but still the most ordinary and movable of furnishings. Compare *Shr.* 2.1.198–9.

315 leaden dagger knife made of a baser metal, too heavy to be useful. Compare 'dagger of lath', 116, and n.

315 pitiful bald crown This surprising substitution for 'cushion' may suggest that as the eye of the subject moves from the bottom (the well-made joint stool) to the top of this monarch, expectations of majesty are increasingly frustrated.

318 in passion with deep emotion. Compare 344 and n.

319 King Cambyses' vein The style of Thomas Preston's *Lamentable Tragedie, mixed full of plesant mirth, containing the Life of Cambises King of Persia* (1569). Both its style and its title were parodied in the entertainment staged by the craftsmen in *MND* called 'A tedious brief scene of young Pyramus / And his love Thisby; very tragical mirth' (5.1.56–7). Falstaff's 'vein' combines extravagant analogies modelled on John Lyly's 'euphuism' with more parody of Puritan sermons.

320 here . . . leg A stage direction: Hal bows to Falstaff as he speaks. Courtiers drew back one leg while bending the other.

FALSTAFF Weep not, sweet Queen, for trickling tears are vain.

HOSTESS O the Father, how he holds his countenance!

FALSTAFF For God's sake, lords, convey my tristful Queen, 325
For tears do stop the floodgates of her eyes.

HOSTESS O Jesu, he doth it as like one of these harlotry players as ever
I see!

FALSTAFF Peace, good pint-pot, peace, good tickle-brain. Harry, I do
not only marvel where thou spendest thy time, but also how thou 330
art accompanied. For though the camomile, the more it is trodden
on the faster it grows, yet youth, the more it is wasted the sooner it
wears. That thou art my son I have partly thy mother's word, partly
my own opinion, but chiefly a villainous trick of thine eye, and a
foolish hanging of thy nether lip, that doth warrant me. If then thou 335
be son to me – here lies the point – why, being son to me, art thou
so pointed at? Shall the blessed sun of heaven prove a micher, and
eat blackberries? A question not to be asked. Shall the son of England prove a thief, and take purses? A question to be asked. There
is a thing, Harry, which thou hast often heard of, and it is known to 340
many in our land by the name of pitch. This pitch – as ancient

324 Father] F; father Qq   325 tristful] *Dering MS., Rowe;* trustfull QqF   327 Jesu] Qq; rare F   332 yet] Qq3–5, F; so
Qq1,2   337 sun] Q1 (sunne); sonne Qq2–5, F

323 **Weep not . . . vain** Weeping queens and
paramours were common in early plays about
tyrants and conquerors. 'Then, daintie damsell,
stint these trickling teares' from Greene's *Alphon-
sus, King of Aragon,* ed. Grosart (1881–6), line
1825, is the closest of many analogues that have
been proposed. Greene probably parodied Tamburlaine's high-flying response to Zenocrate's wet
'passion' (Marlowe, *1 Tamburlaine* 5.135 ff.).
325 **tristful** sorrowful (*OED* sv *a²*). This emendation (Dering *MS.*) has been generally preferred
to 'trustfull' in QqF. Because 'tristful' could also
mean 'trustworthy' (*OED* sv *a¹*), the emendation
retains Falstaff's frequent word-play on loyalty
and truth.
327 **harlotry** knavish, worthless; here and at
3.1.192 used with affection.
329 **pint-pot, tickle-brain** Names suggesting
the hostess' trade; 'tickle-brain' was 'slang for a
kind of strong liquor' (Humphreys).
331–3 **camomile . . . wears** An aromatic
plant with white leaves which proverbially grew
faster the more it was stepped on (Dent C34).
Shakespeare closely parodies Lyly's *Euphues* (ed.
Bond, 1, 196). This ludicrous contrast between
camomile, a creeping ground-cover, and the
Prince's prodigality, launches Falstaff. 'His sus-

tained speech and laborious working out of rhetorical propositions and questions establish his pre-
tended authority; and at the same time, sexual
innuendoes, everyday comparisons, triteness, and
near-nonsense, all mock that authority' (John Russell Brown, ed., *Shakespeare in Performance,* 1976,
p. 151).
333 **thy mother's word** Compare the familiar
expression, 'Ask the mother if the child be like
his father' (Dent M1193). Only in this scene (239
above and here) and only in jest are there references to the mother of the Prince.
334 **trick** characteristic. Compare 5.2.11.
335 **foolish** ridiculous, wanting in judgement.
337–8 **Shall . . . blackberries** An echo of Lyly's
Campaspe, pointed out by Arnold Davenport, *N
& Q* 199 (1954), 19. Hephaestion, the emperor,
rebukes Alexander for desiring the beautiful slave
girl, Campaspe, alleging that 'Bewty is like the
blackberry, which seemeth red when it is not ripe'
(Bond, ed., 2.2.48, noted by Bevington).
337 **micher** truant (*OED* sv *sb* 3).
341–2 **This pitch . . . defile** A pious allusion
to Eccles. 13.1: 'He that toucheth pitch, shalbe
defiled with it.' Lyly alludes to this text in *Euphues
to Philautus,* ed. Bond, 1, 250 and in *Euphues to his
Friend Livia,* 1, 320.

writers do report – doth defile, so doth the company thou keepest.
For, Harry, now I do not speak to thee in drink, but in tears; not in
pleasure, but in passion; not in words only, but in woes also. And
yet there is a virtuous man whom I have often noted in thy com-   345
pany, but I know not his name.

PRINCE What manner of man, an it like your majesty?

FALSTAFF A goodly portly man, i'faith, and a corpulent; of a cheerful
look, a pleasing eye, and a most noble carriage; and, as I think, his
age some fifty, or by'r lady, inclining to three score. And now I   350
remember me, his name is Falstaff. If that man should be lewdly
given, he deceiveth me, for, Harry, I see virtue in his looks. If then
the tree may be known by the fruit, as the fruit by the tree, then
peremptorily I speak it, there is virtue in that Falstaff. Him keep
with, the rest banish. And tell me now, thou naughty varlet, tell me   355
where hast thou been this month?

PRINCE Dost thou speak like a king? Do thou stand for me, and I'll play
my father.

FALSTAFF Depose me? If thou dost it half so gravely, so majestically,
both in word and matter, hang me up by the heels for a rabbit-   360
sucker, or a poulter's hare.

PRINCE Well, here I am set.

FALSTAFF And here I stand. Judge, my masters.

PRINCE Now, Harry, whence come you?

FALSTAFF My noble lord, from Eastcheap.   365

---

343 Harry, now] Q1 *corr.* (Harrie, now) *Huntington Library copy;* Harrie now Q1 *uncorr. British Museum and Trinity
College Cambridge copies*

343–4 For, Harry . . . also The excessive
balance and antithesis of these phrases typifies
euphuism; it also resonates with the repeated use
of 'no more' by King Henry in the first speech of
the play.

343 not . . . in drink Like Falstaff, Cambyses
loved to drink.

344 passion suffering, but also a tragic performance, as in Thisbe's concluding 'passion' (*MND*
5.1.315).

348 portly stately, majestic; compare 1.3.13 and
n.

348 corpulent 'full-bodied – not in the modern
sense of "extremely stout" ' (Kittredge). Falstaff
flatters himself through understatement.

351–2 lewdly given disposed to act wickedly
or lasciviously.

352–3 If . . . tree A popular saying from Matt.
12.33, 'the tre is knowen by the frute'; compare
Luke 6.44 and Dent T497. Lyly alludes to this

saying in *Euphues – The Anatomy of Wit*, ed. Bond,
I, 207): 'No, no, ye tree is knowen by his fruite,
the golde by his touch, the sonne by the sire.'

354 peremptorily decisively.

355–6 And . . . month Falstaff suddenly
changes the subject and adopts the tone of a normal father scolding his young son. The Prince
responds to his question by proposing that they
exchange roles.

360–1 rabbit-sucker baby rabbit, extremely
lean.

361 poulter's hare one hanging in a poulterer's
shop.

362 Well . . . set The Prince takes his place
rapidly, omitting elaborate business with props.
For examples of the extreme variety of attitudes
and responses possible for both Hal and Falstaff
in this sequence, see Introduction, pp. 14, 50–1,
56 and illustration 7.

PRINCE The complaints I hear of thee are grievous.

FALSTAFF 'Sblood, my lord, they are false! Nay, I'll tickle ye for a
   young prince, i'faith.

PRINCE Swearest thou, ungracious boy? Henceforth ne'er look on me.
   Thou art violently carried away from grace. There is a devil haunts   370
   thee in the likeness of an old fat man, a tun of man is thy companion.
   Why dost thou converse with that trunk of humours, that bolting-
   hutch of beastliness, that swollen parcel of dropsies, that huge
   bombard of sack, that stuffed cloak-bag of guts, that roasted
   Manningtree ox with the pudding in his belly, that reverend Vice,   375
   that grey Iniquity, that Father Ruffian, that Vanity in years?
   Wherein is he good, but to taste sack and drink it? Wherein neat and
   cleanly, but to carve a capon and eat it? Wherein cunning, but in
   craft? Wherein crafty, but in villainy? Wherein villainous, but in all
   things? Wherein worthy, but in nothing?   380

FALSTAFF I would your grace would take me with you. Whom means
   your grace?

PRINCE That villainous abominable misleader of youth, Falstaff, that
   old white-bearded Satan.

FALSTAFF My lord, the man I know.   385

PRINCE I know thou dost.

FALSTAFF But to say I know more harm in him than in myself were to

---

367 tickle ye for please you as; perhaps an aside to the onstage audience.

369 ungracious profane, in response to Falstaff's ''Sblood'.

369 Henceforth . . . me In retrospect, we can observe that this statement will apply to Falstaff, but not to the Prince, whose father will never give such a command.

371 tun (1) large barrel for wine or beer, (2) ton.

372 converse keep company with (*OED* sv *v* 2).

372 trunk large chest, with a pun on Falstaff's torso.

372 humours The four bodily fluids: blood, phlegm, choler, and melancholy. In balanced proportions, they maintain health. Here they are morbid and excessive, producing disease.

372–3 bolting-hutch bin used to sift impurities from grain. The hutch retains only those coarse impurities.

373 dropsies diseased condition caused by fluids accumulating in body cavities.

374 bombard large leather vessel for wine.

374 cloak-bag bag used to carry any clothing. The figurative sense of pretence (*OED* Cloak sv *v* 3a) may slip in.

374–5 that . . . belly A roasted ox, its own guts replaced with a bag-pudding or a stuffing of grain or minced meat (vs 'rabbit-sucker', 360–1). In *Christes Teares Over Jerusalem*, 1593 (ed. McKerrow, II, 180), Nashe wrote, 'All the rest of his invention is nothing but an oxe with a pudding in his bellie' (Wilson). Manningtree, a small town near the estuary of the River Stour in Essex, seems to have been noted for Morality plays, probably performed at a fair (Humphreys).

375–6 reverend Vice . . . Vanity in years Morality plays and Interludes portrayed characters known as Vice, Iniquity, and Vanity. Ruffian was a name for the Devil. The Prince plays upon the incongruity between Falstaff's age and behaviour.

378 cleanly adroit or clever in action (*OED* sv *a* 5).

378 cunning skilful.

381 take me with you (1) let me catch up with your meaning or (2) slow down for me. Compare Dent T28.1.

383–4 That . . . Satan The crucial Morality-play role of tempter was frequently taken by evil companions and Vices rather than by the Devil himself.

say more than I know. That he is old, the more the pity, his white hairs do witness it, but that he is, saving your reverence, a whoremaster, that I utterly deny. If sack and sugar be a fault, God 390 help the wicked! If to be old and merry be a sin, then many an old host that I know is damned. If to be fat be to be hated, then Pharaoh's lean kine are to be loved. No, my good lord! Banish Peto, banish Bardolph, banish Poins – but for sweet Jack Falstaff, kind Jack Falstaff, true Jack Falstaff, valiant Jack Falstaff – and therefore 395 more valiant, being as he is old Jack Falstaff – banish not him thy Harry's company, banish not him thy Harry's company. Banish plump Jack, and banish all the world.

PRINCE I do, I will.

[A knocking heard]
[Exeunt Hostess, Francis, and Bardolph]

Enter BARDOLPH *running*

BARDOLPH O my lord, my lord, the Sheriff with a most monstrous 400 watch is at the door.

FALSTAFF Out, ye rogue! Play out the play! I have much to say in the behalf of that Falstaff.

Enter the HOSTESS

HOSTESS O Jesu, my lord, my lord!

PRINCE Heigh, heigh, the devil rides upon a fiddle-stick. What's the 405 matter?

393 lean] Qq2–5, F; lane Q1   399 SD. 1, 2 *A knocking . . . and Bardolph*] Malone; *not in* QqF   405 SH PRINCE] Qq1–3; *Fal.* Qq4, 5, F *subst.; Poyn./ Dering MS.*

389 saving your reverence A polite expression used to introduce disagreement. See Dent R93.

393 Pharaoh's lean kine In Gen. 41 Joseph interprets the Pharaoh's dream, in which seven 'evilfavoured and leane fleshed' cattle devour seven fat ones, by predicting seven years of famine.

399 I do, I will Clearly distinguished in tone and syntax from the earlier verbal attack in which the Prince plays his father, this short line provokes conspicuous, if widely divergent responses from stage Falstaffs. Falstaff may clearly hear the four words or he may not; he may believe the Prince or think he merely jests. There may be a long pause or immediate commotion with the knocking. Some of these choices, even with the same actor, may well vary from day to day. The line offers a timely reminder of the Prince's soliloquy in 1.2. See Introduction, pp. 50, 55, 75.

399 SDs *A knocking . . . running* Most editions and many productions welcome this series of directions proposed by Malone. The knocking can 'ensure that an even keel is restored' (Davison) or replace an intensely personal confrontation with an alarming reminder of the outside world. QqF simply give 'Enter Bardoll running' and at 403 below, 'Enter the hostesse'. Compare 269 SD and n.

401 watch A group of citizens chosen to keep order in the streets, especially at night. In *FV*, the Mayor tells King Henry that the Prince was arrested because, when brawling with his companions outside the 'Eastcheape' tavern, 'neither watchmen nor any other could stay them' (248).

405 devil . . . fiddle-stick A saying or pseudo-proverb possibly invented by Hal (Dent D263). Its nonsense heightens his practical question.

HOSTESS The Sheriff and all the watch are at the door. They are come
to search the house. Shall I let them in?

FALSTAFF Dost thou hear, Hal? Never call a true piece of gold a counterfeit. Thou art essentially made without seeming so.   410

PRINCE And thou a natural coward without instinct.

FALSTAFF I deny your major. If you will deny the Sheriff, so; if not, let
him enter. If I become not a cart as well as another man, a plague on
my bringing up! I hope I shall as soon be strangled with a halter as
another.   415

PRINCE Go hide thee behind the arras, the rest walk up above. Now, my
masters, for a true face, and good conscience.

FALSTAFF Both which I have had, but their date is out, and therefore
I'll hide me.

[Exeunt all but the Prince and Peto]

PRINCE Call in the Sheriff.   420

Enter SHERIFF *and the* CARRIER

---

410 made] Qq, F1, F2; mad F3, F4   419 SD *Exeunt . . . Peto*] *Collier*; *Exit* F; *not in* Qq

409–10 Never . . . so These two short sen-
tences have become one of the most disputed
passages in *1H4*. The general import of the first
sentence, 'Never call . . . counterfeit', seems unex-
ceptionable. The validity of the application of
'true gold' to Falstaff himself may be uncertain,
but it does continue arguments and images he has
repeatedly used. The relation of this first sentence to the second, however, raises difficulties.
Of three problematic words in the second sentence, 'Thou . . . so', two – 'essentially' and 'seeming' – develop from 'true' and 'counterfeit' in the
preceding statement. The third word, 'made' or
'mad', has become a difficult crux.

410 Thou . . . so Perhaps meaning 'You are
basically true/loyal to your friends even if your
last speeches do not show this.' In this second
statement, Falstaff abruptly changes the subject
from himself to the Prince, and attributes to Hal
his own paradoxical sense of truth.

By reading 'made' as 'mad', F3 (followed by
Malone, Wilson, and many other editors) not only
introduced a spelling variant, but suggested other
possibilities for interpretation. Falstaff could be
calling the Prince a madcap who is only playing games no matter how well he acts (compare
192 above). But the earlier Qq reading 'made',
although more difficult at first for modern audiences, has a stronger case. It would apply the preceding metaphors of 'true gold' and 'counterfeit',

which echo earlier word-play on debased metals
(290, 315). Falstaff would again be insinuating that
he has true and real value, developing his 'Banish
plump Jack and banish all the world.'

411 And . . . instinct By echoing Falstaff's
syntax, the Prince yokes 'instinct' with 'seeming',
again rejecting as pretence Falstaff's claim that he
ran away because he recognised the Prince.

412 your major i.e. your fundamental premise
(that I am an 'essential' or natural coward).

412 deny the Sheriff Falstaff quibbles on three
senses: (1) prevent him from entering, (2) reject
his authority, (3) contradict him (as in 'deny your
major').

413 become not do not behave suitably.

413 cart wagon used to expose disgraced crim-
inals while carrying them to the gallows.

414 bringing up (1) breeding or raising, (2)
being summoned before a law court or taken physically to the gallows.

416 arras curtain or tapestry, possibly hanging
from projecting frames on the back wall of the
stage.

418 date is out lease has expired (compare
Dent D42.1).

419 SD *Exeunt . . . Peto* There has been editorial
controversy about whether Peto or Poins should
remain, but Peto is identified three times below as
speaker by QqF. F additionally attributes 448–52
below to Peto.

Now, master Sheriff, what is your will with me?
SHERIFF   First, pardon me, my lord. A hue and cry
          Hath followed certain men unto this house.
PRINCE   What men?
SHERIFF   One of them is well known, my gracious lord,   425
          A gross fat man.
CARRIER   As fat as butter.
PRINCE   The man I do assure you is not here,
          For I myself at this time have employed him.
          And Sheriff, I will engage my word to thee,   430
          That I will by tomorrow dinner-time
          Send him to answer thee, or any man,
          For anything he shall be charged withal.
          And so let me entreat you leave the house.
SHERIFF   I will, my lord. There are two gentlemen   435
          Have in this robbery lost three hundred marks.
PRINCE   It may be so. If he have robbed these men
          He shall be answerable. And so, farewell.
SHERIFF   Good night, my noble lord.
PRINCE   I think it is good morrow, is it not?   440
SHERIFF   Indeed, my lord, I think it be two o'clock.

                                              Exit [*with Carrier*]

PRINCE   This oily rascal is known as well as Paul's. Go call him forth.
PETO   Falstaff! Fast asleep behind the arras, and snorting like a horse.
PRINCE   Hark how hard he fetches breath. Search his pockets.

          [*Peto*] *searches his pockets, and finds certain papers*
          What hast thou found?   445
PETO   Nothing but papers, my lord.
PRINCE   Let's see what they be, read them.

421–7 Now . . . butter] *As verse, Pope; as prose,* QqF   441 SD *with Carrier*] *Hanmer subst.; not in* QqF   443, 446, 461 SH
PETO] QqF; *Poins/ Dering MS., Var. 1773, conj. Johnson*   444 SD *Peto*] *He* QqF

422 hue and cry citizens banded in pursuit of
a criminal.
428 not here True of course only in a literal
sense because Falstaff is behind the arras. The
actor might emphasise 'here', thereby equivocat-
ing to avoid a direct lie.
430 engage pledge.
431–2 I will . . . answer thee This forceful,
unambiguous lie may create insecurity for audiences (in deciding when to believe the promises of
the Prince).

431 dinner-time Usually about noon.
433 withal with (*OED prep.*)
436 three hundred marks Compare 133–4
and n.
442 Paul's The gothic cathedral of St Paul's,
later (like the Boar's Head tavern) destroyed
in the London fire of 1666. It towers over the
City in drawings and prints contemporary with
Shakespeare.

[PETO] [*Reads*] *Item a capon*	2s. 2d.	
Item sauce	4d.	
Item sack two gallons	5s. 8d.	450
Item anchovies and sack after supper	2s. 6d.	
Item bread	ob.	

[PRINCE] O monstrous! But one half-pennyworth of bread to this intolerable deal of sack? What there is else keep close, we'll read it at
more advantage. There let him sleep till day. I'll to the court in the   455
morning. We must all to the wars, and thy place shall be honourable. I'll procure this fat rogue a charge of foot, and I know his death
will be a march of twelve score. The money shall be paid back again
with advantage. Be with me betimes in the morning, and so, good
morrow, Peto.   460
PETO Good morrow, good my lord.

                                     Exeunt

[**3.1**] *Enter* HOTSPUR, WORCESTER, LORD MORTIMER, OWEN
GLENDOWER

MORTIMER These promises are fair, the parties sure,
       And our induction full of prosperous hope.
HOTSPUR Lord Mortimer, and cousin Glendower, will you sit down?
       And uncle Worcester. A plague upon it!

---

448 SH PETO] F; *not in* Qq; *Poin./ Dering MS., Var. 1773, conj. Johnson*   448 SD *Reads*] *Capell; not in* QqF   453 SH
PRINCE] F; *not in* Qq   Act 3, Scene 1   3.1] *Actus Tertius. Scena Prima.* F; *not in* Qq   3–9 Lord . . . heaven] *As verse,
Humphreys,* F *subst., printing line 3 as* Lord . . . Glendower / Will . . . downe?; *as prose,* Qq

451 anchovies Often eaten to increase thirst
and to improve the taste of wine; first use recorded
in *OED*.

452 ob. obolus or halfpenny.

453–4 intolerable exceedingly great (*OED* 1c,
this example).

454 deal portion.

454 close secret, hidden.

454–5 at more advantage at a better time.

457 charge of foot company of infantry.

458–9 The money . . . advantage For this
detail, Shakespeare may be indebted to Stow's
Chronicles (Bullough, p. 219). In *FV*, the Prince
protects the thieves without repaying the stolen
money.

459 advantage interest.

459 betimes early.

Act 3, Scene 1

[**3.1**] The basis of this unhistorical scene is

Holinshed's brief reference (III, 22) to the 'tripartite indenture' sealed by 'deputies' of the lords at
the house of the archdeacon of Bangor in Wales.
Shakespeare brings together the Percys, Mortimer, and Glendower, apparently in Glendower's
home.

2 induction beginning, as in a brief scene
before the main action of a play.

3–10 Lord . . . spoke of Printed as eight lines
of prose by Qq, probably in order to save space;
the F compositor stretched the passage into eleven
lines of text, nine in verse, but printed Hotspur's
reply, 'And . . . of', 9–10, as prose. This edition
follows Humphreys' lineation as irregular verse
because lines 3 and 7 'cannot be reduced to deca-
syllables without producing surplus words which
improperly halt the rhythm'.

3 cousin Compare 1.1.31 and n.

I have forgot the map.

GLENDOWER   No, here it is.   5
Sit, cousin Percy, sit, good cousin Hotspur;
For by that name as oft as Lancaster doth speak of you
His cheek looks pale, and with a rising sigh
He wisheth you in heaven.

HOTSPUR   And you in hell,
As oft as he hears Owen Glendower spoke of.   10

GLENDOWER I cannot blame him. At my nativity
The front of heaven was full of fiery shapes,
Of burning cressets, and at my birth
The frame and huge foundation of the earth
Shaked like a coward.

HOTSPUR   Why, so it would have done   15
At the same season if your mother's cat
Had but kittened, though yourself had never been born.

GLENDOWER I say the earth did shake when I was born.

HOTSPUR And I say the earth was not of my mind,
If you suppose as fearing you, it shook.   20

GLENDOWER The heavens were all on fire, the earth did tremble –

HOTSPUR O, then the earth shook to see the heavens on fire,
And not in fear of your nativity.
Diseasèd nature oftentimes breaks forth
In strange eruptions, oft the teeming earth   25
Is with a kind of colic pinched and vexed
By the imprisoning of unruly wind
Within her womb, which for enlargement striving

9–10 And . . . of] *As verse, Collier; as prose,* QqF   15–17 Why . . . born| *As verse. Pope; as prose,* QqF

7 **Lancaster** The King, referred to by his former title as a duke. See 60 below, where Glendower
again implicitly denies the King's legitimacy by
calling him Henry Bullingbrook.

11–15 **At my nativity . . . coward** Shakespeare expands upon Holinshed's suggestion that
'strange wonders happened (as men reported) at
the nativitie of this man' (III, 21). Holinshed's preceding syntax makes it possible to interpret 'this
man' as Mortimer rather than Glendower.

12 **front** The sky personified as having a face
or forehead.

13 **cressets** torches (*OED* 2). Glendower refers
to an astonishing display of comets or to lights
which may have ominous significance; compare
the beacon in *Per.* 1.4.87.

24–30 **Diseasèd . . . towers** This explanation

of earthquakes may be traced back to Aristotle,
Meteorologica and Pliny, *Natural History*. Gabriel
Harvey, *Pleasant . . . Discourse of the Earthquake in
Aprill Last*, 1580 (ed. Grosart, 1, 52) describes the
'Materiall Cause' as 'great aboundance of wynde,
or stoare of grosse and drye vapors, and spirites
fast shut up, & as a man would saye, emprysoned
in the Caues, and Dungeons of the Earth: which
winde or vapors, seeking to be set at libertie . . . violently rush out' (cited by Humphreys).

25 **eruptions** (1) the bursting out of powerful
natural forces, (2) outbreaks of disease.

25 **teeming** bearing offspring.

28 **enlargement** release from confinement
(*OED* 5a). Hotspur's metaphors associate the
earth's symptoms, and indirectly Glendower, with
flatulence as well as childbirth.

Shakes the old beldam earth, and topples down
Steeples and moss-grown towers. At your birth   30
Our grandam earth, having this distemperature,
In passion shook.
GLENDOWER   Cousin, of many men
I do not bear these crossings. Give me leave
To tell you once again that at my birth
The front of heaven was full of fiery shapes,   35
The goats ran from the mountains, and the herds
Were strangely clamorous to the frighted fields.
These signs have marked me extraordinary,
And all the courses of my life do show
I am not in the roll of common men.   40
Where is he living, clipped in with the sea
That chides the banks of England, Scotland, Wales,
Which calls me pupil or hath read to me?
And bring him out that is but woman's son
Can trace me in the tedious ways of art,   45
And hold me pace in deep experiments.
HOTSPUR I think there's no man speaks better Welsh.
I'll to dinner.
MORTIMER Peace, cousin Percy, you will make him mad.
GLENDOWER I can call spirits from the vasty deep.   50
HOTSPUR Why, so can I, or so can any man,
But will they come when you do call for them?
GLENDOWER Why, I can teach you, cousin, to command the devil.

44 son] Q1 *corr.* (sonne) *British Museum copy*, F; sonne? Q1 *uncorr. Huntington Library and Trinity College Cambridge copies*

29 **beldam** Synonymous with grandam or grandmother, as at 31.

31 **distemperature** disorder of the body (*OED* 2), as in 'colic' (26); compare *Err.* 5.1.81–2, 'At her heeles a huge infectious troop / Of pale distemperatures'.

32 **passion** fit of suffering.

32 **of** from.

33 **crossings** thwartings, contradictions.

37 **frighted** terrified.

41 **clipped in** surrounded by.

42 **chides** chafes with a rough, brawling sound.

43 **Which** Who.

43 **read to** instructed.

45 **trace . . . art** follow my tracks in the demanding discipline of magic.

46 **hold me pace** keep up with me.

47 **no man speaks better Welsh** i.e. the language I cannot understand is better than his English. Hotspur rudely implies that Glendower (1) only boasts, (2) talks too much. The transparent 'compliment' insults all speakers of Welsh.

50 **call** summon, convene (using my art).

50 **vasty deep** huge abyss (*OED* sv *sb* 3c, this example); perhaps also a transposition of 'the depths of vastness', suggesting an unfathomable immensity.

52 **call for** Hotspur twists 'call', 50, which implied success through magic art, into a simple domestic cry, one that may well be futile.

53–4 **teach you, cousin . . . teach thee, coz** Hotspur reduces Glendower's 'you' to 'thee' and 'cousin' to 'coz', giving additional signs of his lack of respect for his older host. These words may imply that Hotspur tries to assume the role of commanding officer. His thrice-repeated 'tell truth'

HOTSPUR And I can teach thee, coz, to shame the devil
            By telling truth. Tell truth, and shame the devil.   55
            If thou have power to raise him, bring him hither,
            And I'll be sworn I have power to shame him hence.
            O, while you live, tell truth, and shame the devil!
MORTIMER Come, come, no more of this unprofitable chat.
GLENDOWER Three times hath Henry Bullingbrook made head   60
            Against my power, thrice from the banks of Wye
            And sandy-bottomed Severn have I sent him
            Bootless home, and weather-beaten back.
HOTSPUR Home without boots, and in foul weather too!
            How scapes he agues, in the devil's name?   65
GLENDOWER Come, here is the map, shall we divide our right
            According to our threefold order taken?
MORTIMER The Archdeacon hath divided it
            Into three limits very equally.
            England, from Trent and Severn hitherto,   70
            By south and east is to my part assigned.
            All westward, Wales beyond the Severn shore,
            And all the fertile land within that bound,

---

54 coz] Q1 (coose); Cousin F

and 'shame the devil' in this short speech suggest how coherent argument is giving way to 'unprofitable chat', 59.

55 Tell … devil Proverbial saying (Dent T566). Hotspur continues to treat Glendower like a childish 'pupil', despite the older man's objections that no living man can instruct him, 41–3 above.

60–3 Three times . . . back Hardyng's *Chronicle*[*s*] (1812 edn, p. 358) say that Henry went three times to Wales in the harvest season and was repeatedly hindered by 'mystes & tempestes'. Holinshed describes the King's successful raid on Wales in 1400 (III, 17), the defeated expedition led by Mortimer in 1402 (20), the King's vain pursuit of Glendower in 1402 (20), a more successful skirmish fought by 'the princes companie' in 1405 (33–4), and a frustrating raid, again led by the King, in 1405 (39–40). Compare 1.3.114–15 and Appendix, p. 232.

60 made head raised an army.

61 my power my forces.

61–2 Wye … Severn Both rivers wind from the Cambrian mountains of Wales towards the Severn estuary. The Severn to the north, and the Wye, farther south, serve in places as the border between Wales and England. In Holinshed, the King penetrates more deeply into Wales (III, 17, 20, 39–40).

63 Bootless (1) Having failed, (2) Empty-handed. In 1400, according to Holinshed, the King returned to England 'with a great bootie of beasts and cattell' (III, 17). In a reversal of Holinshed's viewpoint, Shakespeare's Glendower speaks of Henry as if he were the 'irregular and wild' marauder. Compare 1.1.40.

63 weather-beaten back In Holinshed, Glendower was said to have escaped from the King in 1402 by causing extraordinary 'foule weather' (III, 20).

65 scapes escapes.

66 our right the land we are entitled to.

67 threefold order taken three-way agreement (the 'indentures tripartite', 76 below).

68 Archdeacon The archdeacon of Bangor. See headnote.

69 limits territories (*OED* sv *sb* 3a, this example).

70 Trent The River Trent flows south-east through the Midlands, but turns sharply north-east beyond Burton-on-Trent, through Nottinghamshire and Lincolnshire, entering the estuary of the Humber.

70 hitherto thus far (*OED* 3, this example). Mortimer points out his boundary line.

To Owen Glendower. And, dear coz, to you
The remnant northward lying off from Trent.   75
And our indentures tripartite are drawn,
Which being sealèd interchangeably –
A business that this night may execute –
Tomorrow, cousin Percy, you and I
And my good Lord of Worcester will set forth   80
To meet your father and the Scottish power,
As is appointed us, at Shrewsbury.
My father Glendower is not ready yet,
Nor shall we need his help these fourteen days.
[*To Glendower*] Within that space you may have drawn together   85
Your tenants, friends, and neighbouring gentlemen.

GLENDOWER A shorter time shall send me to you, lords,
And in my conduct shall your ladies come,
From whom you now must steal and take no leave,
For there will be a world of water shed   90
Upon the parting of your wives and you.

HOTSPUR Methinks my moiety, north from Burton here,
In quantity equals not one of yours.
See how this river comes me cranking in,
And cuts me from the best of all my land   95
A huge half-moon, a monstrous scantle out.
I'll have the current in this place dammed up,
And here the smug and silver Trent shall run
In a new channel fair and evenly.
It shall not wind with such a deep indent,   100
To rob me of so rich a bottom here.

---

85 SD *To Glendower*] *Capell; not in* QqF   96 scantle] Qq; cantle F

76 **indentures tripartite** contracts drawn up
in triplicate.
77 **interchangeably** so that each seals all three
copies.
78 **this . . . execute** i.e. we can finish tonight.
82 **Shrewsbury** Town strategically located on
the Severn River, not far from Glendower's residence by the River Dee.
83 **father** father-in-law.
86 **tenants** those who hold land on condition
they provide military support when required.
88 **in my conduct** escorted by me.
92 **moiety** share or portion.
92 **Burton** present-day Burton-on-Trent.

94 **cranking in** winding sharply, zigzagging.
96 **monstrous scantle** large portion. Qq's
'scantle', a small portion or 'scantling', contra-
dicts 'monstrous', thereby implying that Hotspur's objection is part bluff. F's 'cantle' (a projecting corner or angle, *OED* sv *sb* 1b) appears
in *Ant.*: 'The greater cantle of the world is lost'
(3.10.6). The Folio editors or revisers may have
discarded the initial 's' on the assumption that it
was picked up from the last letter of the preceding
word.
98 **smug** smooth, neat (the earliest example of
this sense, *OED* sv *a* 3).
101 **bottom** river-valley.

GLENDOWER Not wind? It shall, it must – you see it doth.
MORTIMER Yea,
       But mark how he bears his course, and runs me up
       With like advantage on the other side,   105
       Gelding the opposèd continent as much
       As on the other side it takes from you.
WORCESTER Yea, but a little charge will trench him here,
       And on this north side win this cape of land,
       And then he runs straight and even.   110
HOTSPUR I'll have it so, a little charge will do it.
GLENDOWER I'll not have it altered.
HOTSPUR   Will not you?
GLENDOWER No, nor you shall not.
HOTSPUR   Who shall say me nay?
GLENDOWER Why, that will I.
HOTSPUR Let me not understand you then, speak it in Welsh.   115
GLENDOWER I can speak English, lord, as well as you,
       For I was trained up in the English court,
       Where, being but young, I framèd to the harp
       Many an English ditty lovely well,
       And gave the tongue a helpful ornament –   120
       A virtue that was never seen in you.
HOTSPUR Marry and I am glad of it with all my heart!
       I had rather be a kitten and cry 'mew'
       Than one of these same metre ballad-mongers.

---

102 wind?] Qq2–5, F; wind Q1   103–7 Yea . . . you] *As verse, Steevens, followed by Humphreys; as verse* Yea . . . course/And . . . side, / Gelding . . . much / As . . . you F; *as prose* Qq   124 ballad-mongers] QqF (balletmongers)

103–7 Yea . . . you Printed by Qq as three lines of prose. This edition follows Humphreys and Davison in using lineation to separate Mortimer's diplomatic 'Yea' from his thoughtful 'But'. Compare the irregularity in 103–4 with the short lines at 110 and 112–14 below. From Mortimer's 'Yea' to Glendower's 'will I', 103–14, the three speakers employ frequent short or split lines, each of which can be effective onstage. F, in contrast, prints 103–7 as four irregular verse lines; the second, 'And . . . side' with its fourteen feet, is unconvincing. See Textual Analysis, pp. 228–30.

104 he the Trent.

106 Gelding . . . continent Cutting off from the opposite bank.

108 charge cost.

108 trench divert by creating a new channel.

117 For . . . court Suggesting that he had been a page or body-squire. Holinshed reports that

Glendower had been 'an apprentice of the law . . . and served king Richard at Flint castell, when he was taken by Henrie duke of Lancaster, though other have written that he served this king Henrie the fourth, before he came to atteine the crowne, in roome of an esquier' (III, 17). See also List of Characters.

119 ditty the words of a song, without the music.

120 gave the tongue a helpful ornament used music and poetry to adorn and enhance the English language.

121 virtue accomplishment (*OED* sv *sb* 5b). 'Virtue' may also refer to a power or energy that Hotspur, being no poet, cannot share.

124 ballad-mongers street pedlars who traffic in ballads. Hotspur travesties Glendower's belief that poetry is an art (as he had magic). He eliminates any sense of the poet's creativity.

I had rather hear a brazen canstick turned,   125
Or a dry wheel grate on the axle-tree,
And that would set my teeth nothing on edge,
Nothing so much as mincing poetry.
'Tis like the forced gait of a shuffling nag.
GLENDOWER Come, you shall have Trent turned.   130
HOTSPUR I do not care, I'll give thrice so much land
    To any well-deserving friend.
    But in the way of bargain, mark ye me,
    I'll cavil on the ninth part of a hair.
    Are the indentures drawn? Shall we be gone?   135
GLENDOWER The moon shines fair, you may away by night.
    I'll haste the writer, and withal
    Break with your wives of your departure hence.
    I am afraid my daughter will run mad,
    So much she doteth on her Mortimer.   *Exit*   140
MORTIMER Fie, cousin Percy, how you cross my father!
HOTSPUR I cannot choose. Sometime he angers me
    With telling me of the moldwarp and the ant,
    Of the dreamer Merlin and his prophecies,
    And of a dragon and a finless fish,   145
    A clip-winged griffin and a moulten raven,
    A couching lion and a ramping cat,

125 canstick] Qq; Candlestick F   127 on] Qq3, 4; an Qq1, 2, 5, F

125 brazen canstick turned The loathsome noise produced by metal-workers as they turned candlesticks on their lathes 'to make them smooth and bright' was mentioned by Stow in his description of Loth ('Lath' or 'Load') berie Street, *Survey*, I, 127.

126 dry wheel Another source of excruciating sound. According to a proverb, 'A dry cart-wheel cries the loudest' (Dent C109.1).

128 mincing tripping along in an affectation of elegance (*OED* sv *ppl*. a2). Compare *MV* 3.4.67–8: 'and turn two mincing steps / Into a manly stride'.

129 forced . . . nag Hotspur demonstrates his contempt for 'metre' ballads, 124, through this caricature of metrical regularity.

134 cavil on wrangle.

135 drawn drawn up, prepared.

137 haste the writer make the scrivener (of the indentures) go faster.

138 Break with Disclose information to.

141 cross contradict; compare 'crossings', 33, and "cross', 166.

142–9 Sometime . . . faith The so-called 'prophecies of Merlin', with their cast of monstrous creatures, flourished whenever the royal succession was in question. Hall and Holinshed scorned the 'blind and fantasticall dreames of the Welsh prophesiers' (III, 23). But in *The Faerie Queene* III (1590), Spenser made Merlin a magus and treated him as a wise and accurate prophet of the Tudor dynasty.

143 moldwarp a mole, which casts up or 'warps' the earth or 'mold'.

144 Merlin The greatest wizard in Arthurian legends, as well as the young Arthur's protector and mentor.

145 dragon The historical Glendower adopted this crest, traditionally associated, according to Geoffrey of Monmouth, with King Arthur and with the last of the British kings, Cadwallader.

146 griffin Fabulous beast with the head and wings of an eagle, the body and hind legs of a lion.

147 couching . . . ramping lying down with head erect (couchant) and rearing on hind legs (rampant). Hotspur burlesques heraldic symbols. Bevington notes that the 'finless', 'clip-winged', and 'moulten' (featherless) creatures of 145–6 are 'deprived of locomotion'.

And such a deal of skimble-skamble stuff
As puts me from my faith. I tell you what –
He held me last night at least nine hours   150
In reckoning up the several devils' names
That were his lackeys. I cried 'Hum', and 'Well, go to!'
But marked him not a word. O, he is as tedious
As a tired horse, a railing wife,
Worse than a smoky house. I had rather live   155
With cheese and garlic in a windmill, far,
Than feed on cates and have him talk to me
In any summer house in Christendom.
MORTIMER In faith, he is a worthy gentleman,
Exceedingly well read, and profited   160
In strange concealments, valiant as a lion,
And wondrous affable, and as bountiful
As mines of India. Shall I tell you, cousin?
He holds your temper in a high respect
And curbs himself even of his natural scope   165
When you come 'cross his humour, faith he does.
I warrant you that man is not alive
Might so have tempted him as you have done
Without the taste of danger and reproof.

---

166 come 'cross] Qq (come crosse); doe crosse F

148–9 And . . . faith Keith Thomas uses this passage as epigraph for his chapter on 'Ancient prophecies', which like Merlin's were rarely believed, he maintains, after the seventeenth century (*Religion and the Decline of Magic*, 1971).

148 skimble-skamble stuff No synonyms can match this exasperated summary of prophetic nonsense.

149 puts . . . faith makes me forget (or deny) my religious belief.

152 lackeys footmen, servile attendants.

152 Well, go to An expression of derisive incredulity (*OED* sv v 93b).

154–5 railing . . . house Both make a man want to rush outside. Similar are Prov. 27.15: 'A continual dropping in the day of raine, and a contencious woman are a like' and Dent H781.

156 cheese . . . windmill i.e. the least desirable food and the noisiest residence. Garlic often stands for foul breath; the windmill, besides its incessant sound, may suggest that Glendower's monologues get nowhere.

157 cates delicacies.

158 summer house An elegant and courtly pavilion in the grounds of a country house or palace. Compare Stowe on the structures springing up in the gardens beyond London's walls: 'fayre summer houses . . . like Midsommer Pageantes, with Towers, Turrets, and Chimney tops', *Survey*, II, 78.

160–1 profited . . . concealments adept at magic or occult arts.

162 wondrous affable remarkably courteous, especially in conversation. Possibly echoing this scene, the Welsh Captain, Fluellen, in *H5* 3.2.127, complains that he has not been used with 'affability' by the hot-tempered Irishman, MacMorris.

163 mines of India Legendary source of wealth since the conquests of Alexander the Great. Compare Marlowe, *1 Tamburlaine* 3.3.263–4.

164 temper disposition; compare *John* 5.2.40: 'A noble temper dost thou show in this.'

165 scope liberty to act.

But do not use it oft, let me entreat you.   170
WORCESTER In faith, my lord, you are too wilful-blame,
    And since your coming hither have done enough
    To put him quite besides his patience.
    You must needs learn, lord, to amend this fault.
    Though sometimes it show greatness, courage, blood –   175
    And that's the dearest grace it renders you –
    Yet oftentimes it doth present harsh rage,
    Defect of manners, want of government,
    Pride, haughtiness, opinion, and disdain,
    The least of which haunting a nobleman   180
    Loseth men's hearts and leaves behind a stain
    Upon the beauty of all parts besides,
    Beguiling them of commendation.
HOTSPUR Well, I am schooled – good manners be your speed!
    Here come our wives, and let us take our leave.   185

       Enter GLENDOWER *with the* LADIES

MORTIMER This is the deadly spite that angers me,
    My wife can speak no English, I no Welsh.
GLENDOWER My daughter weeps, she'll not part with you,
    She'll be a soldier too, she'll to the wars.
MORTIMER Good father, tell her that she and my aunt Percy   190
    Shall follow in your conduct speedily.
    Glendower speaks to her in Welsh, and she answers him in the same

171 **too wilful-blame** (1) to be blamed for excessive wilfulness, (2) deliberately blameworthy. 'To' was often mistaken as 'too'; blame could be understood as an adjective (*OED* Blame sv *v* 6). Humphreys cites, as one of many examples, *2H4* 2.4.361: 'I feele me much too blame'(Q) and 'to blame'(F).

173 **besides** out of.

175 **blood** high spirit.

176 **dearest grace** noblest honour.

177 **present** show, as in 175.

178 **government** self-control.

179 **opinion** arrogance or conceit (*OED* sv *sb* 5c).

180–3 **The least ... commendation** A reminder that the medieval baron's power depended on the trust and support of a personal alliance.

181 **stain** indelible blot. Worcester, like King Henry, argues that dishonour causes an almost physical change in appearance. Compare 1.1.84 and n.

183 **Beguiling** Cheating out of (*OED* Beguile sv *v* 2).

184 **be your speed** give you success or good luck. Hotspur may speak ironically, thinking of a battlefield.

185 **and** Elizabethans could use 'and' to join an affirmation and a command. Compare 5.4.33, 'I will assay thee, and defend thyself.'

186 **spite** vexation.

190 **aunt Percy** Hotspur's wife was in fact sister to the Mortimer who married Glendower's daughter, aunt to the younger Mortimer designated by Richard II as his heir. See 2.3.75 n., and List of Characters.

191 SD Glendower and his daughter may have been played by Welsh actors; perhaps Shakespeare left the selection of Welsh speeches and music to them. W. J. Lawrence (*Welsh Song*, 1922) argues that Shakespeare's lines for Lady Mortimer show he had a boy-actor who could sing well in Welsh.

GLENDOWER She is desperate here, a peevish, self-willed harlotry, one
        that no persuasion can do good upon.
                  The lady speaks in Welsh
MORTIMER I understand thy looks, that pretty Welsh
        Which thou pourest down from these swelling heavens   195
        I am too perfect in, and but for shame
        In such a parley should I answer thee.
                The lady [speaks] again in Welsh
        I understand thy kisses, and thou mine,
        And that's a feeling disputation,
        But I will never be a truant, love,   200
        Till I have learnt thy language, for thy tongue
        Makes Welsh as sweet as ditties highly penned,
        Sung by a fair queen in a summer's bower
        With ravishing division to her lute.
GLENDOWER Nay, if you melt, then will she run mad.   205
                 The lady speaks again in Welsh
MORTIMER O, I am ignorance itself in this!
GLENDOWER She bids you on the wanton rushes lay you down,
        And rest your gentle head upon her lap,
        And she will sing the song that pleaseth you,
        And on your eyelids crown the god of sleep,   210
        Charming your blood with pleasing heaviness,
        Making such difference 'twixt wake and sleep
        As is the difference betwixt day and night,
        The hour before the heavenly-harnessed team

192–3 She ... upon] *As prose, Cam., followed by Humphreys; one line of verse* She ... here, *the remainder as prose* Qq; *as verse* Shee ... heere: / A ... Harlotry, / One ... upon F   197 SD *speaks*] *Malone subst.; not in* QqF

192 **desperate** determined.
192 **harlotry** woman. Glendower uses the term with more compassion than scorn, unlike Capulet, *Rom.* 4.2.14, 'A peevish self [-willed] harlotry it is.'
195 **swelling heavens** tear-filled eyes.
196 **too perfect in** understand only too well.
197 **parley** (1) argument, (2) conference with a military adversary (suggested by 'soldier', 189).
197 **answer** i.e. reply with tears.
199 **feeling disputation** Argument carried on through emotions, rather than words.
202 **highly penned** Written in an exquisite or elegant style.
204 **division** Musical term referring to 'a brilliant passage, of short notes, which is founded

essentially on a much simpler passage of longer notes' (Edward W. Naylor, *Shakespeare and Music*, 1931, p. 28.)
205 **melt** weep.
207 **wanton** profuse, luxuriant (*OED* sv *a* 7a), as in *MND* 2.1.99: 'quaint mazes in the wanton green'.
207 **rushes** Fresh green rushes were used as floor-covering in homes and theatres.
210 **And ... sleep** give sleep absolute power over you.
211 **Charming** Enchanting.
214 **heavenly-harnessed team** horses which pull the chariot, an image that symbolises the sun.

Begins his golden progress in the east.   215

MORTIMER With all my heart I'll sit and hear her sing,

By that time will our book, I think, be drawn.

GLENDOWER Do so, and those musicians that shall play to you

Hang in the air a thousand leagues from hence,

And straight they shall be here. Sit, and attend.   220

HOTSPUR Come, Kate, thou art perfect in lying down.

Come, quick, quick, that I may lay my head in thy lap.

LADY PERCY Go, ye giddy goose.

The music plays

HOTSPUR Now I perceive the devil understands Welsh,

And 'tis no marvel he is so humorous,   225

By'r lady, he is a good musician.

LADY PERCY Then should you be nothing but musical,

For you are altogether governed by humours.

Lie still, ye thief, and hear the lady sing in Welsh.

HOTSPUR I had rather hear Lady my brach howl in Irish.   230

LADY PERCY Wouldst thou have thy head broken?

HOTSPUR No.

LADY PERCY Then be still.

HOTSPUR Neither, 'tis a woman's fault.

LADY PERCY Now, God help thee!   235

HOTSPUR To the Welsh lady's bed.

LADY PERCY What's that?

HOTSPUR Peace, she sings.

---

215 progress journey or tour made by a king or queen, usually ceremonial and spectacular.

217 book the indentures tripartite or documents, 76 above.

218–20 those musicians . . . here How their performance is represented can support or undermine Glendower's claim to control spirits, 50. Zitner suggests two demystified stagings: (1) by a playful gesture, Glendower indicates the musicians visible in the third gallery, the highest tier above the tiring-house; (2) as suggested by Hotspur's response at 224–6, music comes from an invisible source 'below the stage, whence the Devil's infernal music issued in old plays' ('Staging the occult in *1 Henry IV*', in *Mirror up to Shakespeare: Essays in Honour of G. R. Hibbard*, ed. J. C. Gray, 1984, pp. 138–48).

221–43 Come . . . day An uncertain mixture of verse and prose in both Qq and F. The lineation in Q has been followed here, 221–40. See Textual Analysis, pp. 228–30.

225 humorous capricious, implying that the temperament in question has physiological causes. Compare 30–2 above. Q's comma after 'humorous' makes it possible to read the syntax backwards or forwards, applying 'humorous' to 'Welsh' or to 'musician'. On the 'syntactical looseness of English' in the late sixteenth century, see Anne Ferry, *The Art of Naming*, 1988, pp. 63–4.

229 thief A mock-serious charge.

230 I . . . Irish Hotspur ridicules the Welsh lady's allegedly uncouth language and discredits her skill.

230 brach bitch, hunting dog.

233 still silent.

234 Neither . . . fault A punning reply to both of Lady Percy's threats. 'A woman's fault' quibbles upon 'head broken' as 'broken maidenhead'. He also mistakes her meaning of 'still', 233, as sexual passivity.

235 God help thee i.e. no one else can manage you.

Here the lady sings a Welsh song

Come, Kate, I'll have your song too.

LADY PERCY Not mine, in good sooth.   240

HOTSPUR Not yours, in good sooth! Heart, you swear like a comfit-
     maker's wife – 'Not you, in good sooth!' and 'As true as I live!'
     and 'As God shall mend me!', and 'As sure as day!' –
          And givest such sarcenet surety for thy oaths
          As if thou never walk'st further than Finsbury.   245
          Swear me, Kate, like a lady as thou art,
          A good mouth-filling oath, and leave 'In sooth',
          And such protest of pepper-gingerbread,
          To velvet-guards, and Sunday citizens.
          Come, sing.   250

LADY PERCY I will not sing.

HOTSPUR 'Tis the next way to turn tailor, or be redbreast teacher. An
     the indentures be drawn I'll away within these two hours. And so,
     come in when ye will.   *Exit*

GLENDOWER Come, come, Lord Mortimer, you are as slow   255
          As hot Lord Percy is on fire to go.
          By this our book is drawn – we'll but seal,
          And then to horse immediately.

MORTIMER With all my heart.

                                                              Exeunt

---

241–3 Not . . . day] Qq; *as verse* Not . . . sooth? / You . . . Wife: / Not . . . live; / And . . . day: F, *omitting* Heart   256
hot] F; Hot. Qq1–3; Hot, Q4; *Hot* Q5

240 **in good sooth** in truth, a mild oath used to
strengthen an exclamation, as opposed to 'Heart'
('Christ's heart'), 241.

241–3 **Not . . . day** Hotspur parrots the sober
oaths of pious London citizens, who are often
mocked in later plays of the period. In *2H4*, Falstaff snobbishly refers to an obsequious tradesman
who refuses to sell him cloth on credit as a 'yea-
forsooth knave' (1.2.36).

241–2 **comfit-maker** candy-maker, suggesting that her oath is (1) insubstantial, (2) beneath
her rank.

244 **sarcenet surety** a guarantee of certainty
(*OED* Surety *sb* 6), which is no stronger than
sarcenet, a soft, fine silk (*OED* Sarsenet 2b).

245 **Finsbury** Finsbury Fields, north of London beyond Moorfields, popular with citizens as
a place for recreation. It was close to the Curtain
theatre where *1H4* may have been staged. Stow

mentions the traditional archery competitions
held on this site (*Survey*, I, 104; II, 77).

248 **protest of pepper-gingerbread** oaths
that, like hot spiced gingerbread, nip the mouth
instead of filling it.

249 **velvet-guards** Equated with the citizens
who wear trimmings or facings of velvet on their
Sunday clothes.

252 **'Tis . . . teacher** Another mockery of
singing, as at 230. 'Tailors', like weavers, were
noted for singing; they are further disdained by
Hotspur through association with citizens who
wear pretentious clothes ('velvet-guards', 249).
'Redbreast teacher' scoffs at the idiocy of valuing
as art that which robins do better than people.

252 **next** easiest.

257 **seal** To ratify their agreement or 'book' by
affixing their individual seals. Compare 2.4.274–5
and n.

[3.2] *Enter the* KING, PRINCE OF WALES, *and others*

KING Lords, give us leave. The Prince of Wales and I
      Must have some private conference – but be near at hand,
      For we shall presently have need of you.

                                  Exeunt Lords

      I know not whether God will have it so
      For some displeasing service I have done,   5
      That in his secret doom out of my blood
      He'll breed revengement and a scourge for me.
      But thou dost in thy passages of life
      Make me believe that thou art only marked
      For the hot vengeance and the rod of heaven,   10
      To punish my mistreadings. Tell me else,
      Could such inordinate and low desires,
      Such poor, such bare, such lewd, such mean attempts,
      Such barren pleasures, rude society,
      As thou art matched withal, and grafted to,   15

Act 3, Scene 2 3.2] *Scæna Secunda*. F; *not in* Qq

Act 3, Scene 2

[3.2] According to Holinshed, Stow, and other chroniclers, late in the reign of Henry IV (1412) the Prince discovered that he was suspected of planning to usurp the throne. He therefore took the initiative for a meeting with the King and led a group of his followers to the court at Westminster. He reassured his father, professing his loyalty and dismissing his train. The interview in this scene takes place before the battle of Shrewsbury (1403). Without specific historical source, it has been influenced by accounts of the reconciliation in 1412 that *FV* and *2H4* dramatised. It takes place at an unlocalised court, following the summons the Prince received in 2.4.

The entry of these lords (unnamed, of unspecified number, and given no lines), draws attention to the King's suspicion of the Prince and emphasises the intimacy of their meeting.

1 give us leave A polite request for privacy (Dent L.167.1).

2–3 but . . . you This command may suggest that the King anticipates physical violence from his son.

4–17 I know . . . heart The King begins with an indirect reference to his own guilt, but quickly focuses on shaming the Prince. In a second reconciliation scene preceding his death in *2H4* 4.2.311 ff., he will acknowledge more openly by 'what bypaths and indirect crooked ways / I met this crown.'

5 some displeasing service A probable allusion to his responsibility for the death of Richard II.

6 doom judgement.

6 blood children, 'my own flesh and blood'.

7 scourge The human instrument through whom divine punishment functions. Scourges were believed to experience as well as to inflict God's wrath. Compare 8–11 below and *Ham.* 3.4.173–5: 'Heaven hath pleas'd it so / To punish me with this, and this with me, / That I must be their scourge and minister.'

8 thy passages of life your way of living.

11 else i.e. if what I have said is not true.

12 inordinate disorderly and intemperate (another of the King's latinate terms).

13 bare (1) worthless (*OED* sv *a* 10), (2) exposed. Compare *R2* 'detested sins . . . / Stand bare and naked, trembling at themselves' (3.2.44–6).

13 lewd vulgar, base.

13 attempts escapades.

14 rude uncivil, and perhaps violent, barbarous, as in 1.1.41, 'the rude hands of that Welshman'.

15 grafted to joined to. In grafting, a shoot from one tree is literally inserted into another so that the sap can flow into it. The metaphor emphasises the Prince's alienation from his own 'blood' and lineage, 16.

Accompany the greatness of thy blood
And hold their level with thy princely heart?
PRINCE   So please your majesty, I would I could
    Quit all offences with as clear excuse
    As well as I am doubtless I can purge   20
    Myself of many I am charged withal.
    Yet such extenuation let me beg
    As, in reproof of many tales devised,
    Which oft the ear of greatness needs must hear,
    By smiling pickthanks, and base newsmongers,   25
    I may for some things true, wherein my youth
    Hath faulty wandered and irregular,
    Find pardon on my true submission.
KING   God pardon thee! Yet let me wonder, Harry,
    At thy affections, which do hold a wing   30
    Quite from the flight of all thy ancestors.
    Thy place in Council thou hast rudely lost,
    Which by thy younger brother is supplied,
    And art almost an alien to the hearts
    Of all the court and princes of my blood.   35
    The hope and expectation of thy time
    Is ruined, and the soul of every man
    Prophetically do forethink thy fall.

17 hold their level be in an equal position with (*OED* Level sv *sb* 3c).

18–28 So please . . . submission The Prince apologises without explaining himself clearly. He may kneel to his father, as he does in Holinshed (III, 54), but his lines here do not require so literal or so penitent a gesture. He maintains that many of the stories about him are lies and that he should be pardoned even for those others that he readily admits are true.

19 Quit Acquit myself of.

23 in reproof upon disproof.

25 pickthanks 'officious parasites' (Steevens, 1778); those who gain favour or gifts through flattery or by telling tales. Holinshed mentions that servants had tried to create 'discord' between father and son by insinuating that the Prince intended to seize power (III, 53).

25 newsmongers tale-bearers like 'pickthanks'; literally, sellers of news.

28 submission admission or confession. Compare *Wiv.* 4.4.11: 'Be not as extreme in submission as in offence.'

29–91 God . . . tenderness In this sixty-three-line speech, the longest in the play, the King in effect refuses the Prince's request for 'extenuation' of his offences, 22, and judges them in the bleak light of his own political experience.

30 affections inclinations.

30–1 hold . . . flight i.e. take a course quite different from that; the metaphor derives from falconry.

32 Thy place . . . lost The King may allude to a notorious episode in the legend of the wild Prince: reprimanded for drunken brawling, he had cuffed the Lord Chief Justice. In consequence, he was expelled by the King from the Privy Council. The story had been told by Elyot, *The Governor* (1531), and made familiar to audiences through *FV*. On Shakespeare's revision of tales about the Prince, see Introduction, pp. 2, 25–7.

34 art thou art.

36 The hope . . . time 'Your hopeful and promising youth' (Wilson).

37–8 the soul . . . fall The King's statement, if true, confirms the Prince's success in his plan to 'falsify men's hopes', 1.2.171.

Had I so lavish of my presence been,
So common-hackneyed in the eyes of men,   40
So stale and cheap to vulgar company,
Opinion, that did help me to the crown,
Had still kept loyal to possession,
And left me in reputeless banishment,
A fellow of no mark nor likelihood.   45
By being seldom seen, I could not stir
But like a comet I was wondered at,
That men would tell their children, 'This is he!'
Others would say, 'Where, which is Bullingbrook?'
And then I stole all courtesy from heaven,   50
And dressed myself in such humility
That I did pluck allegiance from men's hearts,
Loud shouts and salutations from their mouths,
Even in the presence of the crownèd King.
Thus did I keep my person fresh and new,   55
My presence, like a robe pontifical,
Ne'er seen but wondered at, and so my state,
Seldom, but sumptuous, showed like a feast,
And won by rareness such solemnity.
The skipping King, he ambled up and down,   60

---

59 won] Q1 (wan); wonne F

39 lavish (1) prodigal in spending, (2) wild, as in *Mac.* 1.2.57, 'Curbing his lavish spirit'.

40 common-hackneyed commonplace or vulgar. The sense of 'hackney' as an ordinary horse (*OED* sv *sb* 1) may also suggest some recollection of the effect Bullingbrook produced by entering London on Richard II's horse, roan Barbary. Compare *R2* 5.2.7–11 and 5.5.76–80. Henry contrasts himself with Richard at 54 and 60 below.

42 Opinion Public opinion.

43 to possession i.e. to the possessor, King Richard II.

44 reputeless banishment dishonourable exile. Bullingbrook was literally banished by Richard II for challenging his authority *(R2* 1.3.139–43). The King implies that public 'opinion' ended his exile although, in fact, he created this opinion by returning illegally to England.

45 mark reputation, notice.

47 comet a meteor or shooting star, often viewed as prophetic of disorder on earth. Compare references to meteors by the King, 1.1.10, and by Glendower, 3.1.11–13.

50 And . . . heaven 'Courtesy' refers to (1) the charming humble manner adopted by Bullingbrook, 51–3, and (2) his calculated acquisition of power through courtship, modelled on 'heaven' only insofar as he imitates a comet, 47. Compare the Prince's 'Yet herein will I imitate the sun', 1.2.157. The metaphors chosen by father and son expose striking similarities and differences in their characters and in their conceptions of power.

56–7 My presence . . . wondered at A variation on the saying that 'A Maid oft seen, a gown oft worn, are disesteemed and held in scorn' (Dent, M20, Appendix C).

56 robe pontifical ceremonial vestment of a Pope or high priest. The reference might remind Shakespeare's predominantly Protestant audience that kings, like Catholic priests, could be accused of fostering idolatry.

57 state magnificence (*OED* sv *sb* 17a).

59 solemnity the grandeur characteristic of a great public ceremony.

60 skipping flighty (Wilson).

With shallow jesters, and rash bavin wits,
Soon kindled and soon burnt, carded his state,
Mingled his royalty with capering fools,
Had his great name profanèd with their scorns,
And gave his countenance against his name   65
To laugh at gibing boys, and stand the push
Of every beardless vain comparative,
Grew a companion to the common streets,
Enfeoffed himself to popularity,
That, being daily swallowed by men's eyes,   70
They surfeited with honey, and began
To loathe the taste of sweetness, whereof a little
More than a little is by much too much.
So, when he had occasion to be seen,
He was but as the cuckoo is in June,   75
Heard, not regarded; seen, but with such eyes
As, sick and blunted with community,
Afford no extraordinary gaze,
Such as is bent on sun-like majesty
When it shines seldom in admiring eyes,   80
But rather drowsed and hung their eyelids down,
Slept in his face, and rendered such aspect
As cloudy men use to their adversaries,

---

63 capering] Q1 (capring); Carping Qq2–5, F   71–2 began / To loathe the] *As T. Johnson, Pope;* began to loathe / The QqF

61 rash bavin quickly lighted kindling, soon burnt out.

62 carded his state contaminated his display of power (by mingling with fools, 63). The expression here twists one sense of 'card': to comb impurities from wool or flax; it joins this to a second: to stir or mix (*OED* sv *v*[1] 1 and 2).

65 countenance royal authority. Compare 1.2.24 and note.

65 against his name to the prejudice of his reputation or title.

66 stand the push be prepared to take the thrust. Compare *2H4* 2.2.37, and *Tro.* 2.2.137. The King ironically implies that Richard lacked valour.

67 beardless vain comparative youth who makes trivial jokes. Compare 1.2.64.

69 Enfeoffed . . . popularity Made himself dependent upon the favour and power of the people. A king or lord enfeoffed a vassal by granting him land in return for support. In effect, Richard made himself the vassal.

71 surfeited with honey A familiar expression, as in Proverbs 25.16 and 27 and Dent 11560. Compare the contemptuous references to honey at 1.2.34 and 2.1.62.

75–6 the cuckoo . . . regarded Compare Dent c894, 'No one regards the June (summer) cuckoo's song.' The King here relies on popular expressions to repudiate Hal's association with the common people.

77 community commonness (*OED* 5a), i.e. the experience of seeing the king as an ordinary familiar figure.

78 Afford Bestow, Grant (*OED* 5).

82 in his face in his presence. This affront to the dignity of a ruler is compared to the natural effect of getting too much sun.

83 cloudy Sullen or darkened because no longer reflecting the king's light as do obedient subjects. Compare 'moody', 1.3.18, and 'fair and natural light', 5.1.18.

Being with his presence glutted, gorged, and full.
And in that very line, Harry, standest thou,   85
For thou hast lost thy princely privilege
With vile participation. Not an eye
But is a-weary of thy common sight,
Save mine, which hath desired to see thee more,
Which now doth that I would not have it do,   90
Make blind itself with foolish tenderness.

PRINCE I shall hereafter, my thrice-gracious lord,
Be more myself.

KING   For all the world
As thou art to this hour was Richard then
When I from France set foot at Ravenspurgh,   95
And even as I was then is Percy now.
Now by my sceptre, and my soul to boot,
He hath more worthy interest to the state
Than thou the shadow of succession.
For of no right, nor colour like to right,   100
He doth fill fields with harness in the realm,
Turns head against the lion's armèd jaws,
And being no more in debt to years than thou
Leads ancient lords and reverend bishops on
To bloody battles, and to bruising arms.   105

85 line category, degree. Compare 1.3.166 and n.

87 vile participation fellowship with vile people. The King's abstractions keep the Prince's friends at a distance.

90 that that which.

91 blind itself i.e. by filling with tears, an implicit and self-conscious stage direction. Both in *FV* and in Holinshed, the King weeps sincerely during his reconciliation with the Prince.

92–3 I shall . . . myself The Prince unknowingly repeats his father's self-assertion to the Percys at 1.3.5.

93–128 For all . . . degenerate The King overwhelms the Prince's forceful interjection (92–3) with an apparently premeditated discourse on how history is repeating itself. For a more detailed discussion of the rhythms of this scene, see Introduction, pp. 15–16.

95 Ravenspurgh Former seaport (later submerged by the sea) in Yorkshire where Bullingbrook landed upon his return from exile. Compare 1.3.244 and n.

97 to boot as well.

98–9 He . . . succession i.e. his claim, based on his intrinsic worth, betters yours, based only on inherited right.

100 colour like to semblance of.

101–2 He . . . jaws The King's figures of speech, metonymy (the harness as part of the armour of many men) and heraldic emblem (the lion's jaws symbolising his own power) resemble those which he uses in 1.1.1–33. There they distract attention from personal responsibility for disruption. Here, however, such figures glorify the process controlled by one agent, Hotspur.

102 Turns head Leads a rebel army (*OED* head sv *sb*¹ 29).

103 no . . . thou no older than you are. The historical Hotspur, born in 1364, was really several years older than the King himself, as well as twenty-three years older than the Prince. See List of Characters and Introduction, p. 24.

104 bishops An indication that the King is already aware of the Archbishop of York's confederacy with the rebels. See 4.4.38.

105 bruising crushing. Compare 5.1.13, 'crush our old limbs in ungentle steel'.

What never-dying honour hath he got
Against renownèd Douglas! Whose high deeds,
Whose hot incursions and great name in arms,
Holds from all soldiers chief majority
And military title capital   110
Through all the kingdoms that acknowledge Christ.
Thrice hath this Hotspur, Mars in swaddling clothes,
This infant warrior, in his enterprises
Discomfited great Douglas, taken him once,
Enlargèd him, and made a friend of him,   115
To fill the mouth of deep defiance up,
And shake the peace and safety of our throne.
And what say you to this? Percy, Northumberland,
The Archbishop's Grace of York, Douglas, Mortimer,
Capitulate against us and are up.   120
But wherefore do I tell these news to thee?
Why, Harry, do I tell thee of my foes,
Which art my nearest and dearest enemy?
Thou that art like enough, through vassal fear,
Base inclination, and the start of spleen,   125
To fight against me under Percy's pay,
To dog his heels, and curtsy at his frowns,
To show how much thou art degenerate.
PRINCE Do not think it so, you shall not find it so;
And God forgive them that so much have swayed   130

---

107 renownèd] Qq4, 5, F; renowmed Qq1–3   112 swaddling] Qq1–3 (swathling); swathing Qq4, 5, F

107 Whose Hotspur's.

108 hot incursions sudden attacks, raids, as in 'sallies', 2.3.45.

109–10 Holds . . . capital Holds the reputation of pre-eminent soldier. 'Majority' carries a secondary sense, 'of full age', suggesting that Hotspur has proved his manhood.

112–15 Thrice . . . him Historically Hotspur engaged in three battles against the Douglas family or their representatives: Otterburn (1385) in which the then head of the family was killed and Hotspur himself captured, Nesbit (22 June 1402), and Holmedon (14 September 1402). Shakespeare seems to invent the capturing and releasing of Douglas, a pattern which the Prince follows at 5.5.27–8.

115 Enlargèd Freed.

116 To . . . up The figure of the mouth filled

with a war-cry (another metonymy) conveys Hotspur's readiness to attack.

120 Capitulate Draw up articles (literally 'chapters') of agreement. These articles, circulated by the Percys (5.1.72–4 below and Holinshed III, 23), contained their grievances.

120 up up in arms.

123 dearest Both most cherished and most bitter, as in *Ham.* 1.2.182, 'my dearest foe'.

124 vassal Normally a term for a dependent member of a feudal alliance, but used by the King to suggest social debasement, slavishness. Compare 'Enfeoffed', 69.

125 start of spleen fit of ill humour. Compare 2.3.72 and n.

130 them the 'pickthanks' and 'newsmongers', 25.

Your majesty's good thoughts away from me!
I will redeem all this on Percy's head,
And in the closing of some glorious day
Be bold to tell you that I am your son,
When I will wear a garment all of blood,   135
And stain my favours in a bloody mask,
Which, washed away, shall scour my shame with it.
And that shall be the day, whene'er it lights,
That this same child of honour and renown,
This gallant Hotspur, this all-praisèd knight,   140
And your unthought-of Harry chance to meet.
For every honour sitting on his helm,
Would they were multitudes, and on my head
My shames redoubled. For the time will come
That I shall make this northern youth exchange   145
His glorious deeds for my indignities.
Percy is but my factor, good my lord,
To engross up glorious deeds on my behalf,
And I will call him to so strict account
That he shall render every glory up,   150
Yea, even the slightest worship of his time,
Or I will tear the reckoning from his heart.
This in the name of God I promise here,
The which if He be pleased I shall perform,
I do beseech your majesty may salve   155
The long-grown wounds of my intemperance.

---

154 He . . . perform] Qq; I performe, and doe survive F   156 intemperance] Qq; intemperature F, *Bevington*

132 I will . . . head I will (1) make Percy pay for all this, (2) shift the blame for all this to Percy, (3) use Percy's head to make up for all this. The complex metaphor figuring redemption runs through this crucial promise. See 1.2.177 and n.

135 all of blood Compare the apocalyptic vision of Pyrrhus in *Ham.* 2.2.456–8: 'head to foot / Now is he total gules, horridly trick'd / With blood'. Bevington points out how the image picks up on the sunset of 133, 'reinforcing' a pun upon 'son', 134.

136 favours features, as well as chivalric tokens worn to symbolise great deeds and honours.

137 washed away Like a baptism, immersion in blood may transform character.

138 lights dawns.

139 child youth of gentle birth. Compare 'infant', 113.

141 unthought-of One for whom there are no expectations. This echoes 131 and contrasts with the 'all-praisèd' Hotspur, 140.

142 every . . . helm all the honours that decorate his helmet, like 'favours', 136.

147 factor agent, especially in a commercial transaction.

148 engross up buy up, monopolise.

151 slightest . . . time the least of the honours ('worship') he has earned.

152 reckoning the account prepared and kept by the factor of the wealth belonging to his master.

155 salve heal.

156 intemperance disorderly behaviour. F substitutes 'intemperature', which emphasises the suggestion of disease in 'salve' and 'wounds'. Although this revision is attractive, we retain the copy-text reading.

> If not, the end of life cancels all bands,
> And I will die a hundred thousand deaths
> Ere break the smallest parcel of this vow.
> KING   A hundred thousand rebels die in this.   160
> Thou shalt have charge and sovereign trust herein.

Enter BLUNT

> How now, good Blunt? Thy looks are full of speed.
> BLUNT   So hath the business that I come to speak of.
> Lord Mortimer of Scotland hath sent word
> That Douglas and the English rebels met   165
> The eleventh of this month at Shrewsbury.
> A mighty and a fearful head they are,
> If promises be kept on every hand,
> As ever offered foul play in a state.
> KING   The Earl of Westmoreland set forth today,   170
> With him my son, Lord John of Lancaster,
> For this advertisement is five days old.
> On Wednesday next, Harry, you shall set forward.
> On Thursday we ourselves will march.
> Our meeting is Bridgnorth, and, Harry, you   175
> Shall march through Gloucestershire, by which account,
> Our business valuèd, some twelve days hence
> Our general forces at Bridgnorth shall meet.
> Our hands are full of business, let's away,
> Advantage feeds him fat while men delay.   180

Exeunt

---

161 SD *Enter* BLUNT | F; *after 162* Qq   174–5 march. / Our meeting is| F; march. Our meeting/ Is Qq   175–6 you/ Shall march through| *T. Johnson, Capell;* you shall march/ Through QqF

159 parcel portion.
161 charge leadership.
161 sovereign trust (1) supreme responsibility, (2) my confidence.
164 Mortimer Shakespeare assumes mistakenly that the Scottish Earls of March were Mortimers, like the English Earls of March.
166 the eleventh . . . Shrewsbury This rendezvous, only just planned during the immediately preceding scene, 3.1.82, may suggest the uncanny independence of Welsh from English time – or simply a careless error by the dramatist.
167 head army.
172 advertisement information.
173–8 On Wednesday . . . meet The King

sends the Prince by a roundabout route through Gloucestershire to Bridgnorth in Shropshire. But in 4.2, Hal meets Falstaff near Coventry, suggesting that he may have travelled on a direct course towards the rendezvous. Wilson believes that the reptition of 'Bridgnorth', 'march', and 'business' (179) indicates imperfect revision of this passage.
176–7 by . . . valuèd according to the calculation of the time that our purposes require.
180 Advantage . . . delay Compare the proverb, 'Delay breeds danger' (Dent D195). For discussion of the vivid contrast between the final line of this scene and the first of the next, see Introduction, p. 16 and 3.3.2. n. below.
180 him himself.

[3.3]   *Enter* FALSTAFF and BARDOLPH

FALSTAFF   Bardolph, am I not fallen away vilely since this last action?
Do I not bate? Do I not dwindle? Why, my skin hangs about me like
an old lady's loose gown. I am withered like an old apple-John. Well,
I'll repent, and that suddenly, while I am in some liking. I shall be
out of heart shortly, and then I shall have no strength to repent. And   5
I have not forgotten what the inside of a church is made of, I am a
peppercorn, a brewer's horse. The inside of a church! Company,
villainous company, hath been the spoil of me.

BARDOLPH   Sir John, you are so fretful you cannot live long.

FALSTAFF   Why, there is it. Come, sing me a bawdy song, make me   10
merry. I was as virtuously given as a gentleman need to be. Virtuous
enough. Swore little. Diced not above seven times – a week. Went
to a bawdy-house not above once in a quarter – of an hour. Paid
money that I borrowed – three or four times. Lived well, and in
good compass: and now I live out of all order, out of all compass.   15

Act 3, Scene 3   3.3] *Scena Tertia.* F; *not in* Qq   12 times –] *Staunton;* times QqF   13 quarter –] *Hanmer;* quarter
QqF   14 borrowed –] *Hanmer;* borrowed Qq; borrowed, F

Act 3, Scene 3

[3.3] The entry of the Hostess after 39 below
indicates that the scene takes place at the tavern
in Eastcheap. It has traditionally been called the
second tavern scene.

  1 last action the robbery at Gad's Hill, with the
consequent battle of wits of 2.4. Like the Prince at
2.4.17, Falstaff refers to jest or sport as a serious
military engagement.

  2 bate i.e. abate, decrease in size or bulk (*OED*
sv v^2 4b). Falstaff's first lines counter the King's
last line in 3.2: 'Advantage feeds him fat while
men delay.' For discussion of the changes in the
play which are introduced in this scene and further developed in *Part Two*, see Introduction,
pp. 16–17. Falstaff initiates here the more self-
conscious satiric anatomy or exploration of bodily
analogues for general disorder and death which
will be sustained throughout *2H4*.

  3 apple-john A kind of apple picked around
St John's Day, 24 June (Midsummer), but eaten
long afterwards, and therefore shrivelled. In *2H4*,
Francis the drawer declares that 'Sir John cannot
endure an apple-john' (2.4.2–3).

  4 suddenly immediately.

  4 am in some liking (1) feel like it, (2) am in
fairly good condition. Falstaff plays upon this pun

as he continues.

  5 out of heart (1) disheartened, (2) in poor
condition.

  5 strength both (1) of intention, and (2) of body.

  5 And If.

  7 peppercorn An absurd comparison because
unground pepper is hard, dry, and tiny. Compare
'shotten herring', 2.4.109.

  7 brewer's horse one on its last legs. Compare
Dekker, *If This be not a good Play, the Devil is in It*
(1611): 'as noble-men use their great horses, when
they are past service: sell 'em to brewers and make
'em drey-horses' (cited by Humphreys).

  9 fretful (1) emotionally anxious, (2) physically fretted or worn down (like the gummed velvet, 2.2.2). Bardolph answers Falstaff with another
quibble.

  10 there is it that's the point.

  11 given disposed.

  12–14 Diced . . . times By pausing before 'a
week', 'of an hour', and 'three or four times', stage
Falstaffs often emphasise their self-mockery.

  14–15 in good compass within reasonable
bounds, a proverbial phrase (Dent c577).

  15 out of all compass A quibble: (1) without
any order, (2) too large in girth for belts or girdles,
124–5 below (Dent c577.1).

BARDOLPH Why, you are so fat, Sir John, that you must needs be out
of all compass, out of all reasonable compass, Sir John.

FALSTAFF Do thou amend thy face, and I'll amend my life. Thou art
our admiral, thou bearest the lantern in the poop, but 'tis in the nose
of thee. Thou art the Knight of the Burning Lamp.   20

BARDOLPH Why, Sir John, my face does you no harm.

FALSTAFF No, I'll be sworn, I make as good use of it as many a man
doth of a death's-head, or a *memento mori*. I never see thy face but I
think upon hell-fire, and Dives that lived in purple: for there he is
in his robes, burning, burning. If thou wert any way given to virtue,   25
I would swear by thy face. My oath should be 'By this fire, that's
God's angel!' But thou art altogether given over, and wert indeed,
but for the light in thy face, the son of utter darkness. When thou
ran'st up Gad's Hill in the night to catch my horse, if I did not think
thou hadst been an *ignis fatuus*, or a ball of wildfire, there's no   30
purchase in money. O, thou art a perpetual triumph, an everlasting

26–7 that's God's angel!] Qq3–5; that Gods Angell Qq1, 2; *not in* F

19 admiral flagship.

19 lantern Bardolph's red nose; the jest is echoed in *2H4* 1.2.48 (Melchiori). A lantern was hung in the poop of the flagship to guide the fleet.

20 Knight of the Burning Lamp A parody of the Knight of the Burning Sword, Amadis. Beaumont and Fletcher's later farce, *The Knight of the Burning Pestle* (c. 1607), also mocks the titles given to the heroes of popular romances. Compare Falstaff's reference to 'Phoebus', 'that wandering knight', 1.2.11–12 and n.

23 death's-head a human skull or the representation of one.

23 memento mori an object used to symbolise death. Compare *2H4* 2.4.234–5: 'do not speak like a death's-head, do not bid me remember mine end'.

24 hell-fire . . . Dives An allusion to Christ's parable of the rich man, Dives, and the beggar, Lazarus. The rich man who 'fared wel and delicately' allowed the beggar to starve at his gate. Later Dives learned, too late, that he would burn eternally in Hell, while Lazarus rested in the bosom of Abraham (Luke 16.19–31). Falstaff refers to 'Lazarus in the painted cloth', 4.2.22. He associates Bardolph's nose with the fires of hell in *2H4* 2.4.329–34; and in *H5* 2.3.40–2, he is said to joke on his death-bed about a flea upon Bardolph's nose as a 'black soul burning in hell'.

26–7 By . . . angel A proverbial oath omitted from F as profane. It may refer to the episode of Moses and the Burning Bush in which 'the Angel

of the Lord appeared unto him in a flame of fyre' (Exodus 3.2) or to Psalm 104.4: 'a flaming fyre his ministers'.

28 the son of utter darkness Falstaff repeats 'son(s) of darkness', his transformation at 2.4.145, of 1 Thess. 5.5, and combines it with the 'utter' darkness of Matt. 8.12, 22.13, and 25.30. 'Utter' means 'indefinitely remote' (*OED* sv *a* 1); the King James version substitutes 'outer'.

30 ignis fatuus Latin for 'foolish fire', will o' the wisp, a light that appears to glimmer over marshes and swamps and leads travellers fatally astray.

30 ball of wildfire (1) Translation of *ignis fatuus*, (2) a flaming ball of gunpowder, used both for fireworks and for naval battles, (3) a skin disease, erysipelas (Wilson). In Marlowe, *Dido Queene of Carthage*, Pirrhus is said to be followed by 'his band of Mirmidons, / With balles of wilde fire in their murdering pawes', 2.1.216–17.

31 purchase value.

31 triumph Either a procession celebrating victory or a great public festival, illuminated by the bonfires and torches to which Bardolph's nose is compared, 32 and 33.

31–2 everlasting bonfire-light Bonfires were lit for St John's or Midsummer Eve; compare 'fernseed', 2.1.70, and 'apple-john', 3 above, and nn. An allusion to hell-fire may be suggested, through 'everlasting' and 'bone-fire', which was a current spelling, as well as a word for: (1) the burning of heretics' bones or of proscribed books, (2) a funeral pyre (*OED* sv *sb* 2, 3).

bonfire-light! Thou hast saved me a thousand marks in links and
torches, walking with thee in the night betwixt tavern and tavern.
But the sack that thou hast drunk me would have bought me lights
as good cheap at the dearest chandler's in Europe. I have main-   35
tained that salamander of yours with fire any time this two-and-
thirty years, God reward me for it!

BARDOLPH 'Sblood, I would my face were in your belly!

FALSTAFF God-a-mercy! So should I be sure to be heart-burnt.

Enter HOSTESS

How now, dame Partlet the hen, have you enquired yet who picked   40
my pocket?

HOSTESS Why, Sir John, what do you think, Sir John, do you think I
keep thieves in my house? I have searched, I have enquired, so has
my husband, man by man, boy by boy, servant by servant – the tithe
of a hair was never lost in my house before.   45

FALSTAFF Ye lie, Hostess. Bardolph was shaved and lost many a hair,
and I'll be sworn my pocket was picked. Go to, you are a woman, go!

HOSTESS Who, I? No, I defy thee! God's light, I was never called so in
mine own house before.

FALSTAFF Go to, I know you well enough.   50

---

39 SD *Enter* HOSTESS] F; *after 40* (enquird) Qq1, 2; *after 41* Qq3–5   44 tithe] *Theobald;* tight QqF

32 **marks** Each mark is worth two-thirds of a pound.

32 **links** flares or torches.

34 **me** at my expense.

35 **as good cheap** as a good bargain (but costly under the circumstances) (*OED* sv *sb* 5).

35 **dearest** most expensive.

35 **chandler** maker or seller of candles.

36 **salamander** nose. The belief that this lizard could live in fire because it was cold-blooded derived from Pliny, *Natural History* (cited by Humphreys).

36–7 **two-and-thirty years** No special significance has been found for the exact length of this remarkably long relationship. In *2H4* the Hostess claims to have known Falstaff for twenty-nine years, Justice Shallow for approximately fifty-five (2.4.382–3, 3.2.210).

38 **I . . . belly** A proverbial retort, inviting a speaker to 'eat' his words: 'I wish it were in your belly (for me)' (Dent B299). Falstaff plays upon the literal meaning in his response below.

40 **dame Partlet** A traditional name for a hen, commonly used to designate a scolding woman. In *WT*, Leontes calls Paulina 'Dame Partlet' (2.3.76). The name derived from folktales of Reynard the Fox; 'Dame Pertelote' was the rooster's favourite hen in Chaucer's *Nun's Priest's Tale*.

44 **tithe** tenth part, the traditional assessment for contributions to the church or to charity. Theobald's emendation from QqF 'tight' is made more probable by 'denier' (the tenth of a penny), 62 below.

46 **shaved . . . hair** A quibble on 'tithe of a hair', 44–5. Three more puns on 'shaved' are latent: (1) robbed or cheated, (2) deprived of hair because of venereal disease ('The suggestion of the tavern as a bawdy-house, where customers might suffer this customary double consequence of lechery, is echoed repeatedly in the double entendres of this scene', Bevington); (3) treated in order to eliminate lice. Prisoners in jails traditionally have been shaved.

47, 50 **you are a woman, . . . I know you** Using derogatory connotations of 'woman' and 'know', Falstaff implies that the Hostess is both deceitful and sexually promiscuous.

HOSTESS No, Sir John, you do not know me, Sir John. I know you, Sir John. You owe me money, Sir John, and now you pick a quarrel to beguile me of it. I bought you a dozen of shirts to your back.

FALSTAFF Dowlas, filthy dowlas. I have given them away to bakers' wives. They have made bolters of them.   55

HOSTESS Now as I am a true woman, holland of eight shillings an ell! You owe money here besides, Sir John, for your diet, and by-drinkings, and money lent you, four-and-twenty pound.

FALSTAFF He had his part of it, let him pay.

HOSTESS He? Alas, he is poor, he hath nothing.   60

FALSTAFF How? Poor? Look upon his face. What call you rich? Let them coin his nose, let them coin his cheeks, I'll not pay a denier. What, will you make a younker of me? Shall I not take mine ease in mine inn but I shall have my pocket picked? I have lost a seal-ring of my grandfather's worth forty mark.   65

HOSTESS O Jesu, I have heard the Prince tell him I know not how oft, that that ring was copper.

FALSTAFF How? The Prince is a Jack, a sneak-up. 'Sblood, an he were here I would cudgel him like a dog if he would say so.

Enter the PRINCE *marching* [*with* PETO], *and Falstaff meets him, playing upon his truncheon like a fife*

How now, lad? Is the wind in that door, i'faith, must we all march?   70

68 sneak-up] QQ1, 2 (sneakeup); sneak-cup QQ3–5, F   69 SD.1 *with* PETO] *Theobald subst., not in* QQF   70 How] *Dyce; Falst.* How QQF

53 **to your back** for you to wear.

54 **Dowlas** coarse linen, named after Doulas in Brittany.

55 **bolters** cloths used for sifting meal, i.e. unsuitable for wearing.

56 **holland** fine linen fabric, lawn, originally from the province of Holland in the Netherlands.

56 **ell** 45 inches or 1.1 metres.

57–8 **diet . . . by-drinkings** board (*OED* sv *sb*¹ 5b), and the frequent drinks between meals recorded by Falstaff's IOUs, 2.4.448 ff.

62 **denier** small coin worth one-tenth of a penny; Falstaff may remember the Hostess' 'tithe of a hair' 44–5 above.

63 **younker** a free-spending and gullible young nobleman, eager to be fashionable, but often ruined by bad company. Compare *MV* 2.6.14: 'How like a younger or a prodigal'.

63–4 **Shall . . . inn** Proverbial expression (Dent E 42). Cowl and Morgan cite Harrison, *The Description of England*, 1587, Bk III, chap. 16, on the English innkeeper who 'does not challenge a

lordlie authoritie over his guests . . . sith everie man may use his inne as his owne house in England'.

64 **seal-ring** One decorated with a signet or seal. The sentimental value of such an heirloom is suggested in Sir Thomas Overbury's 'character' of an 'Elder Brother': 'His pedigree and his fathers sealering, are the stilts of his crazed disposition' (cited by Humphreys). Compare the agate-ring, 2.4.61, and the alderman's thumb-ring, 2.4.274–5.

68 **a Jack, a sneak-up** a knave, possibly referring to servile and potentially disloyal pages and serving-men. Compare 2.4.9 and *R3* 1.3.53: 'silken, sly, insinuating Jacks'.

69 SD.1 *with* PETO QQF omit, and some editors follow Johnson in substituting Poins, but the Prince addresses Peto at 164.

69 SD.2 *truncheon* a short thick staff, implied by Falstaff's threat, 69, to cudgel the Prince.

70 **Is . . . door?** Is that (i.e. war) what will happen? A familiar phrase (Dent W419).

BARDOLPH Yea, two and two, Newgate fashion.

HOSTESS My lord, I pray you hear me.

PRINCE What sayest thou, Mistress Quickly? How doth thy husband?
I love him well, he is an honest man.

HOSTESS Good my lord, hear me.   75

FALSTAFF Prithee let her alone, and list to me.

PRINCE What sayest thou, Jack?

FALSTAFF The other night I fell asleep here, behind the arras, and had my
pocket picked. This house is turned bawdy-house, they pick
pockets.   80

PRINCE What didst thou lose, Jack?

FALSTAFF Wilt thou believe me, Hal, three or four bonds of forty
pound apiece, and a seal-ring of my grandfather's.

PRINCE A trifle, some eight-penny matter.

HOSTESS So I told him, my lord, and I said I heard your grace say so.   85
And, my lord, he speaks most vilely of you, like a foul-mouthed
man as he is, and said he would cudgel you.

PRINCE What! He did not?

HOSTESS There's neither faith, truth, nor womanhood in me else.

FALSTAFF There's no more faith in thee than in a stewed prune, nor no   90
more truth in thee than in a drawn fox – and for womanhood, Maid
Marian may be the deputy's wife of the ward to thee. Go, you thing,
go!

HOSTESS Say, what thing, what thing?

FALSTAFF What thing? Why, a thing to thank God on.   95

HOSTESS I am no thing to thank God on, I would thou shouldst know
it, I am an honest man's wife, and setting thy knighthood aside,
thou art a knave to call me so.

73 doth] Qq1–4 *subst.;* does F   92 thing] Qq; nothing F   96 no thing] Q5, F; nothing Qq1–4

71 **Newgate fashion** Prisoners were led in pairs to the City prison, Newgate, or conducted from prison to trial.

82 **bonds** deeds entitling the holder to payment.

90 **stewed prune** Either a prostitute or someone closely linked with prostitution. Stewed prunes were served in brothels or 'stews'; compare *2H4* 2.4.146–7 and *MM* 2.1.90. Like the 'applejohn', 3, the prune may suggest old age.

91 **drawn fox** hunted (drawn from cover), and relying on its cunning to escape. Falstaff, an escape-artist himself, may mix some compliment with his ridicule.

91–2 **Maid Marian . . . to thee** i.e. Compared to you, Maid Marian may be a model of respectability. As a character in morris dances generally performed by a boy or man, Maid Marian became a symbol of grotesque disguise and foppish male dress. But her name was also used as that of the 'loved one', who was given presents in May Day games (Laroque, *Shakespeare's Festive World*, 1993, pp. 124–5). The deputy of a ward would be one of its most respectable citizens.

95 **What thing . . . God on** Having provoked her suspicion that he denies her gender and her morality, Falstaff can slip in an ambiguous compliment which the Hostess takes as a bawdy insult.

97 **setting . . . aside** A polite formula, meaning 'with all due respect to your knighthood'. Falstaff seizes on its literal meanings, 99.

FALSTAFF Setting thy womanhood aside, thou art a beast to say other-
wise.   100

HOSTESS Say, what beast, thou knave, thou?

FALSTAFF What beast? Why – an otter.

PRINCE An otter, Sir John? Why an otter?

FALSTAFF Why? She's neither fish nor flesh, a man knows not where to
have her.   105

HOSTESS Thou art an unjust man in saying so, thou or any man knows
where to have me, thou knave, thou.

PRINCE Thou sayest true, Hostess, and he slanders thee most grossly.

HOSTESS So he doth you, my lord, and said this other day you owed
him a thousand pound.   110

PRINCE Sirrah, do I owe you a thousand pound?

FALSTAFF A thousand pound, Hal? A million, thy love is worth a
million, thou owest me thy love.

HOSTESS Nay my lord, he called you Jack, and said he would cudgel
you.   115

FALSTAFF Did I, Bardolph?

BARDOLPH Indeed, Sir John, you said so.

FALSTAFF Yea, if he said my ring was copper.

PRINCE I say 'tis copper, darest thou be as good as thy word now?

FALSTAFF Why Hal, thou knowest as thou art but man I dare, but as   120
thou art prince, I fear thee as I fear the roaring of the lion's whelp.

PRINCE And why not as the lion?

FALSTAFF The King himself is to be feared as the lion. Dost thou think
I'll fear thee as I fear thy father? Nay, an I do, I pray God my girdle
break.   125

PRINCE O, if it should, how would thy guts fall about thy knees! But

---

109 owed] QqF (ought)   121 prince] Qq; a Prince F   124 an] Qq (and); if F   124 I pray God] Qq; let F

103–4 **An otter . . . flesh** Humphreys cites
Izaak Walton, *Compleat Angler* (1653) 1, 2, on the
inconclusive debate among 'great clerks' over the
nature of otters. Compare the popular saying, 'neither fish nor flesh (nor good red herring)' (Dent
F319). Falstaff has led his listeners to expect a
much more monstrous 'beast', 99.

104–5 **a man . . . her** Understood by the Hostess in the most literal, sexual sense, 106–7, but
perhaps, in addition, another back-handed compliment (compare 90–1 and 95 above): 'She isn't
easy to take advantage of.' The innocent popular
saying, in which 'where to have' means 'how to

understand' (*Oxford Dictionary of Proverbs*,
p. 438), suggests how far both characters have travelled from any simple comprehension.

110 **a thousand pound** Compare 2.4.134 and
n.

121–3 **I fear thee . . . lion** Compare Prov. 19.12:
'The King's wrath is like the roaring of a lyon', and
Prov. 20.2. On the association of royalty with lions,
see 2.4.224–5 and n., and 3.2.102.

124–5 **I pray . . . break** Falstaff's surprising
prayer reworks both Bardolph's 'compass' joke,
16–17 above, and the proverbial saying 'ungirt,
unblessed' (Tilley U10).

sirrah, there's no room for faith, truth, nor honesty in this bosom of thine. It is all filled up with guts and midriff. Charge an honest woman with picking thy pocket? Why, thou whoreson impudent embossed rascal, if there were anything in thy pocket but tavern   130 reckonings, memorandums of bawdy-houses, and one poor penny-worth of sugar-candy to make thee long-winded, if thy pocket were enriched with any other injuries but these, I am a villain. And yet you will stand to it, you will not pocket up wrong! Art thou not ashamed?   135

FALSTAFF Dost thou hear, Hal? Thou knowest in the state of innocency Adam fell, and what should poor Jack Falstaff do in the days of villainy? Thou seest I have more flesh than another man, and there-fore more frailty. You confess then, you picked my pocket?

PRINCE It appears so by the story.   140

FALSTAFF Hostess, I forgive thee, go make ready breakfast, love thy husband, look to thy servants, cherish thy guests, thou shalt find me tractable to any honest reason, thou seest I am pacified still – nay prithee be gone.

Exit Hostess

Now, Hal, to the news at court: for the robbery, lad, how is that   145 answered?

PRINCE O my sweet beef, I must still be good angel to thee – the money is paid back again.

FALSTAFF O, I do not like that paying back, 'tis a double labour.

PRINCE I am good friends with my father and may do anything.   150

141–4 Hostess . . . gone] Qq; *As verse* Hostesse . . . thee: / Go . . . Husband, / Looke . . . Guests: / Thou . . . reason: / Thou . . . still. / Nay . . . gone F   142 guests] Qq2–5, F *subst.*; ghesse Q1   145 court: for] *Theobald;* court for QqF   147–8 O my . . . again] Qq; *as verse* O . . . Beefe: /I . . . thee. / The . . . againe F

127 **bosom** The figurative location of the qualities which have been crowded out ('chest' not 'breast').

128 **midriff** diaphragm (*OED* 1a, this example); what normally separates 'bosom' from 'guts'.

130 **embossed** (1) bulging (*OED ppl. a*¹ 4), (2) foaming at the mouth (like a hunted animal, driven to extremity (*OED v*² 4).

130 **rascal** (1) knave, (2) young male deer, unfit for the hunt (and therefore 'embossed'). Compare 2.2.5.

132 **sugar-candy . . . long-winded** A common prescription to improve stamina, especially of fighting cocks (Wright).

133 **injuries** i.e. the items Falstaff pretends were stolen.

134 **pocket up** submit to. In his word-play upon

a familiar phrase (Dent 170), the Prince mocks Falstaff's pretence of being wronged, puns on his picked 'pocket', and implies, 'You won't even try to hide the injury you have done.'

138–9 **Thou seest . . . frailty** A distortion of the proverbial saying, 'the flesh is frail', Bishops' Bible version of Matt. 26.41 and Mark 14.38; Geneva has 'weake'. Falstaff turns a condemnation of human depravity, symbolised by the body or 'flesh', into a justification.

140 **by** according to.

143 **still** as usual.

146 **answered** taken care of, dealt with.

147 **sweet beef** 'a fattened beast, or its carcass' (*OED* Beef sv *sb* 3) which is still fresh, i.e. not yet preserved with salt. There are many references to Falstaff as meat, living or dead.

FALSTAFF Rob me the exchequer the first thing thou dost, and do it
    with unwashed hands too.

BARDOLPH Do, my lord.

PRINCE I have procured thee, Jack, a charge of foot.

FALSTAFF I would it had been of horse. Where shall I find one that can   155
    steal well? O for a fine thief of the age of two-and-twenty or there-
    abouts! I am heinously unprovided. Well, God be thanked for these
    rebels, they offend none but the virtuous. I laud them, I praise
    them.

PRINCE Bardolph!   160

BARDOLPH My lord?

PRINCE Go bear this letter to Lord John of Lancaster,
    To my brother John, this to my Lord of Westmoreland.

                                    [*Exit Bardolph*]

    Go, Peto, to horse, to horse, for thou and I
    Have thirty miles to ride yet ere dinner-time.   165

                                    [*Exit Peto*]

    Jack, meet me tomorrow in the Temple hall
    At two o'clock in the afternoon.
    There shalt thou know thy charge, and there receive
    Money and order for their furniture.
    The land is burning, Percy stands on high,   170
    And either we or they must lower lie.   [*Exit*]

FALSTAFF Rare words! Brave world! Hostess, my breakfast, come!
    O, I could wish this tavern were my drum.   [*Exit*]

---

156 the age of] Qq; *not in* F   **163** SD *Exit Bardolph*] *Dyce; not in* QqF   **164** Peto] QqF; Poins *Dering MS., Var. 1773, conj. Johnson*   **165** SD *Exit Peto*] *Cam.; Exit Pointz* / *Dyce; not in* QqF   **167** o'] Qq2–5, F (a); of Q1   **171** SD *Exit*] *Dyce; not in* QqF   **173** SD *Exit*] *Capell; not in* Q1; *Exeunt* Qq2–5; *Exeunt omnes* F

151–2 with unwashed hands with no scruples (Dent H125).

157 heinously unprovided infamously ill-equipped. Falstaff blames his poverty, as if it were a crime in itself, on 'paying back', 149, and on the Prince's failure as a thief, 156–7.

157–8 God . . . virtuous Falstaff praises the rebels for giving him a timely chance to make money. He suggests that there is little moral distinction between the rebels and those in power who pretend to 'virtue'. Humphreys summarises Wilson, *Fortunes*, p. 84: 'Falstaff's attitude to war is blatantly, and indeed blasphemously, predatory.' But in recent productions, Falstaff's complex attitude is often close to that of Brecht's Mother Courage.

163 SD, 165 SD *Exit Bardolph, Exit Peto* Q

provides no exits and entrances separating this from the following scene, while Qq2–5, F have only a group exit at the end. Adding these exits for Bardolph and Peto enhances the urgency of the action and leaves the Prince and Falstaff together for the last time until 5.1.121 ff. See Textual Analysis, pp. 221–2.

165 thirty . . . dinner-time 'This fixes the time, of the scene as early morning' (Wilson).

166 Temple hall The hall of the Inner Temple, one of the Inns of Court where students prepared for careers in law.

169 furniture equipment.

173 I . . . drum Hemingway suggests that Falstaff 'may refer to the drum, in its literal sense, as he pounds on the table for his breakfast'. The drum called soldiers into battle.

[4.1] [*Enter* HOTSPUR, WORCESTER, *and* DOUGLAS]

HOTSPUR Well said, my noble Scot! If speaking truth
         In this fine age were not thought flattery,
         Such attribution should the Douglas have
         As not a soldier of this season's stamp
         Should go so general current through the world.   5
         By God, I cannot flatter. I do defy
         The tongues of soothers, but a braver place
         In my heart's love hath no man than yourself.
         Nay, task me to my word, approve me, lord.
DOUGLAS Thou art the king of honour.   10
         No man so potent breathes upon the ground
         But I will beard him.
HOTSPUR   Do so, and 'tis well.

                Enter [MESSENGER] *with letters*

         What letters hast thou there? – I can but thank you.
MESSENGER These letters come from your father.
HOTSPUR Letters from him? Why comes he not himself?   15
MESSENGER He cannot come, my lord, he is grievous sick.
HOTSPUR Zounds, how has he the leisure to be sick
         In such a jostling time? Who leads his power?

Act 4, Scene 1 4.1] *Actus Quartus. Scaena Prima.* F; *not in* Qq 0 SD *Enter* HOTSPUR, WORCESTER, *and* DOUGLAS]
Qq2–5, F *subst.; not in* Q1 1 SH HOTSPUR] Qq2–5, F; *Per. (to line 90)* Q1 12–13 But . . . you] *Capell, followed by
Humphreys;* But . . . him. / Do . . . there? / I . . . you Qq1, 2, F; *one line of verse* But . . . him, *the remainder as
prose* Qq3–5 12 SD *Enter* MESSENGER *with letters*] *Malone subst.; Enter one with letters,* Qq *(after* beard him)*; Enter a
Messenger* F *(after* beard him)

Act 4, Scene 1
[4.1] The characters enter from the same door,
because Hotspur's first words respond to a speech
that he, unlike the audience, has just heard. The
scene takes place in the rebel camp.
  2 fine refined (spoken in a sarcastic tone).
  3 attribution praise, acclaim.
  4–5 As . . . world As no other soldier deserves,
Hotspur uses the metaphor of current coins to
emphasise the universal value of Douglas' heroic
conduct. Compare 2.3.87–8.
  4 stamp The design (a soldier) stamped on
each coin (*OED* sv *sb³* 12b).
  5 general current widely acceptable.
  6 defy distrust, as well as denounce.
  7 soothers flatterers.
  7 braver more worthy.
  9 task test.

  9 approve me put my feeling to the proof.
  11 No man No other man.
  12 beard challenge or defy. The possible
derivation of this sense from seizing the 'beard'
of a lion (*OED* sv *v* 3) is apposite.
  16 grievous sick By delaying this sickness
which, according to Holinshed, came at an earlier
stage of the conspiracy, Shakespeare can emphasise the divergent responses of the rebel leaders.
The chronicle narrative implies that Northumberland's forces would have arrived in time to support his relatives or 'procure a peace', had the King
not marched to Shrewsbury so swiftly (III, 24, 26).
In *2H4* 'Rumour' reports that Northumberland
'Lies crafty-sick' (Induction, 37).
  18 jostling time a time of great contention, of
clashing (as in a joust).

        Under whose government come they along?
MESSENGER His letters bear his mind, not I, my lord.   20
WORCESTER I prithee tell me, doth he keep his bed?
MESSENGER He did, my lord, four days ere I set forth,
        And at the time of my departure thence
        He was much feared by his physicians.
WORCESTER I would the state of time had first been whole   25
        Ere he by sickness had been visited.
        His health was never better worth than now.
HOTSPUR Sick now? Droop now? This sickness doth infect
        The very life-blood of our enterprise.
        'Tis catching hither, even to our camp.   30
        He writes me here that inward sickness –
        And that his friends by deputation could not
        So soon be drawn, nor did he think it meet
        To lay so dangerous and dear a trust
        On any soul removed but on his own.   35
        Yet doth he give us bold advertisement
        That with our small conjunction we should on,
        To see how fortune is disposed to us.
        For, as he writes, there is no quailing now,
        Because the King is certainly possessed   40
        Of all our purposes. What say you to it?
WORCESTER Your father's sickness is a maim to us.
HOTSPUR A perilous gash, a very limb lopped off –
        And yet, in faith, it is not! His present want

---

20 bear| Q7; beares QqF   20 lord| *Capell;* mind QqF   31 sickness –| *Rowe;* sicknesse Q1; Sickness holds him *Capell*
32–3 deputation could not / So| *Capell;* deputation / Could not so QqF

19 government command.

20 bear . . . lord QqF 'beares' is probably a compositor's error. Although 'letters' is at times used as a singular noun by Shakespeare, the presence of 'I', governing the same verb, makes that usage unlikely here. Capell's emendation has been generally accepted.

24 He . . . feared His life was feared for.

31 sickness – The unfinished line in QqF has been thought defective, but may instead express a pause (perhaps staged with a gesture signifying 'you already know about his sickness'). Hotspur, typically impatient, then continues with a hasty but coherent third-person paraphrase of the letter. Proposed completions of the line include

'holds him' (Capell) and 'stays him' (Oxford).

32 by deputation by agents acting in his place.

33 drawn gathered together.

33 meet appropriate, just.

35 On . . . own On anyone less vitally concerned than he (the rallying of 'friends' or allies being a sensitive matter).

36 give . . . advertisement (1) instruct us to be resolute, (2) boldly instruct us.

37 conjunction combination of powers.

37 on i.e. march forward.

40–1 King . . . purposes In Holinshed (III, 23), the King writes an answer to the articles and letters in which the Percys justify their rebellion.

44 want absence.

Seems more than we shall find it. Were it good   45
To set the exact wealth of all our states
All at one cast? To set so rich a main
On the nice hazard of one doubtful hour?
It were not good, for therein should we read
The very bottom and the soul of hope,   50
The very list, the very utmost bound
Of all our fortunes.

DOUGLAS Faith, and so we should. Where now remains
A sweet reversion – we may boldly spend
Upon the hope of what is to come in.   55
A comfort of retirement lives in this.

HOTSPUR A rendezvous, a home to fly unto,
If that the devil and mischance look big
Upon the maidenhead of our affairs.

WORCESTER But yet I would your father had been here.   60
The quality and hair of our attempt
Brooks no division. It will be thought,
By some that know not why he is away,
That wisdom, loyalty, and mere dislike
Of our proceedings kept the Earl from hence.   65
And think how such an apprehension

53–5 Faith . . . in] *Collier³, conj. Walker;* Faith . . . should, / Where . . . reversion, / We . . . in, Qq; Faith . . . should, / Where . . . reversion. / We . . . hope / Of . . . in: F, *Cam. conjectures a missing line after* reversion 55 is] F; 'tis Qq *subst.*

46–7 To set . . . cast To stake the total value of our combined powers on one throw of the dice.

47 main total power (with a serious pun on a stake in gambling).

48 nice precarious.

48 hazard (1) venture, fortune, (2) dice-game.

49–52 for therein . . . fortunes i.e. for we should regard such an action as signifying that we lacked any other source of confidence and had used up any luck we might have.

50 bottom bed of the sea, as in 1.3.201, 'bottom of the deep'.

50 soul essence, exposed or concentrated at the 'bottom'. Wilson notes a quibble on 'sole'.

51 list Synonymous with 'bound', an extreme limit or boundary (*OED* sv *sb³* 8a). Humphreys suggests two puns: a schedule and the selvedge of a cloth.

51 bound This term concludes a series which Mahood, *Wordplay*, 23, recognises as suggesting a naval venture: 'cast' and 'main' (47), 'hazard' (48), 'bottom' (50), 'list' and 'bound' (51).

53–5 Faith . . . in The lineation adopted here avoids irregularities which become inevitable when Douglas' first sentence is either used to complete line 52 or given a line by itself. Qq punctuation by commas throughout is attractive in suggesting the speaker's relief and quick apprehension.

54 reversion possession or wealth that one expects to obtain in the future (*OED* 2a, this example).

56 retirement retreating, as in 5.4.5 (first recorded use in *OED*).

58 look big look threateningly (a common expression).

59 maidenhead of our affairs precarious beginning of our enterprise.

61 hair distinctive character, as in the saying 'of one hair' (*OED* Hair sv *sb* 6).

62 Brooks Tolerates or allows.

64 loyalty By implication, to the King, not to the rebels.

64 mere downright.

66 apprehension conception or idea (*OED* 10), perhaps shading towards the modern sense of uneasy or fearful anticipation.

May turn the tide of fearful faction,
And breed a kind of question in our cause.
For well you know we of the off'ring side
Must keep aloof from strict arbitrement,   70
And stop all sight-holes, every loop from whence
The eye of reason may pry in upon us.
This absence of your father's draws a curtain
That shows the ignorant a kind of fear
Before not dreamt of.

HOTSPUR   You strain too far.   75
I rather of his absence make this use.
It lends a lustre and more great opinion,
A larger dare to our great enterprise,
Than if the Earl were here. For men must think
If we without his help can make a head   80
To push against a kingdom, with his help
We shall o'erturn it topsy-turvy down.
Yet all goes well, yet all our joints are whole.

DOUGLAS As heart can think. There is not such a word
Spoke of in Scotland as this term of fear.   85

Enter SIR RICHARD VERNON

HOTSPUR My cousin Vernon! Welcome, by my soul!
VERNON Pray God my news be worth a welcome, lord.
The Earl of Westmoreland seven thousand strong
Is marching hitherwards, with him Prince John.

HOTSPUR No harm, what more?

VERNON   And further, I have learned,   90
The King himself in person is set forth,
Or hitherwards intended speedily,
With strong and mighty preparation.

---

85 term] QqI–4 (tearme); deame Q5; Dreame F   85 SD RICHARD] F; *Ri:* QqI–4; *Rih* Q5

67 fearful faction conspiracy which causes fear (*OED* Fearful 1).

69 off'ring challenging, aggressive.

70 strict arbitrement rigorous and impartial scrutiny.

71 loop loop-hole, window.

73 draws opens.

74 a kind of fear a doubt, based on 'reason', 72, concerning our cause.

75 strain too far go out of your way to imagine

how people will think.

77 opinion prestige.

80 make a head (1) gather our supporters (compare 1.3.278 and note), (2) advance aggressively.

83 joints limbs.

84 As heart can think A familiar saying (Dent 11300.1).

92 intended (is) on the point of departure.

HOTSPUR He shall be welcome too. Where is his son
            The nimble-footed madcap Prince of Wales,   95
            And his comrades that daft the world aside
            And bid it pass?
VERNON   All furnished, all in arms,
            All plumed like estridges that with the wind
            Bated, like eagles having lately bath'd,
            Glittering in golden coats like images,   100
            As full of spirit as the month of May,
            And gorgeous as the sun at midsummer,
            Wanton as youthful goats, wild as young bulls.
            I saw young Harry with his beaver on,
            His cushes on his thighs, gallantly armed,   105
            Rise from the ground like feathered Mercury,
            And vaulted with such ease into his seat

---

98 with] QqF; wing *Rowe*   98–9 wind / Bated] QqF *subst.; Oxford, Oxford OS, and Bevington conjecture an omission after* wind   99 Bated] Qq1–4 (Baited)*;* Bayted Q5, F*;* Baiting *Oxford, Oxford OS;* Bating *Bevington*

95 nimble-footed Hotspur speaks condescendingly, suggesting cowardice and frivolity, but Shakespeare perhaps noticed praise for the Prince's swiftness in several chronicles (e.g. Holinshed: 'In strength and nimblenesse of bodie from his youth, few to him comparable', III, 133).

96 daft toss(ed) aside carelessly. Humphreys argues that like 'bid', 97, it may be understood as either present or past in tense.

97–110 All furnished . . . horsemanship This choric speech is all the more effective because a rebel leader is so impressed, quite against his own partisan interest, by the Prince's dazzling transformation.

98–9 All plumed . . . bath'd Because of doubtful spelling and punctuation, this splendid passage remains a textual crux.

98 estridges ostriches, referring to the plumes of their crested helmets. Shakespeare probably read the description in Nashe, *The Unfortunate Traveller* (1594), II, 272, of a horse decked out as an ostrich for a ceremonial tilt, with wings which made him as proud 'as he had been some other Pegasus', i.e. the mythical flying horse mentioned in 109 below. Nashe also compared the sound of these artificial wings to that made by 'Eagles . . . pursuing their praie in the ayre'. (G. R. Coffman, *MLN* 13 (1927), 318, cited by Wilson.) 'Estridge' has also been glossed 'goshawk' or 'falcon' (as in Douce, *Illustrations of Shakespeare*, 1807), but such feathers could not have served as plumes.

98–9 that . . . Bated that beat their wings with the wind. 'Bate' is a term from falconry meaning 'to beat the wings impatiently' (*OED* sv *v*¹ 2). Spelled 'Baited' in Qq1–4, it can also, Wilson argues, suggest refreshment, as in Sidney's *Astrophel and Stella* (1598), 39: 'Come sleep . . ., / The baiting-place of wit, the balme of woe' (1–2). Such word-play may anticipate 'bath'd' by implying that the wind invigorated the flying birds. Bevington prefers 'Bating' because 'Baited' may have been contaminated by 'bath'd' in the same line.

99 like . . . bath'd A passage frequently suggested as a source or analogue occurs in Spenser's *Faerie Queene* I, xi, 34 where the Red Crosse Knight (St George), reviving after his first battle with the dragon, is compared to an 'Eagle fresh out of the ocean wave' who tries his 'newly budded pinions'.

100 golden coats shining armour. This epithet recurs in the *Iliad* and the *Aeneid*.

100 images gilded effigies of warriors or illuminated figures in paintings. They may also anticipate the winged deities in 106 and 108 below.

104 beaver helmet, or, strictly, its face-guard.

105 cushes thigh armour, cuisses.

106 feathered Mercury the messenger of the gods in Roman mythology. He was usually represented with wings on heels and cap.

107 vaulted with such ease 'Vaulting fully-armed needed uncommon strength' (Humphreys).

As if an angel dropped down from the clouds
To turn and wind a fiery Pegasus,
And witch the world with noble horsemanship.   110
HOTSPUR No more, no more! Worse than the sun in March,
This praise doth nourish agues. Let them come!
They come like sacrifices in their trim,
And to the fire-eyed maid of smoky war
All hot and bleeding will we offer them.   115
The mailèd Mars shall on his altar sit
Up to the ears in blood. I am on fire
To hear this rich reprisal is so nigh,
And yet not ours! Come, let me taste my horse,
Who is to bear me like a thunderbolt   120
Against the bosom of the Prince of Wales.
Harry to Harry shall, hot horse to horse,
Meet and ne'er part till one drop down a corpse.
O that Glendower were come!
VERNON   There is more news.
I learned in Worcester as I rode along   125
He cannot draw his power this fourteen days.
DOUGLAS That's the worst tidings that I hear of yet.
WORCESTER Ay, by my faith, that bears a frosty sound.
HOTSPUR What may the King's whole battle reach unto?
VERNON To thirty thousand.
HOTSPUR   Forty let it be.   130

108 dropped] Qq2–5, F *subst.;* drop Q1   116 altar] Qq4, 5, F; altars Qq1–3   119 taste] Qq1, 2; take Qq3–5, F   123 ne'er] Qq2–5, F (ne're); neare Q1   123 corpse] QqF (coarse)   126 cannot] Q5 *corr.*, F; can Qq1–4, Q5 *uncorr.*   127 yet] Q5, F; it Qq1–4

109 wind turn. The expert horseman can make his mount wheel around.
109 Pegasus winged horse in Greek and Roman mythology ridden by the hero Perseus.
110 witch bewitch.
111–12 Worse . . . agues The early spring sun was considered strong enough to help breed fevers, by drawing up vapours from undrained marshes (Kittredge).
113 sacrifices . . . trim animals garlanded in preparation for sacrifice. Hotspur continues the classical, heroic idiom of Vernon's speech.
114 fire-eyed . . . war Bellona, Roman goddess of war.
116 mailèd Mars the god of war himself, in armour. Hotspur magnifies Vernon's 'golden coats like images', 100 above.
118 reprisal prize, booty.

119 taste put to the proof, test (*OED* sv v 2).
123 corpse QqF's 'coarse' indicates Elizabethan pronunciation.
126 He . . . days Shakespeare follows Daniel, *Civile Wars* III, st. 99, rather than Holinshed in depriving Hotspur of Welsh support. Compare 3.1.84 where Mortimer intimates that Glendower will not be ready for fourteen days.
129 battle army.
130 To thirty . . . be Hotspur's reply indicates both that success need not be based on numbers (as the later English victory at Agincourt will prove) and that numbers are difficult to establish. Holinshed gives the Percys 14,000 men (III, 24) but provides no figure for the King's side. Humphreys cites Wyntoun's *Cronykil of Scotland* which gives 30,000 for the King, and Hall who says that over 40,000 were engaged on both sides.

My father and Glendower being both away,
The powers of us may serve so great a day.
Come, let us take a muster speedily.
Doomsday is near. Die all, die merrily.

DOUGLAS Talk not of dying, I am out of fear   135
    Of death or death's hand for this one half year.

                                        Exeunt

[4.2] *Enter* FALSTAFF [*and*] BARDOLPH

FALSTAFF Bardolph, get thee before to Coventry. Fill me a bottle of
    sack. Our soldiers shall march through. We'll to Sutton Coldfield
    tonight.

BARDOLPH Will you give me money, captain?

FALSTAFF Lay out, lay out.   5

BARDOLPH This bottle makes an angel.

FALSTAFF And if it do, take it for thy labour – and if it make twenty,
    take them all, I'll answer the coinage. Bid my lieutenant Peto meet
    me at town's end.

BARDOLPH I will, captain. Farewell.   *Exit*   10

FALSTAFF If I be not ashamed of my soldiers, I am a soused gurnet. I

---

134 merrily] Qq2–5, F; merely Q1   Act 4, Scene 2   4.2] *Scœna Secunda.* F; *not in* Qq   0 SD *and*] Qq2–5, F; *not in* Q1
2 Coldfield] *Johnson;* cop-hill Qq 1–5, F *subst.;* Co'fil *Cam.*   11 soused] Qq (souct)

---

132 serve be adequate for.
136 this one half year a little while longer.
Douglas attempts to modify the tone of Hotspur's
fatalistic last line.

Act 4, Scene 2
[4.2] The first three lines locate the scene by
or on the road to Coventry, along the route from
London to Shrewsbury.
2 Sutton Coldfield A town in Warwickshire 20 miles beyond Coventry, well off the
direct route to Shrewsbury and consequently a
long march for Falstaff with his foot soldiers.
This has caused much discussion about whether
Shakespeare wanted Falstaff to avoid Stratford-
upon-Avon. Hemingway's practical suggestion
would resolve the problem of why Falstaff and,
perhaps, the Prince may travel by roundabout
routes: 'the countryside had to be combed for
recruits'. Coldfield was probably pronounced
'Cofil'.
5 Lay out Spend your own money.
6 makes an angel brings expenses to the value
of the gold coin worth between 6s. 8d., and 10s. It
was stamped with the archangel Michael killing a

dragon. 11 or 12s. was a typical weekly wage for a
journeyman (Davison).
7–8 and if . . . coinage Falstaff puns on 'makes'
above; by somehow raising (coining) money Bardolph will profit rather than 'lay out'.
8 Peto Because Hal at 3.3.164–5 tells Peto to
ride with him, Johnson and other editors have
assumed that he cannot serve Falstaff here unless
they replace him with Poins in 3.3. But Peto never
reappears. Shakespeare and his characters seem to
have changed their minds; the Prince enters at 40
below, surprising Falstaff, and there is no further
mention of Peto in the play. Shakespeare indi-
vidualises attendants and companions, but uses
them with great flexibility. See Textual Analysis,
pp. 223–4.
11 soused gurnet pickled gurnet (gurnard),
a small fish with a large spiny head, regarded as
a delicacy. This, with its size and shape, makes
Falstaff's comparison incongruous, like 'poulter's
hare' 2.4.361. After *1H4*, 'soused gurnet' became
a term of contempt (*OED* Gurnard 1b).
11–13 I have . . . pounds As a captain, Falstaff has the power to impress forcibly (or draft)

have misused the King's press damnably. I have got in exchange of
a hundred-and-fifty soldiers three hundred and odd pounds. I press
me none but good householders, yeomen's sons, enquire me out
contracted bachelors, such as had been asked twice on the banns,   15
such a commodity of warm slaves as had as lief hear the devil as a
drum, such as fear the report of a caliver worse than a struck fowl or
a hurt wild duck. I pressed me none but such toasts-and-butter,
with hearts in their bellies no bigger than pins' heads, and they have
bought out their services. And now my whole charge consists of   20
ancients, corporals, lieutenants, gentlemen of companies – slaves as
ragged as Lazarus in the painted cloth, where the glutton's dogs
licked his sores. And such as indeed were never soldiers, but discarded unjust serving-men, younger sons to younger brothers, re-

13 a hundred-and-fifty | Qq (150)   13 three hundred | Qq (300)   17 fowl | *Rowe;* foule Qq 1–3; foole Qq4, 5, F

civilians into the army. His actions reflect current abuse of these practices. See Introduction,
p. 31.
   14 good wealthy, substantial.
   14 yeomen small land-holders rich enough to
purchase their sons' freedom from military service.
   15 contracted engaged to be married.
   15 banns announcements of couples intending
to marry, read out in the established church on
three successive Sundays. QqF 'banes' is a spelling
variant.
   16 commodity parcel or 'lot' of wares (*OED*
7a).
   16 warm slaves contemptible, comfort-loving
civilians (*OED* Warm sv *a* 8).
   17 caliver firearm, light enough to fire without
a rest or support.
   17 struck wounded, a hunting term normally applied to deer. Compare 5.4.106. Johnson
suggested that Shakespeare might have written
'struck sorel' (a young deer), avoiding duplication
by 'hurt wild duck'.
   18 toasts-and-butter milk-toasts, continuing
the satire on civilians. Fynes Morrison's *Itinerary*,
1617, Bk 1, chap. 3, 53, first cited by Malone,
reports that 'Londiners, and all within the sound
of Bow-Bell, are in reproch called Cocknies, and
eaters of buttered tostes' (Kittredge).
   20 bought out their services bribed Falstaff
(or, as in *2H4* 3.2.220–33, perhaps Bardolph) to
release them from the 'press', 12. Steevens (1793)
quotes *The Voyage to Cadiz* (1597) (Hakluyt Soc.)
1, 607: 'A certaine Lieutenant was degraded and
cashiered, &c., for the taking of money by the way
of corruption of certaine prest souldiers in the
countrey, and for placing of others in their roomes,
more unfit for service and of less sufficiency and

abilitie' (cited by Humphreys).
   20 charge company.
   21 ancients (1) The next in command under
a lieutenant, (2) ensigns, standard-bearers. The
'ensign or ancient of a company was an officer of
the highest responsibility and trust' (T. R. Henn,
The Living Image, 1972, p. 107).
   21 gentlemen of companies They held a rank
between ordinary soldiers and officers. Usually
they were exempt from sentinel duty. In *H5* the
disguised King identifies himself as 'a gentleman
of a company' after Pistol challenges him: 'art thou
officer, / Or art thou base, common, and popular?'
(4.1.37–9).
   22–3 Lazarus . . . sores Falstaff refers again
to the parable of the beggar Lazarus and the rich
man; compare 3.3.24 and n. Cowl and Morgan
suggested that pictures painted on cloth were
an inexpensive substitute for tapestry. In *2H4*
2.1.144–5, Falstaff suggests that the Hostess can
pawn her tapestry and replace it with 'a pretty
slight drollery, or the story of the Prodigal, or the
German hunting in water work' (i.e. water colour,
perhaps on paper).
   23–4 discarded unjust discharged for dishonesty. *Sir Thomas More* (1593), 5.2.39 ff., makes it
clear that all discharged servants, even those not
at fault, could be in dire straits.
   24 younger sons to younger brothers They
were doubly removed from any prospect of inheritance which, under the law of primogeniture, only
the eldest living son could claim. Poins says, 'The
worst that they can say of me is that I am a second
brother', in *2H4* 2.2.66–7.
   24–5 revolted tapsters drawers who have run
away from their masters; a reminder of the Prince
and Francis in 2.4.38–40.

volted tapsters, and ostlers trade-fallen, the cankers of a calm world   25
and a long peace, ten times more dishonourable-ragged than an
old fazed ancient. And such have I to fill up the rooms of them as
have bought out their services, that you would think that I had a
hundred-and-fifty tattered prodigals lately come from swine-
keeping, from eating draff and husks. A mad fellow met me on the   30
way, and told me I had unloaded all the gibbets and pressed the
dead bodies. No eye hath seen such scarecrows. I'll not march
through Coventry with them, that's flat. Nay, and the villains
march wide betwixt the legs as if they had gyves on, for indeed I had
the most of them out of prison. There's not a shirt and a half in all   35
my company, and the half shirt is two napkins tacked together and
thrown over the shoulders like a herald's coat without sleeves. And
the shirt, to say the truth, stolen from my host at Saint Albans, or
the red-nose innkeeper of Daventry. But that's all one, they'll find
linen enough on every hedge.   40

Enter the PRINCE, *[and the]* LORD OF WESTMORELAND

PRINCE How now, blown Jack? How now, quilt?

27 old fazed] Q1 (olde fazd); old-fac'd F   29 tattered] QqF *subst.* (tottered)   40 SD *and the*] Qq2–5, F; *not in* Q1

25 **ostlers** stable-men.
25 **trade-fallen** whose business has fallen off.
25 **cankers** (1) worms which destroy leaves and
buds, (2) cancers like the 'sores', 23, that consume
bodies and societies. Compare 1.3.174 and n.
26 **long peace** Often considered unhealthy, as
if society were an organism requiring occasional
drastic cures. Hamlet refers to 'th'impostume of
much wealth and peace, / That inward breaks',
4.4.27–8.
26 **dishonourable-ragged** i.e. dishonourable
because ragged.
27 **old fazed ancient** worn out, fraying ensign
or military banner (*OED* Feaze sv *v*¹ 1a). The F
'old-fac'd Ancient' suggests that the compositor
misread the phrase to mean an elderly officer.
29 **prodigals** Alluding to the parable of the
prodigal son, Luke 15.11–31. Falstaff associates
this story with wall decoration in *2H4* 2.1.144–
5. In *Wiv.* 4.5.7–8, the Hostess describes Falstaff's chamber as 'painted about with the story of
the Prodigal'. On the importance of the story of
the prodigal son as one model for understanding
the Prince's career, see Introduction, p. 10.
30 **draff** swill fed to swine.
30 **husks** a recollection of Luke 15.16 in the
Geneva Bible; the Bishops' and Great Bibles give
'coddes'.

31 **gibbets** gallows.
33 **that's flat** that's for sure.
34 **gyves** leg irons or shackles.
35 **out of prison** Possibly one of the few specific references in this play to a current event or
circumstance: 'The Privy Council emptied the
London prisons in 1596 to furnish recruits for
the Cadiz expedition' (Wilson).
37 **herald's . . . sleeves** A tabard, open at the
sides and emblazoned with the sovereign's coat of
arms. The napkin-shirts resemble the wretched
'tabarte' in Berners, *Froissart* (1523) 1, xii, 12: 'a
tabarte, suche as traytours and theves were wont
to were' (*OED* Tabard 1).
38–9 **Saint Albans . . . Daventry** Towns
between London and Coventry.
39–40 **they'll find . . . hedge** Clothes and
sheets drying on hedges were frequently snatched
by thieves. The song of Autolycus *WT* 4.3.5 ff
shows how familiar this practice would be to the
audience.
41 **blown** (1) swollen, (2) short-winded; compare 'embossed', 3.3.130.
41 **quilt** 'fat man', with a pun on 'Jack', a sleeve-
less padded tunic worn with or as a substitute for
armour (*OED* Jack sv *sb*² 1b; compare Quilt sv
*sb*¹ 2).

FALSTAFF What, Hal! How now, mad wag? What a devil dost thou in
Warwickshire? My good Lord of Westmoreland, I cry you mercy, I
thought your honour had already been at Shrewsbury.

WESTMORELAND Faith, Sir John, 'tis more than time that I were there,   45
and you too, but my powers are there already. The King I can tell
you looks for us all, we must away all night.

FALSTAFF Tut, never fear me, I am as vigilant as a cat to steal cream.

PRINCE I think, to steal cream indeed, for thy theft hath already made
thee butter. But tell me, Jack, whose fellows are these that come   50
after?

FALSTAFF Mine, Hal, mine.

PRINCE I did never see such pitiful rascals.

FALSTAFF Tut, tut, good enough to toss, food for powder, food for
powder, they'll fill a pit as well as better. Tush, man, mortal men,   55
mortal men.

WESTMORELAND Ay, but Sir John, methinks they are exceeding poor
and bare, too beggarly.

FALSTAFF Faith, for their poverty I know not where they had that. And
for their bareness I am sure they never learned that of me.   60

PRINCE No, I'll be sworn, unless you call three fingers in the ribs bare.
But sirrah, make haste. Percy is already in the field.   *Exit*

FALSTAFF What, is the King encamped?

WESTMORELAND He is, Sir John, I fear we shall stay too long.   [*Exit*]

FALSTAFF Well,   65

---

62 SD *Exit*] Qq; *not in* F   64 SD *Exit*] *Capell; not in* QQF   65–7 Well . . . guest] *As verse, Pope; as prose,* QqF

42–3 **What . . . Warwickshire?** Falstaff's question may provoke laughter (has the Prince lost his
way?) and enhance a mood of confusion caused by
the swift, uncertain movement of troops. On the
Prince's plans and journey in relation to Falstaff's,
see 2 and 8 above and nn.

43 **I cry you mercy** I beg your pardon.

47 **must away** must (march) away. The use
of 'away' as a verb-substitute adds urgency, as in
R2 5.1.54, 'With all swift speed you must away to
France'; compare *MV* 3.2.304.

48 **fear** doubt.

48 **vigilant** wakeful and watchful.

49–50 **made thee butter** (1) made butter for
you (out of cream), (2) made you fat. Compare the
melting of butter at 2.4.102–4 and n., and the turning of a bottle into 'angels', 6–8 above. The Prince
may hint that Falstaff functions as and looks like
a churn.

54 **toss** toss on a pike.

54 **food for powder** cannon fodder, something
for the enemy to shoot at.

55 **pit** mass grave on a battlefield.

60 **bareness** Falstaff ignores many possible
meanings of 'bare', 58 (uncovered, threadbare,
destitute, unarmed). He echoes instead the sense
of Hal's earlier joke ('Here comes lean Jack, here
comes bare-bone', 2.4.270).

61 **three fingers** A measure of how fat Falstaff
is. A finger is three-quarters of an inch, or a little
less than 2 centimetres.

64 SD, 67 SD *Exit* Q gives *Exeunt* at the end of
the scene. Falstaff's final speech, however, stands
independent of Westmoreland's and has the qualities of a terminal soliloquy.

65–7 **Well . . . guest** Verse presents more graph-
ically the oppositions included in this proverbial
saying (Dent C547).

To the latter end of a fray, and the beginning of a feast
Fits a dull fighter and a keen guest.   [*Exit*]

[4.3] *Enter* HOTSPUR, WORCESTER, DOUGLAS, [*and*] VERNON

HOTSPUR We'll fight with him tonight.
WORCESTER   It may not be.
DOUGLAS You give him then advantage.
VERNON   Not a whit.
HOTSPUR Why say you so, looks he not for supply?
VERNON So do we.
HOTSPUR   His is certain, ours is doubtful.
WORCESTER Good cousin, be advised, stir not tonight.   5
VERNON Do not, my lord.
DOUGLAS   You do not counsel well.
        You speak it out of fear and cold heart.
VERNON Do me no slander, Douglas. By my life,
        And I dare well maintain it with my life,
        If well-respected honour bid me on,   10
        I hold as little counsel with weak fear
        As you, my lord, or any Scot that this day lives.
        Let it be seen tomorrow in the battle
        Which of us fears.
DOUGLAS   Yea, or tonight.
VERNON   Content.
HOTSPUR Tonight, say I.   15
VERNON Come, come, it may not be. I wonder much,
        Being men of such great leading as you are,
        That you foresee not what impediments

---

67 SD *Exit*] Capell; *Exeunt* QQF   **Act 4, Scene 3   4.3**] *Scæna Tertia*. F; *not in* Qq   0 SD DOUGLAS, *and*] Qq2–5, F; *Doug*:
Q1   **13–14** Let . . . battle / Which . . . fears] F; *as one line* Qq   **16–17** Come . . . much / Being . . . are] As. T. Johnson,
Pope; Come . . . be. / I . . . are QQF *subst*.

Act 4, Scene 3
[4.3] The unlocalised stage makes possible a
rapid juxtaposition of Falstaff's preparations for
battle with those of the rebels.
    1 him the King, whose forces have arrived. In
Holinshed's account, his speed takes the Percys by
surprise, distracting them from a planned attack
on Shrewsbury and compelling Hotspur to exhort
his forces to prepare for battle (III, 24). Compare

Daniel, *Civile Wars*, III, st. 99–100.
    2 then i.e. if you don't fight him tonight. Dou-
glas agrees with Hotspur.
    3 supply reinforcements.
    10 well-respected well-considered (*OED*
Respect sv *v* 2).
    11 hold . . . with am as little moved by.
    17 leading experience in military command.

    Drag back our expedition. Certain horse
    Of my cousin Vernon's are not yet come up,   20
    Your uncle Worcester's horse came but today,
    And now their pride and mettle is asleep,
    Their courage with hard labour tame and dull,
    That not a horse is half the half of himself.

HOTSPUR So are the horses of the enemy   25
    In general journey-bated and brought low.
    The better part of ours are full of rest.

WORCESTER The number of the King exceedeth ours.
    For God's sake, cousin, stay till all come in.

The trumpet sounds a parley

Enter SIR WALTER BLUNT

BLUNT I come with gracious offers from the King,   30
    If you vouchsafe me hearing and respect.

HOTSPUR Welcome, Sir Walter Blunt: and would to God
    You were of our determination!
    Some of us love you well, and even those some
    Envy your great deservings and good name,   35
    Because you are not of our quality,
    But stand against us like an enemy.

BLUNT And God defend but still I should stand so,
    So long as out of limit and true rule
    You stand against anointed majesty.   40
    But to my charge. The King hath sent to know

---

21 horse] Q5, F; horses Qq1–4   28 ours] F; our Qq1–5

19 horse companies of cavalry.

22 pride and mettle natural spirit; the terms are synonyms.

26 journey-bated exhausted or 'abated' by their journey.

29 SD. 1 parley a trumpet-call offstage to announce that the other side desires a conference.

29 SD. 2 BLUNT Shakespeare builds up the role of Blunt, respected by the rebels as well as by the King. See Margaret B. Bryan, ' "Sir Walter Blunt: There's honor for you" ', *SQ* 26 (1975), 292–8. In Holinshed, the Abbot of Shrewsbury and a clerk of the privy seal carry the King's offer of pardon (III, 25).

31 respect consideration. See 10 above.

33 determination settled purpose or resolve (*OED* 10).

34 those some those persons.

35 Envy Begrudge.

36 quality party or side (*OED* sv *sb* 5c).

38 defend but still I should prevent my ever failing to.

39 out of limit beyond a limit or boundary, as in 5.4.89: 'A kingdom for it was too small a bound.' Blunt means that the rebels are not behaving as obedient subjects; they are 'out of place'.

39 true rule (1) the established political order, (2) the legitimate authority of the King.

41–2 The King . . . griefs That the King already knows the grievances proclaimed by the rebels becomes clear at 5.1.72–3. In Holinshed, he reads a final set of rebel 'articles' the day before his offer of pardon, which he makes only once (III, 25). Compare 4.1.40–1 and n. for his earlier responses to the rebels.

The nature of your griefs, and whereupon
You conjure from the breast of civil peace
Such bold hostility, teaching his duteous land
Audacious cruelty. If that the King   45
Have any way your good deserts forgot,
Which he confesseth to be manifold,
He bids you name your griefs, and with all speed
You shall have your desires with interest
And pardon absolute for yourself, and these   50
Herein misled by your suggestion.

HOTSPUR The King is kind, and well we know the King
Knows at what time to promise, when to pay.
My father, and my uncle, and myself
Did give him that same royalty he wears,   55
And when he was not six-and-twenty strong,
Sick in the world's regard, wretched and low,
A poor unminded outlaw sneaking home,
My father gave him welcome to the shore.
And when he heard him swear and vow to God   60
He came but to be Duke of Lancaster,
To sue his livery, and beg his peace
With tears of innocency and terms of zeal,
My father, in kind heart and pity moved,
Swore him assistance, and performed it too.   65

---

42 whereupon on what ground.

43 conjure summon up.

45 Audacious Probably daring, but also shameless. Blunt's language begins to resemble the King's weighty and latinate idiom.

45 If that If.

51 suggestion sinister instigation or temptation.

54–105 My father . . . continuance Hotspur requires 52 lines to express his 'griefs', punctuated with one short, almost rude, interruption by Blunt. Hotspur's survey of recent history may be compared with the representation of events in *R2*. Only his final 13 lines focus on those in *1H4*. Blunt's interruption, 89, implies that the methods by which the King gained power are now beside the point. On the subjective interpretation of their past by different characters, see Introduction, p. 8.

56 six-and-twenty strong Holinshed, II, 853, says 'not past three score persons'. But in *R2*, Northumberland shares intelligence that Bulling-

brook is approaching with 8 noblemen and 3,000 men of war (2.1.279–88).

58 unminded disregarded. In *R2*, several lords eagerly rush to support Bullingbrook (2.2.53–5).

59–61 My father . . . Lancaster In *R2*, Northumberland assists and flatters Bullingbrook before acting as his spokesman. He then uses this vow as a means of reassuring York and King Richard (*R2*. 2.3.148–51; 3.3.105–13). Holinshed describes the oath sworn by Bullingbrook at Doncaster at II, 853.

62 sue his livery make legal suit in the Court of Wards for his dukedom, which had reverted to King Richard upon the death of Bullingbrook's father, John of Gaunt.

62 beg his peace seek reconciliation with the King by confirming mutual obligations (*OED* Peace sv *sb* 1c, cited by Humphreys). In *R2*, York accuses Richard of injustice, both in denying Bullingbrook the right to sue his livery and in repudiating his proffered homage (2.1.201–4).

63 terms of zeal professions of allegiance.

Now, when the lords and barons of the realm
Perceived Northumberland did lean to him,
The more and less came in with cap and knee,
Met him in boroughs, cities, villages,
Attended him on bridges, stood in lanes,   70
Laid gifts before him, proffered him their oaths,
Gave him their heirs as pages, followed him
Even at the heels in golden multitudes.
He presently, as greatness knows itself,
Steps me a little higher than his vow   75
Made to my father while his blood was poor
Upon the naked shore at Ravenspurgh;
And now forsooth takes on him to reform
Some certain edicts and some strait decrees
That lie too heavy on the commonwealth,   80
Cries out upon abuses, seems to weep
Over his country's wrongs – and by this face,
This seeming brow of justice, did he win
The hearts of all that he did angle for.
Proceeded further – cut me off the heads   85
Of all the favourites that the absent King
In deputation left behind him here,
When he was personal in the Irish war.

72 heirs as pages, followed] F4 (Heires, as Pages, followed), *conj. Malone;* heires, as Pages followed QqF *subst.;* heires, as Pagesfollowed Q1 *uncorr. Huntington Library copy*   79 strait] Q1 (streight)   82 country's] *Rowe;* Countrey Q1

68 The more . . . knee Both higher and lower social orders conventionally offered allegiance with hat (or cap) in hand, bending their knees. That Bullingbrook received nearly universal support is emphasised in *R2* 3.2.112–20. The emphasis on 'more and less' seems to eliminate here any class distinction between those who wore hats and those who wore caps.

70 Attended Waited for.

70 lanes files or rows.

72 Gave . . . pages Bevington follows Wilson in arguing that the pages serve as hostages to secure their fathers' loyalty. But the practice of placing children in affiliated households was widespread throughout the middle ages and early renaissance. Here it is meant to indicate the confidence, since lost, of the fathers in Bullingbrook's integrity. Malone's emendation, moving the comma which follows 'heirs' in QqF to follow 'pages', has been widely accepted.

73 golden (1) triumphant, (2) resplendent.

74 as . . . itself i.e. as he realises how to use the power he has acquired. Hotspur's explanation

of how Bullingbrook's ambition escalated may be compared with those of Worcester, 5.1.48 ff., and of the King in *2H4* 4.5.183–5.

75 his vow his promise to seek no more than his inheritance, 60–2 above.

76 his . . . poor (1) his temper was humble, (2) his nature was not royal.

78–80 takes . . . commonwealth Mentioned in Holinshed II, 853, but omitted in *R2*. By claiming to protect the commonwealth, feudal rebels tried to avoid seeming to attack its ruler.

79 strait harsh.

82–3 this face . . . justice Synonyms for hypocrisy.

85–6 cut . . . favourites In *R2* Northumberland silently and willingly carries out Bullingbrook's order to kill the 'favourites' (3.1.35).

87 In deputation As his deputies. King Richard had 'deputed' Bullingbrook's uncle York as lord governor (2.1.220) while Worcester served as steward of the household.

88 was personal in went in person to.

BLUNT Tut, I came not to hear this.

HOTSPUR   Then to the point.
  In short time after he deposed the King,   90
  Soon after that deprived him of his life,
  And in the neck of that tasked the whole state.
  To make that worse, suffered his kinsman March –
  Who is, if every owner were well placed,
  Indeed his King – to be engaged in Wales,   95
  There without ransom to lie forfeited.
  Disgraced me in my happy victories,
  Sought to entrap me by intelligence,
  Rated mine uncle from the Council-board,
  In rage dismissed my father from the court,   100
  Broke oath on oath, committed wrong on wrong,
  And in conclusion drove us to seek out
  This head of safety, and withal to pry
  Into his title, the which we find
  Too indirect for long continuance.   105

BLUNT Shall I return this answer to the King?

HOTSPUR Not so, Sir Walter. We'll withdraw a while.
  Go to the King, and let there be impawned
  Some surety for a safe return again,
  And in the morning early shall mine uncle   110
  Bring him our purposes – and so, farewell.

BLUNT I would you would accept of grace and love.

HOTSPUR And may be so we shall.

BLUNT   Pray God you do.

        [*Exeunt*]

---

113 SD *Exeunt*] F; *not in* Qq

90–1 In . . . life A swift summation of a crisis, dramatised in the final two acts in *R2*. Henry's responsibility for Richard's murder was indirect; compare *R2* 5.4.1–11, 5.6.30–52.

92 in the neck of immediately after.

92 tasked taxed, technically the term for a levy of a 'fifteenth', authorised by the Magna Carta (Humphreys).

93–5 suffered . . . Wales Even Holinshed does not suggest that Henry sent Mortimer to Wales to get rid of him. For Shakespeare's re-fashioning of his source and, consequently, of the King's motivation, see Appendix, pp. 231–2.

94 owner . . . placed i.e. if those entitled to positions always held them.

95 engaged held as hostage. Compare 'impawned' 108 below.

96 lie forfeited remain unreclaimed like a pawned article that has not been redeemed.

98 intelligence The use of spies. 'Perhaps the popinjay (1.3.49 ff.) is meant' (Wilson).

99 Rated Dismissed by berating, recalling the treatment of Worcester, 1.3.14–20.

103 head of safety army for self-defence.

103 withal in addition.

105 indirect (1) acquired by devious means, (2) not in the direct line of succession.

108 impawned pledged as security. Westmoreland will be so 'engaged' (5.2.43).

111 purposes proposals.

113 And . . . shall According to Holinshed, Hotspur 'began to give eare unto the kings offers' (III, 25).

[4.4] *Enter* [*the*] ARCHBISHOP OF YORK [*and*] SIR MICHAEL

ARCHBISHOP Hie, good Sir Michael, bear this sealèd brief
            With wingèd haste to the Lord Marshal,
            This to my cousin Scroop, and all the rest
            To whom they are directed. If you knew
            How much they do import, you would make haste.   5
SIR MICHAEL My good lord,
            I guess their tenor.
ARCHBISHOP   Like enough you do.
            Tomorrow, good Sir Michael, is a day
            Wherein the fortune of ten thousand men
            Must bide the touch. For, sir, at Shrewsbury,   10
            As I am truly given to understand,
            The King with mighty and quick-raisèd power
            Meets with Lord Harry, and I fear, Sir Michael,
            What with the sickness of Northumberland,
            Whose power was in the first proportion,   15
            And what with Owen Glendower's absence thence,
            Who with them was a rated sinew too,
            And comes not in, o'er-ruled by prophecies,
            I fear the power of Percy is too weak
            To wage an instant trial with the King.   20
SIR MICHAEL Why, my good lord, you need not fear,
            There is Douglas, and Lord Mortimer.

Act 4, Scene 4   4.4] *Scena Quarta.* F; *not in* Qq   0 SD *the* | F; *not in* Qq   0 SD *and* | Qq2–5, F; *not in* Q1   0 SD MICHAEL |
Q1 (Mighell) (*and through the scene*)   6–7 My ... do | *As Var. 1773;* My ... tenor / Arch. Like ... do QqF *subst.*

Act 4, Scene 4
    [4.4] Often cut in performance, this brief scene anticipates the continuation of the rebellion in *2H4*. In the Elizabethan theatre, its location need not be fixed, but it is clearly set some distance from the battleground.
    0 SD ARCHBISHOP OF YORK See List of Characters.
    0 SD SIR MICHAEL A member of the Archbishop's household, possibly a knight or priest, who serves as a messenger; he is not a historical figure.
    1 **brief** letter, dispatch (*OED* sv *sb* 4a, citing this line).
    2 **Lord Marshal** Thomas Mowbray, Duke of Norfolk, a leader of the rebels in *2H4*.
    3 **my cousin Scroop** Possibly (1) Sir Stephen Scroop who tells King Richard that his brother

William, the Earl of Wiltshire, has been executed, *R2* 3.2.141–2, or (2) his son Sir Henry, a traitor in *H5* 2.2. On the Archbishop's motives for opposing the King, see 1.3.264–5 and n.
    7 **tenor** drift, general meaning.
    10 **bide the touch** be put to the test, as gold is tested with a touchstone (*OED* sv *sb* 5a).
    15 **in the first proportion** 'the largest of all' (Wilson).
    17 **rated sinew** reckoned to be a mainstay (*OED* Sinew sv *sb* 4).
    18 **o'er-ruled by prophecies** This new motive for Glendower's absence (compare 4.1.126) was invented by Shakespeare. According to Holinshed, Glendower was absent from Shrewsbury, but Welsh fighters did assist the Percys. Daniel says there were no Welshmen present.

ARCHBISHOP No, Mortimer is not there.

SIR MICHAEL But there is Mordake, Vernon, Lord Harry Percy,
     And there is my Lord of Worcester, and a head   25
     Of gallant warriors, noble gentlemen.

ARCHBISHOP And so there is. But yet the King hath drawn
     The special head of all the land together.
     The Prince of Wales, Lord John of Lancaster,
     The noble Westmoreland, and warlike Blunt,   30
     And many more corrivals and dear men
     Of estimation and command in arms.

SIR MICHAEL Doubt not, my lord, they shall be well opposed.

ARCHBISHOP I hope no less, yet needful 'tis to fear,
     And to prevent the worst, Sir Michael, speed.   35
     For if Lord Percy thrive not, ere the King
     Dismiss his power he means to visit us,
     For he hath heard of our confederacy,
     And 'tis but wisdom to make strong against him.
     Therefore make haste – I must go write again   40
     To other friends. And so, farewell, Sir Michael.

                                Exeunt

[**5.1**] *Enter the* KING, PRINCE OF WALES, LORD JOHN OF LANCASTER, SIR WALTER BLUNT, [*and*] FALSTAFF

KING How bloodily the sun begins to peer
     Above yon bulky hill. The day looks pale

---

31 more] QqF *subst.* (mo)   36 not,] Qq2, 3, F; not Qq1, 4, 5   **Act 5, Scene 1**   5.1] *Actus Quintus. Scena Prima.* F; *not in* Qq   0 SD.1–2 LANCASTER, SIR] *Hanmer; Lancaster, Earle of Westmerland, Sir* QqF   0 SD.2 and] Qq2–5, F; *not in* Q1   2 bulky] Q1; busky Qq2–5, F, *Wilson*

28 special head pre-eminent warriors.

31 more Arguments for QqF 'mo' as meaning 'number' while 'more' means 'quantity' rest on an unconvincing distinction. Bevington points out that Shakespeare uses 'more' sixty-one times in *1H4*.

31 corrivals associates.

31 dear worthy, honourable.

32 estimation value.

35 prevent forestall.

37 he means . . . us This prediction is confirmed at 5.5.34–8.

Act 5, Scene 1

[**5.1**] The action in this and the following scenes moves through the battlefield at Shrewsbury.

These scenes rely on a combination of intimate dialogue and violent combat to suggest the battle between large forces. The King's party, in contrast to 1.1 and 1.3, now includes the Prince and Falstaff.

1 How . . . peer A red morning proverbially promises bad weather.

2 bulky large, looming. Humphreys points out that a great 'hump-like mound' represents 'Wrekin hill' on Saxton's 1577 map of Shropshire. Compare 'gross as a mountain', 2.4.189–90. The 'l' of 'bulky' in Q1, although erased at the top, is clearly distinct from the thicker 'ʃ' character. 'Busky' (bosky), meaning 'bushy', (illustrated by *OED*, using this reference), preferred by Wilson and Bevington, is a picturesque, less weighty term.

> At his distemperature.
> PRINCE   The southern wind
> Doth play the trumpet to his purposes,
> And by his hollow whistling in the leaves   5
> Foretells a tempest and a blust'ring day.
> KING   Then with the losers let it sympathise,
> For nothing can seem foul to those that win.
>   *The trumpet sounds*
>
>   *Enter* WORCESTER [*and* VERNON]
>
> How now, my Lord of Worcester! 'Tis not well
> That you and I should meet upon such terms   10
> As now we meet. You have deceived our trust,
> And made us doff our easy robes of peace
> To crush our old limbs in ungentle steel.
> This is not well, my lord, this is not well.
> What say you to it? Will you again unknit   15
> The churlish knot of all-abhorrèd war,
> And move in that obedient orb again
> Where you did give a fair and natural light,
> And be no more an exhal'd meteor,
> A prodigy of fear, and a portent   20

8 SD.2 *and* VERNON] *Theobald; not in* QqF

3 **his distemperature** the physical disorder of the sun. The King's use of personification to suggest that earth and sky may mirror political disorder, as at 7 below, recalls his speech opening the play.

4 **Doth . . . purposes** Like a herald, announces the intentions of the sun.

8 **nothing . . . win** An echo of the proverb, 'He laughs that wins' (Dent I.93).

8 SD.2 *and* VERNON Although he neither speaks nor is spoken to (or even mentioned) in this scene, Vernon's presence here, made probable by his argument with Worcester, 5.2.1–27, is confirmed by his report of the Prince's challenge, 5.2.51–68. Most editors follow Theobald by adding his entry at this point.

12 **easy** comfortable.

13 **crush . . . steel** An implicit stage direction, indicating that all the King's party and their opponents probably now wear armour. In actual history, the King in 1403 was only thirty-six years old. Compare Marlowe, *Edward II*, where an acceleration of the King's age is made to suggest drastic personal and political disruption.

17–18 **And . . . light** An analogy to the Ptolemaic cosmos – stars and planets revolving in fixed orbits or spheres around the earth, the centre of the cosmic system – is used to define the obedience of a mighty subject to the King. Compare *Tro.* 1.3.89–94, where 'the glorious planet Sol / In noble eminence enthron'd and spher'd' is imagined to correct and control the other planets.

19 **exhal'd meteor** An omen or portent, as at 1.1.10 and 3.1.11–15; 'exhal'd' can suggest: (1) the process of the sun's heat drawing a vapour out of the earth and turning it into a meteor, (2) being dragged out or away, i.e. from a proper celestial orbit (*OED* sv v^2), (3) being breathed out or extruded by the earth, anticipating the latent birth metaphors in 'prodigy' and 'broachèd . . . unborn', 20 and 21 below (*OED* sv v^1 5). Compare Bardolph's similar pairing of these terms at 2.4.263–4 (the only other such pairing in *1 H4*) and Hotspur's explanation of earthquakes, 3.1.24–30.

20 **prodigy of fear** omen of evil, synonymous with 'portent', but also a monster or freak of nature (*OED* 2b). Compare *R2* 2.2.64, 'Now hath my soul brought forth her prodigy.'

Of brochèd mischief to the unborn times?
WORCESTER Hear me, my liege.
　　　　For mine own part I could be well content
　　　　To entertain the lag end of my life
　　　　With quiet hours. For I protest   25
　　　　I have not sought the day of this dislike.
KING You have not sought it? How comes it, then?
FALSTAFF Rebellion lay in his way, and he found it.
PRINCE Peace, chewet, peace!
WORCESTER It pleased your majesty to turn your looks   30
　　　　Of favour from myself, and all our house,
　　　　And yet I must remember you, my lord,
　　　　We were the first and dearest of your friends.
　　　　For you my staff of office did I break
　　　　In Richard's time, and posted day and night   35
　　　　To meet you on the way, and kiss your hand,
　　　　When yet you were in place and in account
　　　　Nothing so strong and fortunate as I.
　　　　It was myself, my brother, and his son,
　　　　That brought you home, and boldly did outdare   40
　　　　The dangers of the time. You swore to us,
　　　　And you did swear that oath at Doncaster,
　　　　That you did nothing purpose 'gainst the state,
　　　　Nor claim no further than your new-fallen right,
　　　　The seat of Gaunt, dukedom of Lancaster.   45
　　　　To this we swore our aid. But in short space
　　　　It rained down fortune showering on your head,
　　　　And such a flood of greatness fell on you,

---

21 **brochèd ... times** a calamity released, as by piercing a cask (*OED* Broach *v*¹ 4).

21 **mischief** evil plight, calamity.

24 **entertain** occupy, while away; compare *The Rape of Lucrece* 1361: 'The weary time she cannot entertain.'

29 **chewet** A pun on (1) chough or jackdaw (i.e. a chattering bird), (2) minced-meat pie. Hal's tone may express some pleasure in Falstaff's put-down of Worcester or it may show annoyance at his intrusion. A comparable interruption by Enobarbus (*Ant.* 2.2.103–6) provokes irritation onstage, but laughter followed by some discomfort in the audience.

32–71 **And ... enterprise** Worcester's memory of events in which he was more active than Hotspur can be compared with Hotspur's account

(4.3.54–105), with pertinent scenes in *R2*, and with the versions of Daniel and the chroniclers.

32 **remember** remind.

34–5 **For you ... time** Mentioned by Holinshed (II, 855), and emphasised in *R2* 2.2.58–9 and 2.3.26–8.

35 **posted** travelled in haste, possibly with relays of horses.

38 **Nothing** Nowhere near (adverb).

42 **that oath** Compare 4.3.62 and note. The articles sent by the Percys to the King at Shrewsbury charged him with 'manifest perjurie' in violating this vow (Holinshed, III, 25).

44 **new-fallen right** Inheritance through the recent death of his father, John of Gaunt.

45 **seat** estate.

What with our help, what with the absent King,
What with the injuries of a wanton time,   50
The seeming sufferances that you had borne,
And the contrarious winds that held the King
So long in his unlucky Irish wars
That all in England did repute him dead.
And from this swarm of fair advantages   55
You took occasion to be quickly wooed
To gripe the general sway into your hand,
Forgot your oath to us at Doncaster,
And being fed by us, you used us so
As that ungentle gull the cuckoo's bird   60
Useth the sparrow – did oppress our nest,
Grew by our feeding to so great a bulk
That even our love durst not come near your sight
For fear of swallowing. But with nimble wing
We were enforced for safety's sake to fly   65
Out of your sight, and raise this present head,
Whereby we stand opposèd, by such means
As you yourself have forged against yourself,
By unkind usage, dangerous countenance,
And violation of all faith and troth   70
Sworn to us in your younger enterprise.
KING   These things indeed you have articulate,
Proclaimed at market crosses, read in churches,
To face the garment of rebellion

---

65 safety's] QqF (safety)   72 articulate] Qq; articulated F

50 **injuries** abuses.
50 **wanton** anarchic, badly managed.
51 **sufferances** wrongs.
56 **occasion** opportunity.
60–4 **ungentle . . . swallowing** The cuckoo lays its eggs in the nests of other smaller birds; when hatched, the aggressive and ungrateful young cuckoo crowds out or even eats up the host family. Compare *Lear* 1.4.215–16.
60 **ungentle . . . bird** i.e. that rough nestling, the cuckoo's offspring. Both 'gull' (*OED* sv *sb*², citing this passage) and 'bird' (*OED* sv *sb* 1a) refer to unfledged or very young birds.
64 **swallowing** being swallowed.
65–8 **to fly . . . against yourself** Most editions omit Q's comma after 'means', 67. The addition of a comma after 'opposèd' clarifies the passage in

linking 'by such means' to 'fly' and 'raise', thus emphasising that the Percys are not merely provoked by the King; they have been driven to use his own methods.
69 **unkind** (1) 'ungentle' (60), (2) unfamilial or unnatural.
69 **dangerous countenance** menacing attitude and appearance. Worcester returns the King's charge against him at 1.3.18.
70 **troth** vow or plighted word.
71 **younger** earlier, referring to his initial claim, 44.
72 **articulate** set forth, item by item, in articles.
74 **face** trim or decorate to disguise the nature of the 'garment' underneath. Compare 'velvet-guards', 3.1.249.

With some fine colour that may please the eye   75
Of fickle changelings and poor discontents,
Which gape and rub the elbow at the news
Of hurly-burly innovation.
And never yet did insurrection want
Such water-colours to impaint his cause,   80
Nor moody beggars starving for a time
Of pell-mell havoc and confusion.

PRINCE In both your armies there is many a soul
Shall pay full dearly for this encounter
If once they join in trial. Tell your nephew,   85
The Prince of Wales doth join with all the world
In praise of Henry Percy. By my hopes,
This present enterprise set off his head,
I do not think a braver gentleman,
More active-valiant or more valiant-young,   90
More daring or more bold, is now alive
To grace this latter age with noble deeds.
For my part, I may speak it to my shame,
I have a truant been to chivalry,
And so I hear he doth account me too.   95
Yet this before my father's majesty –
I am content that he shall take the odds
Of his great name and estimation,
And will, to save the blood on either side,
Try fortune with him in a single fight.   100

83 your] Qq; our F   88 off] F; of Qq   90 active-valiant . . . valiant-young] *Theobald;* active, valiant . . . valiant yong QqF *subst.*

75 colour A quibble on (1) outward pretence, (2) the literal colour of the fabric used as trim.

76 fickle changelings and poor discontents unpredictable persons inclined to change their masters or abandon their lords and leaders.

77 gape gaze foolishly, with open mouth.

77 rub the elbow 'hug themselves (with pleasure), arms crossed and hands on elbows. Joy supposedly made the elbows itch' (Humphreys).

78 hurly-burly innovation violent commotion and change, 'turning the world upside down'.

79 want lack.

80 water-colours i.e. deceptions. Like thin or cheap paints, they hide nothing from judicious observers and are easily washed off.

81 moody sullen.

81–2 beggars . . . confusion The 'changelings'

and 'discontents' (76) have come down in the world. Compare their alleged hunger for an insurrection which will feed them with Falstaff's enthusiasm for war, 3.3.157–9.

82 havoc general devastation, originally from the military order to pillage or plunder (*OED* sv *sb* 1).

83–100 In . . . fight This chivalric speech ending in a challenge seems to be Shakespeare's invention, perhaps suggested partly by Hotspur's speech in Daniel, III, st. 101–2. See Introduction, p. 17.

83 your i.e. the King's and the rebels'. Some editions adopt 'our' from F.

88 set off his head not counted against him. Compare 3.2.132.

92 latter later, more recent.

KING And, Prince of Wales, so dare we venture thee,
    Albeit considerations infinite
    Do make against it. No, good Worcester, no,
    We love our people well, even those we love
    That are misled upon your cousin's part,   105
    And will they take the offer of our grace,
    Both he, and they, and you, yea, every man
    Shall be my friend again, and I'll be his.
    So tell your cousin, and bring me word
    What he will do. But if he will not yield,   110
    Rebuke and dread correction wait on us,
    And they shall do their office. So, be gone.
    We will not now be troubled with reply.
    We offer fair, take it advisedly.
           Exeunt Worcester [and Vernon]

PRINCE It will not be accepted, on my life.   115
    The Douglas and the Hotspur both together
    Are confident against the world in arms.
KING Hence, therefore, every leader to his charge,
    For on their answer will we set on them,
    And God befriend us as our cause is just!   120
           Exeunt; the Prince and Falstaff remain

FALSTAFF Hal, if thou see me down in the battle and bestride me so, 'tis
    a point of friendship.
PRINCE Nothing but a Colossus can do thee that friendship.
    Say thy prayers, and farewell.
FALSTAFF I would 'twere bed-time, Hal, and all well.   125

---

114 SD *and Vernon*] *Theobald subst.; not in* QqF   120 SD *the Prince and Falstaff remain*] QqF *subst.* (*manent Prince, Falst.*)   121–4 Hal . . . farewell] *As prose,* Pope; *as verse,* Hal . . . battel / And . . . friendship. / Prin. Nothing . . . friendship, / Say . . . farewell QqF *subst.*

102 **Albeit** Although. Compare 1.3.126 and n.
105 **cousin** kinsman, meaning his nephew, Hotspur.
106 **grace** pardon.
111 **wait on us** attend me, await my (royal) command.
112–14 **So . . . advisedly** The King briefly combines royal dignity and generosity with an assertion of power and, perhaps informally, a threat: 'If you know what's good for you, take my offer.'
119 **on their answer** i.e. 'as soon as they refuse', almost certainly not 'whatever they reply'. The King's conciliatory language and twice-proffered pardon to the rebels make his desire here for peace seem unequivocal. Some recent produc-

tions, however, treat this line as evidence of bad faith.
121 **bestride me** stand over me in order to protect me. Compare *Err.* 5.1.191–2: 'the service that long since I did thee, / When I bestrid thee in the wars'.
123 **Colossus** A giant or a gigantic statue of a man. The statue of Apollo at Rhodes, one of the seven wonders of the ancient world, was reputed to have stood astride the harbour entrance.
125 **bed-time** An exceptionally simple and straightforward moment. Falstaff, in response to 'Say thy prayers', here speaks as if he were still a small child.

PRINCE Why, thou owest God a death.   [*Exit*]

FALSTAFF 'Tis not due yet – I would be loath to pay him before his day.
What need I be so forward with him that calls not on me? Well, 'tis
no matter, honour pricks me on. Yea, but how if honour prick me
off when I come on, how then? Can honour set to a leg? No. Or an   130
arm? No. Or take away the grief of a wound? No. Honour hath no
skill in surgery then? No. What is honour? A word. What is in that
word honour? What is that honour? Air. A trim reckoning! Who
hath it? He that died a' Wednesday. Doth he feel it? No. Doth he
hear it? No. 'Tis insensible, then? Yea, to the dead. But will it not   135
live with the living? No. Why? Detraction will not suffer it. Therefore I'll none of it. Honour is a mere scutcheon – and so ends my
catechism.   *Exit*

[**5.2**] *Enter* WORCESTER, [*and*] SIR RICHARD VERNON

WORCESTER O no, my nephew must not know, Sir Richard,
     The liberal and kind offer of the King.

VERNON 'Twere best he did.

WORCESTER   Then are we all undone.
     It is not possible, it cannot be,

---

126 SD *Exit*] *Hanmer; not in* QqF   129 Yea, but] Qq; But F   130 then? Can] Qq2, 3, F; then can Qq1,4,5   135 will it]
Qq2–5, F; wil Q1   Act 5, Scene 2   5.2] *Scena Secunda*. F; *not in* Qq   0 SD *and*] Qq2–5, F; *not in* Q1   3 undone] Q5, F;
under one Qq1–4

126 **thou . . . a death** Proverbial saying (Dent
G237), with a quibble on 'debt'.

126 SD *Exit* QqF provide no exit for the Prince.
After his 'farewell', 124, Hal is in a hurry to be
off; clearly, by 128 Falstaff is talking to himself
and to the theatre audience. The opening lines of
his soliloquy might be addressed to the departing
Prince.

129 **pricks me on** spurs me on.

129–30 **prick me off** mark me down for death.
Falstaff's pun refers to the practice of making
holes as marks on a list of names. Compare *JC*
4.1.1: 'These many then, shall die; their names are
prick'd.' In *2H4* 3.2.110–78, the repeated 'prick-
ing' of recruits turns into farce.

130 **set to a leg** set a broken or disjointed leg.

131 **grief** pain.

133 **trim reckoning** fine account (ironic).

135 **insensible** not perceptible to the senses
(and perhaps senseless).

136 **Detraction** Slander.

136 **suffer** permit.

137 **scutcheon** The most humble of heraldic
devices, a tablet or canvas panel representing a
coat of arms which could be carried in a funeral
procession or hung in a church to honour the dead.
It is comparable to the 'hatchment' mentioned by
Laertes in *Ham.* 4.5.215: 'No trophy, sword, nor
hatchment o'er his bones'.

138 **catechism** A common method of religious
instruction which uses an established question-
and-answer format.

Act 5, Scene 2

1–2 **O . . . King** Worcester's treachery is based
on Holinshed (III, 25), but Shakespeare invents his
motives and self-justification, 4–25 below.

3 **undone** ruined. This Q5, F reading has been
widely accepted. Wilson follows Pollard in suggesting that Shakespeare may have written 'und
one', which the Q printer mistakenly 'corrected'.

The King should keep his word in loving us.   5
He will suspect us still, and find a time
To punish this offence in other faults.
Supposition all our lives shall be stuck full of eyes,
For treason is but trusted like the fox,
Who, never so tame, so cherished and locked up,   10
Will have a wild trick of his ancestors.
Look how we can, or sad or merrily,
Interpretation will misquote our looks,
And we shall feed like oxen at a stall,
The better cherished still the nearer death.   15
My nephew's trespass may be well forgot,
It hath the excuse of youth and heat of blood,
And an adopted name of privilege –
A hare-brained Hotspur, governed by a spleen.
All his offences live upon my head   20
And on his father's. We did train him on,
And, his corruption being ta'en from us,
We as the spring of all shall pay for all.
Therefore, good cousin, let not Harry know
In any case the offer of the King.   25

Enter [HOTSPUR *and* DOUGLAS]

VERNON Deliver what you will; I'll say 'tis so.
        Here comes your cousin.
HOTSPUR   My uncle is returned;

---

8 Supposition] QqF; Suspicion *Rowe, Bevington*   12 merrily] Q1 (merely)   25 SD *Enter* HOTSPUR *and* DOUGLAS]
Rowe (after cousin *line 27); Enter Percy* Q1; *Enter Hotspurre* F (*after* Cosin *line 27*)

6 still always.
7 in when he punishes.
8 Supposition Following Rowe, many editors have emended the QqF reading to 'Suspicion'; the line will be hypermetric in either case. 'Supposition' is more consistent with Worcester's own readiness to formulate the mistaken thoughts and inferences of others at 1.3.281 and 4.1.62–75.
8 stuck full of eyes The notion of an allegorical figure 'full of eyes' probably derives from the 'Fama' (Rumour) of Virgil's *Aeneid* (IV. 181–3), a monster covered with as many eyes, tongues, mouths, and ears as she has feathers. Gibbons comments on *MM* 4.1.56 'millions of false eyes' that they suggest 'artificial eyes on the robes of a pageant or emblem figure'.

10 never so no matter how.
11 trick trait.
12 or ... or whether ... or.
13 misquote misconstrue.
18 an adopted ... privilege a nickname that gives him a special licence.
19 spleen rash impulse. Compare 2.3.72, 3.2.125 and nn.
21 train draw on by art or allure (*OED* sv v^1).
23 spring source.
25 SD Many editors follow F in placing this entrance after 27; directors must decide the exact timing. A larger group of rebels should be onstage for Hotspur's exhortations at 75, 81, and 92 below.

        Deliver up my Lord of Westmoreland.
        Uncle, what news?
WORCESTER The King will bid you battle presently.   30
DOUGLAS Defy him by the Lord of Westmoreland.
HOTSPUR Lord Douglas, go you and tell him so.
DOUGLAS Marry, and shall, and very willingly.   *Exit*
WORCESTER There is no seeming mercy in the King.
HOTSPUR Did you beg any? God forbid!   35
WORCESTER I told him gently of our grievances,
        Of his oath-breaking – which he mended thus,
        By now forswearing that he is forsworn.
        He calls us rebels, traitors, and will scourge
        With haughty arms this hateful name in us.   40

              Enter DOUGLAS

DOUGLAS Arm, gentlemen, to arms! For I have thrown
        A brave defiance in King Henry's teeth,
        And Westmoreland that was engaged did bear it,
        Which cannot choose but bring him quickly on.
WORCESTER The Prince of Wales stepped forth before the King,   45
        And, nephew, challenged you to single fight.
HOTSPUR O, would the quarrel lay upon our heads,
        And that no man might draw short breath today
        But I and Harry Monmouth! Tell me, tell me,
        How showed his tasking? Seemed it in contempt?   50
VERNON No, by my soul, I never in my life
        Did hear a challenge urged more modestly,
        Unless a brother should a brother dare
        To gentle exercise and proof of arms.
        He gave you all the duties of a man,   55
        Trimmed up your praises with a princely tongue,
        Spoke your deservings like a chronicle,

50 tasking] Q1; Talking Qq2–5, F

28 **Deliver . . . Westmoreland** The identity, not heretofore important, of the 'surety' required at 4.3.109.

31 **Defy . . . Westmoreland** i.e. Have Westmoreland carry your defiance to the King.

33 **Marry, and shall** Yes, I will.

34 **no seeming** no appearance of.

38 **forswearing** denying with a false oath.

42 **brave** bold.

43 **engaged** held as hostage.

44 **cannot choose but** must of necessity.

49 **Harry Monmouth** i.e. the Prince of Wales. Monmouth, the Welsh town where the Prince was born, is sometimes used as his name.

52 **urged** proposed.

54 **proof** test or trial.

55 **duties of a man** marks of respect owed to true manhood.

Making you ever better than his praise
By still dispraising praise valued with you,
And, which became him like a prince indeed,   60
He made a blushing cital of himself,
And chid his truant youth with such a grace
As if he mastered there a double spirit
Of teaching and of learning instantly.
There did he pause. But let me tell the world –   65
If he outlive the envy of this day,
England did never owe so sweet a hope
So much misconstrued in his wantonness.

HOTSPUR Cousin, I think thou art enamoured
On his follies! Never did I hear   70
Of any prince so wild a liberty.
But be he as he will, yet once ere night
I will embrace him with a soldier's arm,
That he shall shrink under my courtesy.
Arm, arm with speed! And fellows, soldiers, friends,   75
Better consider what you have to do
Than I that have not well the gift of tongue
Can lift your blood up with persuasion.

Enter a MESSENGER

[FIRST] MESSENGER My lord, here are letters for you.
HOTSPUR I cannot read them now.   80
O gentlemen, the time of life is short!
To spend that shortness basely were too long
If life did ride upon a dial's point,
Still ending at the arrival of an hour.

---

71 a liberty] Qq1–4 (a libertie), at libertie Q5, F *subst.*, a libertine *Capell*   79 SH FIRST | *This edn; not in* QqF

59 dispraising . . . you (1) making you the standard of what is worth praising, (2) valuing you more than words can express.

61 blushing modest (probably not meant literally).

61 cital reproof or impeachment (*OED* 2, this example).

64 instantly simultaneously.

66 envy malice.

67 owe own.

68 wantonness unruliness.

71 liberty lawlessness, licence.

73–4 I will embrace . . . courtesy This

contemptuous response to the Prince's challenge parodies its chivalric, fraternal spirit by promising a brutal encounter.

74 shrink (1) cower, (2) shrivel up.

76–8 Better . . . persuasion i.e. reflect well, yourselves, and you will act better than I, with my weak skills in argument, can persuade you to do by raising your spirits.

82–4 To spend . . . hour i.e. a base life would be too long if it lasted only an hour.

83 If Even if.

83 dial's point the pointed hand of a clock.

And if we live, we live to tread on kings,   85
If die, brave death when princes die with us!
Now, for our consciences, the arms are fair
When the intent of bearing them is just.

Enter another [MESSENGER]

(SECOND) MESSENGER My lord, prepare, the King comes on apace.
HOTSPUR I thank him that he cuts me from my tale,   90
For I profess not talking. Only this –
Let each man do his best. And here draw I
A sword whose temper I intend to stain
With the best blood that I can meet withal
In the adventure of this perilous day.   95
Now, Esperance! Percy! and set on!
Sound all the lofty instruments of war,
And by that music let us all embrace,
For, heaven to earth, some of us never shall
A second time do such a courtesy.   100
Here they embrace, the trumpets sound

                                                    [*Exeunt*]

[5.3] *The* KING *enters with his power. Alarum to the battle. Then enter*
DOUGLAS *and* SIR WALTER BLUNT [*disguised as the King*]

BLUNT What is thy name that in [the] battle thus

---

88 SD MESSENGER] F; *not in* Qq   89 SH SECOND] *Capell; not in* QqF   92–3 Let . . . stain] *As Pope;* Let . . . sword, /
Whose . . . staine QqF   100 SD. 1 *Here . . . sound*] QqF (*not separated from opening* SD *of* 5.3)   100 SD. 2 *Exeunt*] *Rowe; not
in* QqF   Act 5, Scene 3   5.3] *Capell; not in* QqF   0 SD. 2 *disguised as the King*] *Wilson subst.; not in* QqF   1–3 What . . .
head?] *As Hanmer;* What . . . me, / What . . . head? QqF   1 the] *T. Johnson, Hanmer; not in* QqF

87 **for** as regards.
87 **fair** justifiable.
90 **cuts . . . tale** stops me telling my story.
91 **I profess not** I claim no skill at.
93–4 **A sword . . . blood** The idea of augment-
ing the 'temper' or hard metallic composition of a
sword by blood occurs in *Beowulf*, 1460, and is an
epic commonplace.
95 **adventure** chance, but as weighted here
with the sense of a chivalric enterprise, extremely
challenging and hazardous.
96 **Esperance** The Percy battle-cry, meaning
'Hope, my comfort.' Compare 2.3.65 and n.
99 **heaven to earth** i.e. I'll wager heaven
against earth, or 'the odds are as heaven is to earth'
(Humphreys).

Act 5, Scene 3
0 SD The action is continuous in QqF and
stage directions run on (i.e. combine directions for
the exiting party with those for the entering).
These give no '*Exeunt*' or any other break between
the sounding of trumpets (5.2.100 SD) and the
King's entry. The scene change, first suggested
by Capell, has been retained here only for convenience of reference. Onstage, the foregrounding
of an individual can be emphasised both through
contrast with group fighting and through battle
sounds; compare Falstaff's solitary entry following '*Alarum*' at 29 SD below.
0 SD. 1 *Alarum* A call to battle by drums or
trumpets. In the theatre, this usually preceded the
entry of groups of soldiers.

Thou crossest me? What honour dost thou seek
Upon my head?

DOUGLAS   Know then my name is Douglas,
And I do haunt thee in the battle thus
Because some tell me that thou art a king.   5

BLUNT   They tell thee true.

DOUGLAS   The Lord of Stafford dear today hath bought
Thy likeness, for instead of thee, King Harry,
This sword hath ended him: so shall it thee
Unless thou yield thee as my prisoner.   10

BLUNT   I was not born a yielder, thou proud Scot,
And thou shalt find a king that will revenge
Lord Stafford's death.

They fight; Douglas kills Blunt

Then enter HOTSPUR

HOTSPUR   O Douglas, hadst thou fought at Holmedon thus
I never had triumphed upon a Scot.   15

DOUGLAS   All's done, all's won. Here breathless lies the King.

HOTSPUR   Where?

DOUGLAS   Here.

HOTSPUR   This, Douglas? No, I know this face full well.
A gallant knight he was, his name was Blunt,   20
Semblably furnished like the King himself.

DOUGLAS   A fool go with thy soul, whither it goes!
A borrowed title hast thou bought too dear.
Why didst thou tell me that thou wert a king?

HOTSPUR   The King hath many marching in his coats.   25

DOUGLAS   Now, by my sword, I will kill all his coats!

---

16 won. Here] Qq2, 3 (won: here); won here, Q1; won, here Qq4, 5, F   22 A fool go] *Capell;* ah foole, goe Qq; Ah foole:
go F

7–9 **The Lord . . . him** Shakespeare synthe-
sises distinct bits of information from Holinshed
(III, 25–6): (1) that Blunt, the standard-bearer, and
Stafford were both killed when Hotspur and Douglas tried to slay the King himself in a 'violent
onset', (2) that when the King later broke through
enemy ranks, Douglas struck him down and killed
'Sir Walter Blunt, and three other, apparelled in
the kings sute and clothing'. Daniel, III, st. 111–12,
makes it explicit that historically there were two
Blunts. Compare *2H4* 1.1.16–17: 'both the Blunts
/ Kill'd by the hand of Douglas'.
    7–8 **bought thy likeness** paid for his similarity
to you.

16 **breathless** dead.
    21 **Semblably furnished like** Dressed and
armed to resemble.
    22 **A fool . . . soul** i.e. 'You are a fool', a
common gibe. Compare Dent G150.1 and Jonson,
Volpone, 'Rooke goe with you, raven' (1.4.124).
Capell's emendation of Qqf's 'Ah' makes the
idiomatic expression recognisable and has been
widely accepted.
    25 **coats** sleeveless surcoats bearing heraldic
devices, worn over armour. Compare 4.2.37 and
n.

I'll murder all his wardrobe, piece by piece,
Until I meet the King.
HOTSPUR   Up and away!
Our soldiers stand full fairly for the day.

[Exeunt]

Alarum. Enter FALSTAFF *alone*

FALSTAFF Though I could scape shot-free at London, I fear the shot   30
here, here's no scoring but upon the pate. Soft! Who are you? Sir
Walter Blunt – there's honour for you! Here's no vanity! I am as hot
as molten lead, and as heavy too. God keep lead out of me, I need no
more weight than mine own bowels. I have led my ragamuffins
where they are peppered. There's not three of my hundred-and-   35
fifty left alive – and they are for the town's end, to beg during life.
But who comes here?

Enter the PRINCE

PRINCE   What, stand'st thou idle here? Lend me thy sword.
Many a nobleman lies stark and stiff
Under the hoofs of vaunting enemies,   40
Whose deaths are yet unrevenged. I prithee
Lend me thy sword.
FALSTAFF O Hal, I prithee give me leave to breathe a while. Turk

29 SD.1 *Exeunt*] F; *not in* Qq   **29** SD.2 *Enter* FALSTAFF *alone*] Qq (*Enter Falstaffe solus*); *and enter Falstaffe solus* F   **34** ragamuffins] *Capell;* rag of Muffins QqF   **35–6** hundred-and-fifty] QqF (150)   **38** stand'st] Qq2–5, F *subst.;* stands Q1   **39** nobleman] F; noble man Qq   **41** I prithee] Qq (preethe); Prethy F

29 stand . . . day are well on their way to victory.

30 shot-free A quibble: (1) without being wounded or shot at, (2) without paying the tavern reckoning or 'shot', by making a mark or notching a tally stick.

31 scoring charging to a tavern account. In battle, the word refers to slashing or notching the head or 'pate'.

32 Here's no vanity! The actor can speak ironically, in the manner of his 'catechism' (5.1.127–38), implying that death for honour is the ultimate folly ('If this isn't futile, what is?'). Or he can recognise the battlefield reality of sudden death, far from the 'vanity' of 'shot-free' London.

34–5 I have led . . . peppered 'Falstaff leads his "charge" to a hot corner, and then himself takes cover, in order that he may pocket the pay of those killed' (Wilson). Humphreys cites contemporary attacks upon this common form of military corruption.

36 town's end outskirts of a town where rubbish was dumped and beggars gathered.

41–52 I prithee . . . dally now A 'mixture of prosy verse and versy prose' (Humphreys). Hal breaks the regular cadence of his verse, while Falstaff speaks rhythmical, orderly prose.

43–4 Turk Gregory 'Turk' could be a synonym for an outrageously violent man. Two different Popes have been identified as this 'Gregory': (1) Hildebrand, who became Gregory VII (1073–85), and was denounced for his fury by Protestant writers, especially John Foxe in *Acts and Monuments*, 1563, p. 14 (cited by Humphreys), or (2) Gregory XIII (1572–85) who 'blessed if he did not instigate the Massacre of St Bartholomew, and promised plenary indulgence to anyone who would murder Elizabeth' (Wilson). See also Henry IV's letter of 1408 to Gregory XII (1406–15), complaining of policies prolonging schism in the church (Holinshed, III, 47).

Gregory never did such deeds in arms as I have done this day. I
have paid Percy, I have made him sure.   45
PRINCE He is indeed, and living to kill thee.
           I prithee lend me thy sword.
FALSTAFF Nay, before God, Hal, if Percy be alive thou gets not my
     sword, but take my pistol if thou wilt.
PRINCE Give it me. What, is it in the case?   50
FALSTAFF Aye, Hal, 'tis hot, 'tis hot. There's that will sack a city.
           The Prince draws it out, and finds it to be a bottle of sack
PRINCE What, is it a time to jest and dally now?
           He throws the bottle at him   *Exit*
FALSTAFF Well, if Percy be alive, I'll pierce him. If he do come in my
     way, so. If he do not, if I come in his willingly, let him make a
     carbonado of me. I like not such grinning honour as Sir Walter   55
     hath. Give me life, which if I can save, so. If not, honour comes
     unlooked for, and there's an end.   [*Exit*]

[**5.4**] *Alarum. Excursions. Enter the* KING, *the* PRINCE, LORD JOHN OF
LANCASTER, [*and*] EARL OF WESTMORELAND

KING I prithee, Harry, withdraw thyself, thou bleedest too much.
           Lord John of Lancaster, go you with him.
LANCASTER Not I, my lord, unless I did bleed too.
PRINCE I beseech your majesty, make up,
           Lest your retirement do amaze your friends.   5

57 SD *Exit*| F; *not in* Qq   Act 5, Scene 4   5.4| *Capell; Scena Tertia* F; *not in* Qq   0 SD.2 *and*| F; *not in* Qq

45 paid killed, with a pun on 'settled his score'.
45 made him sure (1) got rid of him, (2) made
him secure. The Prince picks up the second meaning.
51 'tis hot i.e. from repeated firing.
51 sack destroy, with a pun on the contents of
his case.
53 pierce Pronounced 'perse' and allowing a
pun on 'Percy', as an instrument of violence.
55 carbonado a piece of fish or flesh scored
across, ready for grilling (*OED* sv *sb¹*). Compare
Marlowe, *1 Tamburlaine* 4.4.43–4: 'I will make
thee slice the brawnes of thy armes into carbona-
does, and eat them.'
57 there's an end (1) to life, (2) to my speech,
as in 'so ends my catechism' 5.1.137–8.
57 SD Q provides no exit for Falstaff, and there
is no evidence whether the corpse of Blunt is
removed or remains onstage.

Act 5, Scene 4
0 SD.1 *Excursions* Raids. The exchange between
two characters gives way to the busy movement of
unidentified soldiers and the noise of battle before
the King and his leaders enter.
1 I prithee ... much This extra-metrical line
(Q1) may convey a sense of haste.
1 thou bleedest too much Holinshed
describes how the Prince, hurt in the face by
an arrow, refused to leave the field when several
nobles tried to escort him off (III, 26).
4 make up bring your forces forward, as at 57
below.
5 retirement falling back.
5 amaze alarm, fill with consternation (*OED*
sv *v* 3).

KING I will do so. My Lord of Westmoreland,
       Lead him to his tent.
WESTMORELAND Come, my lord, I'll lead you to your tent.
PRINCE Lead me, my lord? I do not need your help,
       And God forbid a shallow scratch should drive   10
       The Prince of Wales from such a field as this,
       Where stained nobility lies trodden on,
       And rebels' arms triumph in massacres!
LANCASTER We breathe too long: come, cousin Westmoreland,
       Our duty this way lies: for God's sake, come.   15
                     [Exeunt Lancaster and Westmoreland]
PRINCE By God, thou hast deceived me, Lancaster,
       I did not think thee lord of such a spirit:
       Before, I loved thee as a brother, John,
       But now I do respect thee as my soul.
KING I saw him hold Lord Percy at the point   20
       With lustier maintenance than I did look for
       Of such an ungrown warrior.
PRINCE O, this boy lends mettle to us all!   *Exit*

                 [Enter DOUGLAS]

DOUGLAS Another king! They grow like Hydra's heads.
       I am the Douglas, fatal to all those   25
       That wear those colours on them. What art thou
       That counterfeitest the person of a king?
KING The King himself, who, Douglas, grieves at heart
       So many of his shadows thou hast met,

6–7 I . . . tent] *As Capell; as one line* Qq; *I . . . so: / My . . . Tent* F   15 SD *Exeunt Lancaster and Westmoreland]* *Capell subst.; not in* QqF   22–3 Of . . . all] QqF; *Of . . . warrior. Prince. O . . . boy (as one line) /* Lends . . . all *Pope, followed by Humphreys*   23 SD.2 Enter DOUGLAS] F; *not in* Qq

6–7 I . . . tent Printed as a single line in Qq; compare 1 above.

12 stained i.e. by blood and dirt. The Prince wants to belittle his scratch by comparison with the blood of those massacred, 13, not suggest that they are dishonoured. Compare 'stain my favours in a bloody mask', 3.2.136.

14 breathe pause for breath.

15 SD This '*Exeunt*', not given in QqF, could be delayed until 19 or until the Prince leaves at line 23. The praise from the Prince and the King, 16–23, would then become direct compliment to Lancaster.

21 lustier maintenance more energetic bearing (*OED* Maintenance *sb* 1, this example).

23 mettle spirit, courage.

24 Another king Compare 5.3.7–9 and n. In Holinshed (III, 26) Douglas strikes down the King and his decoys when the King is in the van of battle; here he finds Henry retired.

24 Hydra's heads The many heads of Hydra grew back as soon as Hercules cut them off. This analogy is commonly used to characterise evil when it spreads as fast as it is destroyed.

26 colours the colours of the 'coats' Douglas vowed to kill, 5.3.26.

29 shadows (1) delusive semblances, (2) reflections or mirror images, (3) those who play or act the King. Because many of these 'shadows' have been slain, the grieving King may also suggest that they are phantoms or shades.

And not the very King. I have two boys   30
Seek Percy and thyself about the field,
But seeing thou fallest on me so luckily
I will assay thee, and defend thyself.
DOUGLAS I fear thou art another counterfeit,
And yet, in faith, thou bearest thee like a king –   35
But mine I am sure thou art, whoe'er thou be,
And thus I win thee.
                They fight, the King being in danger

                Enter PRINCE OF WALES

PRINCE Hold up thy head, vile Scot, or thou art like
Never to hold it up again! The spirits
Of valiant Shirley, Stafford, Blunt are in my arms.   40
It is the Prince of Wales that threatens thee,
Who never promiseth but he means to pay.
                They fight; Douglas flieth
Cheerly, my lord, how fares your grace?
Sir Nicholas Gawsey hath for succour sent,
And so hath Clifton – I'll to Clifton straight.   45
KING Stay and breathe a while.
Thou hast redeemed thy lost opinion,
And showed thou mak'st some tender of my life
In this fair rescue thou hast brought to me.
PRINCE O God, they did me too much injury   50
That ever said I hearkened for your death.

33 thee, and] Qq2–5; thee and Q1; thee: so F

30 **very** true, real.
33 **assay** test.
36 **mine** my conquest.
37 SDs Daniel credits the Prince with saving his
father's life from Douglas: 'Hadst thou not there
lent present speedy ayd / To thy indaungerde
father nerely tyrde, / Whom fierce incountring
Dowglas overlaid, / That day had there his trou-
blous life expirde' (III, st. 111).
40 **Shirley** Listed ('Shorlie') among the slain by
Holinshed (III, 26), along with Gawsey (Gausell)
and Clifton, who are fighting fiercely at 44 and 45
below.
42 **Who . . . pay** i.e. Who keeps his word. The
Prince's assertion resonates with many different
expressions of obligation and redemption in the
play, including his own vow to 'pay the debt I
never promisèd' (1.2.169), Hotspur's allegation

that 'the King / Knows at what time to promise,
when to pay' (4.3.52–3), and Falstaff's grim puns
on death as a final reckoning or payment (5.1.127,
5.3.30–1).
43 **Cheerly** A terse encouraging shout.
47 **opinion** reputation. Compare 3.2.42:
'Opinion, that did help me to the crown'.
48 **thou mak'st some tender of** i.e. you care
to preserve from harm (*OED* sv *sb* 3).
50–1 **they . . . your death** There are echoes
of such slander at 3.2.25 and 124–26 but no support for it in *1H4*. In *FV*, however, the Prince
frankly hopes for his father's death, 93–4, 455–7,
and 479–81.
51 **hearkened for** lay eagerly in wait for. Compare *Shr.* 1.2.258: 'The youngest daughter, whom
you hearken for'.

If it were so, I might have let alone
The insulting hand of Douglas over you,
Which would have been as speedy in your end
As all the poisonous potions in the world,   55
And saved the treacherous labour of your son.
KING   Make up to Clifton, I'll to Sir Nicholas Gawsey.   *Exit*

Enter HOTSPUR

HOTSPUR If I mistake not, thou art Harry Monmouth.
PRINCE   Thou speakest as if I would deny my name.
HOTSPUR My name is Harry Percy.
PRINCE   Why then I see   60
A very valiant rebel of the name.
I am the Prince of Wales, and think not, Percy,
To share with me in glory any more.
Two stars keep not their motion in one sphere,
Nor can one England brook a double reign   65
Of Harry Percy and the Prince of Wales.
HOTSPUR Nor shall it, Harry, for the hour is come
To end the one of us; and would to God
Thy name in arms were now as great as mine.
PRINCE   I'll make it greater ere I part from thee,   70
And all the budding honours on thy crest
I'll crop to make a garland for my head.
HOTSPUR I can no longer brook thy vanities.
They fight

Enter FALSTAFF

FALSTAFF Well said, Hal! To it, Hal! Nay, you shall find no
boy's play here, I can tell you.   75

60–1 My . . . name] *As Rowe¹*; My . . . Percy. / Why . . . name QQF (*subst.*)   67 Nor] F; Now QQ

53 **insulting** scornfully triumphant.
57 **Make up** Move your forces forward.
64 **Two stars . . . sphere** In the Ptolemaic system, each star kept within its own orbit. Compare
the King's use of this analogy at 5.1.17 and Dent
s992: 'Two suns cannot shine in one sphere.'
65 **brook** endure. Hotspur repeats the word at
73 and 77 below.

67 **Nor** QQ's 'Now' would be an error easily
made by a printer and is clearly wrong.
71 **honours on thy crest** Literally, the chivalric favours decorating Hotspur's helmet; figuratively, his glorious reputation, as in 'proud titles',
78 below.
73 **vanities** vain boasts.
74 **Well said** Well done.

Enter DOUGLAS; *he fighteth with Falstaff,* [*who*] *falls down as if he were dead*
                                                                    [*Exit Douglas*]

The Prince killeth Percy

HOTSPUR O Harry, thou hast robbed me of my youth!
I better brook the loss of brittle life
Than those proud titles thou hast won of me.
They wound my thoughts worse than thy sword my flesh.
But thoughts, the slaves of life, and life, time's fool,   80
And time, that takes survey of all the world,
Must have a stop. O, I could prophesy,
But that the earthy and cold hand of death
Lies on my tongue. No, Percy, thou art dust,
And food for –   85

[He dies]

PRINCE For worms, brave Percy. Fare thee well, great heart!
Ill-weaved ambition, how much art thou shrunk.
When that this body did contain a spirit,
A kingdom for it was too small a bound.
But now two paces of the vilest earth   90
Is room enough. This earth that bears thee dead
Bears not alive so stout a gentleman.
If thou wert sensible of courtesy
I should not make so dear a show of zeal,
But let my favours hide thy mangled face,   95

75 SD.1 *who* | F; *he* Qq   75 SD.2 *Exit Douglas* | Capell; *not in* QqF   75 SD.3 *killeth Percy* | QqF; *mortally wounds Hotspur /
Humphreys*   80 thoughts, | Q1; thought's Qq2–5, F   85 for – | F; for. Qq1, 2; for Qq3–5   85 SD *He dies* | Rowe; *not in*
QqF   91 thee | Q7; the Qq1–5, F, Q6

75 SD.2 *Exit Douglas* Not indicated by QqF.
The later report by the Prince that Douglas
'saw . . . The noble Percy slain' means that he
understood this death to be part of his bad fortune, 5.5.17–20, not that he felled Falstaff, then
stayed onstage as a mere by-stander while the
Prince killed Hotspur.

75 SD.3 *The Prince killeth Percy* The Prince
gives a mortal wound to Hotspur, who does not
die until 85 below. QqF use 'Percy' *subst.* here,
but 'Hotspur' in all other stage directions and
speech headings of 5.4. In Holinshed, the King
is responsible, but only indirectly, for Hotspur's
death: 'The other on his part [i.e. the other warriors on the King's side] incouraged by his doing,
fought valiantlie and slue the lord Persie, called
Sir Henrie Hotspurre' (III, 26). For stagings of
this combat and its aftermath, see Introduction,
pp. 48, 52, 59.

80 thoughts The Q1 reading is preferable to
Qq2–5, F 'thought's' because it links 'thoughts'
grammatically with 'life' 80, and 'time' 81, as sub-

jects of 'Must have a stop' (i.e. Come to an end),
82.

82 prophesy On the proverbial ability of dying
men to develop foresight, compare Dent M514,
'Dying men speak true', and *R2* 2.1.5–16 and 31–
9.

85 SD *He dies* QqF give no explicit direction.

87 Ill-weaved (1) loosely or poorly woven and
therefore apt to shrink, (2) woven with evil purpose.

92 stout valiant.

93 sensible of able to recognise.

94 so . . . zeal so heartfelt a display of admiration.

95 favours tokens of honour or personal favour
worn on the helmet. Herbert Hartman, 'Prince
Hal's "shew of zeale"', *PMLA* 46 (1931), 720–3,
suggests that the Prince lays his plumes (4.1.98)
upon Hotspur's face. C. W. Scott-Giles, *Shakespeare's Heraldry*, 1950, p. 91, proposes 'a torse of
silk of his own colours, white and blue, which he
unbound from his helm for the purpose'.

And even in thy behalf I'll thank myself
For doing these fair rites of tenderness.
Adieu, and take thy praise with thee to heaven!
Thy ignominy sleep with thee in the grave,
But not remembered in thy epitaph.   100
          He spieth Falstaff on the ground
What, old acquaintance, could not all this flesh
Keep in a little life? Poor Jack, farewell!
I could have better spared a better man.
O, I should have a heavy miss of thee
If I were much in love with vanity.   105
Death hath not struck so fat a deer today,
Though many dearer, in this bloody fray.
Embowelled will I see thee by and by,
Till then in blood by noble Percy lie.   *Exit*
          Falstaff riseth up

FALSTAFF Embowelled? If thou embowel me today, I'll give you leave   110
to powder me and eat me too tomorrow. 'Sblood, 'twas time to
counterfeit, or that hot termagant Scot had paid me, scot and lot
too. Counterfeit? I lie, I am no counterfeit. To die is to be a counterfeit, for he is but the counterfeit of a man who hath not the life of
a man. But to counterfeit dying, when a man thereby liveth, is to be   115
no counterfeit, but the true and perfect image of life indeed. The

---

97 rites] Qq2–5, F; rights Q1   106 fat] Q1, F; faire Qq2–5

104 heavy sorrowful, with a faint pun on the notion of weight.
107 dearer (1) more valiant, (2) more truly admired. The Prince puns on 'deer', 106, and ironically echoes his praise of Hotspur, 94 above. Compare Antony's metaphor for the murdered Caesar, *JC* 3.1.204: 'Here wast thou bay'd, brave hart.'
108 Embowelled Disembowelled, in prepara- tion for embalming and burial. A punning allu- sion to the 'assay' or ceremony of disembowelling a deer after the hunt is noted by Humphreys.
109 in blood i.e. in the blood of the slain Hot- spur. Humphreys points out that the Prince speaks truer than he knows, for a hunted deer, said to be 'in blood', is vigorously alive, like the shamming Falstaff.
109 SDs If Falstaff's resurrection follows a brief pause after the Prince's exit, it will surprise those in the audience who are ignorant of his trick and increase the anticipation of those who are not. If his 'death' is obviously faked through the whole sequence, Falstaff becomes a more theatrical

clown, detached from the tragic implications of this sequence.
111 powder (1) embalm, (2) preserve (like veni- son). In both cases a process of steeping in brine was employed.
112 termagant savage or violent. The imagi- nary deity, Termagant or Mahound, represented in earlier miracle plays, became a by-word for bul- lying bluster. Compare Hamlet's criticism of the players for 'o'erdoing Termagant, it out-Herods Herod', *Ham.* 3.2.13–14. In Jean Bodel's widely known French version (thirteenth-century) of the *Ludus super Iconia Sancti Nicolai*, an actor con- cealed within 'Termagaunt' roars when this idol is beaten.
112 paid killed. Compare 5.3.45 and 5.4.42.
112 scot and lot in full, a commonplace (Dent s159). Falstaff puns on death as final payment, using a quibble on 'scot', meaning Douglas. Com- pare 1.3. 212–13.
116–17 The better . . . discretion Falstaff puts into memorable form the idea (compare Dent D354) illustrated by Cowl and Morgan from

better part of valour is discretion, in the which better part I have
saved my life. Zounds, I am afraid of this gunpowder Percy, though
he be dead. How if he should counterfeit too and rise? By my faith,
I am afraid he would prove the better counterfeit. Therefore I'll   120
make him sure, yea, and I'll swear I killed him. Why may not he rise
as well as I? Nothing confutes me but eyes, and nobody sees me.
Therefore, sirrah [*Stabbing him*], with a new wound in your thigh,
come you along with me.

> *He takes up Hotspur on his back*

> *Enter* PRINCE [*and*] JOHN OF LANCASTER

PRINCE Come, brother John, full bravely hast thou fleshed   125
   Thy maiden sword.
LANCASTER   But soft, whom have we here?
   Did you not tell me this fat man was dead?
PRINCE I did, I saw him dead,
   Breathless and bleeding on the ground. Art thou alive?
   Or is it fantasy that plays upon our eyesight?   130
   I prithee speak, we will not trust our eyes
   Without our ears. Thou art not what thou seemest.
FALSTAFF No, that's certain, I am not a double-man. But if I be not
  Jack Falstaff, then am I a Jack. There is Percy!

> [*He lays the body on the ground*]

---

123 SD *Stabbing him*] *Malone; not in* QqF   124 with me] Qq; me F   124 SD.2 PRINCE *and* JOHN] Qq2–5, F; *Prince John*
Q1   125–6 Come . . . sword] Qq; *as prose* F   134 SD *He lays the body on the ground*] *This edn; He throws the body down /*
Var. 1773, Capell subst.; not in QqF

Vincentio Saviolo, 'Of Honour', *Saviolo His Prac-*
tice (1595), signature Bb: 'The wisdom and discretion of a man, is as great a vertue as his
magnanimitie and courage . . . without them a man
is not to be accounted valiant, but rather furious.'
 117 part quality or role, as well as portion.
 122 Nothing . . . eyes 'Only an eye-witness
could prove me a liar' (Humphreys). The fact that
so many 'eyes' do observe Falstaff's actions always
shapes the playing of the scene.
 123 thigh The significance of the thigh has been
disputed. The armour would protect the front of
the leg, but probably not its rear. (Could this suggest that Hotspur was fleeing?) Fatal thigh wounds
were familiar to audiences in the 1590s: Philip Sidney was known to have died of a thigh wound at
Zutphen in 1588; more mythically, Adonis dies
of such a wound inflicted by a boar in *Venus and*
Adonis (1593), 1052–3.

 125 fleshed initiated. The metaphor derives
from 'the practice of "entering" a young hound
by allowing it to taste the flesh of the animal it was
being trained to hunt' (Cowl and Morgan).
 133 double-man (1) apparition or wraith, (2)
two men (referring to his appearance with Hotspur on his back).
 134 SD *He lays the body on the ground* Variants
of the stage direction, *He throws the body down*,
present vivid examples of an intrusive SD that
has strongly influenced readers and spectators
for three hundred years. It has, however, no early
textual authority other than 'There is Percy!'
(134). A more neutral verb in the SD permits
readers and directors to choose the degree of
force in his gesture and the tone in which he
delivers the line.

If your father will do me any honour, so. If not, let him kill the next   135
Percy himself. I look to be either earl or duke, I can assure you.

PRINCE Why, Percy I killed myself, and saw thee dead.

FALSTAFF Didst thou? Lord, Lord, how this world is given to lying! I
grant you I was down, and out of breath, and so was he, but we rose
both at an instant, and fought a long hour by Shrewsbury clock. If   140
I may be believed, so. If not, let them that should reward valour
bear the sin upon their own heads. I'll take it upon my death, I gave
him this wound in the thigh. If the man were alive, and would deny
it, zounds, I would make him eat a piece of my sword.

LANCASTER This is the strangest tale that ever I heard.   145

PRINCE This is the strangest fellow, brother John.
Come, bring your luggage nobly on your back.
For my part, if a lie may do thee grace,
I'll gild it with the happiest terms I have.

A retreat is sounded

The trumpet sounds retreat, the day is ours.   150
Come, brother, let us to the highest of the field,
To see what friends are living, who are dead.

Exeunt [Prince of Wales and Lancaster]

FALSTAFF I'll follow, as they say, for reward. He that rewards me, God
reward him! If I do grow great, I'll grow less, for I'll purge, and
leave sack, and live cleanly as a nobleman should do.   155

Exit [bearing off the body]

148–9 For . . . have] *As* QqF; *an aside to Falstaff* / *Wilson, Humphreys*   150 ours] Qq2–5, F; *our* Q1   152 SD *Prince of Wales and Lancaster] Cam.; not in* QqF   155 nobleman] Qq4, 5, F; *noble man* Qq1–3   155 SD *bearing off the body] Capell; not in* QqF

140 **at an instant** simultaneously.

140 **long hour . . . clock** Mock precision, as if real warriors patiently timed their battles. But compare 1.3.99 (suggested by Brian Gibbons).

142–3 **I . . . thigh** Falstaff supports his lies with one true statement.

148–9 **For my . . . I have** Wilson and Humphreys regard this line as an aside to Falstaff. For examples of productions which treat the Prince's generosity as morally problematic, see Introduction, pp. 54, 59.

148 **do thee grace** help you to gain credit

or favour. Evidently it does, because in *2H4* 1.2.148–9, the Lord Chief Justice tells Falstaff: 'Your day's service at Shrewsbury hath a little gilded over your night's exploit on Gadshill.'

149 **happiest** most favourable.

153 **I'll follow . . . reward** Wilson suggests that this expression links Falstaff to the hounds who are rewarded after the hunt with portions of the deer. Compare 108 above and n.

154 **purge** (1) become spiritually pure through expiating sins, (2) lose weight by taking purgative medicines.

[**5.5**]   *The trumpets sound. Enter the* KING, PRINCE OF WALES, LORD
JOHN OF LANCASTER, EARL OF WESTMORELAND, *with* WORCESTER
and VERNON *prisoners*

KING   Thus ever did rebellion find rebuke.
        Ill-spirited Worcester, did not we send grace,
        Pardon, and terms of love to all of you?
        And wouldst thou turn our offers contrary?
        Misuse the tenor of thy kinsman's trust?   5
        Three knights upon our party slain today,
        A noble earl, and many a creature else
        Had been alive this hour
        If like a Christian thou hadst truly borne
        Betwixt our armies true intelligence.   10
WORCESTER   What I have done my safety urged me to,
        And I embrace this fortune patiently,
        Since not to be avoided it falls on me.
KING   Bear Worcester to the death, and Vernon too.
        Other offenders we will pause upon.   15
                     [*Exeunt Worcester and Vernon guarded*]
        How goes the field?
PRINCE   The noble Scot, Lord Douglas, when he saw
        The fortune of the day quite turned from him,
        The noble Percy slain, and all his men
        Upon the foot of fear, fled with the rest,   20
        And falling from a hill he was so bruised
        That the pursuers took him. At my tent
        The Douglas is – and I beseech your grace
        I may dispose of him.
KING   With all my heart.
PRINCE   Then, brother John of Lancaster, to you   25

Act 5, Scene 5   5.5] *Capell; Scæna Quarta.* F; *not in* Qq   15 SD *Exeunt Worcester and Vernon guarded*] *Theobald; Exeunt
Worcester and Vernon* F; *not in* Qq   25–6 Then . . . belong] *As Pope;* Then . . . Lancaster, / To . . . belong QqF

Act 5, Scene 5
  0 SD *trumpets sound* Although this is a triumphant royal entry, the trumpets may well be
restrained in order to introduce the sober tone of
the opening lines.
  1 rebuke (1) disgrace, (2) reprimand.
  5 tenor habitual condition (*OED sb*[1] 3b).

5 thy kinsman i.e. Hotspur.
  6–7 Three . . . else Shakespeare minimises
the casualties. Holinshed reports as slain on the
King's side 10 knights in addition to the Earl of
Stafford, and 1,600 soldiers; 4,000 were 'greevous-
lie wounded' (III, 26).
  20 Upon . . . fear In flight motivated by panic.

        This honourable bounty shall belong.
        Go to the Douglas and deliver him
        Up to his pleasure, ransomless and free.
        His valours shown upon our crests today
        Have taught us how to cherish such high deeds,   30
        Even in the bosom of our adversaries.
LANCASTER I thank your grace for this high courtesy,
        Which I shall give away immediately.
KING Then this remains, that we divide our power.
        You, son John, and my cousin Westmoreland,   35
        Towards York shall bend you with your dearest speed
        To meet Northumberland and the prelate Scroop,
        Who, as we hear, are busily in arms.
        Myself and you, son Harry, will towards Wales,
        To fight with Glendower and the Earl of March.   40
        Rebellion in this land shall lose his sway,
        Meeting the check of such another day,
        And since this business so fair is done,
        Let us not leave till all our own be won.

                                     Exeunt

32–31 . . . immediately] Qq1–4; *not in* Q5, F   36 bend you] Qq4, 5, F; bend, you Qq1–3   41 lose] Q1 (loose)   41 sway]
Q1; way F

  26 honourable bounty the honour of bestowing the reward for honour (to Douglas).
  27–8 Go . . . free The Prince's generosity contrasts with the King's severity in executing Vernon along with the more treacherous Worcester.
  36 bend you direct your way.
  36 dearest greatest.
  40 To fight . . . March The play ends, as

it begins (1.1.38–40) with references to Mortimer and Glendower. In Holinshed, the King goes directly to York where he makes peace with Northumberland (III, 26).
  43–4 And . . . be won The concluding lines may point towards a second play, however firm the closure provided by the victory at Shrewsbury.

TEXTUAL ANALYSIS

On 25 February 1598, *The First Part of King Henry the Fourth* (called simply *Henry IV*) was entered in the Stationers' Register to the bookseller, Andrew Wyse. The title page of the quarto printed later in the same year by Peter Short reads:

THE / HISTORY OF / HENRIE THE / FOVRTH; / With the battell at Shrewsburie, / *betweene the King and Lord* / Henry Percy, surnamed / Henrie Hotspur of / the North. / *With the humorous conceits of Sir* / John Falstalffe.

This first quarto, now generally known as Q1, and a fragment rediscovered in the nineteenth century, known as Q0, provide the only authoritative copy-texts for this play. Q1 appears to be an exceptionally faithful reprinting of Q0; both are widely acknowledged to be among the most carefully printed quartos of any play by Shakespeare. Their textual reliability is striking when compared with that of the six other good quartos of his plays which were first published in 1597–1600. For example, the earliest quarto of *King Richard the Second* (1597) omitted the deposition scene because of censorship; it was restored by the fourth quarto (1608) and much improved in the First Folio (F), printed in 1623, by collation with a manuscript presumably 'clean and superior to the quarto version' (Gurr, p. 176). Not only were there a great many press corrections to the only quarto of *The Second Part of King Henry the Fourth* (1600); the Folio also added 'eight longer passages, totalling over 160 lines', while omitting eight passages or twenty-three lines, most with 'marked sexual innuendoes' (Melchiori, pp. 190–1).

In contrast, subsequent quartos of *The First Part of King Henry the Fourth* (Q2, 1599; Q3, 1604; Q4, 1608; Q5, 1613; Q6, 1622) lack authority; they make minor revisions and add numerous errors. Each subsequent quarto is closely based upon the one preceding it. No recent editor takes seriously the claim of 'Newly corrected' on the title page of Q2. Q5 probably reflects some familiarity with actual performance in correcting the misattribution to Northumberland of Hotspur's lines at 1.3.199–206, and in clarifying Worcester's reply to Vernon at 5.2.3. Other improvements are negligible.

The Folio text (1623), probably based upon an edited copy of Q5, owes what limited authority it has to two factors: (1) a reflection of theatrical changes occurring subsequent to early performances, and (2) reliance on a copy-text characterised by spellings believed by some editors to be more typical of Shakespeare's usage than those in Qq01. F's act and scene divisions, which may well be evidence of Jacobean staging even if added by the F editors, have been generally adopted and are followed here, with the exception of the division proposed by Capell in 5.3 after line 100; F's 5.3 and 5.4 consequently become 5.3, 5.4, and 5.5. Selected examples of F's thorough but still incomplete excision of oaths and biblical passages, interesting primarily as evidence about responses to the 1606 law against profanity on stage, have been recorded in the Collation at several points. F's other changes, including those which may depend on consultation of QqO1 or which correct errors in QqO–5, will be described in more detail below. None of these corrections, it should be stressed, adds or deletes passages longer than one line. They are accompanied by the perpetuation of old errors and the addition of many new ones, created by the processes of editing and printing the Folio text.

The printing of QO and QI

QO, an eight-page fragment found by J. O. Halliwell 'some years' before 1867 in the binding of William Thomas' *Rules of Latin Grammar* (1567) and now held in the Folger Shakespeare Library, provides the basic textual authority for 1.3.199 to 2.2.93. Charlton Hinman (1966) has shown that both QO and QI came from the printing-house of Peter Short. He observed that the same stock of types, including some distinctive ornaments, was employed for both quartos, and he surmised that QI 'was printed directly from QO' because the two texts share 'so many typograph-ical and textual peculiarities' (p. viii), such as the omission of the speech heading 'Hotspur' at 1.3.199, leading to the misattribution already mentioned. That QI is an accurate reprint rather than the original text is indicated by its compression, which is relatively greater than that of QO. QI ends with K4 ᵛ, the final page of its tenth sheet, whereas QO, according to Hinman, 'must have required at least one leaf of an eleventh sheet L'. QI makes only one clearly negligent error, omitting 'fat' from 'How the fat rogue roared' (2.2.93); it corrects 'whip' to 'whipt' (1.3.236) and replaces 'my owne' with 'mine owne' (2.2.29).[1]

The obvious care taken in printing QO and QI, together with the unusually early publication relative to first performance, may have represented one means of assuring the Cobham family that the name of Oldcastle had been removed from Shakespeare's play. But such assurance seems to have been perfunctory. Although 'Falstaff' replaces 'Oldcastle' in dialogue and speech headings (Q of *The Second Part of King Henry the Fourth* preserves an 'Old.' speech heading at 1.2.96), Oldcastle lingers on in the Prince's address to 'my old lad of the castle' (1.2.34) and in Gadshill's cryptic reference to the safety of stealing in the good company of 'old Sir John' (2.1.55) and other 'burgomasters and great oneyres' (62): 'We steal as in a castle, cock-sure' (2.1.69–70). Other names which may well have given offence survive through QqF when Poins refers to 'Falstalffe Harvey, Rossill, and Gadshil' (1.2.130–1); Qq1–5 retain speech headings for 'Ross.' at 2.4.147, 149, and 153, corrected by F to 'Gad.'.

When Shakespeare completed the manuscript of a play, he turned it over, with or without revision, to his acting company. Authorial manuscripts, known as 'foul papers' (but not necessarily messy or 'foul') are believed to have furnished the basis for many quarto and for some Folio texts. Shakespeare or his company might also have arranged for a scribe to make a fair copy of his manuscript for the convenience of the 'book-keeper' or prompter.

[1] W. W. Greg in Hinman, Preface, p. vii.

That the manuscript of *The First Part of King Henry the Fourth* submitted for printing by Short was a scribal copy of Shakespeare's work rather than his own corrected foul papers or revised transcription seems probable. Not only is it less likely that Shakespeare, as opposed to a scribe, could have overlooked and failed to replace 'Harvey', 'Rossill', and 'Ross.'. It is also doubtful that his company would have chosen to use the time of their major playwright on the large task posed by changing many names. (The *Textual Companion* editors judge that some 330 alterations would have been required.)

Controversy has arisen over two questions raised by the surmised existence of such a transcript: its proximity to the realities of staged performances, and its uncharacteristic orthography. The first of these matters requires a more careful consideration of how the manuscript might have functioned in the playhouse. The second has been linked with recent arguments for the validity of readings which are based on F. It will therefore be addressed as a key element in the current revaluation of F's authority.

The first quartos and stage practice

Surviving copies of playtexts which may have been used as prompt-books suggest that prompters were able to work directly from authorial handwriting; the actors would not always have needed stage directions which added to or clarified those provided by the playwright.[1] Individual actors' parts would have been copied out and distributed. In some cases, actors may have begun to study their parts and may have started performing while the playwright continued to revise.[2] Approaching the copy-text for *The First Part of King Henry the Fourth* in the light of this complex theatrical process will help to explain its nature.

Qq01 exhibit features which are often found in quartos known to have been printed from foul papers, like *The Merchant of Venice* and *Much Ado About Nothing*. At the same time, they show signs of having been printed from a copy regularised by a scribal hand. Whatever the case may be, the quarto texts reflect a stage in the producing of *Part One* which is earlier than the revision of controversial names. The evidence that Qq01 originate from foul papers is not necessarily stronger than that for a fair, scribal copy, but it does highlight the question of the text's usefulness in the theatre. The two most conspicuous foul-paper characteristics have been thought to be (1) permissive or absent stage directions, and (2) indecisive treatment of minor characters. Recent editors seem to agree that had a play-book or prompter's copy served as the basis of the first quartos, these defects or oddities would not have been so apparent.[3] What this consensus may overlook is the possibility that some of the features deemed inadequate from an editorial viewpoint might not present great problems in the theatre itself.

[1] See Scott McMillin, *The Elizabethan Theatre and 'The Book of Sir Thomas More'*, 1987, p. 49 and William B. Long, 'Stage directions: a misinterpreted factor in determining textual provenance', *TEXT* 2 (1985), 121–37.
[2] In *The Stability of Shakespeare's Text*, 1965, pp. 19–20, E. A. J. Honigmann mentions Sir Henry Herbert's criticism of actors for commencing work before their play-book had been officially licensed.
[3] See Hinman, p. ix, Humphreys, p. lxvi, and Bevington, p. 87.

QQoI's treatment of entrances and exits provides a number of examples which support this possibility. Act 3, Scene 3 omits four exits within fifteen lines, including a terminal exit for Falstaff, while 4.1 begins with no entrance formula whatsoever for Hotspur, Worcester, and Douglas. The omission of these exits, however, would be unlikely to confuse actors, while the omission of the entrance is, in theatrical terms, much more impracticable. This one is so plainly faulty that it is more likely to have been caused through a corruption of the manuscript by a scribe or compositor than by Shakespeare himself. Of the exits omitted in 3.3, two, those of Bardolph and Peto, are emphatically implied by the words of the Prince when he gives sharp orders, 'Bardoll. / Go beare this letter' and 'Go Peto, to horse, to horse.' For Bardolph or Peto to simply remain onstage might well cause raucous laughter and spoil the effect of the rousing couplet with which the Prince concludes his speech. This presumably signals his own exit, before Falstaff's final, antiphonal couplet, balancing the Prince's call to arms with a call for breakfast. Accustomed to a convention of separating scenes by general exits, an actor playing Falstaff would be unlikely to linger while Hotspur and the others come on.

Q1 repeatedly omits exits that clear the stage at the end of a scene, as do many other quarto and Folio texts. Skipping an exit direction which has been clearly referred to by speeches can seldom be judged a serious flaw in a script intended primarily for playhouse performance. Shakespeare could have designed other scenes which obviously require exits but have left the timing indeterminate. For example, a contemporary editor must furnish exits for Bardolph and the Hostess in 2.4.399, where the action of the scene generates confusing bustle. Here we have evidence that Shakespeare, to quote Stanley Wells, was 'writing sketchily' as in 1.2 of *Much Ado About Nothing*.[1]

QQoI's omissions of entrances are potentially more disruptive for theatrical production. Characters left out of entrances preceding the first lines of scenes include Sir Walter Blunt (1.1), Bardolph (2.2), and Vernon (5.1). Douglas abruptly appears, without an entrance, eager to attack 'Another king', 5.4.24, after the Prince exits with his brother John and King Henry remains alone. In a more problematic example, the King's phrase, 'Here is . . . Sir Walter Blunt' (1.1.62–3) may be an implicit stage direction, indicating either that Blunt has been present from the beginning, or that he has entered belatedly (surprising the other lords, if not the King himself). Bevington and Oxford suggest that 'here' means 'here in the court' (and can therefore be no guide to action on the stage). Only a director can make a final decision about Blunt's stage presence. Bardolph, as the evidence of speech headings (see below) also suggests, provides fairly clear signs that Shakespeare was confused about a minor role, in ways which are similar to those found in foul papers. Shakespeare seems at first not to have distinguished him firmly from Gadshill or decided upon his function.[2] The cases of both Blunt and Bardolph, it might be noted, occur early, while Shakespeare could be trying out various possibilities. Those of Vernon and Douglas may be accounted for, in part, as theatrical casualties of the military crisis Shakespeare was orchestrating.

---

[1] 'Editorial treatment of foul paper texts: *Much Ado About Nothing* as test case', *RES* 31 (1986), 13.
[2] See John Jowett, 'The thieves in *1 Henry IV*', *RES* 38 (1987), 325–33.

Three other features of Qqo1 suggest near-readiness for theatrical presentation: (1) lively, descriptive stage directions, (2) light punctuation, apt as a guide to pauses when speaking in the theatre, and (3) relatively accurate speech headings. Vivid directions are distributed throughout the text after the first Act: 'Enter a Carrier with a lanterne in his hand' (2.1), 'Here they rob them and bind them' (2.2), 'Enter Bardoll running' (2.4), 'He spieth Falstalffe on the ground', and 'He takes up Hotspur on his backe' (5.4). William Long regards such information as 'playwrights' advisory directions' which could be adapted or entirely ignored by experienced professional actors.[1]

Contemporary directors, notably Audrey Stanley, have argued that the punctuation of Q1 provides far more effective guidance to actors speaking verse than does either F or any modern text.[2] For example, Q1's comma in mid-phrase for 'what saies sir John Sacke, and Sugar Iacke?' (1.2.91–2) appears to suggest a balance of elements while leaving the syntactic distribution of meaning open to a range of voice inflections. This edition follows Q1 in deleting several commas from the King's speech at the beginning of 1.3, and in restoring a comma at the end of its penultimate line: 'And therefore lost that title of respect, / Which the proud soul ne'er pays but to the proud' (8–9). For silent reading, no pause after 'respect' is required. But to speak lines 8 and 9 on one breath might deprive the King's repetitive conclusion of its weighty and measured pace.

Speech headings in Qqo1 are far more consistent, as well as more accurately adjusted to speeches and to speakers' names, than is common for plays derived from foul papers, particularly *The Second Part of King Henry the Fourth* (Humphreys, p. lxvii). But as Humphreys (p. lxviii) and Davison (p. 248) have argued, the exceptional necessity to revise names could have caused Shakespeare (or his representative) simply to make corrections on the foul papers themselves. Such confusion as exists pertains largely to Bardolph and Gadshill; the speech by the Prince at 2.4.146 is erroneously attributed in Qqo1 to 'Gad', while 'Ross.' (the abbreviation for Bardolph's earlier name, Rossill), speaks lines at 2.4.147, 149, and 153 attributed by F to Gadshill. As in the case of Bardolph's missing entrances in 2.2 and 2.4, such errors are likely to have reflected Shakespeare's indecision as recorded in his manuscript. It is true that quartos set from foul papers generally reveal Shakespeare's propensity to tinker with the actual names of his minor figures (apparent in Hand D of *The Book of Sir Thomas More*, which is believed to be Shakespeare's writing). Their speech headings also tend to be more variable. Here the names themselves remain stable, while the slight changes in abbreviations and, occasionally, spellings of speech headings never interfere with a quick and reliable identification of a character.

Indeed, a cursory examination of the order of these headings shows that full or longer forms usually precede shorter abbreviations: Prince/Prin./Pr.; Falst./Fal.; Wor./Worst.; and Poines/Poynes/Poy./Po./Poin. Someone has taken the trouble to avoid confusing Pr. with Po. or Prin. with Poin., which in the italic face used for speech headings could easily mislead a reader, especially in 1.2 where both characters

---

[1] Long, 126–7.
[2] Stanley supported her view in a lecture given at the Pacific Northwest Renaissance Conference, 1979.

first appear. That this someone is more likely to have belonged to the theatre than to the print-shop is suggested by the fact that Po. does conserve space in some cases, as in the speeches beginning at 1.2.121 and 136, but that it also appears at 110, 142, and 154 where there was space to spare. And it was not used for 91 where it would have saved a line.

The most conspicuous variant speech heading, 'Per.' for 'Hotsp.' and 'Hot.', could be assigned, with almost equal probability, to author or to compositor. This variant occurs ten consecutive times starting with his first speech in 4.1, before 'Hot.' reappears for the remainder of the scene. Because both forms of his name are used so frequently and regularly in *Part One* ('Percy' or 'Percys' forty-six times, 'Hotspur' ten times), the 'Per.' of Act 4 is unlikely to have expressed or caused confusion. Interestingly, neither 'Hotspur' nor 'Percy' occur in the dialogue of Act 4. Either Shakespeare or a scribe might simply have had the alternative form 'Per.' in his mind as he set down the speech headings.

One other feature of the play which may be mentioned in connection with the copy for Qq01 is the disappearance of Poins from the action after 2.4.419, and the sudden prominence of Peto as the Prince's attendant at the ends of 2.4 and 3.3. Fredson Bowers agrees with Dr Johnson's decision to replace Peto with Poins, on the theory that Shakespeare's original intentions can thereby be served. Bowers regards the 'substitution' of Peto for Poins in 2.4 as theatrically creaky, because, he reasons, the Sheriff would be more likely to recognise Peto than Poins (whom the Travellers of course never see).[1] He apparently forgets both the 'vizards' provided by Poins and the darkness before dawn at Gad's Hill, suggesting that Shakespeare's muddle with his thieves can become contagious for his bibliographers and editors.[2]

In summary, analysis of Qq01 suggests that their copy-text must have been more suitable for staging than many editors and scholars have judged. The manuscript submitted for printing omits a number of exits and entrances, but few of these omissions would have created confusion in the playhouse. In most cases, the manuscript seems to have been sensitive to stage requirements, clearly indicating exits through dialogue. An actor playing Falstaff does not need a stage direction after the Prince's 'Farewell, the latter spring! Farewell, All-hallown summer!' (1.2.128). Francis has to pop on and off because of his job. A degree of indecision about the coming and going of characters who serve as messengers, delegates, and followers might reflect the exigencies of a company sometimes reduced in size for summer touring, not merely the drafting phase of composition.

The facts that Shakespeare's company could easily add minor roles and that Shakespeare often handled such parts inconsistently are more problematic for editors than for actors.[3] More accurate and consistent speech headings such as we find in *Part One* have usually been considered characteristic of 'literary' fair copies rather

---

[1] 'Establishing Shakespeare's text: Poins and Peto in *1 Henry IV*', *SB* 34 (1981), 189–98.
[2] Compare the discussion of 'Russell/Peto', *Textual Companion*, p. 331.
[3] Arthur Colby Sprague repeats Cumberland Clark's view that Peto may have come into being because three men would not be quite enough for two to 'set upon' in 'Shakespeare's unnecessary characters', *S.Sur.* 20 (1967), 80.

than of playwrights' manuscripts. Surely, however, the preparation of parts clearly aligned with speech headings would have been more important for the players than for the printer, even if the Oldcastle controversy did provoke Shakespeare into more carefully identifying and renaming some roles in his play.

What, then, of the evidence that the copy for Qq01 could indeed have been a fair copy made by a scribe, rather than Shakespeare's corrected papers or a transcript incorporating his revisions and written in his own hand? To begin with, editors and textual scholars have noticed, following Alice Walker's *Textual Problems of the First Folio*, an occasional formality or stiffness in Qq01.[1] Where a more colloquial elision might well be expected, the text uses instead 'Before the game is afoote thou still letst slip' (1.3.272) or Falstaff's 'All is one for that' (2.4.130). Walker attributed such 'pedantry' to a compositor rather than a scribe. As Humphreys has shown, however, any argument from Qq01's treatment of elisions strongly confirms their authority as copy-texts. Where there are merely a handful of unelided and sometimes irregular forms, there are 'scores' of elided ones, correctly set, it would appear, by the compositors. Hereward Price has argued that Shakespeare exercised special care in eliding weak past verb forms for metrical purposes.[2] Humphreys applies Price's conclusions from *Titus Andronicus* to *The First Part of King Henry the Fourth*: 'of past forms in the verse portions (the only ones to which the test applies) Qq01 rightly elide 168 and rightly leave unelided 33; they wrongly elide 1 . . . and wrongly leave unelided 10'.[3]

Yet such accuracy need not exclude the hypothesis of a scribal transcript. Humphreys ruled it out because the text seemed to him better, in regard to punctuation and elision, than any transcript was likely to be, and because he considered that the revision of names would 'not appreciably mess up the MS or make it unusable' (p. lxviii). Recent bibliographical study of Qq01's orthography suggests that an exceedingly faithful scribal transcript has become a slightly stronger possibility than the alternatives. Particularly persuasive is the evidence amassed by the editors of the *Textual Companion*, which includes: Qq01's departure from Shakespeare's preference for 'between' in favour of 'betwixt'; its predominant use of 'prithee', when Shakespeare (before 1600) preferred 'pray thee'; its anomalously high incidence of 'ye' and 'y'; and its preference for 'yea', when Shakespeare's 'most authoritative texts' prefer 'I' ('ay').[4]

While no one would assert that editions should adjust Shakespeare's spelling in individual plays to match statistical norms for his entire career, the editors of the *Textual Companion* do argue that such norms, defined by computer study, may be employed as support for readings based upon the Folio text of *Part One* rather than on Qq01. By re-opening the question of the Folio's substantive authority, so

[1] Alice Walker, 1953, p. 111.
[2] 'The first quarto of *Titus Andronicus*', in *English Institute Essays 1947*, 1948, pp. 137–68.
[3] Humphreys, pp. lxviii–lxix.
[4] *Textual Companion*, pp. 329–30. See also MacD. P. Jackson, 'Two Shakespeare quartos: *Richard III* (1597) and *1 Henry IV* (1598)', *SB* 35 (1982), 173–91 and 'The manuscript copy for the quarto (1598) of Shakespeare's *1 Henry IV*', *N&Q* 33 (1986), 353–4.

emphatically denied by Hinman and earlier editors, they have reminded us that the QqoI origins of the text cannot be the end of its story. The play, like Shakespeare's spelling, continued to evolve.

The Folio text

In her pioneering examination of the Folio text for *Part One*, Alice Walker classified the kinds of corrections and errors which could be attributed to its two compositors, A and B. Although the number of compositors responsible for what was thought to be A's stint has grown like Falstaff's men in buckram, Walker's findings remain a useful point of departure for considering the Folio text. She begins by listing twenty-six variants between F and its copy-text, Q5, which actually restore QI readings, later corrupted in Q2–5, such as 'fat' for 'faire' at 5.4.106. She also lists F's correction of cumulative QI–5 errors.[1] F has long been credited with such minor improvements as replacing Q's 'present' (2.4.27) with 'president' (precedent) and 'Now' with 'Nor' (5.4.67). Although Walker's main contribution was to identify the extensive errors committed by Compositor B, she did show that F bore evidence of having checked earlier readings.

Yet in spite of having consulted its predecessors, the editors or copy-setters of F failed to supply many of the speech headings and stage directions missing in QqoI. Gadshill's 'Speak, sirs, how was it?' (2.4.146) has now been correctly attributed to the Prince, while Peto has been given a speech heading at 2.4.448. Falstaff is provided with an exit at 5.3.57 (although the scene remains undivided); so, too, are Worcester and Vernon at 5.5.15, while group exits have been added at the ends of 2.1 and 4.3. They have also been eliminated in several other places, repeating the omissions in Qq4–5. Douglas gets an entrance at 5.4.23, but the '*Etc.*' which probably included Bardolph at the beginning of 2.2 has been dropped. The exits of Bardolph and the Hostess in 2.4 are still unspecified, as are the entrances of Blunt in 1.1 and Vernon in 5.1. The inappropriate group '*Exeunt*' employed by Qq2–5 to conclude 3.3 has been kept, with the addition of a pointless '*omnes*'. The inference from F's treatment of speech headings and stage directions has generally been that the copy from which F was set contained some annotations based on familiarity with the theatre, but that a prompt-book cannot have been collated. Again, this consensus may reflect the doubtful assumption that the 'book' for a play would have given clear and consistent instructions to actors. Still, Bevington's observation about 'the First Folio editor's inability or unwillingness to provide any meaningful clarification of stage action' (p. 93) seems justified. The provision of an incorrect entrance for Poins at the beginning of 1.2 appears to be evidence of careless editing, although Qq4–5's mistaken treatment of Falstaff's welcoming 'Poins!' as a speech heading (1.2.86) probably added to the confusion. Another clearly erroneous entry is the inclusion of the offstage Westmoreland at the beginning of 5.1.

Although it would be pointless to cite the many misreadings introduced by F, it may be more fruitful to understand one of their causes. Paul Werstine has shown

---

[1] 'The Folio text of *1 Henry IV*, *SB* 6 (1954), 45–59.

that Compositor B, thought by Walker to be the source of many substitutions, omissions, and interpolations in F, was relatively accurate in his work on other Folio texts, and that his mistakes on this text are partly caused by the way the copy he set had been previously cast off.[1] In casting off copy, a printer judges in advance the number of manuscript pages needed to fill a sheet or a group of sheets when they are printed. It seems that inadequate space in the overall sequence of plays was allotted for the printing of the last part of *King Richard the Second*, and the two parts of *King Henry the Fourth*, and that supplementary sheets had to be added, resulting in more space than the printers needed. The individual manuscript pages seem at this point to have been unevenly cast off, burdening the compositors with the task of adjusting copy to spaces which might be too great here, too small there. Some of the errors introduced under these circumstances were probably editorial. Werstine also points to one example which is of particular interest because it suggests that a proof-reading correction has been made which relies upon a corrected manuscript source. F's 'I, but tis like' seems to have been a late replacement for the Qq form 'Yea but tis like' (1.2.140), as is indicated by the abnormally large space which seems to have been left between the speech heading 'Prin.' and 'I'. Although we cannot exclude the correction of some other error as the cause of such a space, it does seem possible that one anomalous 'yea' typical of Qq01 copy has here been brought into line with F's preference for 'I'.

Whether such changes reflect in some degree the authority of Shakespeare or of his manuscripts as used in the theatre is the question that has been raised by the newest bibliography. F's revisions in 1.3, which Walker surmised to be signs of editorial intervention and, in fact, 'singularly pointless' (i.e. the replacement of Qq01's 'Either envie therefore' with F's 'Who either through envie' at 1.3.26) are believed by the Oxford editors to reflect 'deliberate authorial changes incorporated from the manuscript'.[2] Such judgements rely on the presence, within a few lines of the 'authorial changes', of undoubted restorations of Qq01, on the clustering of the changes in a scene where numerous elisions have been introduced, and on the editors' confidence in the statistical norms for Shakespearean spellings which diverge, as we have seen, from the usage of the first quartos.

Cruxes

In this edition, each word or passage considered to be a crux has been discussed in the Commentary when it appears. Of five cruxes that are particularly important, four – 'oneyres', 2.1.62, 'elf-skin', 2.4.203, 'scantle', 3.1.96, and 'estridges', 4.1.98 – are unlikely to have presented problems for audiences at early performances. In each case, the actor speaks an unusual word which is made roughly intelligible by its context. This edition has adopted the copy-text readings of these four words as both plausible and attractive.

---

[1] 'Compositor B of the Shakespeare First Folio', *AEB* 2 (1978), 241–63.
[2] *Textual Companion*, p. 333, note on 1.3.26; compare p. 333, note on 1.2.165.

One crux, however, at 2.4.410 presents a choice between familiar words and their senses: 'Thou art essentially made' (QqF1–2) and 'Thou art essentially mad' (F3). Not only would the words have been spelling variants in 1597; the actor playing Falstaff could also, through intonation and gesture, have delivered the phrase in very different ways. Indeed, the choice between conveying the sense of 'made' or of 'mad' might well have been the kind of decision which would vary from performance to performance. Not surprisingly, stage history seems to offer no clear examples of such choices in specific productions. Where original production is concerned, two points may be worth bearing in mind: (1) that we cannot be sure how actors would have pronounced the word, and (2) that Falstaff almost certainly means his phrase to be a compliment, whether he implies one or both senses of the word in question.

Lineation

The same pressure to save space that led the compositors of Qq01 to omit terminal exits and speech headings probably caused them at times to end one speech and begin another on one line. It has also been conjectured that Shakespeare's foul papers crowded speeches together. Junctures of two or three short lines (i.e. those having less than five metrical stresses) or of shorter with longer lines, all spoken by different characters, invite editorial decisions as to how such dialogue should be represented in contemporary editions: flush with speech headings near the left-hand margin, or distributed across the page on subsequent lines which have been visually linked to reflect the metre.[1] Given Shakespeare's growing tendency to use more short lines of verse, combined either with longer verse lines or with prose passages, and the fact that, as Wright shows, he 'modulates back and forth between the forms', it becomes evident that editors will often agree on the expressive variety created by his style, but disagree on how to represent it through lineation.[2]

Act 1, Scene 3 of *Part One* can illustrate the editorial options for representing short lines and suggest how such lines enrich dialogue.[3] If we consider only lines that begin and end speeches, Qq01 print twenty-nine lines as short. Of these, this edition prints twenty-six as shared between speakers (thirteen pairs), leaving only three as separate short lines which immediately follow the speech heading. Bevington uses ten pairs, leaving nine separate short lines, while Humphreys combines line 264 with 263 – thus including three speakers in a single line and leaving only two short lines separate. When an iambic line, however irregular, has apparently been divided between speakers, the separate components of the metrical unit have been spaced apart vertically but numbered as one line. For example, 210–11:

HOTSPUR I cry you mercy.
WORCESTER   Those same noble Scots
            That are your prisoners –
HOTSPUR   I'll keep them all!

[1] G. Wright demonstrates that the use of short and of shared lines is an important part of Shakespeare's 'metrical repertoire' (p. 117).
[2] See G. Wright, p. 110.
[3] Other scenes of great interest in this respect include 3.1, 4.1, and 4.3.

Q1 prints Worcester's words, 'Those . . . prisoners –', as one long irregular line. F, apparently not pressed for space, splits Worcester's reference to the Scots where it is divided here, but like Q1, begins the speech immediately after the speech heading. F also gives Worcester (just before Hotspur's 'I cry you mercy') an extraneous short line, 'And list to me', which most editors reject. It thereby prints five short lines in a row.

Early in 1.3, Shakespeare uses a group of split lines in a way which quickly clarifies the troubled relationship between King Henry, Worcester, and Northumberland. At 14, the King cuts off Northumberland and seems to ignore his brief line, 'My lord –', in order to command the complaining Worcester, 'get thee gone . . .' The King then turns, seven lines later, to Northumberland with 'You were about to speak', a line which Northumberland completes: 'Yea, my good lord.' Northumberland's half lines dissociate him from his brother (whose haughty last line in 13 remains short even after Northumberland addresses the King with 'My lord –'). They also seem to frame the speech in which the King dismisses Worcester, pointing up the King's outburst and Northumberland's strategic obedience as he waits to say his piece in an attempt to justify his son.

Hotspur, interrupting again and again, is responsible for the largest number of short lines in this scene. Each of the eleven split lines from 128 until the end of Scene 3 includes a speech by Hotspur. These lines are often as unpredictable and energetic as Hotspur himself. Of particular interest are the linked speeches (210–11) which were cited above to illustrate typographical options. The use of split lines here suggests Hotspur's lack of control in the dialogue. Unable to keep the promise implied by 'I cry you mercy', he cries out in his next half line, 'I'll keep them all.' His interruptions here and at 216 seem to speed up the process by which Worcester becomes the wily historical expert, 'training' his nephew on. At 275, Worcester answers Hotspur's question, 'To join with Mortimer, ha?' and completes his line, 'And so they shall'. When Hotspur cuts off Worcester's, 'Hear you, cousin, a word', with the long and regular 'All studies here I solemnly defy', 225, he seems to ignore Worcester, as the King ignored Northumberland. But, unlike Hotspur, the King was keeping his channels of communication open. Northumberland and Worcester again complete Hotspur's short lines at 155, 185, and 214. By linking these exchanges, we have tried to make more evident the surprising interplay among the characters. Of course, no edition can hope to rival the theatre as a medium for expressing what Wright has called 'that condition of being bound together in a common action that the play as a whole affirms'.[1]

Hotspur's last words at 5.4.85, 'And food for –', clearly break off without finishing his thought or his line. The Prince, who has refused to share glory with Hotspur, does however appear to share the thought with which he ends, 'For worms, brave Percy'. Yet he does not really split or divide a line with his rival after all. His own line continues, 'Fare thee well, great heart!', composing thereby a measured, independent pentameter which leaves Hotspur's 'for' hanging in the air – an extra

[1] G. Wright, p. 139.

beat which somehow assures us that the Prince cannot have fully mastered Hotspur's spirit.

Whether the stylistic contexts for short lines are verse, prose, or a mixture hovering between the two, such lines often signal swift and important shifts of emotion and purpose, as in 'I do, I will' (2.4.399). Although considerations of space may help us to understand why QqF printed part of the verse exchange between Hotspur and Lady Percy in 2.3 as prose, it is helpful to notice that their interview begins with a number of short lines. Early compositors could well have been responding to the near-indeterminacy and the lively imbalance of a style which fully exercises actors' voices and readers' ears.

APPENDIX: SHAKESPEARE AND HOLINSHED

This edition treats as 'sources' for *1 Henry IV* those passages or details about characters or events which Shakespeare probably used. For Holinshed, however, there is special value in extending the possibilities of relationship between texts to include the methods and ambience of chronicle history. Often it will also prove illuminating to recognise what Shakespeare has left out of his play.

The Holinshed writers presented their readers with many opportunities to assess opinions which they recorded with little or no comment. This method served well the purposes of a playwright whose characters would not or could not obtain reliable information. A significant example of how Shakespeare adapted Holinshed's indecisiveness occurs in Act 1, Scene 3, where an argument over Mortimer provides one of the causes of eventual civil war. In the order of their occurrence, Holinshed's explanations for the defeat and defection of Mortimer are:

But coming to trie the matter by battell, whether by treason or otherwise, so it fortuned, that the English power was discomfited, the earle taken prisoner, and above a thousand of his people slaine in the place. (III, 20)

Edmund Mortimer earle of March, prisoner with Owen Glendouer, whether for irksomnesse of cruell captiuitie, or feare of death, or for what other cause, it is vncerteine, agreed to take part with Owen, against the king of England, and tooke to wife the daughter of the said Owen. (III, 21)

Thomas Persie earle of Worcester, whose studie was euer (as some write) to procure malice, and set things in a broile, came to the king vnto Windsore . . . and there required of him, that either by ransome or otherwise, he would cause to be deliuered out of prison Edmund Mortimer . . . their cousine germane, whome (as they reported) Owen Glendouer kept in filthie prison, shakled with irons, onelie for that he tooke his part, and was to him faithfull and true. (III, 22)

Although Holinshed conveys the mystery of Mortimer's actions and attitudes, he leaves little doubt about the motives of English politicians. His King considers Mortimer's claim to the English crown before answering the Percys with the 'fraudulent excuse' that Mortimer deliberately gave in to Glendower. Whereupon Hotspur comments, 'Behold, the heire of the relme is robbed of his right, and yet the robber with his owne will not redeeme him' (III, 22). Shakespeare, however, turns the opportunistic rationalisations of the parties in Holinshed into a less premeditated, more volatile conflict by involving his characters personally in the Mortimer puzzle. The King's concern over Mortimer's lineage becomes an explanation offered by Hotspur only after the fact of the King's anger, which seems to be directed more at Hotspur than at Mortimer.

The King's surmise that Mortimer has indeed betrayed him emerges in connection with his statement, perhaps also news to the Percys, that 'as we hear', Mortimer has just married Glendower's daughter. Hotspur answers the King's surmise with a more generous one of his own, stressing the 'deadly wounds' Mortimer received during hand-to-hand combat with Glendower. In turn, Hotspur's justification of his brother-in-law enrages the King, who calls it a lie: 'I tell thee, he durst as well have met the devil alone / As Owen Glendower for an enemy' (1.3.114–15). Glendower's later statement (3.1.60) that he has fought off King Henry's attacks three times eventually makes possible a reassessment of how both the King and Hotspur behave: the King may have lost his temper in response to Hotspur's tactless vision of Mortimer as Glendower's military equal, provoking Hotspur into recollecting Mortimer's claim to the crown. In this instance, Holinshed's detached method of admitting uncertainty about Mortimer becomes a method of portraying characters who seem unable to tolerate uncertainty about one another.

As he condensed political events between 1400 and 1403, Shakespeare omitted materials which tended to simplify or sensationalise the rebellion. The Percys appear much more devious in Holinshed, where they are said to envy the King's 'wealth and felicitie' (III, 22). Worcester's 'studie was euer (as some write) to procure malice, and set things in a broile' (III, 22). Glendower, constantly 'robbing and spoiling within the English borders' (III, 20), is downright treacherous; his people contrive to hide a terrible device with 'three long prickes' of iron under the royal bed. Only by chance does Henry discover it before lying down. Holinshed comments at length upon the likely perturbation of a monarch who finds death in his 'secret chamber' and 'bed of downe': 'Oh what a suspected state therefore is that of a king holding his regiment with the hatred of his people, the hart grudgings of his courtiers, and the peremtorie practises of both togither?' (III, 18–19).

Holinshed's King has to reckon as well with sporadic danger from the French, who do cancel their plans to invade England when they learn of King Richard's death, but are later involved in attacks upon the Isle of Wight, Plymouth, and Cornwall. Twice in the period between 1400 and the battle of Shrewsbury, Richard himself is rumoured to be alive, by conspirators who 'wished the kings death' in 1402 (III, 19), and again by the Percys as they march towards Shrewsbury. This tale, says Holinshed, reflecting on the consequences of the usurpation and the ultimate rooting out of all the factions involved, 'bred variable motions in mens minds, causing them to wauer, so as they knew not to which part they should sticke' (III, 24).

Understandably, Shakespeare omitted details which might have detracted from the economy of his plot. Within the span of years his play dramatised, the English negotiated the return to England of Richard's Queen (who had been considered a desirable match for the Prince of Wales) and the King married the Duchess of Brittany. Holinshed also reports the visit of the Emperor of Constantinople who seeks help against the Turk, the business of successive parliaments, the burning of Lollards, the spectacular fiery comet of 1402, and the appearance of the Devil in an Essex church, dressed as a Grey Friar, which is linked to the conspiracy mentioned above. As the Devil behaves 'outrageouslie', the church roof blows off in a tempest (III, 20).

The England presented by Holinshed resembles Shakespeare's in being vulnerable to repeated invasions and disturbed by warring nobility. It differs because it seems to be in contact with a wider world, both political and spiritual. Because Shakespeare concentrates upon the King's responses to his limited options, Shakespeare's England may appear more parochial. Compared with Holinshed, Shakespeare seems to deprive the King of popular support; he emphasises Henry's disdain for 'vile participation' and omits all mention of how the people actively reinforced their King's authority by killing conspirators and beating away the French.

READING LIST

This list contains a selection from the books and articles referred to in the Introduction and Commentary, with some additions that may serve as guides to further study of the play.

Auden, W. H. *The Dyer's Hand and other Essays*, 1962

Bahktin, Mikhail. *Rabelais and His World*, trans. Helene Iswolsky, 1984

Barber, C. L. *Shakespeare's Festive Comedy*, 1959

Barber, C. L. and Richard P. Wheeler. *The Whole Journey: Shakespeare's Power of Development*, 1986

Barton, Anne. *Essays, Mainly Shakespearean*, 1994

Bate, Jonathan (ed.). *The Romantics on Shakespeare*, 1992

Bentley, Eric. *The Life of the Drama*, 1965

Berg, James E. 'This dear, dear land: "dearth" and the fantasy of the land-grab in *Richard II* and *Henry IV*', *English Literary Renaissance* 29.2 (1999), 225–45

Bevington, David (ed.). *Henry IV, Parts I and II: Critical Essays*, 1986

Bloom, Harold. *Shakespeare: The Invention of the Human*, 1999

Booth, Stephen. 'The Shakespearean actor as kamikaze pilot', *SQ* 36 (1985), 553–70

Breight, Curtis. 'Elizabethan world pictures' in John Joughin, ed., *Shakespeare and National Culture*, 1997, pp. 295–325

Brennan, Anthony. *Shakespeare's Dramatic Structures*, 1986

Bristol, Michael D. *Carnival and Theatre: Plebeian Culture and the Structure of Authority in Renaissance England*, 1985

Brookes, Douglas A. 'Sir John Oldcastle and the construction of Shakespeare's authorship', *Studies in English Literature* 38 (1998), 333–61

Brown, J. R. (ed.). *Shakespeare in Performance: An Introduction Through Six Major Plays*, 1976

Bullough, Geoffrey (ed.). *Narrative and Dramatic Sources of Shakespeare*, IV, 1962

Bulman, J. C. 'Shakespeare's Georgic histories', *S.Sur.* 38 (1985), 37–47

Bulman, J. C. and H. R. Coursen (eds.). *Shakespeare on Television*, 1988

Burnett, Mark Thornton and Wray, Ramona. *Shakespeare and Ireland: History, Politics, Culture*, 1997

Cohen, Derek. 'History and the nation in *Richard II* and *Henry IV*', *Studies in English Literature* 42.2 (2002), 293–315

Cox, John D. *Shakespeare and the Dramaturgy of Power*, 1989

Crowl, Samuel. 'The long goodbye: Welles and Falstaff', *SQ* 31 (1980), 369–80

David, Richard. *Shakespeare in the Theatre*, 1978

Davies, Michael. 'Falstaff's lateness: Calvinism and the Protestant hero in *Henry IV*', *RES* n.s. 56 (2005), 351–78

De Grazia, Margreta and Wells, Stanley. *The Cambridge Companion to Shakespeare*, 2001

Dean, Paul. 'Forms of time: some Elizabethan two-part history plays', *Renaissance Studies* 4.4 (1990), 410–30

Dutton, Richard. 'Shakespeare and Lancaster', *SQ* 49 (1998), 1–21

Dutton, Richard and Howard, Jean E. *A Companion to Shakespeare's Works: The Histories*, 2003

Empson, William. *Essays on Shakespeare*, 1986

Erskine-Hill, Howard. *Poetry and the Realm of Politics: Shakespeare to Dryden*, 1996

Everett, Barbara. 'The fatness of Falstaff: Shakespeare and character', *PBA* 76 (1991), 109–28

Foakes, R. A. *Shakespeare and Violence*, 2003

Goldberg, Jonathan. 'The commodity of names: "Falstaff" and "Oldcastle" in *1 Henry IV*' in Jonathan Crewe, ed., *Reconfiguring the Renaissance: Essays in Critical Materialism*, 1992

Goldberg, Jonathan. *Sodometries: Renaissance Texts, Modern Sexualities*, 1992

Goldman, Michael. *Shakespeare and the Energies of Drama*, 1972

Grady, Hugh. 'Falstaff: subjectivity between the carnival and the aesthetic', *MLR* 96 (2001), 609–23

Greenblatt, Stephen. *Shakespearean Negotiations: The Circulation of Social Energy in Renaissance England*, 1988

Griffin, Benjamin. *Playing the Past: Approaches to English Historical Drama 1385–1600*, 2001

Hapgood, Robert. *Shakespeare the Theatre-Poet*, 1988

Hattaway, Michael. (ed.). *The Cambridge Companion to Shakespeare's Histories*, 2002

Hawkes, Terence. 'Bryn Glas' in Ania Loomba and Martin Orkin, eds., *Post-Colonial Shakespeares*, 1998, pp. 117–40

Helgerson, Richard. *Forms of Nationhood: The Elizabethan Writing of England*, 1994

Highley, Christopher. 'Wales, Ireland, and *1 Henry IV*', *Renaissance Drama* n.s. 21 (1990), 91–114

Hodgdon, Barbara. *The End Crowns All: Closure and Contradiction in Shakespeare's History*, 1991

Holderness, Graham. *Shakespeare's History*, 1985

Holderness, Graham (ed.). *Shakespeare's History Plays: Richard II to Henry IV*, 1992

Holderness, Graham. *Shakespeare Recycled: The Making of Historical Drama*, 1992

Howard, Jean E. and Rackin, Phyllis. *Engendering a Nation: A Feminist Account of Shakespeare's English Histories*, 1997

Howlett, Kathy M. 'Utopian revisioning of Falstaff's tavern world: Orson Welles's *Chimes at Midnight* and Gus van Sant's *My Own Private Idaho*' in Lisa S. Starks and Courtney Lehmann, eds., *The Reel Shakespeare: Alternative Cinema and Theory*, 2002, pp. 165–88

Hunter, G. K. *Dramatic Identities and Cultural Tradition*, 1978

Hunter, G. K. (ed.). *King Henry IV Parts 1 & 2: A Casebook*, 1970

Hunter, G. K. 'Truth and art in history plays', *S.Sur.* 42 (1990), 15–24

Hutson, Lorna. 'Not the King's two bodies: reading the "body politic" in Shakespeare's *Henry IV, Parts 1* and *2*', in Victoria Kahn and Lorna Hutson, eds., *Rhetoric and Law in Early Modern Europe*, 2001, pp. 166–97

Ives, E. W. 'Shakespeare and history: divergencies and agreements', *S.Sur.* 38 (1985), 19–35

Johnson, Samuel. *Johnson on Shakespeare*, ed. Arthur Sherbo, 1968

Jones, Emrys. *Scenic Form in Shakespeare*, 1971

Jones, Emrys. *The Origins of Shakespeare*, 1977

Kahn, Coppelia. *Man's Estate: Masculine Identity in Shakespeare*, 1981

Kastan, David Scott. *Shakespeare After Theory*, 1999

Kastan, David Scott. *Shakespeare and the Shapes of Time*, 1982

Laroque, François. 'Shakespeare's 'Battle of carnival and lent': the Falstaff scenes reconsidered (*1 & 2 Henry IV*)' in Ronald Knowles, ed., *Shakespeare and Carnival: After Bakhtin*, 1998, pp. 83–96

Laroque, François. *Shakespeare's Festive World: Elizabethan Seasonal Entertainment and the Professional Stage*, 1993

Levine, Nina. 'Extending credit in the *Henry IV* plays', *SQ* 51 (2000), 403–31

Lindenberger, Herbert. *Historical Drama: The Relation of Literature and Reality*, 1975

Mahood, M. M. *Bit Parts in Shakespeare's Plays*, 1992

McAlindon, Tom. 'Perfect answers: religious inquisition, Falstaffian wit', *S.Sur.* 54 (2001), 100–107

McAlindon, Tom. 'Testing the new historicism: "Invisible bullets" reconsidered', *Studies in Philology* 92 (1995), 411–38

McLoughlin, Catherine T. *Shakespeare, Rabelais, and the Comical-Historical*, 2000

McMillin, Scott. *Shakespeare in Performance: Henry IV, Part One*, 1991

Melchiori, Giorgio. 'The corridors of history: Shakespeare the remaker', *PBA* 72 (1986), 67–85

Merlin, Bella. *With the Rogue's Company: Henry IV at the National Theatre*, 2005

Montaigne, Michel de. *Complete Works*, trans. Donald M. Frame, 1958

Morgann, Maurice. *Shakespearean Criticism*, ed. Daniel A. Fineman, 1972

Muir, Kenneth. *The Sources of Shakespeare's Plays*, 1978

Ornstein, Robert. *A Kingdom for a Stage: The Achievement of Shakespeare's History Plays*, 1972

Patterson, Annabel. *Reading Holinshed's Chronicles*, 1994

Patterson, Annabel. *Shakespeare and the Popular Voice*, 1989

Pechter, Edward. 'Falsifying men's hopes: the ending of *I Henry IV*', *MLQ* 41 (1980), 211–30

Poole, Kristen. *Radical Religion: From Shakespeare to Milton. Figures of Nonconformity in Early Modern England*, 2000

Rabkin, Norman. *Shakespeare and the Common Understanding*, 1967

Rackin, Phyllis. *Stages of History: Shakespeare's English Chronicles*, 1990
Read, David. 'Losing the map: topographical understanding in the *Henriad*' in *Modern Philology* 94 (1996/7), 475–495
Rossiter, A. P. *Angel with Horns: Fifteen Lectures on Shakespeare*, 1961
Ruiter, David. *Shakespeare's Festive History: Feasting, Festivity, Fasting and Lent in the Second Henriad*, 2003
Saccio, Peter. *Shakespeare's English Kings*, 1978
Sant, Gus van. *Even Cowgirls Get the Blues and My Own Private Idaho*, 1993
Shannon, Laurie. *Sovereign Amity: Figures of Friendship in Shakespearean Contexts*, 2002
Smidt, Kristian. *Unconformities in Shakespeare's History Plays*, 1982
Tillyard, E. M. W. *Shakespeare's History Plays*, 1944
Tomlinson, Michael. 'Shakespeare and the Chronicles reassessed', *Literature and History* 10 (1984), 46–88
Wilders, John. *The Lost Garden: A View of Shakespeare's English and Roman History Plays*, 1978
Wiles, David. *Shakespeare's Clown: Actor and Text in the Elizabethan Playhouse*, 1987
Wilson, John Dover. *The Fortunes of Falstaff*, 1943
Wright, George T. *Shakespeare's Metrical Art*, 1991

Printed in the United States
By Bookmasters